RELIGION IN THE PUBLIC SPHERE

Canadian Case Studies

The place of religion in the public realm is the subject of frequent and lively debate in the media, among academics and policymakers, and within communities. This collection of essays brings together important case studies from across Canada that focus on understandings of the "public" and "private" spheres in regard to religious groups and practices.

Religion in the Public Sphere explores a number of contemporary issues, including the public perception of religious minority groups, legal debate about "reasonable accommodation," and the role of religion in public services and institutions such as health care and education. Offering a wide range of contributions from scholars in the fields of religious studies, political science, theology, and law, *Religion in the Public Sphere* sheds new light on the complex relations between religion, civil society, the private sector, family, and the state.

SOLANGE LEFEBVRE is a professor and the Chair of Religion, Culture, and Society in the Faculty of Theology and Religious Studies at the Université de Montréal.

LORI G. BEAMAN is a professor and Canada Research Chair in the Contextualization of Religion in a Diverse Canada in the Department of Classics and Religious Studies at the University of Ottawa.

EDITED BY SOLANGE LEFEBVRE
AND LORI G. BEAMAN

Religion in the Public Sphere

Canadian Case Studies

UNIVERSITY OF TORONTO PRESS
Toronto   Buffalo   London

© University of Toronto Press 2014
Toronto Buffalo London
www.utppublishing.com
Printed in Canada

ISBN 978-1-4426-4862-3 (cloth)
ISBN 978-1-4426-2630-0 (paper)

∞

Printed on acid-free, 100% post-consumer recycled paper with
vegetable-based inks.

Library and Archives Canada Cataloguing in Publication

Religion in the public sphere : Canadian case studies / edited by Solange Lefebvre and
Lori G. Beaman.

Includes bibliographical references and index.
ISBN 978-1-4426-4862-3 (bound).—ISBN 978-1-4426-2630-0 (pbk.)

1. Religion and state – Canada – Case studies.   2. Religion and
sociology – Canada – Case studies.   3. Religion and law – Canada –
Case studies.   I. Lefebvre, Solange, 1959–, editor of compilation
II. Beaman, Lori G. (Lori Gail), 1963–, editor of compilation

BL65.S8R44   2014 322'.10971   C2014-900126-6

This book has been published with the help of a grant from the Canadian
Federation for the Humanities and Social Sciences, through the Awards to Scholarly
Publications Program, using funds provided by the Social Sciences and Humanities
Research Council of Canada.

University of Toronto Press acknowledges the financial assistance to its
publishing program of the Canada Council for the Arts and the Ontario
Arts Council.

Canada Council   Conseil des Arts
for the Arts   du Canada

ONTARIO ARTS COUNCIL
CONSEIL DES ARTS DE L'ONTARIO
50 YEARS OF ONTARIO GOVERNMENT SUPPORT OF THE ARTS
50 ANS DE SOUTIEN DU GOUVERNEMENT DE L'ONTARIO AUX ARTS

University of Toronto Press acknowledges the financial support of the
Government of Canada through the Canada Book Fund for its publishing activities.

Contents

Figures and Tables

Figures

Tables

Contributing Authors

Solange Lefebvre (co-editor) is a member of the Royal Society of Canada, the Research Chair in Religion, Culture and Society and a professor in the Faculté de Théologie et de Sciences des Religions at the Université de Montréal. She was also the founding director (2000–2008) of the Centre for the Study of Religions at the Université de Montréal. Her most recent publications include "Disestablishment of the Church and Voluntary Culture: The Case of Francophone Roman Catholics in Canada" in *Quebec Studies* 2012; "Roman Catholics and Same-Sex Marriage in Quebec" (with Jean-François Breton) in *Faith, Politics, and Sexual Diversity in Canada and the United States* (edited by David Rayside and Clyde Wilcox, UBC 2011); "Storia sociale delle religioni" in *Dizionario del sapere storico-religioso del novecento*, Volume II (edited by Alberto Melloni, Il Mulino, 2010), the edited collections *Le programme d'éthique et culture religieuse* (with M. Estivalèzes, 2012), *Les religions sur la scène mondiale* (with Robert R. Crépeau, Laval, 2010), *Le Patrimoine religieux du Québec: Éducation et transmission du sens* (Laval, 2009) and the book *Cultures et spiritualités des jeunes* (Bellarmin, 2008). She is the principal investigator of a nine-member international research team whose focus is religious identities and state regulations (www.crcs.umontreal.ca).

Lori G. Beaman (co-editor), PhD, is the Canada Research Chair in the Contextualization of Religion in a Diverse Canada and a professor in the Department of Classics and Religious Studies at the University of Ottawa. Her publications include *Defining Harm: Religious Freedom and the Limits of the Law* (UBC Press, 2008); "Is Religious Freedom Impossible in Canada?" *Law, Culture, and the Humanities* 6(3) 2010: 1–19; "'It was all slightly unreal': What's Wrong with Tolerance and Accommodation in the Adjudication of Religious Freedom?" *Canadian Journal of Women and Law* 23(2) 2011: 442–63; "Religious Freedom and Neoliberalism: From Harm to Cost-Benefit," in *Religion and Neoliberal Policy and Governance,* edited by F. Gauthier and T. Martikainen, Ashgate, 2012: 193–210; and "Battles over Symbols: The 'Religion' of the Minority Versus the 'Culture' of the Majority," *Journal of Law and Religion* 28(1) 2012/3: 101–38. She is co-editor, with Peter Beyer, of *Religion and Diversity in Canada* (Leiden: Brill Academic Press, 2008). She is principal investigator of a 37-member international research team whose focus is religion and diversity (religionanddiversity.ca).

Paul Allen is an associate professor in the Department of Theological Studies at Concordia University. He is the author of *Theological Method: A Guide for the Perplexed* (T&T Clark, 2012); *Catholicism and Science* (with Peter M. J. Hess, Greenwood, 2008); and *Ernan McMullin and Critical Realism in the Science-Theology Dialogue* (Ashgate, 2006). He also has contributions to the European Society for the Study of Science and Theology's *Studies in Science and Theology* series and forthcoming publications in the edited volume *Augustine and Science* as well as the journal *Zygon.*

Clark Banack is an assistant professor in the Department of Political Science at York University, where he is completing a book that explores the influence of religion on political thought in Alberta, both historically and more recently. He is also in the initial stages of a new research project co-sponsored by SSHRC and York University that explores religious rights and education policy across the Canadian provinces. His broader research interests include religion and politics in Canada and the United States, Canadian political thought, Provincial politics, Canadian regionalism and federalism, and Western-Canadian populism.

Peter Beyer is a professor of religious studies at the University of Ottawa, Canada. His publications include *Religion and Globalization* (Sage, 1994); *Religions in Global Society* (Routledge, 2006); *Religion, Globalization, and Culture* (edited with L. Beaman, Brill, 2007); and *Religion and Diversity in Canada* (edited with L. Beaman, Brill, 2008). Since 2001 he has been conducting research on the religious expression of second-generation immigrant young adults in Canada. Based on this research, he is principal author of *Growing Up Canadian: Muslims, Hindus, Buddhists* (edited with R. Ramji, McGill-Queen's, 2013).

Paul Bowlby is a professor in the Department of Religious Studies at Saint Mary's University. His publications include *World Religions Today: Canadian Edition* (with John L. Esposito, Darrell J. Fasching, and Todd Lewis, Oxford UP, 2009); "Shaping and Re-Shaping Urban Landscapes in Halifax: The Recent Contributions of Immigrant Religious Communities" (with Nancie Erhand, in *Our Diverse Cities 2*, 2006); and *Religious Studies in Atlantic Canada: A State-of-the-Art Review* (Wilfrid Laurier UP, 2001).

Yolande Cohen is a professor in the Department of History at the Université de Montréal, and a member of the Royal Society of Canada. Her publications include "The Migrations of Moroccan Jews to Montreal: Memory, (Oral) History, and Historical Narrative" *Journal of Modern Jewish Studies* 10(2) 2011; *Femme Philanthropes: Catholiques, protestantes et juives dans les organisations caritatives au Québec* (Montréal, 2010); and the edited collection *Identités Sépharades et Modernité* (with Jean-Claude Lasry and Joseph Lévy, Lavel, 2007).

Phillip Connor is a research associate at the Pew Research Center's Forum on Religion & Public Life, specializing in religion and migration. He studies patterns of migration and immigrant adaptation (immigrants' adjustment to their new societies) around the world. Prior to joining the Pew Forum, Phillip was a fellow at the Social Sciences and Humanities Research Council of Canada as well as a graduate fellow at Princeton's Center for the Study of Religion.

Pascale Fournier is an associate professor and Vice-Dean (Research) at the University of Ottawa, Faculty of Law. She holds a University of Ottawa Research Chair in Legal Pluralism and Comparative Law. Her recent publications include "Honour Crimes and the Law—Public Policy in an Age of Globalization" *Canadian Criminal Law Review* 16(2), 2012 (Guest Editor's Introduction to the Special Issue on Crimes of Honour); "Calculating Claims: Jewish and Muslim Women Navigating Religion, Economics and Law in Canada" *International Journal of Law in Context* 8(1), 2012; and the book *Muslim Marriage in Western Courts: Lost in Transplantation* (Ashgate, 2010).

Matthias Koenig is a professor of sociology/sociology of religion at the University of Göttingen, Germany and a Max Planck Fellow at the Max Planck Institute for the Study of Religious and Ethnic Diversity. His recent publications include *International Migration and the Governance of Religious Diversity* (edited with Paul Bramadat, McGill-Queens, 2009); *Democracy and Human Rights in Multicultural Societies* (edited with Paul de Guchteneire, 2007); and articles in journals such as *Acta Sociologica*, *Ethnic and Racial Studies*, and *International Sociology*.

Margarita A. Mooney is an associate research scientist in the Department of Sociology at Yale University. Her book *Faith Makes Us Live: Surviving and Thriving in the Haitian Diaspora* (University of California Press) was published in 2009. Her current research focuses on relationships, religion, and resilience among young adults who have experienced traumatic events.

Nancy Nason-Clark is a professor in the Department of Sociology at the University of New Brunswick. She is the director of the RAVE project www.theraveproject.org and the author of several books, including *No Place for Abuse* (with Catherine Clark Kroeger, Intervarsity, 2010) and the edited collection *Responding to Abuse in Christian Homes: A Challenge to Churches and their Leaders* (with Catherine Clark Kroeger and Barbara Fisher-Townsend, Wipf and Stock 2011). Currently she is serving as the director of the Muriel McQueen Fergusson Centre for Family Violence Research.

Kamala Elizabeth Nayar is a lecturer in South Asian studies at Kwantlen Polytechnic University. She is the author of *The Punjabis in British Columbia: Location, Labour, First Nations, and Multiculturalism* (McGill-Queens, 2012); *The Socially Involved Renunciate: Guru Nanak's Discourse to the Nath Yogis* (with Jaswinder Singh Sandhu, SUNY, 2007); *Hayagriva in South India: Complexity and Selectivity of a Pan-Indian Hindu Deity* (Brill, 2004); and *The Sikh Diaspora in Vancouver: Three Generations Amid Tradition, Modernity, and Multiculturalism* (Toronto, 2004).

Rubina Ramji is an associate professor in the Department of Philosophy and Religious Studies at Cape Breton University. She is the author of numerous articles and chapters including "A Letter to Students: Beware the Perils and Pitfalls of Studying Religion" in *Religion and Canadian Society: Contexts, Identities, and Strategies* (ed. Lori G. Beaman, Canadian Scholars' Press, 2012) and "Being Muslim and Being Canadian: How Second Generation Muslim Women Create Religious Identities in Two Worlds" in *Women and Religion in the West: Challenging Secularization* (eds. Kristin Aune, Sonya Sharma and Giselle Vincett, Ashgate, 2008).

Yann Scioldo-Zürcher is a French historian working in the CNRS (National Centre for Scientific Research, and a member of MIGRINTER Laboratory (International Migrations UMR 73-01) based in Poitiers, France. His research program focuses on the contemporary post-colonial migrations, in particular on the "Repatriated" population of French who were settled in the colonies and obliged to return to metropolitan France at the end of the Empire. He also works, in a comparative way, on the Migrants Jews from Maghreb settled in France, Canada and Israel. In a methodological way, he adapts geographical methods to his historical thoughts.

Erica See is a doctoral student in law at the University of Ottawa. Her research focuses on the ways in which narratives of gendered and religious identities are articulated in the context of refugee determination hearings. She holds a Juris Doctorate from the University of Wisconsin and an LLM with Concentration in Women's Studies from the University of Ottawa.

RELIGION IN THE PUBLIC SPHERE

Canadian Case Studies

Introduction

Religion and the Public Sphere

LORI G. BEAMAN AND SOLANGE LEFEBVRE

Religion is frequently referenced in relation to its presence or absence from the public sphere, or its relegation to the private sphere.[1] In part, the often easy use of the terms "public" and "private" in relation to religion inspired the creation of this volume. Despite the fact that private and public are regularly invoked in discussions about religion, there is little systematic reflection on the meaning of these terms, specifically on the boundaries between them or what, exactly, we mean when we use them. For instance, religion is said to be "private," or "religion in the public sphere" is identified as requiring discussion. Indeed, one of the final meetings of the Religion and Society Programme, a large research initiative based in the United Kingdom, had as its core theme "New Forms of Public Religion."[2] In 2012, the comparative European project RELIGARE published a collective book on that topic, entitled *Religion in Public Spaces: A European Perspective* (Ferrari and Pastorelli 2012). Yet, scholarly reflection on what it means to link or distinguish between "religion" and "public" and "private" remains relatively rare outside of specific and isolated contexts. Thus, we frequently see reference to the idea of religion being "privatized" or "pushed to the private sphere," but little reflection on where the boundaries of the private sphere are. It seems that the public/private distinction has become essential to any discussion on religion. The chapters in this volume show how subtle, complex, and changing the frontier between the two can be.

Religion has become the subject of frequent and lively debate in a wide range of places: in the media; among academics, policy makers, and communities; and within social institutions. This increase in attention has resulted in a reconsideration of religion and its place in society, raising the question of whether religion is enjoying a resurgence.

Of course, increased attention does not mean increased religiosity, and there are a number of factors to consider, including the growing religious diversity that has come with immigration to various Western democracies, including Canada. In addition, a broadening of the scope of inquiry about what constitutes religion, including the curious inclusion of atheism in conversations about religion and religious diversity, is reshaping the sorts of questions social scientists are asking. The dramatic rise in numbers of religious nones (those who have no religious affiliation) showing up on census data is posing new challenges to scholars of religion, who must re-equip their intellectual toolkits to explore the diverse ways that religion manifests in the murky spaces of "public" and "private."

In this complex context, one of the most interesting paradoxes to emerge is the decline of traditional institutional religion at the same time as a greater public presence of religiously orthodox individuals. Certainly, our view of religion has changed. We are more anxious about the possibility of religious fanaticism, of which we are reminded day after day in the news. Requests for religious freedom and for recognition of religious identities regularly come before the courts and public tribunals. Growing pluralism and diversification of practices, or at least awareness of the multiplicity of ways that people live out their faith commitments, have challenged stagnant theories of religion. And there exists among some a nostalgia for a past that is imagined to be more cohesive, imbued with collective practices and a shared belonging.

This book sheds light on a number of perspectives on religion in Canada, and as such it makes a contribution to an existing body of literature that has examined religion and society in Canada. During the past decade or so there have been a number of important contributions to this field of study that help situate this volume. Lyon and Van Die's edited collection *Rethinking Church, State, and Modernity: Canada between Europe and America* (2000) and Van Die's edited book *Religion and Public Life in Canada* (2001) situate Canada in a comparative and historical context. The 2000 book endeavours to reflect on various aspects of the Christian churches and their relations with the state and with public life, relations that, since the 1960s, have been on shaky ground. The book analyses a number of paradoxes, including declining religious practice and belief coupled with tenacious religious affiliations, as well as the public assertion of multiculturalism coupled with the persistence of a strong Christian influence – complicated by

the fact that both Catholic and Protestant churches, historically designated as the twin "shadow establishments" (4), are now undergoing
disestablishment. The comparative perspective taken by Lyon and Van
Die situates Canada in an in-between position (between Europe and
the United States), without a clear church/state separation but also
without a clearly established religion (Christiano 2000; Martin 2000). It
explores the features of Canada's evangelical Christianity (with its less
radicalized views on such issues as same-sex marriages) and finds it
to be more moderate than that of the United States (Reimer 2000). The
book observes that there is still a strong correlation between political
allegiance and political choice (Stackhouse 2000). In keeping with sociology of religion of the 1980s and 1990s (Hervieu-Léger and Champion 1986; Hervieu-Léger 1993; Beyer 1994; Martin 1978), the book is
above all concerned with examining the deregulation, relocalization,
and pluralization characteristic of changes in religious practices and
beliefs.

The edited collection *Religion and Canadian Society* (Beaman 2012b)
considers the ways in which the Canadian religious landscape is
changing by examining the themes of contexts, identities, and strategies through an exploration of historical traditional religions and their
place in contemporary Canada. The authors in that collection reflect on
the ways in which religious identities are shaped and understood, both
within religious groups and by outsiders, and the strategies that scholars use to understand religion in Canada. Above all else, the book asks
crucial methodological questions at a time when studies on religion are
getting their second wind in a number of disciplines. The methodological issues considered in that volume range from the researcher's relationship to the groups she studies to the collection and interpretation of
data on Canadian religiosity.

Responding to a need for more information about the principal religious groups present in Canada, Bramadat and Seljak have published
two edited collections that offer introductions to the main world religions in Canada and to the Canadian Christian churches and their
ethnic backgrounds (Bramadat and Seljak 2005, 2008). Their volumes
examine the diversity of religious expression in Canada. What is important in both these volumes is that the authors dig below the surface of
religions and denominations within Canada to explore their diversity.
For example, the authors examine the many forms Buddhism takes in
Canada as well as the links between Anglicanism in Canada and the
global community.

As religion seems to be gaining a greater presence in the public sphere (or perhaps just greater attention), there has been a corresponding focus on religious diversity and its "management." Beaman and Beyer's edited collection *Religion and Diversity in Canada* (2008) examines some of the controversial aspects of diversity in Canada, while keeping religion in the foreground. From Wicca to the Bouchard-Taylor Commission process, that volume considers the path through issues of accommodation and equality, in part by examining religion in global context and in part by examining cases specific to Canada.

Context

Important controversies regarding majority and minority groups continue to take place. For example, seeming to back away from its formerly expansive approach to the inclusion of religious minorities, in 2009 the Supreme Court of Canada ruled for the province of Alberta against a small group of Hutterites who wished to be exempt from having their photographs on their drivers licences.[2] More recently British Columbia's Supreme Court debated the legality of the practice of polygamy by fundamentalist Mormons in the province, ultimately deciding to forbid this practice (Beaman 2012a; Beaman 2013; Beaman 2014). Shortly thereafter, Canadians became captivated by the trial of the Shafia family (originally from Afghanistan) accused in the deaths of four of their own family members (all women) under circumstances entangling culture, religion, and family honour. The debate over whether "honour killing" is a special class of crime and the need for public declarations that it is not part of Canadian values continues. Prayer and the display of the crucifix in municipal meetings have also been debated in Québec, with a recent Court of Appeal decision upholding the display of the crucifix and the recitation of prayer in the city of Saguenay. Each of these examples raised important issues around the idea of the public sphere, as well as the construction of boundaries between the public and the private.

In this context we identified the need for a continued and more detailed exploration of religion vis à vis the notions of public and private. In November 2010, we organized a workshop under the core theme "Religion in the Public Sphere." Our goal was to bring together a wide range of scholars from a number of disciplines, including sociology, religious studies, applied theology, demography, and history, to reflect on the public/private divide, specifically in relation to religion. One of the interesting consequences of that workshop was the realization that these terms are used in myriad ways, and that the public and the private are not always easily divided. While not a new realization, our shared puzzling over the divide raised interesting insights about the flexible boundaries of the public and the private and the power relations that influence the shaping of those boundaries. So, for example, domestic violence in religious families is at once a matter that has been hidden in the shadows of the private sphere and a matter for public concern and response. The creation of laws restricting the wearing of religious clothing in the public sphere may result in the expansion of the definition of the public sphere into areas that were previously thought to be private or into an in-between zone. The chapters in this volume reflect the realization that the boundary between the public and the private is blurred in some instances, while reinforced in others, and that the important site of questioning lies in the exploration of how and why the boundary shifts. Our volume makes a unique contribution to scholarly literature in that it develops case studies that lend a deeper insight into the links among the religious, the private, and the public. Moreover, themes such as secularization, diversity, pluralism, multiculturalism, interculturalism, and identity add new dimensions to the discussion.

We would be remiss if we did not mention that another important contextualizing factor for the volume is the Bouchard-Taylor Commission and its subsequent report (2008). This consultation commission had a mandate to examine accommodation practices related to cultural differences (McAndrew, Milot, Imbeault, and Eid 2008; Gaudreault-DesBiens 2009; Adelman and Anctil 2011). Although largely perceived as relating predominantly to Québec, the discussions surrounding the hearings and the language of accommodation had a Canada-wide impact. Indeed, the impact of the report has moved beyond Canada to the European context where the language of interculturalism and accommodation has gained traction (Foblets and Kulakowski 2010; Ferrari and Pastorelli 2012). Previously relegated primarily to employment law cases, the language of "reasonable accommodation," for example, took on a life of its own and has become a key discursive pillar in discussions of religious diversity and its so-called management in Canada.

However, debates about religion in the public sphere did not begin in Québec with the Bouchard-Taylor Commission. A commission on religion in schools made fundamental changes to Québec's confessional public education system (Proulx 1999; Lefebvre 2000). The Québec school boards were secularized in 1998 and, after public hearings in 2000, the schools were also secularized. In 2008, the minister of education announced that a neutral program on religious culture would be implemented. With these changes came a rebirth of interest in issues concerning religion in the public sphere (Lefebvre 2005; Milot 2002). A plethora of books was produced, including academic reflections and teaching guides for the new ethics and religious culture course that was eventually introduced in all schools (both public and private) in 2008 (Estivalèzes and Lefebvre 2012; Ouellet 2005). Again, to see these developments as being solely related to Québec would be a mistake: the question of religion in the public sphere is a pan-Canadian phenomenon, and indeed an issue that is now hotly debated in most Western democracies.

Moreover, historically Québec had the nearest thing to a religious establishment of any province in Canada. This intriguing circumstance has had lasting reverberations into the present, including the question of what shape secularism should take and to what extent secularism should prevail. There is an ongoing debate concerning the future of Québec's religious heritage that has taken place against a background of decline in religious and faith communities (Commission de la culture du Québec 2006; Lefebvre 2009; Noppen and Morisset 2005). These debates are also present in other parts of Canada, but for the most part lack the intensity that they have in Québec. Québec has a long history of generating cases that have acted as benchmarks for standards of religious freedom beyond its borders – two of the three most important recent Supreme Court of Canada decisions on religious freedom originated in Québec. Although it would be an overstatement to frame this volume as a response to the Bouchard-Taylor proceedings and subsequent report, they have influenced our choice of themes. Québec remains an important laboratory for the examination of religion and the public sphere and thus Québec receives sustained attention in this volume.

Approach Taken by This Book

Two key approaches are taken in this volume. First, we concentrate on the ways that religion illuminates *the complex relations between the public and the private spheres*. The authors in this book do not conclude that the privatization of religion is inevitable, a solution that is often evoked whenever contemporary society is agitated by conflicts of values.

Through case studies and illustrations based on religious groups and practices, as well as examples drawn from jurisprudence, the authors of this book re-examine and question the classic distinction between the public and the private, whether by observing the break-up of the frontier between public and private as in Beaman; the importance of managing diversity in the workplace as in Lefebvre; or the transformation of secularization under the effect of human rights charters as in Bowlby. Fournier and See clearly outline the contradictory nature of the Québec project of Bill 94 (which was abandoned after few months of debate), which planned to ban wearing the full face veil in public, under the auspices of gender equality, while at the same time banishing from the public sphere and even imprisoning women who wear the face veil. Banack shows how Alberta's proverbial defiance of the state is strongly linked to its religious heritage. Mooney's chapter, as well as the chapter by Connor and Koenig, reminds us that religion can have a positive impact on the well-being of populations and the successful integration of new citizens. Allen argues that political contexts generally require a deep assessment of religion and religious pluralism that cannot be achieved by the empirical and distant religious studies alone; it requires a complementary theological approach from "inside" religion. Nason-Clark reveals how churches and community groups develop extensive networks and strategies to deal with domestic violence, whereas Cohen and Scioldo-Zürcher discover a link between matrimonial strategies and the integration of migrants. Nayar and Ramji explore the subcultures of young Sikhs and Muslims who cross the public/private frontier by public protest and by intensive and individualized use of the internet.

In addition to our commitment to illustrating the complexity of the relations between the public and private spheres, in this volume we strive to look *beyond the conventional image of a singular Canada*, not only by paying attention to its provincial and regional differences but also by presenting several case studies of recent immigrants. Admittedly, we cannot possibly be comprehensive in our coverage of Canada; however, the case studies we have included span from coast to coast and give a sense of the range of issues and geographies that intersect with the theme of religion and the public sphere. A number of chapters touch on issues that are specific to Québec, including an analysis of the debates surrounding the niqab and Muslim women (Fournier and See); a study of religious accommodations in businesses in the private sector (Lefebvre); a comparative study on the role of religion in the insertion of Haitian Catholic communities (Mooney); and an examination of the strategies of integration used by Montréal's Jewish immigrants to ensure that exogamic marriages will not compromise their community's ethnic and religious continuity (Cohen and Scioldo-Zürcher). The contributors to this volume also examine many of Canada's other regional particularities: the unique character of Alberta's civil society, which jealously guards its freedom against the state (Banack); the impact of the large Sikh community in British Columbia (Nayar); and the Victorian and softly secularized spirit of the Maritimes (Bowlby). On a broader and more pan-Canadian theme, two chapters consider national data sets, including national statistical survey research, offering insight into both specific provinces and regions as well as a pan-Canadian picture (Connor and Koenig) and research on multiculturalism and religion among young adult second-generation Canadians (Beyer).

The study of religion and society is changing rapidly: religious diversity has increased, the secularization thesis has lost much of its appeal, the contours of the post-9/11 era have become more clearly defined, and so too have those of globalization. This new era means that innovative approaches to the study of religion must be developed in addition to reliance on our already substantial body of knowledge. To that end, we have included case studies that we believe offer new insights on these themes. We have also included historical reflections that lend a deeper understanding of the social and cultural location of current challenges. We have divided the chapters in this volume into four parts: Part I: The Public/Private Divide; Part II: Private Life; Part III: The Public/Private Continuum; and Part IV: Public Life. As one might expect, the themes spill across and between the chapters, creating opportunities for dialogue and hints at broader implications when seen in conversation with each other.

The Public/Private Divide

Although we introduced the public sphere as the touchstone for conversation in our workshop and in this volume, the idea of the public sphere necessarily relies on a dualism that is more fully articulated as the public/private divide. Mapping onto this divide is another binary – the sacred or religious and the secular. There is no neat division or overlay between these two binaries – in other words, despite the claims of some that the religious has been relegated to the private sphere, this is not and has never been the case. The more interesting analysis is the exploration of how and under what circumstances the boundaries between them are constructed.

Both Bowlby and Beaman rely on the notion of a public imaginary, Bowlby in the more communitarian sense, following Benedict Anderson and Charles Taylor, and Beaman drawing from critical theory to think about the ways in which such imaginaries shape how privilege, exclusion, and inclusion are formed. Beaman introduces the idea of competing imaginaries and frames the discussion of religion in the public sphere as a contest over which of these imaginaries will prevail. Bowlby maps a shift from one dominant imaginary to another. In both cases, however, there is no "fixed" imaginary; rather the ways in which peoples imagine themselves or the narratives they tell about themselves change.

Another key intersecting factor is "multiculturalism," a word which carries with it multiple meanings and which garners strong reaction. Although multiculturalism is commonly understood to include both ethnic and religious diversity, the latter comes, as Beyer points out in his chapter, with stronger qualifications for public presence. Law's response to religion is very clearly tied to a legal imaginary about multiculturalism, although that has shifted as the courts imagine themselves less as defenders of multicultural ideals and more as enforcers of security policies. In this way, multiculturalism as an ideology acts as a filter through which religion is imagined and shaped in the public sphere.

Spatial analysis can help us to think more fully about what we mean when we talk about the public sphere. Beaman's chapter, "Between the Public and the Private: Governing Religious Expression," considers the ways in which religion lies between the public and the private sphere and the implications this has for its governance and its practice. She recalls that the history of a Christian shadow establishment informs the debates about religion in the public sphere in contemporary Canada. Drawing from recent Supreme Court of Canada case law, which has dealt with the public/private divide in very spatial ways, she pays attention to the space that religion occupies as a key, yet often ignored, aspect of the negotiation of the public and the private and the space in between.

Bowlby's chapter, "Canadian Social Imaginaries: Re-examining Religion and Secularization," reflects on the ongoing debate about the differences between the European, American, and Canadian versions of secularization. The failure of the Victorian, Christian social imaginary to adequately cultivate equality among diverse Christian churches and ethnicities was the driving force behind the emergence of a new social imaginary centred on a version of state neutrality in relation to religious difference, based on the *Canadian Charter of Rights and Freedom*. The education and religion debates in the Maritimes during the early post-Confederation period in Canada serve as an illustration in Bowlby's chapter, which demonstrates the importance of understanding the historical context of discussions of religion in the public sphere in contemporary society.

In Canada, the complex relationship between the private and the public is commonly perceived as a moderate secularism, according to Beyer in his chapter, "Regional Differences and Continuities at the Intersection of Culture and Religion: A Case Study of Immigrant and Second-generation Young Adults in Canada." Analyzing results from research conducted in urban centres located in the five regions of British Columbia, the Prairies, Ontario, Québec, and Atlantic Canada, he examines regional variations and continuities among focus groups of immigrant and second-generation young adults from different religious and cultural backgrounds. The analysis sheds light on the degree to which differences that are publicly considered salient (region, language, religion, majority/minority status, culture) actually make a difference in the concrete religious and cultural lives of important segments of the population.

Private Life

Although a core theme in this volume is the fluidity of the boundary between the public and the private, a focus on the private as it is imagined in particular circumstances reveals other facets of the public presence of religion. It also allows us to further query the boundary between the public and the private and the purposes for which it is constructed. The three chapters in this part each offer very different insights into the private sphere and its embeddedness in the public.

For many years violence against women was ignored completely, for reasons that rested largely in the sanctity of the home and the protection of it as private space offered by a patriarchal approach that saw a man's house as his castle. The social imaginary that sustained the idea that family was a safe haven has given way in some measure to the recognition of the sustained violence to which women are often subjected. As the personal became increasingly political, to borrow an idea from the feminist movement, violence that took place in the privacy of the home became increasingly exposed to public scrutiny. The home and "private" space play an important role in religion, but it becomes complicated when violence is involved, or, in a different direction, when we are thinking about the internet. The internet, often accessed in private, allows the user to enter a public domain. This in-between space plays an important role in the construction of religious identity.

The construction and maintenance of identity can be thought to begin with the individual, but, as Ramji's chapter illustrates, individual identity is intimately linked to family, and also to broader, indeed global, communities. Who we are shapes and is shaped by social relations and social location. Thus, to imagine identity as a purely private matter is impossible, whether we are talking about relations between men and women in the family setting, marriage outside of one's religious group, or the use of the internet to build or maintain a religious identity. Whether the individual and the authentic can be equated remains an open question – in other words, is the only authentic path one in which the individual constructs identity, or what, exactly, does it mean when religious participants imagine themselves as being authentic, and how does this relate to the public and the private? The layers of context require careful examination, such as that offered by Cohen and Scioldo-Zürcher when they explore the "private" and intimate decision to marry, the community requirement for conversion of non-Jewish spouses, and the influence of Québec political culture in the creation of a franco-Sephardic subculture that is perceived to be more congruent with a public imaginary of a Québec nation. The private is indeed rather public in this instance, despite a beginning place in intimate relations and love.

Paying attention to the in-between of the public and the private spheres, Nason-Clark's chapter, "Talking about Domestic Violence and Communities of Faith in the Public Sphere: Celebrations and Challenges," offers both a theoretical and practical contribution to the discussion by considering points of intersection between domestic violence and communities of faith. This research demonstrates that, whether an abuser or a victim, a person's faith tradition has a profound impact on both the way domestic violence is understood and the person's subsequent journey toward healing and wholeness. Building a bridge between secular and sacred frameworks is understood as an important starting point. Although her primary focus is on Atlantic Canada, Nason-Clark explores the ways that the sacred intersects with the secular in a number of geographic locations. Her finding that programs for men who abuse in the United States have a high completion rate when a faith leader is involved in the monitoring of the abuser has important implications for approaches to intervention with abusers. Findings from research in Jamaica highlight the intertwining of sacred and secular responses, while research in Croatia shows the opposite trend. Nason-Clark's chapter is an illustration of the ways in which private/public and sacred/secular matrices intersect. Most significantly, her research demonstrates that this is not simply an intellectual exercise – that the manner in which boundaries are shaped impacts the lives of real people in profound, indeed, life-and-death, ways.

Ramji's chapter, "Maintaining and Nurturing an Islamic Identity in Canada – Online and Offline," shows how innovations involving the internet have impacted the way Muslim youth in Canada understand and practise their faith. This "private" activity of internet exploration is melded with the very public space that the internet has become. She explores the attitudes of second-generation Muslims toward religion and their participation in their faith community. As a whole, the group interviewed felt at ease in Canadian culture, having been raised to have a number of identities (Islamic, parent's ethnic-cultural background, Canadian culture, etc.). Over 50 per cent of this group reported using on-line sources in order to better understand their faith and the majority chose not to turn to their elders, local mosque, or community for guidance. Websites dedicated to Islam cater to a highly individualized understanding of faith that is evident among those she interviewed.

In their chapter, "Maghrebi Jewish Migrations and Religious Marriage in Paris and Montréal, 1954–1980," Cohen and Scioldo-Zürcher show the importance of post-war migration movements for the redefinition, renewal, and even survival of the Jewish communities in both France and Québec, through a comparison of the marriages celebrated in three synagogues. During a short-term period, these North African Jewish migrations had an influence on matrimonial strategies: migrant men and women easily entered into exogamic marriages. However, these personal choices took on community significance and conversion became an expectation. The complexity of religion, ethnicity, community, and nation are enmeshed in this chapter, which attempts to unravel some of the dynamics of Jewish migration through the study of the private and intimate act of marriage.

Although we have framed these chapters as exploring the private, we recognize that in fact the private quickly folds over into the public. This is our intention – to demonstrate that even as we keep these categories as heuristic devices, they cannot act as stand-alone concepts. Moreover, the cultural and social context, which may well transcend the immediate geography in which religion operates, is a vital part of understanding religion in the public sphere.

The Public/Private Continuum

The chapters in this part continue the blurring we explore in Part II, but through examples that are not situated in family life or the private endeavour of individual identity construction (at least not overtly). Here we examine the world of employment, the perspective of religious communities and their integration, and religion in social institutions that are usually thought of as secular. The worlds of work, school, and community are at least nominally public, but retain within them the private worlds of their participants. Workplace participation can take place in so-called private companies, but a failure to adequately respond to religious requests have decidedly public implications or can invoke public sanction and action. Religious communities may negotiate between a closed, more private world and engagement with a broader public. Sometimes the broader public sphere is closed to them, as Mooney argues of Haitian immigrants. And religion may indeed be banished from the sphere of education in an attempt to equalize groups and individuals. It is perhaps in this part that we see the boundaries between the secular and the sacred or religious most clearly drawn, and the tension between the secular and the religious most clearly.

In her chapter, "Beyond Religious Accommodation in the Workplace: A Philosophy of Diversity," Lefebvre examines how private enterprises manage cultural and religious diversity. The question emerged in the aftermath of the Bouchard-Taylor public inquiry, which focused primarily on issues of cultural and religious accommodation within public and semi-public institutions and community organizations. She finds an interesting and broad approach to diversity, with religion being "one more" factor of diversity among others, such as gender, sexual orientation, disabilities, ethnicity, age, and generation. Lefebvre's chapter raises the important issue of the overemphasis on religion that can occur when it is highlighted as an identity marker. For many religious people, their religious identities are not necessarily something they wish to foreground. It is in this context, then, that companies must respond to religious diversity, acknowledging and accommodating those who wish to have their religious identities protected, and ensuring that those who wish to remain "private" with their religious beliefs and practices can do so. This is not an easy balance to strike and brings with it its own challenges of negotiating the public/private divide. Her chapter also raises, as do a number of others, the impact of intersecting identity characteristics, such as ethnicity and religion, a theme picked up in Mooney's chapter.

Drawing on her fieldwork in Montréal, Mooney's chapter, "Religion and the Incorporation of Haitian Migrants in Montréal," examines the role of Catholic organizations in the incorporation of Haitian immigrants in Montréal, through comparisons with their counterparts in Miami and Paris. The view that religion belongs in the private sphere contributes to the marginalization of Haitian immigrants and the religious organizations that support them. Haitian immigrants in Montréal are caught in a system that claims neutrality toward religion but in practice is suspicious of religious institutions conflicting with Québec's national identity and secularity. Religious organizations, which could facilitate the integration process, are viewed as representing an era that has passed in Québec, and little space is left for the positive role that they might play in smoothing the process of integration. This leads us to the question of whether this is a phenomenon specific to Québec, with its admittedly unique approach to religion in the public sphere or whether the trends evidenced in Québec represent a more universal phenomenon.

On the other side of the country, Sikhs in British Columbia form a significant minority population. In the last four decades British Columbia has seen the increase, and greater visibility, of its diverse Asian religious landscape. The Sikh community has emerged as the largest non-Christian group living in the BC Lower Mainland. Nayar's chapter, "The Intersection of Religious Identity and Visible Minority Status: The Case of Sikh Youth in British Columbia," examines the situation in Surrey and analyzes the ways in which Sikh youth relate to the public sphere. In 2008, about twenty students wore Khalistan T-shirts to their local public high school in Surrey, BC, where they were told that, due to the shirts' "violent" nature, the shirts were inappropriate and forbidden at school. Nayar raises the question as to whether wearing these shirts was really about Khalistan politics or about other feelings of marginalization. Her chapter illuminates the complex intertwining of global politics, ethnic alienation, and religious minority status. What happens when the politics of resistance enters the schoolyard? What must be kept "private" and how can youth convey discontent to generate a public message? And, more broadly, what happens when the public message received is not the message intended? Nayar addresses these questions, systematically unpacking a superficial read of this incident that dominated public discourse to offer a much deeper interpretation of identity, religious practice, and political message.

We continue on in the education setting, but this time at the university level with Allen's chapter, "Curricular Heresy: Theological Religious Studies and the Assessment of Religious Pluralism in Canada," which reflects on several examples of the ways in which theology and religious studies are developing in Western universities. There is a concern that a social scientific approach, without complementary humanistic theological inquiry, will lead to management goals that are not sympathetic to understanding the plausibility structures of religious belief in a multicultural context. Although religious studies has offered much in the way of a "thick description" of religion, this chapter argues that the political context requires a deep assessment of religion and religious pluralism, one that requires a complementary theological approach. Allen calls this approach "theological religious studies." This chapter argues that because of their role in shaping polity and culture, Canadian universities should play a lead role in the development of theological religious studies. Allen's chapter foregrounds the secular/sacred divide and the ways the sacred are framed as "off limits" in the university setting. As "public" institutions, universities have engaged in the interesting balancing act of avoiding religious truth claims while allowing space for religious activism and practice on campuses. This is not an easy balance to achieve and it illustrates again the intersections of public, private, religious, and secular.

Public Life

Our final part emphasizes more fully the idea of the public, and in particular the ways in which religion, law, and public policy intersect. Of course, what may seem to be public – such as a law related to the regulation of clothing in public space – may in fact relate also to the realm of the private, or may, as is the case with Bill 94, substantially shift the boundary between public and private. Moreover, the very notion of the public sphere must be understood as a complicated reality that is perhaps too often simplistically rendered. This was often the case during the Bouchard-Taylor Commission hearings, and, as Banack's chapter demonstrates, has often been the case in the way that Alberta's public sphere is portrayed. Understanding broad trends, such as the integration of immigrants who highlight religion as an important part of their identities, can help to develop sound public policy and can also highlight areas of social rupture. Alienating religious minorities, whether among recent immigrant communities or longer-settled groups, can have devastating effects both on individuals and on communities.

Alienation and exclusion is a key theme in Fournier and See's chapter, "The 'Naked Face' of Secular Exclusion: Bill 94 and the Privatization of Belief," which considers the case of Québec's Bill 94, proposed in March 2010. Bill 94 is one of many recent bans on the wearing of the niqab discussed in the West. The chapter explores a peculiar manifestation of "secularism" with the concurrent existence of "governance feminism," in which the privatization of belief goes hand in hand with and is perversely reinforced by a colonial discourse on gender equality, leaving some already marginalized women out of the public gaze. Fournier and See argue that Bill 94 extends the realm of the public into spaces that might previously have been considered to be private or largely beyond the purview of state regulation, particularly for something like women's clothing. Their chapter offers insight into the power relations embedded in shifting boundaries of the public and the private, and raises broader questions about the place of the state in liberal democracies in relation to the regulation of a public sphere that is, in theory, supposed to invite multiple perspectives, beliefs, and practices. The Bill 94 situation also highlights an alignment between secular/public and religious/private, giving credence to the argument of some religious minorities that religion is being banned from the public sphere.

The control of the public sphere does not always rest in government, though, as is illustrated by Clark Banack in his chapter, "Conservative Christianity, Anti-statism, and Alberta's Public Sphere: The Curious Case of Bill 44." Banack looks at the case study of Bill 44, *The Human Rights, Citizenship and Multiculturalism Amendment Act* adopted by Alberta in 2009. The Act included both a symbolic recognition of "sexual orientation" as protected ground from discrimination under Alberta's human rights legislation and a parental rights clause that essentially prevents the introduction of any form of compulsory "gay-friendly" instruction in public schools. Although the popular perception of Alberta is that of a province dominated by conservative Christian sentiment that fuels an overt hostility towards homosexuality, this chapter argues that the actual nature of Alberta's public sphere is far more complicated. Conservative Christianity has strongly influenced the political culture of Alberta, but a more pervasive product of Alberta's conservative Christian heritage is a particular suspicion of government itself, an anti-statist perspective that favours community and family-level solutions to communal problems.

Our final chapter places some of the discussion of immigrants in the volume in a broader context. Drawing on the US/European comparison of religion as either a bridge (US) or a barrier (Europe) for immigrant integration, Connor and Koenig's chapter, "Religion and the Socio-economic Integration of Immigrants across Canada," lays out a series of hypotheses of how religious contextual differences in Québec and English Canada may lead immigrants to experience different levels of integration based on their religious affiliation and religious participation. Picking up on a theme introduced in Mooney's chapter, which explored integration from an individual and community perspective, this chapter uses data from Statistics Canada's 2002 Ethnic Diversity Survey. The most important contribution of this chapter, however, is that it demonstrates, perhaps contrary to expectations, that while the contexts of Québec and the other Canadian provinces differ, affiliation and participation operate in very similar ways across Canada. We introduced this idea at the very beginning of the volume by noting that Québec offers an important laboratory for the exploration of religion and the public sphere. To be sure, there are important differences that should not be too readily dismissed, but our final chapter highlights the similarities in the intersections of integration, religion, and immigration.

Our hope and expectation is that this volume will encourage a continuation of the scholarly exploration of the issues the contributors have raised. We do not pretend that the volume is comprehensive or the last word on religion in Canada. Rather, in reflecting on the complex relationship between the private and the public spheres and in encouraging a detailed examination of the social construction of these realms, we might rethink the easy use of the phrase "religion in the public sphere" and generate further reflection on the work that this binary does in scholarly research.

NOTES

1 The editors would like to acknowledge the support of the following SSHRC-funded projects and programs: the Aid to Scholarly Publications Program; the Religion and Diversity Project (University of Ottawa); and

Lori G. Beaman's Canada Research Chair in the Contextualization of Religion in a Diverse Canada (SSHRC). We are grateful for funding from SSHRC for the workshop, "Religion in the Public Sphere," at which these papers were initially presented. Thank you to K. Gandhar Chakravarty for his assistance with the SSHRC application and the workshop organization. We would also like to express our deep gratitude for the editorial assistance provided by Tess Campeau and Dr. Heather Shipley. Our University of Toronto Press editor, Doug Hildebrand, has been unwavering in his support for this volume. Last but not least, we would like to thank the contributors to this volume for their intellectual generosity and commitment to engaging with the theme of the volume.
2 *Alberta v. Hutterian Brethren of Wilson Colony*, 2009 SCC 37, [2009] 2 S.C.R. 567.

REFERENCES

Adelman, Howard, and Pierre Anctil. 2011. *Religion, Culture, and the State: Reflections on the Bouchard-Taylor Report*. Toronto: University of Toronto Press.
Beaman, Lori G. 2008. *Defining Harm: Religious Freedom and the Limits of the Law*. Vancouver: UBC Press.
Beaman, Lori G., ed. 2012a. *Reasonable Accommodation: Managing Religious Diversity*. Vancouver: UBC Press.
Beaman, Lori G., ed. 2012b. *Religion and Canadian Society: Contexts, Identities, Strategies*. Toronto: Canadian Scholars Press.
Beaman, Lori G. 2013. "Introduction: Is Polygamy Inherently Harmful?" In *Polygamy's Rights and Wrongs: Perspectives on Harm, Family, and Law*, edited by Gillian Calder and Lori G. Beaman, 1–20. Vancouver: UBC Press.
Beaman, Lori G. 2014. "Opposing Polygamy: A Matter of Equality or Patriarchy?" In *Of Crime and Religion: Polygamy in Canadian Law*, edited by D. Koussens, S. Bernatchez, and M-P. Robert. Sherbrooke: Éditions Revue de droit de l'Université de Sherbrooke.
Beaman, Lori G., and Peter Beyer. 2008. *Religion and Diversity in Canada*. Leiden: Brill.
Beyer, Peter. 1994. *Religion and Globalization*. London: Sage Publications.
Bouchard, Gérard, and Charles Taylor. 2008. "Building the Future: A Time for Reconciliation." *Commission de consultation sur les pratiques d'accommodement reliées aux différences culturelles*. Québec: Québec Government Printing Office, 22 May.
Bramadat, Paul, and David Seljak. 2005. *Religion and Ethnicity in Canada*. Toronto: Pearson Longman.

Bramadat, Paul, and David Seljak. 2008. *Christianity and Ethnicity in Canada.* Toronto: University of Toronto Press.

Calder, Gillian, and Lori G. Beaman. 2013. *Polygamy's Rights and Wrongs.* Vancouver: UBC Press.

Christiano, Kevin J. 2000. "Church and State in Institutional Flux: Canada and the United States." In *Rethinking Church, State, and Modernity: Canada between Europe and America,* edited by David Lyon and Marguerite Van Die, 69–89. Toronto: University of Toronto Press.

Commission de la culture du Québec. 2006. "Croire au patrimoine religieux du Québec." Report, Secrétariat des commissions de l'Assemblée nationale du Québec, Juin.

Estivalèzes, Mireille, and Solange Lefebvre, eds. 2012. *Le programme d'éthique et culture religieuse: De l'exigeante conciliation entre le soi, l'autre et le nous.* Québec: Presses de l'Université Laval.

Ferrari, Silvio, and Sabrina Pastorelli. 2012. *Religion in Public Spaces: A European Perspective.* Surrey/Burlington: Ashgate.

Foblets, Marie-Claire, and Christine Kulakowski. 2010. *Les assises de l'interculturalité 2010.* Bruxelles: Ministère de l'Emploi et de l'Égalité des Chances.

Gaudreault-DesBiens, Jean-François. 2009. *Le droit, la religion et le "raisonnable": Le fait religieux entre monisme étatique et pluralisme juridique.* Montréal: Éditions Thémis.

Hervieu-Léger, Danièle. 1993. *La religion pour mémoire.* Paris: Cerf.

Hervieu-Léger, Danièle, and Françoise Champion. 1986. *Vers un nouveau christianisme?: Introduction à la sociologie du christianisme occidental (Sciences humaines et religions).* Paris: Cerf.

Lefebvre, Solange. 2000. *Religion et identités dans l'école québécoise. Comment clarifier les enjeux.* Saint-Laurent: Fides.

Lefebvre, Solange. 2005. *La religion dans la sphère publique.* Montréal: Presses de l'Université de Montréal.

Lefebvre, Solange, ed. 2009. *Le patrimoine religieux du Québec. Éducation et transmission du sens.* Québec: Presses de l'Université Laval.

Lyon, David, and Marguerite Van Die, eds. 2000. *Rethinking Church, State, and Modernity: Canada between Europe and America.* Toronto: University of Toronto Press.

Martin, David A. 1978. *A General Theory of Secularization.* New York: Harper & Row.

Martin, David A. 2000. "Canada in Comparative Perspective." In *Rethinking Church, State, and Modernity: Canada between Europe and America,* edited by David Lyon and Marguerite Van Die, 22–33. Toronto: University of Toronto Press.

McAndrew, Marie, Micheline Milot, Jean-Sébastin Imbeault, and Paul Eid, eds. 2008. *L'accommodement raisonnable et la diversité religieuse à l'école publique. Normes et pratiques*. Montréal: Fides.

Milot, Micheline. 2002. "Laïcité dans le nouveau monde: Le cas du Québec." *Bibliothèque de l'École des hautes études. Sciences religieuses*, vol. 115. Turnhout: Brepols.

Noppen, Luc, and Lucie K. Morisset. 2005. *Les églises du Québec: Un patrimoine à réinventer*. Sainte-Foy: Presses de l'Université du Québec.

Ouellet, Fernand. 2005. *Quelle formation pour l'éducation à la religion?* Québec: Presses de l'Université Laval.

Proulx, Jean-Pierre, and Task Force on the Place of Religion in Schools in Québec. 1999. *Religion in Secular Schools: A New Perspective for Québec*. Québec: Ministère de l'éducation, Gouvernement du Québec.

Reimer, Samuel. 2000. "A Generic Evanglicalism? Comparing Evangelical Subcultures in Canada and the United States." In *Rethinking Church, State, and Modernity: Canada between Europe and America*, edited by David Lyon and Marguerite Van Die, 228–47. Toronto: University of Toronto Press.

Shachar, Ayelet. 2001. *Multicultural Jurisdictions Cultural Differences and Women's Rights*. Cambridge: Cambridge University Press.

Stackhouse, John G. Jr. 2000. "Bearing Witness: Christian Groups Engage Canadian Politics since 1960s." In *Rethinking Church, State, and Modernity: Canada between Europe and America*, edited by David Lyon and Marguerite Van Die, 113–29. Toronto: University of Toronto Press.

Van Die, Marguerite, ed. 2001. *Religion and Public Life in Canada: Historical and Comparative Perspectives*. Toronto: University of Toronto Press.

CASES

Alberta v. Hutterian Brethren of Wilson Colony, 2009 SCC 37, [2009] 2 S.C.R. 567
Reference re: Section 293 of the Criminal Code of Canada, 2011 BCSC 1588

PART I

The Public/Private Divide

1 Canadian Social Imaginaries

Re-examining Religion and Secularization

PAUL BOWLBY

I propose to use the notion of social imaginary as developed by Benedict Anderson (1991) and Charles Taylor (2004, 2007) as a conceptual
framework within which to reconsider the secularization debate as
it applies to Canada. Underlying the reconsideration is the question,
Why has secularization in Canada unfolded neither in the European
versions nor in those of its neighbour to the south, the United States?
As David Martin (2005) and José Casanova (2006) have compellingly
shown, modernity has spawned many versions of modernization and
its offspring, secularization. Canada's story is one among many.

Modernization in Canada is framed first within a Victorian social
imaginary of a Christian nation conceived in different versions by
Anglo-Protestants and French Roman Catholics. Within these versions
of the imaginary is a fundamental limitation centred on the debate
about equality among peoples of different religious, ethnic, and racial
backgrounds. Imagined alternatives range across segregation, assimilation, or accommodation of difference, however identified. The failure
of the Victorian social imaginary to realize sufficient equality among
citizens opens up the possibility for a new imaginary, the post-1982 version of a "secular nation" based in the 1982 Constitution and *Charter
of Rights and Freedoms*. The *Charter*, with its introduction of a shared
language of human rights, has as one of its objectives to more equi-
tably accommodate ethnic, racial, national, and religious differences.
The historic debate and contemporary silence in the Maritimes over
the place of religion in public education will illustrate these two social
imaginaries.

To develop these themes, I will first examine the secularization
debate as it has been discussed in the Canadian context and the puzzle

posed by its differences from the American and the European debates. That will open a place to reframe the debate using social imaginaries as a framework within which to re-examine the meaning of secularization in Canada. The third part will briefly apply the social imaginary view of secularization to the historic and contemporary debates about the place of religion in public education in the Maritimes. The fractious debates between religious communities about public education will illustrate the good reasons why the Victorian social imaginary collapsed. The failure to recognize any place for religion in public education will raise the question of whether the secular social imaginary can encompass a sufficiently broad and inclusive equality for its citizens.

Secularization in Canada: The Puzzling Middle between Europe and the United States

José Casanova has identified three "connotations" that define standard secularization theory. Secularization posits "a *decline of religious beliefs and practices* in modern societies," "the *privatization of religion*," and "*the differentiation of the secular spheres* (state, economy, science), usually understood as 'emancipation' from religious institutions and norms" (Casanova 2006, 7; emphasis in original). Casanova's tripartite description of secularization seems to have much to commend it in contemporary Canada. There is evidence for decline. Census data and analyses by sociologists of religion in Canada show a well-developed decline in participation in religious worship and membership in church organizations (see Appendix One). There is ample evidence of privatization of the religious. Continuing attachments to church denominations are retained invisibly (Beyer 2000, 189–210). Invisible religion is also evident beyond the believing-without-belonging sector connected to the church denominations. It is also evident in the frequent use of "spirituality" as an alternative terminology to "religion," which has been so usefully analysed by Carrette and King in *Selling Spirituality* (2005). Invisible religion in whatever form it takes is by definition religious life for the private sphere. At every turn the private individual refuses any notion of religious practice that involves a public or corporate identification with religions or denominations. As for differentiation, there is again significant evidence for it in the pervasive handing over to public control of historic religious institutions in the areas of education, health care, and social services (O'Toole 2000, 2006).

Whether or not these examples imply emancipation from religious control is a question that muddies the secularization debate. Christian churches have voluntarily divested themselves of their oversight of or partnership with governments in education, social services, and health care at least in part because the costs of continuing in these roles in the wake of rapidly increasing population were prohibitive. Emancipation as a necessary outcome of differentiation, perhaps more than any other aspect of secularization theory, may in the final analysis be more in the eye of the beholder than a necessary characteristic of secularization in Canada.

At the same time as there is considerable evidence of secularization, there is also evidence for the view that religion is thriving in some sectors and engaging in a lively participation in the public sphere. Post-1960s immigrant populations have given significant vitality to a spectrum of world religions resident in Canada. According to the census data in 2001 the fastest-growing religions in Canada include culturally and ethnically diverse versions of Islam, Hinduism, Sikhism, Buddhism, and new Christian denominations like the Eastern Orthodox churches and multi-ethnic Pentecostal churches (see Appendix Two).

While there is some evidence for the aspiration to relegate all aspects of religion to the private sphere, religion's public participation has been both frequent and controversial. Discussions of abortion and same-sex relations and marriages have been and continue to be routinely public. Other issues like the niqab, the hijab, and the kirpan – to pick only a few – suggest that the wish to liberate the public sphere entirely of religion has not succeeded and probably cannot. Muslim, Jewish, and Christian columnists routinely publish their views in the *Globe and Mail*, Canada's presumptive national newspaper. The *Charter of Rights and Freedoms'* guarantee of the fundamental freedom of conscience and religion and the adjudication of that freedom by the courts and human rights commissions assures that a secular desire to relegate religion to the private sphere cannot be achieved.

The mixture of evidence about secularization in Canada provides a clear indication of an elaborate process of change going on with regard to religion. Whether or not those processes fit classical notions of secularization theory is not entirely clear. There is at least room for reconsideration.

Reconsideration of secularization theory is not novel. Peter Berger threw down the gauntlet in his typically clear way over ten years ago: "My point is that the assumption that we live in a secularized world is false" (Berger 1999, 2). Berger took up the secularization debate again in 2008 with Grace Davie and Effie Fokas to compare secularization in Europe and in America. In passing, Berger mentions Canada as a country occupying a middle ground between the two continental poles. He states:

> America is indeed "exceptional" but with regard to religion it is very much like the rest of the world – namely, very religious. The exception is Europe. (To be precise, western and central Europe; the Orthodox east is a very different story. And "America" here refers to the United States; English-speaking Canada, as one might expect, is about half-way between the United States and Britain in terms of religion, while rapidly secularizing Québec looks like a curious extension of Europe.) Most of the world today is characterized by an explosion of passionate religious movements. (Berger, Davie, and Fokas 2008, 9–10)

It is not self-evident what being "half-way" between the United States and Europe on the secularization scale might mean in relation to the three dimensions of secularization theory identified by Casanova, nor indeed what complexities are introduced into the debate by Canada's *Charter*-grounded tri-nationalism (Aboriginal, French, and English nations), together with its much-heralded and much-debated policy of multiculturalism.

Canada as the puzzling middle has been a subject that has engaged Canadian scholars as well. In their seminal conference and publication, David Lyon and Marguerite Van Die, along with a leading cohort of scholars, took up the issue in *Rethinking Church, State and Modernity: Canada between Europe and America* (2000). The papers include several comparative studies as well as those that seek to uncover the changing character of religion in Canada, especially with regard to the Christian churches. These studies provide a foundational exploration of the intersections of modern secularization and religions in Canada. The three characteristics of secularization identified by Casanova each receive their due, making clear that there are significant developments in Canada along all three lines. Nonetheless, David Lyon in his introductory summation notes, "The point is that secularization, understood as religious decline, deflects attention from the ways that the religious impulse is being reflected, and religious activities restructured. It might also obscure the peculiar paths that the uncoupling of church-and-state take [*sic*] in specific social settings" (Lyon 2000, 10). He argues that secularization theory is much abused as an explanatory device for modernization and calls for a "rethinking of secularization" by examining the "ways in which the religious is restructured and relocated" (Lyon 2000, 10).

In another important reflection on the changing face of religious diversity in Canada, Paul Bramadat and David Seljak have edited two books that illuminate religious change. The first, *Religion and Ethnicity in Canada* (2009 [originally published in 2005]), and the more recent *Christianity and Ethnicity in Canada* (2008) document the impact of the immigration of peoples after 1960 on religious diversity in Canada. The first book surveys the religions experiencing significant growth, such as Islam, Hinduism, Sikhism, Buddhism, and Judaism. The second book documents the lament embedded in what the authors call a "discourse of loss" among historic Canadian denominations experiencing a significant decline in membership overall. They also document the much less visible – but not invisible – changes that immigration is bringing to those denominations. Among the churches, to take one example, growing numbers of Presbyterians are Korean Christians. Both Presbyterians and other church denominations have developed national or ethnically populated parishes and congregations to serve Asian, African, and Latin American populations. Ordained leadership either comes from countries of origin or is developed in Canada. Alongside the local, national, and international organizations of the Protestant, Orthodox, and Roman Catholic churches are vibrant organizations to provide public voices for Muslims, Jews, Buddhists, Hindus, and Sikhs. Taken together, all of this evidence of religious change reiterates the importance of Lyon's call to reconsider the type of secularization occurring in Canada as one among many versions occurring worldwide.

What does seem clear is that the vibrant religious traditions established by the post-1960s immigrants, now citizens of long standing, or the long-established Canadian denominations, albeit with diminished membership, have not abandoned the public sphere for the private. Religions and their diverse members are exploring the meaning of the *Charter* and its freedoms of conscience and religion (Section 2) for a new understanding of how religions are to participate in public life. Within the theoretical debate, the story of secularization in Canada as the puzzling middle is still unresolved. Lyon's call for reconsideration is not out of date. In light of the remarkable changes in the nature of religious diversity in Canada it seems clear that the formations of the secular in Canada are an unfinished story. Our contribution to that discussion centres on the notion of social imaginary as a lens through which to view the processes of change.

Canada's Social Imaginaries

For Benedict Anderson, the nation "is an imagined political community – and imagined as both inherently limited and sovereign." He continues, "It is *imagined* because the members of even the smallest nation will never know most of their fellow-members, meet them, or even hear of them, yet in the minds of each lives the image of their communion" (Anderson 1991, 6). Such nations are *limited* because they are bounded both in space and time; they are *sovereign* as creations of a post-enlightenment awareness of the pluralism of religions and the need for a "place" in which to create freedom for all in the nation's midst. Finally, the nation or state is imagined as a *community* – "a deep horizontal comradeship" symbolized most deeply in the willingness to fight or die for that community and its state (Anderson 1991, 7).

Charles Taylor takes up Anderson's notion of social imaginary with a view to making clear that he is not creating another political or social theory for intellectuals to debate: "I am thinking, rather, of the ways people imagine their social existence, how they fit together with others, how things go on between them and their fellows, the expectations that are normally met, and the deeper normative notions and images that underlie these expectations" (Taylor 2004, 23; see also Taylor 2007, 159ff). Anderson and Taylor are exploring the sense that living is made up of expectations embedded in shared practices that are inscribed in notions and images. Taken together, living in a social imaginary – a political community – is made up of a "repertory" of such practices, notions, and images that make the place what it is. Taylor illustrates this repertory through the practices of an election that carry the very meaning of freedom in them. Not the least of such practices, for example, is the visit to one's door by candidates for election. Standing there with the door ajar, the householder and the candidate greet one another, while shaking hands, and ask how each other is before embarking on discussion first of the weather and then the political matters at hand. Such met expectations, and the learned skills they represent, are the social imaginary at work.

The repertoire of expectations and their collectively understood practices evokes a "deep horizontal comradeship" binding an otherwise disparate people into a sovereign nation designed to create their version of freedom. Consider how English-speaking Protestants described Canada in 1867. They used the word "dominion." The story is told that "Dominion of Canada" was suggested by Sir Leonard

Tilley based on Psalm 72:8 (King James Version): "May He have dominion from sea to sea, and from the river to the ends of the earth." The reference is still inscribed on the Canadian coat of arms. Just as significant as the biblical reference for English Protestants, "dominion" was an imperial term first used to describe lands appropriated to the British Crown and after Confederation for self-governing nations in the British Empire. Only after the colonial conference in 1907 was Canada recognized as a "dominion" in the British Empire. The dual references inscribed by the word "dominion," – biblical and imperial – expressed the social imaginary of the majority, English-speaking and mostly Protestant settlers and early citizens of Canada. For them the accent was on the historic connection with Britain and the importance of federal institutions with the capacity to implement assimilative policies designed to enhance nation building. Such an emphasis was reinforced in the reading of the Christian scriptures in the King James Version in worship in the churches built by the congregation and often by the larger community for every town and village across the land. Dominion named the social imaginary arising out of colonial victory over France and out of a Protestant view of the nation, which, as we shall see, presumed its colonial heritage as inherently good for the state and its denominations as the proper form of religion for inclusion in the public sphere.

The version of Anderson's "comradeship" implemented in the Dominion of Canada was for the most part limited to the contending religious and ethnic groups – Protestant and Catholic, English and French speaking – in the provinces and in the Confederation as a whole. Parliamentary democracy provided a structure for contained competition within which it was essential to maintain political arrangements and practices that would permit acceptance by, and integration of, the losing side in elections. Loss is a dimension of freedom as much as winning – with the second clearly being preferred to the first. Sovereign nations emerging in post-enlightenment, post-colonial settings have had varying degrees of success in dealing with competition, most especially when majorities sought to impose solutions, the effect of which was to assimilate minorities by limiting their capacity to be engaged citizens or by placing their communal identity at risk. Such instances were frequent in the Canadian context. Women were not persons under the law; Acadians were exiled; Black Loyalists were relegated to marginalized ghettoes and Aboriginal peoples to reserves. These instances of exclusion, among many others involving Sikhs, Hindus, and East Asians, from the "comradeship" of shared citizenship are clearly among the most egregious limitations that Anderson identified in the development of social imaginaries.

From its inception in Canada, the social imaginary developed in two languages and employed two repertoires of social convention. If the English Protestant spoke biblically and imperially about "dominion," the alternate voice was in French and was Roman Catholic. Consider Wilfrid Laurier's evocation of social imaginary through the word "cathedral": "The cathedral is made of marble, oak and granite. It is the image of the nation I would like to see Canada become. For here I want the marble to remain the marble; the granite to remain the granite; the oak to remain the oak; and out of all these elements I would build a nation great among the nations of the world" (cited in Weinfeld 2001, 7). Here the accent is on the preservation of difference. The Anglo-Protestant urge to assimilate embedded in "dominion" was both complemented and resisted by the French Roman Catholic urge to preserve the distinctive voice and character of partners in Confederation.

Evoked in Laurier's version of the social imaginary is a repertoire arising from the long colonial heritage of Roman Catholic churches in every village of Québec, the masses and liturgies, the religious communities, and also the clerical hierarchy and its role in the Québec establishment. Laurier's description had its root in Québec but also envisioned metaphorically the religious diversity symbolized in the marble, granite, and oak. All must remain what they are for the vibrancy of the whole. Such a description served to perpetuate the minority francophone people until the Quiet Revolution. The description expressed both the strength of that understanding and its limitation representing the minority voice within Confederation.

Dominion and Cathedral brought with them Victorian repertoires adapted to the Canadian regional landscape. Dominion and Cathedral named imaginaries within which it was possible to construct varieties of community expectations and practices reflecting the religious and ethnic pluralism of the citizens colonizing the nation. Included in its construction were those who emigrated from the homeland of the British Empire and the Loyalists from the United States for whom "duty" lay in an ongoing allegiance to the British Empire. Lives lost in the Boer War and the First and Second World Wars gave expression to the power of that sense of allegiance. Those who gave their lives for freedom envisioned a religious diversity freed of one established church and filled by a relatively limited range of denominations, both Roman Catholic and Protestant, whose task was both the cultivation of the religious life of the community and the building of the nation(s) in the English-speaking and French-speaking regions of the nation.

Every community participated in the building of churches and shared in the religious and social centering of life that most of those buildings provided. Churches were often situated close to the public buildings that encapsulated governmental power, allowing church members to move with relative ease from their offices of state to the offices of worship. So imagined, communities built education systems, social services, and healthcare systems in which denominational allegiance provided both a significant motive and the ground for divisive opposition as Protestants and Catholics competed for public support and funding. At the level of practices and expectations, denominational difference provided the structures within which otherness was recognized, given legitimate competitive expression, and ultimately limited in its socially destructive potential. For some, like the Aboriginal peoples, the South Asians, and the East Asians who arrived on the west coast in the late nineteenth and early twentieth centuries, otherness was the ground for continuing exclusion. Sovereignty as a way to structure freedom in the social imaginary of Canada as a Christian nation was not universal or shared equally.

After the Second World War, the limitations of the Victorian Christian social imaginary became intolerable and, led by the new wave of modernization of the marketplace from its wartime industrial roots, it gave way to the emergence of the secular society. The repatriated Constitution and the *Charter of Rights and Freedoms* (1982) provided the capstone for an emerging understanding of sovereignty designed to provide all individuals with their rights and freedoms. Freedom of conscience and freedom of religion were situated in the *Charter* among other fundamental freedoms. Adjudication of how the freedoms would be interpreted in the event of conflicting claims was a matter for the courts and Parliament to resolve through judicial decisions or legislation. The "plural establishment" of the main-line denominations gave way to corporate establishment, with the state taking a more neutral position on religions. The secular social imaginary aspired to provide a more inclusive freedom for Canadian citizens, superseding the imaginary of the Christian nation with its inherent limitations. In the twenty-eight years since the new constitution came into force, courts, human rights commissions, and public debate have been engaged in the transitional explorations of the secular and its adequacy for a renewed experience of freedom and equality within Canadian sovereignty. Evident throughout the social imaginaries at work in Canada is the unresolved tension between the aspiration to assimilate difference, with its roots in the Anglo-Protestant vision of a dominion, and the need for civil society to accommodate difference, reflected in Laurier's image of the Cathedral and continuing in the *Charter of Rights and Freedoms*.

The Social Imaginaries at Work in Atlantic Canada

British North America Act, Section 93 Education

In and for each Province the Legislature may exclusively make Laws in relation to education, subject and according to the following Provisions:

(1) Nothing in any such Law shall prejudicially affect any Right or Privilege with respect to Denominational Schools which any Class of Persons have by Law in the Province at the Union:

(2) All the Powers, Privileges and Duties at the Union by Law conferred and imposed in Upper Canada on the Separate Schools and School Trustees of the Queen's Roman Catholic Subjects shall be and the same are hereby extended to the Dissentient Schools of the Queen's Protestant and Roman Catholic Subjects in Québec.

The Victorian Christian social imaginary in the Maritimes took its shape both in the pre- and post-Confederation "dominion" of Canada. The social imaginary exploited the full duality of the meaning of dominion, pointing both toward the Christian denominations present among the citizens and to the imperial, colonial mores and attachments. To paraphrase Taylor, the social existence of how diverse people were to fit together took shape across the colonial regimes of France, then Great Britain, and post-Confederation Canada. At issue throughout were the public policy choices that were required to shape how things were to go between peoples. Segregation, assimilation, and accommodation provide the spectrum across which many of those choices were made. It is far beyond the scope of this paper to enumerate all of the choices; our focus instead will be on the post-Confederation development of public education and the place of religion within it.

The dominant social imaginary in the Maritimes was the Anglo-Protestant Victorian Christian social imaginary. From within that imaginary the problem was to resolve the religious differences among citizens at the level of public policy. After 1867, the issue to be worked out within the imaginary came down to a question of religious equality among the denominations and their members, in particular between Roman Catholics and Protestants. Was equality possible given the inherited animosities among religious groups still embedded in their colonial, competitive history and still carrying their links to English, Scottish, and Irish nationalities? The formation of education systems in the Maritimes became a major exercise in the exploration of the notion of equality and how to teach each generation the practices required to live among equal citizens.

Public education is a principal requirement of modernization for any state. Literacy and numeracy are among the bedrock skills required, not to mention the more advanced skills required of scientists, engineers, navigators, and so on. Education was not, and probably is not, however, conceived as a value-neutral institution in which persons learn those sorts of skills. As William Katerburg puts it, "perhaps the most obvious place where religious identities, social order, and politics overlapped was in public schools. Besides academic subjects, English Canadian and American public schools promoted progress, capitalism, individualism, good citizenship, and consensus Protestantism" (2000, 286). Education's task was, and presumably still is, in some measure, to create the best kind of citizen, one who is capable of functioning within the democratic institutions of the state and society at large. The kind of citizens required within the Victorian Christian imaginary were educated persons, deeply rooted in the practices and virtues of the various Christian churches, with the skills necessary for a modernizing society. How, and to what extent, therefore could provincial policies incorporate the kinds of education required both for skilled labour and for citizenship in a Christian nation? What ensued from such questions was the debate over religion in the schools.

Section 93 of the *British North America Act* (BNA Act) set the terms for the exploration of the meaning of equality. It designated education as a provincial responsibility. This meant that the provinces could determine unique policies about the place of religion and religious practices in the schools. This policy served the interests of Québec certainly and was a condition insisted upon for entry into Confederation. Section 93 of the BNA Act was apparently a repudiation of the objective of assimilation as formulated, for example, in Lord Durham's Report (1838). The issue of an established Anglican Church had been rejected and the clergy reserves dispersed (1840). This was particularly important in Nova Scotia where the Anglican Church had been the established religion of the province/region. Thereafter the plurality of denominations in Canada was given state recognition that took specific constitutional shape in the BNA Act of 1867 in the section on education. It stated: "Nothing in any such Law shall prejudicially affect any Right or Privilege with respect to Denominational Schools which any Class of Persons have by Law in the Province at the Union" (Section 93.1).

The appearance of constitutionally grounded accommodation of religious difference in education was, however, forcefully contested within the Victorian Christian social imaginary in the Maritimes. Protestant majorities, however small, as in the case of Prince Edward Island, struggled vehemently against tax support for Roman Catholic schools. Every legal technicality was used to avoid the seemingly obvious meaning of Section 93 in the BNA Act. The popular Protestant view in the Maritime Provinces was that education was an area of such importance that it could be used as a public policy tool to demonstrate Protestant precedence over the minority Roman Catholic populations. In contrast, Roman Catholics sought to implement the guarantees for denominational schools as suggested in the BNA Act. Nonetheless, Protestants resisted the provision of tax-based funding for denominational schools while advocating limited inclusion of Bible reading – often to be done without comment – and religious exercises at the beginning and end of the school day.

In the 1860s and 1870s across the Maritimes the legislated solutions developed excluded public funding of denominational schools. Sir Charles Tupper led the opposition to denominational schools in Nova Scotia successfully. In doing so he brought to an end the dual system of Roman Catholic and Protestant schools established in 1840. After the *Common School Act* in 1871 in New Brunswick, the teaching of the catechism, the wearing of religious symbols, and funding for Catholic schools were prohibited. In Prince Edward Island, the *Public School Act* in 1877 permitted Bible reading without comment and optional attendance at religious exercises, but denied funding for Roman Catholic schools.

The story does not end with the legislatures and their repudiation of the guarantees in the BNA Act. Whether it was the riot in 1875 led by disaffected Roman Catholics in New Brunswick or the civic compromise in Halifax, the legislated results did not work. There was, to paraphrase Charles Taylor (2004, 23), a problem with the reality of how citizens could fit together when the education system entrenched a failure to accommodate. As a result, in New Brunswick the compromise involved an understanding of how school systems would be administered. Any child could go to any school, permitting religiously based clusters of pupils in a school; religious orders were allowed to teach in schools; and religious instruction could take place after regular class hours. Textbooks were reviewed to remove religious offense. In Nova Scotia, the school boards found another way to work around the legislation. The boards rented Roman Catholic schools for the use of public education. The result was the creation of a unified public education system with a religiously dual practice. This administrative solution endured until the 1960s with the result that by 1967 this system had evolved to include fourteen Roman Catholic schools in which 98 per cent of the students were Catholic and seventeen "public" schools in which over 97 per cent of the students were Protestant or of no Christian denomination. Religious orders routinely taught in the Roman Catholic schools. As in the case of New Brunswick, religious instruction could be offered outside of normal class hours (Cutting 2003).

At work in the legislative arena and in the arena of social and religious compromise is the formation of the practices designed to form a limited version of equality in the Maritimes. It incorporates the exercise of majority rule and power, on the one hand, with a kind of discretionary administrative practice designed to make a kind of equality possible on the other. There are profound risks inherent to the kind of solutions developed in the Maritimes. While it created a measured equality in educational opportunity for the predominantly Irish Roman Catholic population in Halifax, it also illustrated how the Victorian Protestant imaginary worked when groups were deemed not to fit together with the majority population. Thus for the descendants of the Loyalist Black population who ended up in segregated settlements such as "Africville" on the Bedford Basin in Halifax, there was no administrative accommodation. "The Old School" in Africville began in 1883, funded by the residents of Africville. It provided education in Africville for children up to grade eight and, upon graduation, students moved on to north-end public schools with limited success (Clairmont and Magill 1974, 110–11). Even more distant from the urban compromise solution in Halifax was the assimilationist educational policy of the federal government for Aboriginal peoples on reservations, culminating in the residential school system administered by the Christian denominations. There were no residential schools in New Brunswick or Prince Edward Island. The residential school at Shubenacadie, Nova Scotia, ran from approximately 1922 through 1968 and was administered by the Roman Catholic Church through two religious orders, the Sisters of Charity of Saint Vincent de Paul and the Missionary Oblates of Mary Immaculate.

38   Paul Bowlby

The administrative solutions point to the inherent limitation in the Victorian Christian social imaginary in its Maritime version. In education a measured equality was dispensed by the privileged majority. It is not sufficient however to see in the solutions a kind of pragmatism designed to make society with its religious differences work. The policy debates on the place of religion in education were an exploration into the meaning of equality that tended in the direction of accommodation of difference, but could not realize it. That it lasted over one hundred years into the late 1960s is no small measure of the habitual acceptance of such forms of consensus between majority and minority constituencies. Within its limitations, however, the imaginary framed modernization for the Maritimes.

Conclusion

For good reasons, the Victorian Christian imaginary gave way to the secular imaginary. William Katerburg (2000, 283–301) rightly argues that the imaginary no longer functions to legitimate the relationship between social mores and the public sphere. It failed, in the terms of this argument, to sufficiently institutionalize equality for Canadian citizens. Unfortunately, in a post-*Charter*, secular Canada, the old habit of exclusion endures. The place of religion in contemporary schools illustrates the limitation, this time of the secular social imaginary.

Whereas the administrative solution to denominational diversity, principally between Catholics and Protestants, permitted funding of schools across the religious divide, in the secular system, religion is largely ignored and severely limited, if not excluded. There are two different kinds of exception to this exclusion. In Halifax, for example, there is a remnant of the denominationally plural public school system. It is still possible to offer religious education outside of normal school hours if parents will organize it and find a teacher willing to teach it and obtain parental consent. Such courses are rarely offered, and when they are offered, they are modeled on catechism classes rather than on the study of religions. The second exception is school-initiated courses on world religions. The origins of this exception lie with teachers at St. Patrick's High School and its Protestant equivalent, Queen Elizabeth High School, two schools that were located only a few hundred meters from one another in downtown Halifax. World religions courses were started in the schools and taught successfully for several years. The curriculum was developed by individual teachers and was approved by the school administration and the Halifax school board. Both of these schools are now closed and have been replaced by Citadel High

School, which does not offer courses on world religions. Halifax West High School continues this tradition of world religions courses initiated by teachers at the school and approved only for that school. Beyond that, religion has virtually been eliminated from the curriculum of the schools and from the social studies curriculum. The province has no plans to develop a provincially approved world religions curriculum.

Religious education and world religions are routinely offered by private religious schools such as Sacred Heart School for girls and the boys' school, the Fountain Academy of the Sacred Heart. The Muslim Academy integrates Qur'an studies into the otherwise provincially approved curriculum. Contemplative practice is taught in the Shambhala School sponsored by the Shambhala Buddhist community in the city. In summary, there is little or no felt urgency to accommodate the study of world religions in the public school curriculum, leaving only the private schools to offer world religions courses.

Unlike other regions, however, out-migration of the populations has predominated over the limited in-migration. In base numbers, the region has not developed a sufficiently diverse ethnic and religious population. In other regions there is a vigorous debate about what can and should be accommodated. So, for example, there appears to be no move on the part of the Department of Education to develop an approved curriculum for world religions. Such a proactive step in the creation of a welcoming society would recognize the fact that those immigrant communities that have come to the Maritimes have identified their religious life as a primary value by building sanctuaries in which to worship and hold community gatherings (Bowlby and Erhard 2008). Hindus, Sikhs, Buddhists, Muslims, Coptic Christians, and Greek and Lebanese Orthodox all have created their own sacred spaces at their own communal expense. In this respect, these post-1960s communities have done what Christians and Jews did historically in the Maritimes and across Canada: they have invested in their communities through the construction of their religious sanctuaries. A curriculum on world religions could give positive recognition to the diversity of religious communities in the Maritimes, even as it enhances the understanding of the whole population about the diversity in its midst.

To view classic secularization theory in Canada through the lens of social imaginary provides an illuminating perspective. In the context of the Victorian Christian social imaginary, the groundwork was established for modernization, industrialization, and the education necessary for a modern nation-state. Victorian Christianity played an integral and varied role in the development of that modern state. It is not obvious that the modernization brought an end to that Victorian imaginary. Rather, the inherent limitations of the construction of that imaginary press toward their limits around the issues of ethnic and religious difference. Public policies that segregate, assimilate, and fail to accommodate gave formal definition to those limits. The question remains: can a secular social imaginary actually deliver on those issues on which the Victorian Christian imaginary so clearly failed?

REFERENCES

Anderson, Benedict. 1991. *Imagined Communities* (rev. ed.). London: Verso.
Belanger, A., and É. Caron Malenfant, with the collaboration of L. Martel, Y. Carriere, C. Hicks, and G. Rowe. 2005. "Population Projections of Visible Minority Groups, Canada, Provinces and Regions 2001–2017." Ottawa: Statistics Canada, Demography Division.
Berger, Peter L., ed. 1999. *The Desecularization of the World: Resurgent Religion and World Politics*. Washington, DC: Ethics and Public Policy Center, William B. Eerdmans Publishing Company.
Berger, Peter, Grace Davie, and Effie Fokas. 2008. *Religious America, Secular Europe?: A Theme and Variations*. Aldershot: Ashgate Publishing Limited.
Beyer, Peter. 2000. "Modern Forms of the Religious Life: Denomination, Church and Invisible Religion in Canada, the United States and Europe." In *Rethinking Church, State and Modernity: Canada between Europe and America*, edited by David Lyon and Marguerite Van Die, 189–210. Toronto: University of Toronto Press.
Bowlby, Paul, and Nancie Erhard. 2008. "Shaping and Re-Shaping Urban Landscapes in Halifax: The Recent Contributions of Immigrant Religious Communities." *Our Diverse Cities* 5: 95–9.
Bramadat, Paul, and David Seljak, eds. 2008. *Christianity and Ethnicity in Canada*. Toronto: University of Toronto Press.
Bramadat, Paul, and David Seljak, eds. 2009. *Religion and Ethnicity in Canada*. Toronto: University of Toronto Press [First published in 2005 by Pearson].
Carrette, David, and Richard King. 2005. *Selling Spirituality: The Silent Takeover of Religion*. London: Routledge.
Casanova, José. 2006. "Rethinking Secularization: A Global Comparative Perspective." *The Hedgehog Review* 8(1–2): 7–22.
Clairmont, Donald, and Dennis William Magill. 1974. *Africville: The Life and Death of a Canadian Black Community*. Toronto: McClelland and Stewart Limited.
Craig, Gerald M. 2006. *Lord Durham's Report, New Edition*. Montréal and Kingston: McGill-Queen's University Press.

Cutting, Christopher. 2003. "Multicultural Accommodation or Selective Tolerance? Religion in the Education System of Canada's Maritime Provinces." Unpublished honours thesis in Religious Studies, Saint Mary's University, Halifax.

Katerburg, William H. 2000. "Consumers and Citizens: Religion, Identity, and Politics in Canada and the United States." In *Rethinking Church, State and Modernityy: Canada between Europe and America*, edited by David Lyon and Marguerite Van Die, 283–301. Toronto: University of Toronto Press.

Lyon, David. 2000. "Introduction." In *Rethinking Church, State and Modernity: Canada between Europe and America*, edited by David Lyon and Marguerite Van Die, 3–19. Toronto: Toronto University Press.

Lyon, David, and Marguerite Van Die, eds. 2000. *Rethinking Church, State and Modernity: Canada between Europe and America*. Toronto: University of Toronto Press.

Martin, David. 2005. *On Secularization: Towards a Revised General Theory*. Aldershot: Ashgate.

Nation's Encyclopedia. (n.d.). "Nova Scotia." Available at http://www.nationsency clopedia.com/canada/Alberta-to-Nova-Scotia/Nova-Scotia.html/

O'Toole, Roger. 2000. "Canadian Religion: Heritage and Project." In *Rethinking Church, State and Modernityy: Canada between Europe and America*, edited by David Lyon and Marguerite Van Die, 34–51. Toronto: University of Toronto Press.

O'Toole, Roger. 2006. "Religion in Canada: Its Development and Contemporary Situation." In *Religion and Canadian Society: Traditions, Transitions, and Innovations*, edited by Lori G. Beaman, 7–21. Toronto: Canadian Scholars' Press.

Statistics Canada. 1993. "Religion: Catholic and Protestant Religions Continued to Decline." *The Daily*, 1 June 1, 3–4.

Taylor, Charles. 2004. *Modern Social Imaginaries*. Durham: Duke University Press.

Taylor, Charles. 2007. *A Secular Age*. Cambridge: The Belknap Press of Harvard University Press.

Weinfeld, Morton. 2001. *Like Everyone Else ... But Different*. Toronto: McClelland & Steward Ltd.

LEGISLATION

British North America Act, 1867, 30–31 Vict., c. 3 (U.K.)
Canadian Charter of Rights and Freedoms, Part I of the *Constitution Act, 1982*

APPENDICES

Appendix One

Table 1.1. Religious affiliation, Canada

	1891	1901	1911	1921	1931	1941	1951	1961	1971	1981	1991
					Percentage Distribution						
Catholic	41.6	41.7	39.4	38.7	41.3	43.4	44.7	46.7	47.3	47.3	45.7
Roman Catholic	41.6	41.7	39.4	38.7	39.5	41.8	43.3	45.7	46.2	46.5	45.2
Ukrainian Catholic	–	–	–	–	1.8	1.6	1.4	1.0	1.1	0.8	0.5
Protestant	56.5	55.6	55.9	56.0	54.4	52.2	50.9	48.9	44.4	41.2	36.2
United Church (1)	–	–	–	0.1	19.5	19.2	20.5	20.1	17.5	15.6	11.5
Anglican	13.7	12.8	14.5	16.1	15.8	15.2	14.7	13.2	11.8	10.1	8.1
Presbyterian (1)	15.9	15.8	15.6	16.1	8.4	7.2	5.6	4.5	4.0	3.4	2.4
Lutheran	1.4	1.8	3.2	3.3	3.8	3.5	3.2	3.6	3.3	2.9	2.4
Baptist	6.4	5.9	5.3	4.8	4.3	4.2	3.7	3.3	3.1	2.9	2.5
Pentecostal	–	–	–	0.1	0.3	0.5	0.7	0.8	1.0	1.4	1.6
Other Protestant (2)	19.1	19.3	17.3	15.5	2.3	2.4	2.5	3.4	3.7	4.9	7.9
Eastern Orthodox	–	0.3	1.2	1.9	1.0	1.2	1.2	1.3	1.5	1.5	1.4
Jewish	0.1	0.3	1.0	1.4	1.5	1.5	1.5	1.4	1.3	1.2	1.2
No Religion (3)		0.1	0.4	0.2	0.2	0.2	0.4	0.5	4.3	7.3	12.4
Other (4)	1.8	1.9	2.0	1.9	1.6	1.5	1.4	1.2	1.2	1.5	3.2

1. Between 1911 and 1931, the United Church denomination was formed through an amalgamation of Methodists, Congregationalists, and about one half of the Presbyterian group. For 1931, and thereafter, the figures for Presbyterian reflect the segment that did not amalgamate with the United Church.
2. Other Protestant denominations include Methodists and Congregationalists up to 1921, and other denomination such as Adventist, Churches of Christ, Disciples, and the Salvation Army. The "Other" group also includes a certain proportion of smaller Protestant denominations.
3. In 1891, "No religion" is included in "Other;" in 1971, the introduction of self-enumeration methodology may have been in part a cause of the large increase in the proportion of the population reporting "No religion." However, the 1971, 1981, and 1991 figures for this group are comparable.
4. In 1981, many of these smaller denominations were disaggregated and are counted in the "Other Protestant" category. The remainder of the "Other" group includes Eastern non-Christian religions.
Source: Statistics Canada (1993, 3).

Appendix Two

Table 1.2. Major religious denominations, Canada, 1991 and 2001

	2001 Number	2001 Percentage	1991 Number	1991 Percentage	Percentage change
Roman Catholic	12,793,125	43.2	12,203,625	45.2	4.8
Protestant	8,654,845	29.2	9,427,675	34.9	−8.2
Christian Orthodox	479,620	1.6	387,395	1.4	23.8
Christian (other) (2)	780,450	2.6	353,040	1.3	121.1
Muslim	579,640	2.0	253,265	0.9	128.9
Jewish	329,995	1.1	318,185	1.2	3.7
Buddhist	300,345	1.0	163,415	0.6	83.8
Hindu	297,200	1.0	157,015	0.6	89.3
Sikh	278,415	0.9	147,440	0.5	88.8
No religion	4,796,325	16.2	3,333,245	12.3	43.9

1. For comparability purposes, 1991 data are presented according to 2001 boundaries.
2. Includes persons who report "Christian," as well as those who report "Apostolic," "Born-again Christian," and "Evangelical."

Source: Belanger et al. 2005.

Appendix Three

Table 1.3 Canadian population, 2003

Estimated 2003 population	936,000
Population change, 1996–2001	−0.1%
Percentage urban/rural population	
Urban	55.8%
Rural	44.2%
Foreign-born population	4.6%
Population by ethnicity	
Canadian	425,880
Scottish	263,060
English	252,470
Irish	178,585
French	149,785
German	89,460
Dutch (Netherlands)	35,035
North American Indian	28,560
Welsh	12,245
Italian	11,240
Acadian	11,180
Métis	4,395

Source: Nations Encyclopedia (n.d.)

2 Between the Public and the Private

Governing Religious Expression

LORI G. BEAMAN

Debates about the public presence of religion have been intense and varied of late, not only in Canada, but in many Western democracies. In Switzerland, for example, twenty-two of twenty-six cantons voted to ban the building of new minarets;[1] in Italy the presence of the crucifix in classrooms preoccupied not only the Italian courts, but subsequently the European Court of Human Rights;[2] in England the wearing of a cross in the workplace was held to be unnecessary to the Christian faith and an employer's request that it be removed was deemed reasonable;[3] and in France, of course, head coverings continue to attract legal sanction and controversy.[4] The fact that the debates about the presence of religion in the public sphere extend to so many Western liberal democracies suggests that they may be linked and that it might be useful to seek to understand them by thinking about possible patterns of similarity between nation-states, rather than isolating the analysis to individual nation-states. It is in this context and with a view to broader patterns and implications that I consider religion in the public sphere in Canada.

To begin, it is important to explicate the terms of reference for the reflections that follow. While there is much discussion of the "public sphere," there is little reflection on what falls within the definition of "the public." In many cases there is an unreflexive association of the public with the state and state institutions. But this does not completely capture the nuance of "the public" and what, for many of us, seems like public space in the course of our daily lives. What do we mean by the "public sphere"? We may walk to work on public streets, take public transit, enter a private business that is accessible to the general public, eat our lunch in a restaurant that is open to the public, wave to our neighbour from our balcony that is visible to the public, pick up our children from a public school (or a private school that is publicly accessible for those who have the means), interact with publicly funded service providers, and so on. Each of these settings may have different rules, regulations, and social expectations regarding the presence of religion, thus rendering impossible a discussion of "the" public sphere as a uniform space.

Further, the notion of the "public" is frequently positioned as part of the binary "public/private." Indeed, it is questionable whether either of these terms has meaning without the other. And the private is equally fraught with conceptual challenges, as was laid bare by the feminist slogan "the personal is political." Robert Orsi (2003) has also challenged the idea that religion is ever "private," noting that even prayer in the solace of one's own home is public. The blurring of the boundaries between the public and the private is a dynamic phenomenon, revealing them as socially constructed concepts that are dependent on social actors and power relations.

Contests over religion in the public sphere, then, are embedded in these shifting boundaries, and in part the contest is almost always over the line between what is visible to others and what remains out of view. There is a wide range of issues and behaviours included in these contests: the meeting of Raelians in a local pub; the saying of prayers at the beginning of a municipal council meeting; the presence of niqab-wearing women on the streets, in the courtroom, and in hospitals; the wearing of a kirpan in school, on an airplane, or in a government building; the presence of a succah on the balcony of a high-end condominium building; or an eruv in a predominantly orthodox Jewish neighbourhood. There are issues of quantity and context – how many Raelians are too many? How many niqab-wearing women can be present before fear and panic are generated? Where is the line between participation and presence in the public sphere and forcing others to engage in religious behaviour that is not their own? Can the presence of dominant religious symbols be experienced as force or coercion? In order to begin to answer these questions it is important to consider the social context from which they emerge.

This chapter will consider the ways in which religion lies between the public and the private, and the implications for its governance and its practice. In the first section I briefly discuss the shadow establishment in Canada and the positive and negative contributions of a predominantly Christian church to Canada. This history in turn informs the debates about religion in the public sphere in contemporary Canada.

I then draw from recent Supreme Court of Canada case law that has dealt with the public/private divide in very spatial ways. In other words, the space that religion occupies – on a balcony, in a school yard, on the streets – is a key, yet often ignored, aspect of the negotiation of the public, the private, and the space in-between. The third part considers Canada's debates about religion in the public sphere in the context of other Western democracies.

Religion in the Public Sphere in Canada

The largely and historically Christian population of Canada has meant that, for the most part, religion in the public sphere has been dominated by the presence of Christianity. Social institutions are embedded with Christian symbols and practices: the *Canadian Charter of Rights and Freedoms* includes mentions of the supremacy of God, tax exemptions have largely benefited Christian churches, and public holidays are often religious and/or entirely Christian. It is important to be honest about the presence of Christianity in the public sphere, as well as to reflect carefully on the effects of a dominant religion's presence in the public sphere in a country that has (at least until recently) purported to be proud of its (ever-increasing) diversity. This diversity has been carefully propogated, both at home and internationally, through the ideology of multiculturalism. There has never been a full-fledged Christian establishment in the Canadian context (neither Protestant nor Catholic), but nor has there been a disestablishment. Perhaps the best description of the Canadian position has been what David Martin (2000) described as a "shadow establishment," although this may not adequately describe the historical position of the Roman Catholic Church in Québec (see also Seljack 2008 for the idea of residual Christianity).

Religious groups in Canada have contributed and continue to contribute to the welfare of Canadians in both material and spiritual senses, as well as to public debates on a range of issues.[5] So, for example, the Salvation Army continues to run shelters for the homeless across Canada, and various church-based programs run soup kitchens and food banks. The positive presence of Christianity in the public sphere has been rendered more complex by the negative contributions, including Christianity's involvement in residential schools, the abuse of children by clergy, and the denial of equality to women in church hierarchies. These negative contributions have created painful memories of religion for many people and indeed have contributed to a more negative perception of religion overall, even for those who have never directly experienced harm. Their influence over present debates about religion in the public sphere should not be underestimated (Gagnon-Tessier 2012). Perhaps nowhere is this more in evidence than in Québec, where, while 45.3 per cent of Québécers still identify themselves as Roman Catholic (Statistics Canada 2011), there is a cautious if not overtly hostile attitude toward the church's involvement in the public sphere. During the Bouchard-Taylor Commission hearings, open hostility toward the church and anything short of a laïque society was often framed in terms of memory of past injustices, especially toward women. This has been carried forward by the Conseil du Statut de la femme (2011) in their staunch opposition to the *laïcité ouverte* called for by the Bouchard-Taylor Commission and their insistence on "real" laïcité.[6]

> Aussi, nous allons démontrer qu'un Québec respectueux de l'égalité entre les sexes ne peut continuer de s'avancer sur la voie de la « laïcité ouverte ». Pour le Conseil, la « laïcité ouverte », c'est la laïcité ouverte aux atteintes à l'égalité des femmes. Comme le notait le rapport de la Commission de réflexion sur l'application du principe de laïcité dans la République (Rapport Stasi) remis au président français: « Aujourd'hui, la laïcité ne peut être conçue sans lien direct avec le principe d'égalité entre les sexes ». C'est avec cette préoccupation de préservation et d'amélioration des droits des femmes que nous allons montrer que l'affirmation de la laïcité de l'État québécois en tant que principe structurant est nécessaire, autant que l'adoption de mesures qui devraient l'accompagner ...
>
> Pour cela, nous allons d'abord constater que, de tout temps, religion a rimé avec oppression des femmes. Les trois grandes religions monothéistes ont toujours été et continuent d'être discriminatoires à l'égard des femmes. Ensuite, nous verrons qu'à mesure que l'État s'est dissocié de la religion, les femmes ont progressé sur le chemin de l'égalité. Au Québec, la présence de l'Église catholique au cœur de la société a longtemps nui à la marche des femmes vers l'égalité. La laïcisation de la société a levé un obstacle de taille à la reconnaissance de leurs droits. (Conseil du statut de la femme 2011, 11–12)

This combined positive and negative history of the traditional majority religion (Christianity) in Canada forms an important contextualizing factor in thinking about religion in the public sphere. Challenges to Christian hegemony are often met with accusations of anti-Christian motivations or, more recently, framed as threats to Canadian values.[7]

As dominant power relations are disrupted for a host of reasons (some of which will be discussed in more detail later), religion in the public sphere becomes a more urgently contested matter of whose religion is given public voice and under what conditions. It is important to recognize that not everyone is an equal negotiator in this process. Thus, in the process of working toward a fair distribution of access to and presence in the public sphere, two things seem to be especially important: (1) to consider carefully and honestly the impact of the traditionally dominant religion on the ways in which religion is present in the public sphere and (2) to avoid throwing the baby out with the bathwater – the baby in this instance being Christianity. Thus, for example, in Québec, while narratives about the oppression of women under the *de facto* Roman Catholic establishment abound, the same attention is now paid to the ways in which women have also found community and support in the church.

Despite the majority presence and influence of Christianity at all levels of Canadian society, some attempt has been made in recent years to redefine Christianity as a minority position in Canada, mostly by conservative Christians. The move to include same-sex couples in the marriage regime of Canada was hotly contested by religious conservatives from a range of traditions. While the argument was made from a majoritarian position about the place and purpose of marriage (marriage always has and should only include opposite sex couples), the discourse subsequent to the *Reference re Same-Sex Marriage*[8] has been framed in terms of religious minority rights. There is also a general concern about the erasure of Christian symbols from the public sphere, and it is here that these groups may find more support. The question that emerges from all of this is whether Christian groups are seeking to have a place in the religious mosaic or to restore or preserve a Christian Canada (Blaikie 2011; Suderman 2011).

The struggle over religion in the public sphere is presented as one among competing religious voices and interests. But religion in the public sphere is not simply about making room for other, non-hegemonic religions or, put another way, making a place for minority religions alongside the majority religion. It is also making space for the non-religious, atheists, humanists, and those for whom religion does not form part of their identities. Renewed attention on religion and spirituality has generated an approach that imagines everyone as having religious or spiritual needs ("we are all religious now" as Winnifred Sullivan [2009b] puts it) or what I have described (following Foucault) as the will to religion (Beaman 2013). The need to confess or reveal our spiritual needs and the assumption that we all have spiritual needs have infiltrated social institutions such as hospitals, schools, and prisons.

If we were to reduce the situation in Canada regarding religion in the public sphere to its simplest terms we might describe it this way: we are in the midst of a struggle that imagines the presence of religion in Canada in a number of ways. One of these imaginaries is in some measure linked to the imaginary of a multicultural Canada that includes a multiplicity of religious voices, symbols, and practices with as fluid a boundary as possible between the public and the private. A second model is a rigid separation between the public and the private, with religion relegated to the private sphere, a "true" laïcité similar to that of France. A final model is one in which Christianity remains the dominant religious discourse, intertwined with Canadian values, and permits, within the range of tolerance and accommodation, the expression of other religious practices and beliefs. Like any ideal type, none of the models are found in pure form, but intertwined with each other in various places in public and institutional discourses. In the following section I'll focus on the ways in which law has understood the relationship between religion and the public/private.

Recent Case Law and Debates over Religion in the Public Sphere

Case law arguably represents some of the more pressing debates about religion in the public sphere and for that reason it provides interesting examples that offer a way to examine the negotiation of the boundaries of the public/private divide as well as the limits on religion in the public sphere. Three of the most recent cases to come before the Supreme Court of Canada illustrate some interesting facets of the intertwining of the public and religion, and also demonstrate the shifting boundaries of the private and the public.

Since the ideas of public and private are closely intertwined with the notion of space, in this section I'll draw from the work of Kim Knott (2005, 2009), who has crafted a particularly insightful theoretical/ methodological tool for the analysis of religion from a spatial perspective. Like Knott, I don't wish to suggest that a spatial analysis can be reduced simply to geography, landscape, and place. But, by beginning with space and imagining how it is implicated in discussions about religion and religious freedom, we may in turn better understand the ways in which the public and the private are constructed. Space in this context is "a medium, a methodology and an outcome" (Knott 2009, 3). Space plays an important role in any discussion over religion in the public sphere, whether we are thinking about the Jehovah's Witnesses who hand us a brochure in a park or come to our door on a Saturday morning, the presence of a crucifix in a national assembly, or the temporary colonizing of auditory space by church bells, for example. By thinking more explicitly about space, the divide between the public and the private is exposed as being, at the very least, socially constructed. The church bells intrude into my living room; the Jehovah's Witnesses intrude into my "personal space," even in a public park; and the crucifix brings the religious beliefs of the majority into a space that is supposed to be public in that it represents all citizens. The case explorations that follow invite the reader to engage with a troubling of the public/private divide, in part by thinking about the space involved and the ways in which narratives about what is public or what is private are negotiated, imagined, and constructed.

The first case is *Amselem*,[9] which was decided in 2004. The claimant was an Orthodox Jew who lived in a condominium building in Montréal. Under the terms of the by-laws in the declaration of co-ownership, decorations, alterations, and constructions on the balconies were prohibited. During the festival of Succot he wished to build a succah – a structure resembling a tent – on his balcony, which was prohibited by co-ownership by-laws. Although there was some evidence that a communal succah would fulfill the requirements of his religion, the claimant's interpretation was that he should build his own succah on his balcony. This intrusion into public space was supported by the Supreme Court, which held that aesthetics should not outweigh religious freedom. The analysis began with as assessment of the sincerity of belief of the claimant. Once the Court established that he was sincere, it had no problem erasing the divide between the private, an intensely personal version of religious commitment it recognized through sincerity, and the public space of the balcony. If we think about the decision spatially, the *Amselem* case endorses the presence of religion in a public domain. Indeed, the aesthetic vision of the high-end condo building is disrupted by the dissolution of the public/private divide.

Two years later the *Multani*[10] case came before the Court. In this case a Sikh schoolboy sought the right to wear a kirpan to school, a right protected under the religious freedom provisions of the Québec *Charter of Human Rights and Freedoms*. The parents and the school board had entered into an agreement that contained the conditions under which the boy could wear his kirpan. The conditions were rigorous and rendered the symbol both invisible and impotent. Nonetheless, the school board took issue with the agreement. The Supreme Court of Canada upheld Mr. Multani's right to wear a kirpan. After a brief excursion through the "sincerity" query, the Court considered numerous factors, including questions of security. That a relatively small proportion of Sikhs are orthodox or fully observant was not considered by the Court, suggesting that the individualized vision of religion introduced in *Amselem* was also accepted in *Multani*. Again, though, the Court decoupled "individual" and "private," allowing the bringing of a religious symbol into the public sphere of the school.

Finally, in 2009, the Supreme Court decided the *Hutterian Brethren* case,[11] in which a small group of Hutterian Brethren who live communally in Alberta sought an exemption from having their photographs on their driver's licences, which they believe contravenes the Bible. They had been granted an exemption for thirty years, but the government of Alberta revoked the exemption. The Supreme Court upheld the government's decision and believed its evidence that exempting the Hutterites would compromise the security of the driver's licence system and risk identity theft.

The *Hutterian Brethren* case may seem a peculiar inclusion in this discussion as it is not about the presence of a symbol or the incursion of a religious structure into public space, as were the *Multani* and *Amselem* cases, but the case does deal with the participation of a religious group in a "public" regulatory regime and, as the case has been framed, a request for an exemption from that regime. Further, the decision of the Supreme Court in this instance marks a dramatic and radical shift from the previous cases, which were characterized by their expansive and inclusive approach to religious minorities. Both *Multani* and *Amselem* approached religion in a somewhat paradoxical manner – beginning with the individual and his (in both cases) religious commitment and then ensuring that commitment has full expression in what might be considered the public arena – a balcony visible to all and a school yard. The boundary between public and private in these cases is dissolved or at least significantly blurred. The *Hutterian Brethren* case takes another tack, framing the Hutterian Brethren as "other" whose religious commitment has no place in a public regulatory regime. Indeed, because of their communal lifestyle the decision has the effect of establishing a rather more rigid boundary between the Hutterian Brethren and the surrounding community.[12]

In many ways the *Hutterian Brethren* case signaled a shift in the public/private divide for religion. Developments subsequent to that case suggest that this shift may be somewhat widespread. For example, the introduction of Bill 94 in Québec marks, as suggested by Pascale Fournier and Erica See in this volume, a significant extension of the public domain. The upholding of the Criminal Code provisions against polygamy in a British Columbia case explicitly excludes polyamourous relationships from scrutiny.[13] It is only when multiple marriages and religion intersect that the court is concerned. Here the boundary of the public extends into religiously motivated family life to outlaw it. Further, the Canadian Minister of Citizenship and Immigration recently announced that in order to take the citizenship oath, one's face must be completely exposed.[14] How are we to understand these developments in the Canadian context?

Common Ground?

As I suggested in the introduction to this chapter, it might be useful to think about the emergence of contests about religion in the public sphere a bit more broadly. To view Canada in isolation would be to ignore some trends with a global resonance. This is not to deny that national economic, political, and social landscapes are relevant, but rather to suggest that a transformation is underway in relation to religion and the negotiation of religion in both public and private spheres, as well as the boundaries between those spheres, which, as already noted, are constantly in flux in any event. We might then consider four emerging trends – the discourse of the postsecular, the shift to culture, a move toward interculturalism, and the increased regulation of women's bodies – that are shaping the ways in which religion in the public sphere is imagined, both in its existence and in terms of its "management." These trends are not necessarily in harmony with each other and do not necessarily produce a coherent or consistent picture in terms of religion in the public sphere.

The Discourse of the Postsecular

In his 2011 Presidential Address to the Society for the Scientific Study of Religion, James Beckford took issue with the current infatuation with and scholarly currency given to the idea of the "postsecular," a term that, as he pointed out, seems to fluctuate in meaning depending on context. This way of framing current events around religion is having

a number of interesting effects, including a rather self-serving justification for entire disciplines in their ignoring of religion as an important
social fact in many people's lives. The notion of the postsecular assumes
that the secular was at some point realized and that now we may be
experiencing an unraveling of sorts. Beckford has cautioned against a
whole-hearted scholarly embrace of the idea of the postsecular, arguing
that "any focus on the postsecular is likely to obfuscate – or divert attention from – questions about the involvement of states in shaping and
regulating public responses to religious diversity. These questions, in
turn, relate to issues of freedom, equality and justice" (Beckford 2011).
I agree with Beckford, and think that while there may be something
afoot, the idea of postsecularism is too linked to past social science and
philosophical and theological misfortune to avoid distracting us from
the focus on "freedom, equality and justice."

Why should we care about the postsecular narrative? What effect does
it have on understanding and negotiating religion in the public sphere?
If we understand the idea of the postsecular as, in part, an attempt to
explain scholarly ignorance and in part as a recognition of religion's
persistence, we must also recognize the consequences of embarking on
a voyage down this path. Insight about the lessons that might be learned
from the scholarly preoccupation with "the secular" might be drawn
from the incredible amount of scholarly and public energy invested in
the proof of the secular, even as religion has persisted, albeit in some
cases in altered forms with altered functions (a process that is dynamic
and ongoing). Aside from distracting, as Beckford points out, from
more important questions, an acceptance of the notion that we live in a
postsecular society can reframe our understanding of public life to necessarily involve or implicate religion. This may be what the new atheists
have (so badly) reacted to. Moreover, we run the risk of essentializing
religious groups and flattening the complex texture of religion as it is
interwoven with day-to-day life. Finally, there is a continuing tendency
to assess the desirability of religious presence in rather Christian terms
and in institutional rather than "lived" manifestations of religion. From
a spatial perspective, the notion of postsecularism may disrupt the
public/private divide through a "religion is everywhere" imaginary.

What we may want to consider is what Peter Beyer (2013 a; 2013b)
has called post-Westphalianism. The Peace of Westphalia was actually
a complicated series of agreements and discussions that ended nearly
a century of religious wars and is often noted as demarcating the birth
of the idea of nation. It created, argues Beyer, the state and religion

as foundational, putting in the hands of the king the right to declare the religion of the nation. The sovereignty and the spirituality of states were thus linked. Although as Beyer himself acknowledges the term "post-Westphalian" has had currency in political theory for some time (see, for example, Elizabeth Hurd 2011), it has had little careful examination in relation to the global shifts we can observe in relation to religion. Beyer's observation is that as migration has increased, so too has the global flow of religion, resulting in more intensely diverse societies. The strength of Beyer's argument is that it does not buy into the "once upon a time there was religion, then there were secular societies, and then there was religion again" narrative that is espoused or implied by postsecularism. His account demands a more complicated understanding of the ways in which religion in the public sphere is imagined and responded to.

The Shift to Culture

Elsewhere I have made the argument that a rhetoric of culture is emerging around what have previously been dominant religions or shadow establishments. This rhetoric includes a claim to universalism or national values; such was the case in *Lautsi*[15] from Italy (in which an atheist family sought to have the crucifix removed from a classroom wall), where arguments were made to establish Christianity (specifically in that case Roman Catholicism) as a core and inextricable part of Italy's history. A similar claim to universalism was made by an evangelical prison program that claimed not to be violating the establishment clause of the US Constitution (Sullivan 2009a). In Québec the language of culture and heritage has played an important role in preserving the public presence of Roman Catholic religious symbols. Despite the recommendation of the Bouchard-Taylor Commission Report that the crucifix be removed from the Salon Bleu of the Assemblée Nationale, its members voted unanimously (on the day the report was released) to retain the crucifix as an important symbol of Québec's heritage and culture (Charest 2008). An interesting twist in the religion-to-culture move is the denial of the same protection for religious minorities. The wearing of hijab, the practice of polygamy, and other minority religious practices are framed as being cultural and thus not worthy of protection under constitutional and human rights regimes.[16]

If what was previously known as religion is recast as culture, then a majority "religion" becomes invisible in the public sphere, transformed into a matter of culture, heritage, and values. This has the effect of making minority religions' claims to public space even more visible – for, while "ours" is culture, part of our heritage and values, theirs is "religion" and foreign. Hegemonic religion can thus claim physical space in the guise of culture. This is also, of course, how the language of accommodation has been able to overtake both legal and public discourse about religious minority claims and their presence in the public sphere. There is no pretense of equality or a right to equality in Europe, and equality is fast disappearing as a legitimate mode of negotiating and adjudicating difference in the North American context.

The Intercultural Move

In the 2008 Bouchard-Taylor Commission Report, interculturalism rather than "Canadian multiculturalism" (coupled with laïcité ouverte) was highlighted as the dominant ideological umbrella for understanding how Québec should manage diversity. Although this idea finds most support in Québec, according to Gérard Bouchard (one of the co-authors of the Bouchard-Taylor Commission Report) in a talk he gave at University of Ottawa on 23 September 2011, when he is speaking of interculturalism outside of Québec, the response from his audience is frequently "we need more of that." In other words, while multiculturalism is seen to deny majority culture, interculturalism in its most simplistic form both recognizes and preserves majority culture.[17] This notion of interculturalism was picked up in the final report of the Belgian commission of 2010, with the accompanying idea that while majority culture is to be protected, a duty to accommodate minorities should be part of the social and legal milieu (Foblets and Kulakowski 2010).

The status of multiculturalism in Canada is in flux. In the *Hutterian Brethren* case the Supreme Court backed away from multiculturalism as a value to a descriptive reality of the Canadian demographic. The language of multiculturalism has largely disappeared from political discourse under the current regime. Canadian multiculturalism has been viewed by some as one of our most important contributions to global discourse on diversity and its management. Will Kymlicka (1995, 2005) is perhaps its best-known ambassador internationally. Nationally, multiculturalism is supported at the level of policy and public opinion,[18] legislatively by the *Canadian Multiculturalism Act*, and constitutionally by Section 27 of the *Canadian Charter of Rights and Freedoms*, which states, "This *Charter* shall be interpreted in a manner consistent with the preservation and enhancement of the multicultural heritage of Canadians." Thus, there is arguably a local as well as a political accommodation, to use the words of Vertovec and Wessendorf (2010), of immigrant practices, most often around religion.

What implications does this have for religion in the public sphere? It is difficult to determine this at the moment, partly because the exact content of multiculturalism as an ideology has been notoriously difficult to assess, and partly because most of the indicators of pull back have been at the political and legal levels, leaving a gap in knowledge about what is happening on the ground. However, we can speculate that because multiculturalism has been popularly viewed as a positive initiative that recognizes the value of diversity, support for the presence of multiple religious symbols and practice in the public sphere will decline if multiculturalism is rejected or undermined. Although unique in its history because of the establishment-like presence of the Roman Catholic Church, developments in Québec (particularly the move to refuse services to women wearing the niqab and the move toward "real laïcité" [Lefebvre 2012]) should serve as signals of what may be to come. The overt rejection of multiculturalism by many European nations should also be treated as a signal, although Vertovec and Wessendorf (2010) would caution against a simplistic assessment based on political rhetoric.

At Your Pleasure ... the Regulation of Women's Bodies

Although by no means the exclusive sites of contest, women's bodies have become a fighting ground on which the battle over religion in the public sphere is being fought. Bill 94 in Québec, while ostensibly about everyone having a "naked face" (as my colleague Pascale Fournier so provocatively puts it; Fournier and See, this volume), would grossly disproportionately affect Muslim women. The recent shift in Canadian government policy for those taking the oath of citizenship to have a fully exposed face also is predominantly directed at women. The polygamy reference in British Columbia was ostensibly about the protection of women.[19] The Bouchard-Taylor Commission Report highlights the protection of women and "égalité hommes-femmes" as being paramount in any resolution of contests over religious difference. There are some interesting assumptions underlying this – that Western democracies have actually achieved equality between men and women (a questionable position at best) and so are best positioned to examine the practices of others, and that equality, visually, "looks" a particular way.

Lost or minimized in these discussions is the agency of religious women. Women who choose to cover their faces are imagined as oppressed, unenlightened, and (this is key) unavailable. Implicated in all of this are orientalist assumptions, racist undertones (Sherene Razack [2008] would argue that race is the key issue here), and Western patriarchy. These collude to impact the ways in which the boundary between the public and the private is shaped. For example, as Fournier and See point out, the realm of the public is significantly extended in the case of Bill 94. Feminism, which has frequently had difficulty with religious women and the idea that they make choices, has colluded in the forced "emancipation" of women through its collaboration with the state in what Lefebvre (2011) describes as "republican feminism." To be sure, the oppression of women has happened and does happen in religious contexts, and religious doctrine has been and is used to justify that experience, but to gloss all religious women's experiences as "oppressed" is to simplify a complex set of experiences.[20]

It is particularly important to acknowledge that it is the Muslim woman's body that is the current object of obsession regarding the regulation of the body and its coverings. Natasha Bakht (2012) systematically reviews the myriad ways in which the veil has become an object of regulation and obsession. Bakht's analysis draws on examples from a number of Western democracies, pointing to the widespread targeting of women's bodies beyond the Canadian context and the consistent way in which the same objections arise repeatedly.[21] France, Belgium, the Netherlands, and Italy have all moved to ban or restrict Muslim women's head coverings in public spaces.[22]

Conclusions

Contests over religion in the public sphere signify, in many ways, an adjustment to new social and political realities that are shaped by increased population and therefore religious diversity, human rights expectations, transnational flows and relations, neoliberalism, and economic restraint and uncertainties. As Beyer argues, this period is marked by uncertainty of direction, tenuousness about what the post-Westphalian arrangement/s will be.[23] The brief exploration of four cross-border trends that shape the negotiation of religion in the public sphere may offer a few clues. However, these trends exhibit what may

be an inherent contradiction: the increasing currency of the discourse
of the postsecular opens space for religious voices and would seem to
support a widening of the public sphere in relation to religion. However, what may be a rise of interculturalism, the policing of (Muslim)
women's bodies, and the shift of historical majority religion to "culture" marks a retrenchment of sorts. It may be then that the postsecular
is opening space for only a particular kind of religion, although this
remains to be seen.

The spatial aspects of this discussion are intended to raise the question of who can claim presence and how in any given circumstance.
The ways in which public and private are imagined are often linked
to space in a very literal way. But "in the privacy of your own home"
may not, as I have argued, be so "private" after all. And if we associate
the idea of accessibility with the notion of the public, this too is challenged by the banning of certain citizens from certain spaces because
they wear religious symbols. We imagine that we know what constitutes the public and the private, but discussions about religion in the
public sphere disrupt those ideas both ideologically and spatially.

These issues are not simply fodder for academic discussion and
debate. Their importance is underscored by the fact that legislation
such as Bill 94 (and now the proposed *Québec Charter of Values*) and its
equivalent in other countries impacts the everyday lives of citizens.[24]
Discussions about the regulation of religion in the public sphere can
create space for dialogue, but, as the Bouchard-Taylor Commission
hearings demonstrated, can also reveal conflicting visions about what
a society is and what it should be. Canada is not, as I have argued,
the only nation-state struggling with these issues. Rather debates about
religion in the public sphere are common to Western democracies.

NOTES

1 See BBC News (2009), CBC News (2009), and Cumming-Bruce and
  Erlanger (2009).
2 See *Lautsi v. Italy* App. no. 30814/06, Eur. Ct. H.R. 2009; *Lautsi and Others v.
  Italy* App. no. 30814/06, Eur. Ct. H.R. 2011.
3 See *Chaplin v Royal Devon and Exeter Hospital NHS Foundation Trust* [2010] ET
  1702886/2009 (21 April 2010); BBC News (2010a); and *The Guardian* (2010).
4 See *Loi interdisant la dissimulation du visage dans l'espace public* no. 524; see
  also Associated Press (2010), Reuters (2011), and Samuel (2011).

5 See Allen (1971), Baum (1980), Christie and Gauvreau (2001), Dickey Young (2006), McGowan and Clark (1993), Struthers (1994), Tindal (2011), and Trothen (2000).
6 Also see Lefebvre (2012).
7 See the following for some of the media coverage of the requirement to have a bare face to take the oath of citizenship and its link to Canadian values: Citizenship and Immigration Canada (2011), *The Globe and Mail* (2012), and *Toronto Star* (2011).
8 *Reference re Same-Sex Marriage* [2004] 3 S.C.R. 698, 2004 SCC 79.
9 *Syndicat Northcrest v. Amselem*, 2004 SCC 47, [2004] 2 S.C.R. 551.
10 *Multani v. Commission scolaire Marguerite-Bourgeoys*, 2006 SCC 6, [2006] 1 S.C.R. 256.
11 *Alberta v. Hutterian Brethren of Wilson Colony*, 2009 SCC 37.
12 The Supreme Court of Canada used what is known as the *Oakes* test in the Hutterian Brethren case to determine whether the requirement of a photograph is a reasonable limitation on religious freedom. The discussion of that test falls under the rubric of what I would describe as "legal" analysis, which is not what my discussion is intended to do here. While this volume was in the process of going to press the N.S. case (*R. v. N.S.* 2012 SCC 72), which involved a Muslim woman who wished to wear her niqab to give evidence in criminal court, was decided. The Supreme Court discussed issues of "the private" and "the public" in its decision, but that discussion is beyond the scope of this chapter.
13 *Reference re: Section 293 of the Criminal Code of Canada,* 2011 BCSC 1588.
14 See National Post (2011), Payton (2011), and Quinn (2011).
15 *Lautsi v. Italy* App. no. 30814/06, Eur. Ct. H.R. 2009 and *Lautsi and Others v. Italy* App. no. 30814/06, Eur. Ct. H.R. 2011.
16 For discussions of the ways in which religion and culture are used in this way, see Brown (2006), Phillips (2007), and Song (2007).
17 Critical theorists of multiculturalism have argued that it is really a front for majority culture hegemony (see Bannerji 2001; Day 2000; and Kernerman 2005).
18 See Adams (2008).
19 *Reference re: Section 293 of the Criminal Code of Canada,* 2011 BCSC 1588.
20 See Alvi, Hoodfar, and McDonough (2003) for an excellent collection of essays that document the complex reasons women wear hijab.
21 Bakht (2012) writes: "Those who favour banning the niqab put forward the following arguments: (1) the niqab shows a refusal by Muslims to integrate into broader society; (2) such clothing is a testament to the oppression of Muslim women; (3) the display of religious symbols is an affront to secular

societies; (4) the veil is intimidating or off-putting and this is exacerbated in certain settings; (5) covering portions of one's body is a security or safety concern; (6) not showing one's face is impolite; (7) covering one's face is a barrier to communication and incongruent to social relations; (8) identification becomes problematic if women cover their faces; (9) the niqab is incompatible with tolerance and respect of others; and (10) Islam does not impose a religious requirement for women to cover their faces." (p. 76).

22 For information on the ban in Belgium, see BBC (2010b) and Traynor (2010); in France, see Associated Press (2010), Reuters (2011), and Samuel (2011); in The Netherlands, see Reuters (2012); in Italy, see Associated Press (2011) and Squires (2010).

23 A perhaps more dramatic version of the uncertainty than Beyer's can be found in Wendy Brown's (2011) *Walled States, Waning Sovereignty*.

24 On 6 November 2013, the *Québec Charter of Values* was officially renamed under Bill 60 as the *Charter Affirming the Values of Secularism, State Religious Neutrality, and the Equality of Men and Women and the Framing of Accommodation Requests*. The proposed law would, among other things, prohibit the wearing of headscarves, yarmulkes, turbans, and larger-than-average crucifixes by those offering public services (see Canadian Press 2013; Drainville 2013).

REFERENCES

Adams, Michael. 2008. *Unlikely Utopia: The Surprising Triumph of Multiculturalism*. Toronto: Penguin.

Allen, Richard. 1971. *The Social Passion: Religion and Social Reform in Canada, 1914–28*. Toronto: University of Toronto.

Alvi, Sajida H., Homa Hoodfar, and Sheila McDonough, eds. 2003. *The Muslim Veil in North America: Issues and Debates*. Toronto: Women's Press.

Associated Press. 2010. "French Senate Bans Burka." *CBC News*, 14 September. Available at http://www.cbc.ca/news/world/story/2010/09/14/france-burka-ban.html

Associated Press. 2011. "Italy Approves Draft Law to Ban Burka." *The Guardian*, 3 August. Available at http://www.guardian.co.uk/world/2011/aug/03/italy-draft-law-burqa

Bakht, Natasha. 2012. "Veiled Objections: Facing Public Opposition to the Niqab." In *Reasonable Accommodation: Managing Religious Diversity*, ed. Lori G. Beaman, 77–108. Vancouver: UBC Press.

Bannerji, Himani, ed. 2001. *The Dark Side of the Nation: Essays on Multicultural-
   ism, Nationalism and Gender*. Toronto: Canadian Scholars' Press.
Baum, Gregory. 1980. *Catholics and Canadian Socialism: Political Thought in the
   Thirties and Forties*. Toronto: J Lorimer.
BBC News. 2009. "Swiss Voters Back Ban on Minarets." *BBC News*, 29 Novem-
   ber. Available at http://news.bbc.co.uk/2/hi/8385069.stm
BBC News. 2010a. "Devon Nurse Loses Crucifix 'Ban' Claim at Tribunal." *BBC
   News*, 7 April. Available at http://news.bbc.co.uk/2/hi/uk_news/england/
   devon/8605700.stm
BBC News. 2010b. "Belgian Lawmakers Pass Burka Ban." *BBC News*, 30 April.
   Available at http://news.bbc.co.uk/2/hi/8652861.stm
Beaman, Lori. G. 2013. "The Will to Religion: Obligatory Religious Citizen-
   ship." *Critical Research on Religion*, special issue *Critical Sociology of Religion*
   1(2): 141–57.
Beckford, James A. 2011. "Public Religions and Post-Secularity: Critical Reflec-
   tions." Paper presented at the annual meeting for the Society for the Scien-
   tific Study of Religion, Milwaukee, Wisconsin, October 28–30.
Beyer, Peter. 2013a. "Multiculturalism and Religious Pluralism in Canada:
   Intimations of a 'Post-Westphalian' Condition." In *Multiculturalism and Religious Identity: Perspectives from Ottawa and Delhi*, edited by Sonia Sikka and
   Lori G. Beaman. Montréal: McGill-Queen's University Press.
Beyer, Peter. 2013b. "De-Privileging Religion in a Post-Westphalian State:
   Shadow Establishment, Organization, Spirituality, and Freedom in Can-
   ada." In *Varieties of Religious Establishment*, edited by Winnifred F. Sullivan
   and Lori G. Beaman. London: Ashgate.
Blaikie, Bill. 2011. *The Blaikie Report: An Insider's Look at Faith and Politics*.
   Toronto: United Church Publishing House.
Bouchard, Gérard. 2011. "Interculturalism and the Management of Ethno-
   Cultural Diversity in Québec." Paper presented at Critical Thinkers in Law,
   Religion and Social Theory lecture series, University of Ottawa, Ottawa,
   23 September.
Bouchard, Gérard, and Charles Taylor. 2008. "Building the Future: A Time for
   Reconciliation." *Commission de Consultation sur les pratiques d'accommodement
   reliées aux différences culturelles*. Québec: Québec Government Printing
   Office, 22 May.
Brown, Wendy. 2006. *Regulating Aversion: Tolerance in the Age of Identity and
   Empire*. Princeton: Princeton University Press.
Brown, Wendy. 2011. *Walled States, Waning Sovereignty*. Cambridge: MIT
   Press.

Canadian Press. 2013. "PQ Values Charter Given Complicated, 28-word Name."
    The Globe and Mail, 6 November. Available at http://www.theglobeandmail
    .com/news/politics/pq-values-charter-given-complicated-28-word-name/
    article15294865/
CBC News. 2009. "Swiss Vote to Ban New Mosque Minarets." *CBC News*,
    30 November. Available at http://www.cbc.ca/news/world/story/
    2009/11/29/swiss-minarets.html
Charest, J. 2008. "Réitérer la volonté de l'Assemblée de promouvoir la langue,
    l'histoire, la culture et les valeurs de la nation québécoise, de favoriser
    l'intégration de chacun et de témoigner de son attachement au patrimoine
    religieux et historique." In *Québec. Assemblée nationale. Journal des débats
    (Hansard) of the National Assembly*, 38th legislature, 1st sess.
Christie, Nancy, and Michael Gauvreau. 2001. *A Full-Orbed Christianity: The
    Protestant Churches and Social Welfare in Canada, 1900–1940*. Montréal and
    Kingston: McGill-Queen's University Press.
Citizenship and Immigration Canada. 2011. "Speaking Notes for The Honour-
    able Jason Kenney, P.C., M.P. Minister of Citizenship, Immigration and Mul-
    ticulturalism," 12 December. Available at http://www.cic.gc.ca/english/
    department/media/speeches/2011/2011-12-12.asp
Conseil du statut de la femme. 2011. "Avis Affirmer la laïcité, un pas de plus
    vers l'égalité réelle entre les femmes et les hommes." Québec: Conseil du
    statut de la femme.
Cumming-Bruce, Nick, and Steven Erlanger. 2009. "Swiss Ban Building of
    Minarets on Mosques." *New York Times*, 29 November. Available at http://
    www.nytimes.com/2009/11/30/world/europe/30swiss.html
Day, Richard J. F. 2000. *Multiculturalism and the History of Canadian Diversity*.
    Toronto: University of Toronto Press.
Dickey Young, Pamela. 2006. "Same-sex Marriage and the Christian Churches
    in Canada." *Studies in Religion/Science Religieuses* 35(3): 2–23.
Drainville, Bernard. 2013. "Projet de loi no 60 Charte affirmant les valeurs
    de laïcité et de neutralité religieuse de l'État ainsi que d'égalité entre les
    femmes et les hommes et encadrant les demandes d'accommodement."
    Québec: Éditeur officiel du Québec.
Foblets, Marie-Claire, and Christine Kulakowski. 2010. *Les assises de
    l'interculturalité*. Report, edited by M. d. l. E. e. d. l. É. d. Chances, Bruxelles.
Gagnon-Tessier, Louis-Charles. 2012. "Archives et spectres du catholicisme
    dans les mémoires de la commission sure la religion à l'école et Bouchard-
    Taylor." Paper presented at Catholicisme, religion culturelle, institutions
    et diversité religieuse. Problématiques contemporaines et comparatives
    France / Québec. Université de Montréal, 20 January.

The Globe and Mail. 2012. "Muslim Women Must Show Faces when Taking Citizenship Oath." 6 September. Available at http://m.theglobeandmail .com/news/politics/muslim-women-must-show-faces-when-taking-citizenshipoath/article1357177/?Service=mobile

The Guardian. 2010. "Christian Nurse Loses Battle to Wear Crucifix at Work." *The Guardian*, 6 April. Available at http://www.guardian.co.uk/uk/2010/ apr/06/christian-nurse-loses-battle-crucifix

Hurd, Elizabeth S. 2011. "Secularism and International Relations Theory." In *Religion and International Relations Theory*, edited by Jack Snyder, 60–90. New York: Columbia University Press.

Kernerman, Gerald P. 2005. *Multicultural Nationalism: Civilizing Difference, Constituting Community*. Vancouver: UBC Press.

Keung, Nicholas. 2011. "Women Could Be Asked to Unveil before Ottawa's New Rule." *Toronto Star*, 13 December. Available at http://www.thestar .com/news/investigations/2011/12/13/women_could_be_asked_to_ unveil_before_ottawas_new_rule.html

Knott, Kim. 2005. *The Location of Religion: A Spatial Analysis*. London: Equinox.

Knott, Kim. 2009. "From Locality to Location and Back Again: A Spatial Journey of the Study of Religion." *Religion* 39(2): 154–60.

Kymlicka, Will. 1995. *Multicultural Citizenship: A Liberal Theory of Minority Rights*. Oxford: Oxford University Press.

Kymlicka, Will. 2005. *Multicultural Odysseys: Navigating the New International Politics of Diversity*. Oxford: Oxford University Press.

Lefebvre, Solange. 2011. "Cross-Cultural Religion: Women and Laïcité." Paper presented at the annual meeting of the Association for the Sociology of Religion, Las Vegas, Nevada, 19 August.

Lefebvre, Solange. 2012. "L'approche québécoise, entre laïcité et sécularité. Histoire sémantique d'un débat." In *Le programme d'éthique et culture religieuse: De l'exigeante conciliation entre le soi, l'autre et le nous*, edited by Mireille Estivalezès and Lori G. Beaman. Québec: Presses de l'Université Laval.

Martin, David. 2000. "Canada in Comparative Perspective." In *Rethinking Church, State and Modernity: Canada between Europe and America*, edited by David Lyon and Marguerite Van Die, 22–33. Toronto: University of Toronto Press.

McGowan, Mark G., and Brian P. Clark. 1993. *Catholics at the Gathering Place*. Toronto: Dundurn.

Orsi, Robert A. 2003. "Is the Study of Lived Religion Irrelevant to the World We Live In?" *Journal for the Scientific Study of Religion* 42(2): 169–74.

National Post. 2011. "Niqabs, Burkas Must Be Removed During Citizenship Ceremonies: Jason Kenney." *National Post*, 12 December. Available at http://news.nationalpost. com/2011/12/12/niqabs-burkas-must-be-removed-during-citizenship-ceremonies-jason-kenney/

Payton, Laura. 2011. "Face Veils Banned for Citizenship Oaths." *CBC News*, 12 December. Available at http://www.cbc.ca/news/politics/story/2011/12/12/pol-kenney-citizenship-rules.html

Phillips, Anne. 2007. *Multiculturalism without Culture*. Princeton: Princeton University Press.

Quinn, Ben. 2011. "Burqa Wearing Banned in Canada for Taking Citizenship Oath." *The Guardian*, 12 December. Available at http://www.guardian.co.uk/world/2011/dec/12/burqa-wearing-banned-canada

Razack, Sherene. 2008. *Casting Out: Race and the Eviction of Muslims from Western Law and Politics*. Toronto: University of Toronto Press.

Reuters. 2011. "France Begins Ban on Niqab and Burqa." *The Guardian*, 11 April. Available at http://www.guardian.co.uk/world/2011/apr/11/france-begins-burqa-niqab-ban

Reuters. 2012. "Netherlands Plans to Ban Muslim Face-covering Veils Next Year." *The National Post*, 27 January. Available at http://news.nationalpost.com/2012/01/27/netherlands-plans-to-ban-muslim-face-covering-veils-next-year/

Samuel, Henry. 2011. "Burka Ban: French Woman Fined for Wearing Full-face Veil." *The Telegraph*, 22 September. Available at http://www.telegraph.co.uk/news/worldnews/europe/france/8781241/Burka-ban-French-women-fined-for-wearing-full-face-veil.html

Seljak, David. 2008. "Secularization and the Separation of Church and State in Canada." Report for the Strategic Policy, Research and Planning Directorate, Multiculturalism and Human Rights Program, Department of Canadian Heritage, Ottawa, 7 January.

Song, Sarah. 2007. *Justice, Gender and the Politics of Multiculturalism*. Cambridge: Cambridge University Press.

Squires, Nick. 2010. "Muslim Woman Fined £430 for Wearing Burka in Italy." *The Telegraph*, 4 May. Available at http://www.telegraph.co.uk/news/worldnews/europe/italy/7676367/Muslim-woman-fined-430-for-wearing-burka-in-Italy.html

Statistics Canada. 2011. "Religions in Canada." National Household Survey. Available at http://www12.statcan.gc.ca/nhs-enm/2011/as-sa/99-010-x/99-010-x2011001-eng.cfm#a6

Struthers, James. 1994. *The Limits of Affluence: Welfare in Ontario, 1920–1970*. Toronto: University of Toronto.

Suderman, Brenda. 2011. "Faith Relevant in Political Arena, Blaikie says." *Winnipeg Free Press*, 5 November. Available at http://www.winnipegfree

press.com/opinion/fyi/faith-relevant-in-political-arena-blaikie-says-
133288003.html

Sullivan, Winnifred F. 2009a. *Prison Religion: Faith Reformers and the Constitution*. Princeton: Princeton University Press.

Sullivan, Winnifred. F. 2009b. "We Are All Religious Now. Again." *Social Research* 76(4): 1181–98.

Tindal, Mardi. 2011. "Non-violent Civil Disobedience." *WonderCafe.ca.*, 6 August. Available at http://www.wondercafe.ca/blogs/moderator-mardi-tindal/non-violent-civil-disobedience

Traynor, Ian. 2010. "Belgium Moves toward Public Ban on Burka and Niqab." *The Guardian*, 31 March. Available at http://www.guardian.co.uk/world/2010/mar/31/belgium-public-ban-burqa-niqab

Trothen, Tracy J. 2000. "A Social Ethical Analysis of the United Church of Canada's Historical Approach to Human Sexuality." *Studies in Religion/Sciences Religieuses* 29(3): 325–39.

Vertovec, Steven, and Susanne Wessendorf, eds. 2010. *The Multiculturalism Backlash*. New York: Routledge.

LEGISLATION

Canadian Charter of Rights and Freedoms, R.S.C., 1985 Appendix II, No. 44. *see also* Part I (ss. 1 to 34) of the *Constitution Act, 1982*.

Canadian Multiculturalism Act (R.S.C., 1985, c. 24 (4th Supp.)) *Loi interdisant la dissimulation du visage dans l'espace public* n° 524.

CASES

Alberta v. Hutterian Brethren of Wilson Colony, 2009 SCC 37.

Chaplin v. Royal Devon and Exeter Hospital NHS Foundation Trust [2010] ET 1702886/2009 (21 April 2010).

Lautsi v. Italy App. no. 30814/06, Eur. Ct. H.R. 2009.

Lautsi and Others v. Italy App. no. 30814/06, Eur. Ct. H.R. 2011.

Multani v. Commission scolaire Marguerite-Bourgeoys, 2006 SCC 6, [2006] 1 S.C.R. 256.

Reference re: Section 293 of the Criminal Code of Canada, 2011 BCSC 1588.

Reference re Same-Sex Marriage [2004] 3 S.C.R. 698, 2004 SCC 79.

Syndicat Northcrest v. Amselem, 2004 SCC 47, [2004] 2 S.C.R. 551.

3 Regional Differences and Continuities at the Intersection of Culture and Religion

A Case Study of Immigrant and Second-Generation Young Adults in Canada

PETER BEYER

In much of the public discourse in Canada today, religious and cultural diversity appear in an ambiguous light. On the one hand, one hears that they are a great asset to this country; that the future prosperity of Canada is dependent on the continued arrival of immigrants from all over the world who are generating these diversities; and, moreover, that such diversity is also a question of Canadian identity (Citizenship and Immigration Canada 2011; Dib, Donaldson, and Turcotte 2009; Kymlicka 2010). We are said to be a society characterized by this diversity, whether we call that character multicultural or intercultural (Bouchard and Taylor 2008a). On the other hand, these diversities are said to produce potential problems as Canadian societies may have difficulty absorbing these differences into a cohesive and integrated social whole. The result, some suggest, threatens to be a divided and even perhaps chaotic society in which contradictory and isolated differences live in often conflictive silos, side by side but not sufficiently connected for a peaceful and prosperous society (cf. Bissoondath 1994; Karim 2009; Ryan 2010; Sibley 2008; Steyn 2006).

This latter view appears to be shared in important portions of parallel public debates happening in other countries such as Australia, the United States, and Western European countries (Foner and Alba 2008; Jupp 2002; Lucassen, Feldman, and Oltmer 2006; Metcalf 1996; Portes and Rumbaut 2001). The issue is therefore not just a Canadian one, but rather one that has emerged in a broad range of countries around the world that are receiving a good portion of the intense transnational migration that has characterized this world since the middle of the twentieth century (Castles and Miller 2003). It is in many respects a global issue, both in the sense that it is an issue in many countries around the world and in the sense that the diversities represent the rest of the world: religious and cultural diversity represent and embody the fact that all countries are tied into global society, are expressions of it, and therefore are forced to incorporate global differences in globally shared ways. Transnational migration is one of these ways but is, of course, by far not the only one.

In this context, I suggest that there is behind this dilemma or ambiguous regard a transitional state in which both society, but above all the self-descriptions of societies, are moving from an almost exclusively national societal view to include also a relational global view. Religious and cultural diversity mark an important aspect of what Roland Robertson has called the "relativization of national societies in the global field" (Robertson 1992). This "relativization" manifests itself in the current debate about religious and cultural diversity. One the one hand, Canada, and Québec within it, are said to be welcoming of these diversities, indicating that both "national societies" are open to the differences that come from being situated in a global societal world. On the other hand, the debate also insists that these differences have to be "integrated" into these societies and that this integration assumes "shared" culture or values as a necessary basis. The role of religion in this "shared" or common culture remains ambiguous, but the prevailing position in the public discourse on this matter styles both Canada and Québec as "secular" societies, meaning principally that the religion need not be shared. It remains an open question, however, whether that means that religion in its diversity must therefore be restricted, in particular to the so-called "private sphere," perhaps to the point of "public" invisibility but certainly to the point of "public" irrelevance, or whether that shared culture still includes at least the cultural vestiges of a once-dominant religion – here Christianity – that should therefore still be part of the "public sphere."

Certain portions of the populations of Canada more clearly embody the ambiguity and possible dilemma that is thus felt; these are people who are both "within" and "without" and cannot be only one or the other convincingly, namely those who are deemed from one aspect to be from "away" and from another from "here." These are the second generation of immigrants and those who have comparable socialization experiences ("1.5ers" or those who have spent the bulk of their lives in the country to which they or their parents migrated). They embody the religious and cultural diversity that is a consequence of Canada being open to the relativizing forces of the global world, but they are also born/bred "Canadian" and/or "Québécois" and therefore should also embody the "shared" component of integrated "national societies."

In this chapter, I present results from a research project currently being completed and involving this segment of the Canadian population. The research project has asked of them: how do they see their situation in terms of being socially and as concerns personal identity from "here" and yet also ineluctably from "away"? How do they do this in terms of culture and religion, both of which together and independently are deemed to be social spaces where difference and identity are primarily inscribed or lived? These are, of course, very general and abstract questions, and therefore the project adopted a specific strategy for specifying and operationalizing them. These are evident in the main features of the research design, which can be briefly described.

Project Research Design

Data gathering for the project was conducted from fall 2008 to summer 2010 in six Canadian cities, namely Vancouver, Edmonton, Toronto, Ottawa, Montréal, and Sydney, NS. The project held 36 focus groups, with 98 (follow-up) individual interviews, spread across these six urban areas. Participants were mostly immigrants or children of post-1970s immigrants, almost all of whom had lived in Canada for at least eight years, and were 18–30 years old. Recruitment was done mostly on university and community college campuses, but also in some cases through specific religious organizations and other means such as snowballing or through contacts in specific groups. Twenty-nine of the focus groups were organized along ethnic and religious lines, such that each consisted of people from specific cultural and specific religious identities. Thus there were groups consisting of, for instance, Turkish Muslims, African Christians, Tamil Hindus, Punajbi Sikhs, Chinese Christians, and so on, but not of Muslims, Christians, Hindus, or Sikhs of various ethnic background. These groups were held in Vancouver, Toronto, Ottawa, and Montréal. Four focus groups were of mixed composition, both with respect to ethnicity and religion, and three were structured as "controls," consisting of people who were simply between 18 and 30 years old, irrespective of immigrant, cultural, or religious identity. These seven were held in Edmonton and Sydney, NS. Because the project was also the second phase of a two-phase project, the first of which concentrated on Muslims, Buddhists, and Hindus (Beyer and Ramji 2013), the focus groups for this project targeted Christian and Sikh identities more strongly, with relatively few being composed of other religious identities. We thus arrived at 20 Christian groups, subdivided into African/Caribbean (6), Chinese (5), Korean (2), Filipino (2), Eastern European/West Asian (2), and Latin American (1). The remaining 16 groups consisted of 4 Punjabi Sikh groups; 2 Tamil Hindu; 2 Muslim, 1 Somali, and 1 Turkish group; 1 Southeast Asian mostly Buddhist group; 4 mixed groups; and 3 control groups. Of the 36, 2 were conducted in Sydney, 6 in Montréal, 5 in Ottawa, 11 in Toronto, 5 in Edmonton, and 7 in Vancouver. The numbers attending the groups ranged from 3 to 18, with most clustered in the 7–10 range. The follow-up interviewees were drawn unevenly from these groups, with the inclusion of a number of independent individual interviews, that is, with people who fit the descriptions but did not actually attend one of the groups. All focus groups and interviews in Montréal were conducted in French, whereas those in the rest of the country were conducted in English.

The questions that structured the focus groups sought to discover how the participants regarded their place in Canada, both culturally and religiously; how they viewed the country in general in terms of its management and incorporation of religious and cultural differences; and to what degree they felt that Canada overall, and their region in particular, enabled the free and complete practice of religion, and whether the religions were treated equally in this regard. To concretize these aims, participants were asked what they thought of the policy and reality of Canadian multiculturalism; in Montréal we also asked about their degree of identification as Québécois and Canadians, and their view of Québec culture and society in terms of their place in it. We further asked how multiculturalism, in Québec also interculturalism, could be improved, and whether there was a Canadian or Québec culture and, if so, in what it consisted. On the religious side we asked if they felt that religious freedom existed in Canada; whether they felt that they could practice their religions fully and without constraint; and whether all religions were treated equally in Canada, and if not, which ones were privileged or disadvantaged and why.

The results reported here are from detailed analysis of only the 36 focus groups; the 98 follow-up interviews did not ask the same questions, and therefore their analysis with regard to these issues is left to other occasions.[1]

Multiculturalism

The attitudes displayed in almost all the focus groups toward the idea of cultural diversity, particularly in the concept of multiculturalism, were what one might call "critically positive." This means that *most* of the participants approved of both the ideal and the reality of a society in which cultural differences existed, were valued and maintained, and in which there was not the expectation that everyone conform to an existing dominant culture of whatever description. Clearly positive assessments of Canada in this regard took several forms, but here is one from a member of a Chinese Christian focus group held in Vancouver:

> [W]hen I was little, I remember thinking about multiculturalism in Canada and in school, and I remember feeling really proud that Canada was a multicultural country – whatever that meant. And I think now ... [i]f ... someone asked me ... why is Canada multicultural, ... I'd probably say something like, "like a country that is made up of all different cultural backgrounds from different places in the world and we're all living here and we're all under the same government and we're working together and we live side by side; and even if we are somewhat segregated sometimes because it's easier to work with our own group or whatever, like that's okay, and everyone is close enough that we can get to know each culture a bit better."

The clear majority of opinions on this issue were, however, significantly more critical, and almost uniformly the critique of the multicultural reality in Canada, including Québec, targeted its lack of fulfillment, the fact that it had not been realized or that it was superficial, not that it was a bad idea. This lack of realization was seen to manifest itself in two ways. On the one hand, a number pointed to how dominant, European-originated populations had not adequately accepted the multicultural reality, a criticism discussed under headings like "discrimination" and "racism." With the notable exception discussed below, however, such discrimination was not overly severe, at least in large urban areas. A participant in the Somali Muslim group held in Ottawa put this "yes, but ..." aspect nicely:

> I like the fact that ... there's a lot of multiculturalism here. And that's something that Canada is known for. At the same time, though, I find that issues that are like race issues, problematic issues ... are harder to bring to light, I would say because people just say that Canada is a multicultural

country. That's what we're known for. But at the same time, like, there is a lot of tension between certain races or certain racial issues ... ones that do exist here in Canada ... that are kind of glossed over because "we're Canada, we're multicultural."

In this regard, a further common observation was that multiculturalism was a different matter in urban Canada – especially the very large cities like Montréal, Toronto, and Vancouver – than it was in the smaller centres with relatively few immigrants and members of visible minorities. The policy was one thing, but the reality of multiculturalism varied from place to place. As a participant in one of the Sikh groups put it:

[W]hen we are driving from Toronto to Ottawa and you stop at some places ... where it's regionally a white community, ... I went into Tim Horton's and it's not obvious discrimination but you can feel it. They are looking at you like "Ooh, we don't really have an Indian community in our town." So, they kind of view us differently because they are not used to it.

This Montréal/Toronto/Vancouver (especially Toronto) versus the smaller-city/rural Canada difference was, however, not simply a matter of the multicultural reality being restricted to the large urban centres. Another critical orientation toward that reality worried that in cities with high densities of different cultural and religious groups, multiculturalism has resulted or can result in "silo formation" or enclaving, an outcome that the participants generally, but not always, evaluated negatively. As another participant in the same Sikh group put it:

Yeah, well it depends on where you say multiculturalism is. Like ... is it multicultural to have a bunch of different cultural groups in the same area, only hanging out with each other? Like, is that multiculturalism? Or, is it ... people from different communities hanging out with different communities? Because, that's what you don't see. Like, ... when I am in Toronto, like I go to Brampton ... my parents take me [t]o see the places where Sikhs live. And, my friend, whenever he is in Toronto ... he's in North York. And, he's like, "All of the Chinese people, all of the Viet[namese] people are there." If that's multiculturalism, then I guess you see it everywhere. But here, that's why I like Ottawa at least a little bit better because it's not like that ... You see more groups ... hanging out together. I don't see people, like separate kind of thing.

Another, more pointed version came from two of the participants in an African/Caribbean Christian group in Toronto:

Chantal: And I also find that people are sticking with their ...
Samantha: ... yeah, you know, in their group. So you can go to different parts of the city and see Chinese, and see just Indian, and then just Filipino. And there's no togetherness, I find. Because everybody's just finding their culture, their background and kind of gravitating over there.

Sometimes this criticism referred to sheer numbers: the more people there were in a city or region of a particular cultural identity, the more likely or possible it was to "stick to one's own." In other cases, this criticism carried a generational aspect: it was the recent arrivals and the parental generation who were singled out for particular criticism. Put differently, the view of multiculturalism was that it was insufficient unless the cultural differences interacted and "learned from each other," meaning that the process should and would result in a fair amount of "compromise" or "hybridization" of the different cultural identities. Moreover, quite a number of participants across the groups considered multiculturalism to be an ongoing project, one that did not have a clear endpoint of fulfillment but was rather a process. To quote one Korean Christian participant: "It [multiculturalism] can always be worked on; it won't be perfect." At the same time, there seemed to be comparatively little concern that this process would actually endanger the cultural differences, that it would amount to "assimilation" and the erasure of those differences. Yet it also did not seem to mean the construction of a new, uniquely Canadian, cultural identity either, except insofar as that meant one characterized by this unity within difference. The prevailing view was the ideal, if not the reality, of Canadian multicultural society as a "salad," not a "soup," the mythic "mosaic" as opposed to "melting pot." These words were actually used by a number of participants, but the issue was put in a variety of ways, including the following opinion from a participant in the Vancouver Chinese Christian group:

I think that ... what multiculturalism boils down to is just respect for other cultures, like obviously if all these cultures are living together in a similar geographical space then there can't be – each culture can't be what it is, fully. And so they have to learn to live together and that is what multiculturalism is – that space when they're living together.

At least three sorts of partial exception to this general pattern need to be highlighted, however. One concerns those who felt excluded, one concerns those who did not want to be included, and the third concerns those who wanted the immersion of differences in a Canadian or Québécois national cultural identity. Although significant numbers of participants in most of the focus groups reported having experienced some sort of discrimination on the basis of their differences, it is only among three of the seven "Black" groups (six Christian, one Muslim) and among one of the four Sikh groups that this sometimes amounted to the conviction that they were generally excluded from the wider society. The theme of exclusion came up clearly in the Caribbean Christian group in Toronto, in the two Haitian groups in Montréal, and in one of the Vancouver Sikh groups.

In the Toronto group, the general tenor of this complaint was that "race" made it more difficult for participants to be fully included. As one participant put it, "we're always going to ... going to have to work harder than the Caucasians to get what we need to do, even if we're more educated than them, or we're more talented than them, we always have to work harder than them to show them that we're – there." To this, however, others responded that concerted effort on their part could overcome these barriers, that racist attitudes could be and were being overcome, and that therefore multiculturalism would work for them as well. Here is how one woman in the group put it (a tiny excerpt from a long intervention):

[L]ike my mom, she's like that. She's starting to grow out of it because all her kids are born in Canada and we grew up very different. But she's coming from that background where like "yeah, we were always slaves and we'll always be slaves." And she's very hard core on that. And if some white lady runs over her foot with the trolley in the frigging grocery store, she'll be like, "oh you're just trying to keep me down!!" [Laughter from the group]. "No, no mom–it was an accident. Just let it go." You know? Come on.

[M]y mom, she's starting to realize, like when we go out now she's not so boisterous and she's not so, like, "oh frigging white people!" She's more like, "oh, I'm sorry about that, ma'am." And the white lady's like, "oh no, it's my fault." And then they get into conversation. And that's how they meet people and that's how you break the barriers. You know what I mean? If you play into this whole stereotype – and I find there's a lot of black youth who play into the stereotype, because they're influenced by their parents, who are influenced by their parents, and other generations. And that's why it may seem like "oh, they're still putting us down." Well no, not really.

Of particular note in this quote is the expressed optimism that racism and discrimination, while real, can be overcome and that the possibility of it being otherwise is seen as "old country" thinking that denies that Canada is a "different country" in which inherited assumptions do not necessarily apply. The "differences" can be better "integrated" here.

Something like the reverse was the case with the Montréal groups: the minority thought it was only a matter of trying harder; for the majority the barriers were pretty firm: they were pessimistic about ever being accepted as full and equal members of Québec society. For some this was a simple matter of discrimination, but others located the problem not so much or just there, but in the existence of a strong Québécois identity that modeled itself on people who looked a certain way and who spoke a certain language in a certain way. One participant illustrated the point by contrasting the possibilities of her adopting either a Canadian or a Québécois identity:

> Moi personnellement, je me sens canadien avant tout, puis je trouve que c'est beaucoup plus facile ... partout où tu es, de dire que t'es Canadien que de dire que t'es Québécois, même ici ... Comme [un autre participant] disait tout à l'heure, ici si tu dis que t'es Québécois, mais c'est comme si on regarde pour voir si c'est vrai, que tu prouves que t'es Québécois. Quand t'es Canadien, t'es Canadien, tout le monde est Canadien, t'a pas besoin de prouver rien.

Another focused specifically on what they perceived to be the requirement to assimilate. Referring to visible minorities appearing on the English and French television networks, another member of the group made this contrast, which includes an implicit understanding of multiculturalism as the maintenance of difference without assimilation:

> Moi je pense que le point du multiculturel ... Ça se voit à la télé. Pour moi, je trouve que le multiculturalisme, tu le vois plus à la télé. Tsé, genre quand tu vois *Salut-Bonjour*,[2] pis que tu 'switch' à CBC, c'est plus possible que tu vois un 'black-dude' qu'à *Salut-Bonjour* le matin. Tsé, un Haïtien à *Salut-Bonjour*, ça serait une première. ... [rire général] C'est pour ça que moi le multiculturalisme au Québec, j'y crois pas encore, tsé. ... [À]

Salut-Bonjour, ... un 'black-dude' là, il est comme assimilé, tsé, il faut qu'il parle joual. Il est pas resté qu'est-ce qu'il était au début, tsé, il a dû changé. Tsé, François de Météo Média,[3] [une des animatrices], elle a un petit peu changé, elle parle un peu joual, elle est pas resté Haïtienne, tsé. Pis ça que je trouve au Québec, on dirait qu'on essaie comme de nous faire devenir Québécois, tsé vraiment. Tandis qu'aux États-Unis aussi, qu'est-ce que j'entend de ma famille aux États pis même des gens qui vont en Ontario, j'ai une cousine qui est rendue à Toronto, pis elle est restée Haïtienne, tsé, elle a pas eu à changer son attitude ou au niveau du langage ou au niveau de son comportement, tsé ...

There was therefore a noticeable difference with respect to this question between the Toronto and Montréal groups that consisted of Christians of, broadly speaking, African ancestry. Both of these, however, contrasted in their attitudes with two other African Christian groups consisting of Ghanaians in Vancouver and a mix of Africans in Montréal. These latter groups presented themselves as fairly positive about multiculturalism, although they felt, like many others, that it was a phenomenon restricted to the large cities and that there was room for improvement. That said, they were also fairly positive that improvement was both possible and happening. They did not feel excluded:

Interviewer: Est-ce que c'est une bonne chose pour vous le multiculturalisme canadien?
[several voices]: Ben oui!!! On se sent pas exclus ...

To what degree such differences reflect "national" differences, in this case the differences between people of Haitian and other "African" origins, is a question that will have to remain open. It is certainly possible, as Margarita Mooney's chapter might also suggest.

The Vancouver Sikh groups presented another variant on the exclusion theme. Here the participants were generally negative about multiculturalism, saying it mostly was a sham or didn't work. As two of them put it succinctly when asked about Canadian multiculturalism:

First participant: I don't think it exists.
Second participant: No.
First Participant: Totally – like, as the way it sounds, the way Canada advertises it ...

Second Participant: Still a lot missing. ... I mean I'm not bashing it completely but ... whenever in my mind I think of when people are trying to
sell Canada as so multicultural and Canada has a large understanding,
you know, that term tolerance – not in my personal experience.

The main fault, according to these participants, lay with "white"
Canadians, who they felt largely did not accept diversity, but kept their
attitudes to themselves so as not to be accused of racism. As a third participant said, "people sort of – it's not politically correct to actually say
this but they sort of think it, they don't say it. And that's pretty broadly
held across society." There was however, another component to their
negative attitude, and that was the tendency of the immigrant minority
populations to isolate themselves in enclaves and not get involved in
the larger society. Here is how a further participant put it:

I think a lot of it is being involved – I think a lot of people especially in Surrey,[4] I think it's their fault in a way, because they actually aren't involved.
And they are sort of self-ghettoized. They don't really care what's going
on or in terms of at the community level, or are in their own sort of world.
So I think in order to be Canadian and sort of actually be a pure Canadian
is that you have to sort of be involved and be aware of how maybe the
government works, how the society functions – being actively involved
at a certain level. I think a lot of people across the board aren't involved;
everyone is sort of in their own zone, in their own personal lives.

The contrast with the Toronto Sikh group could not have been more
stark. Here we find the dominant "critically positive" attitude of felt
inclusion, but with the necessity for Canada to keep working towards a
genuinely multicultural society. Here are excerpts from the responses to
the issue about whether Canadian multiculturalism exists and whether
it works:

First Participant: I think it does. Right? I think it's, um, it's come to a point
where everyone respects each other's, you know, their identity and their
space. There is curiosity between groups ... a lot of people are open to
change or different aspects of different cultures.
Second Participant: I think it has gone a long way and it's getting better
day-by-day. Because before maybe people were picked on because of
having the turban or whatever reason, but I think it's getting better day-
by-day.

Taken together, the African/Black and Sikh groups demonstrate not just that different people have different attitudes and experiences, but also the possibility of real local cultural difference that one also finds among Montréal, Toronto, and Vancouver. It may be that not just the urban/rural or largest/smaller city distinction makes a difference, but that *which* largest city also does.

Ironically, the exceptions of not really wanting to be included and that of wanting a higher degree of immersion of differences were noticeable in the two groups with an Eastern Christian religious identity. In Toronto, a focus group of Serbian Orthodox Christians thought that Canada was very welcoming and a great place to live: "Everybody who's immigrated to this country is thankful ... *[several in background: 'yeah!']* for allowing us to come here and have these opportunities and things like that. I know I am for sure." On the whole, however, participants in this group prioritized their Serbian roots and culture, with a good segment expressing the wish to go back to Serbia, even if they had been born or had grown up in Canada. Of the six in the group, none of them identified with Canada and most wanted to live elsewhere, often Serbia itself. By contrast, a Montréal group consisting of Eastern Christians of various stripes (Armenian, Bulgarian, Russian, Syrian Orthodox, and Coptic Christian) came the closest to saying that immigrants to Canada, in this case very much and specifically Québec, should be expected to immerse themselves in Québécois culture and maintain their differences only to the extent that doing so did not contradict this immersion process. Using the soup-and-salad metaphor, several in this group felt that the "ingredients" didn't make a salad without the binding "dressing":

> Il faut quand même mettre les ingrédients de la salade ensemble, dans le même bol. C'est ça que je dis, on est même pas dans le même bol. On est chacun dans une assiette à part, parfois même sur des tables à part et on décide d'évoluer chacun de son côté et y a pas ce bol. Moi je suis d'accord avec toi, la salade ... mais la vinaigrette, il faut qu'elle prenne.

In consonance with this orientation, this was also the only group in which the majority put their Québec identity ahead of either their "ethnic" or their "Canadian" identity. Most were Québécois, perhaps *montréalais*, first, Canadian second. Only one of nine declared their Canadian identity to come first. By contrast, the other five groups in Montréal – the two Haitian, one African, one Southeast Asian, and one

Latin American – were dominated by those with a shifting and fluid sense of identity. A large number of them felt differently depending on whom they were with and where they found themselves. They could feel Québécois(e), Canadian, neither, or closer to their "ethnic" identity, depending on circumstances. One variant of this orientation was expressed like this by a participant in the Latin American group: "Moi, ça va dépendre d'où je me trouve. Si je suis à l'étranger je vais dire que je suis Canadien; si je suis ici j'aurai plus tendance à me dire Québécois pour éviter d'offenser ceux qui sont super souverainiste et qui vont dire 'Moi, je suis pas Canadien, je suis Québécois'." Another, from the Southeast Asian group, was more expansive:

> Moi, pour ma part, c'est sûr que je dirais que je suis Québécoise d'origine vietnamienne, sauf qu'avant tout, je suis Montréalaise. Je suis attachée à Montréal ... Je vis maintenant dans le quartier Villeray, c'est important pour moi le quartier, la vie communautaire, sortir dans la rue et entendre parler espagnol, vietnamien, anglais, français, tsé, c'est important pour moi. Mais ça dépend aussi à qui je parle. C'est beaucoup une question d'interlocuteur. C'est sûr que je suis Québécoise, le français c'est important pour moi, mais je parle 4 langues quand même, j'ai travaillé, j'ai étudié en espagnol, en anglais aussi, ça fait que si je m'adresse à un Canadien, c'est sûr que je vais lui faire part du fait français, mais je suis aussi Canadienne. Pour moi, il n'y a pas une dichotomie d'identité: c'est une identité à plusieurs volets. Puis je suis Canadienne, je suis Québécoise, je suis Montréalaise ...

As these quotes indicate, however, the great majority of those in the Southeast Asian and Latin American groups, but also many of those in the African Christian group, felt very comfortable in Québec/Montréal society, not excluded as was the majority opinion in the two Haitian groups.

Canadian/Québec Culture

The example of the Eastern Christian group in Montréal finds further resonance in responses to questions surrounding the existence and character of Canadian and Québec culture. Without exception, the six Montréal groups were very clear in their conviction that there was a Québec culture, that it was different from the dominant culture in other parts of Canada, and that this culture was centred in the difference of language, history, North American minority status, and in the place of and orientation toward religion. Here are three expressions of the difference taken from three different focus groups in Montréal:

> Si tu voyages un peu dans le Canada, tu te rends compte que les Québécois sont totalement différents par leurs habitudes, leurs façon de parler, leurs valeurs positives. (African Christian group)
>
> Historiquement, les Canadiens sont les loyalistes américains et puis les Québécois sont les colons français. Donc c'est sûr qu'ils ont différentes cultures. Moi je suis allé à Calgary cet été, c'est pas la même chose que Montréal, c'est beaucoup plus cowboy, c'est différent ... Ils ont leur fierté propre d'être Canadiens. Ici au Québec, on remarque plus la fierté québécoise. Il existe donc deux cultures. (Latin American Christian group)
>
> Moi j'aimerais ajouter une chose qui est très différente et qui pour moi est très importante. C'est tout ce qui est en lien avec la culture, la musique, euh, c'est ça, toute la culture qui existe au Québec, que je trouve très riche. Qu'ailleurs, si on va en Ontario, c'est différent. Y a des groupes de musique ici qui me représentent, quand je vais là-bas, ce n'est pas pareil. (Orthodox Christian group)

By contrast, the Montréal groups and those in the rest of Canada gave quite varied responses when asked about both the existence and the characteristics of a Canadian culture. Some thought there was no such thing. As one participant in the Serbian Orthodox group in Toronto put it bluntly: "There is none." A participant in the Turkish Muslim group in Ottawa said the same but introduced the comparative aspect: "When you say you want ... to know what Canadian culture is like, compared to my cultural background, I don't see a culture." Similarly, one of those in the Montréal Southeast Asian group said, "Ben, je vois plus qu'il y a une culture québécoise que canadienne. Ben, je sais pas, je suis pas capable d'imaginer la culture canadienne."

Understanding Canadian culture in comparative or relative terms was in fact the more dominant orientation expressed in most of the groups across the country, and this comparison was very often quite positive. The dominant comparative references were, however, not Québec and Canada, but the United States and the countries of origin. One person put the Canada/America comparison like this: "I'm not really sure what Canadian culture is, but I just know it's not what I used to think, it's not just a pale imitation of American culture it's something else" (Edmonton Mixed Group 2). The two comparisons were mentioned separately and in combination. Here is a particularly revealing version in how it combines the two, and implicitly, the relation to multiculturalism:

> I think, just from traveling across Canada, that the bigger the city is, the more willing and proud people are of the fact that they are from a different culture and for the difference between Canada and the US; in Canada you are more likely to hear someone describe themselves as whatever their homeland is and Canadian, so like if they are Italian-Canadian, Chinese-Canadian, it's whatever they were, and Canadian. Whereas in the US, they just say I'm an American and that's it. In a lot of ways it's good because you get to see and experience a bunch of different diversities and cultures and you get exposed to other things but again it's – you do run the risk of being segregated from other groups. (Edmonton Mixed Group 1)

Quite a number of participants focused specifically on multiculturalism as a defining characteristic: "What is Canada? ... You know, the first thing that probably comes to mind is multiculturalism. Oh it's sort of a little bit of this and a little bit of that" (Ottawa Korean Christian group). Another said, "My friends ask what is Canadian culture and I'm like 'mixture of every other culture?'" (Vancouver Korean Christian group). For these participants, "integrating" into Canadian culture was almost entirely unproblematic because living their own differences, their own hyphenated identities, their own mélange or hybridity in itself already constituted Canadian culture. One might say that these participants had internalized the myth of Canadian multiculturalism to the extent that they considered themselves to be proper embodiments of it, to be proper Canadians one might say, whereas those who did not participate in the mélange were not. Another version of this attitude expressed itself in the idea that Canadian culture was a kind of background condition that didn't have or need a lot of positive definition and content. As one participant in the Ottawa Somali Muslim group put it:

> I find whenever especially someone's like, "Oh, I'm Canadian ... my grandparents are Canadian." Everyone is just like – bored, you know? They pass the conversation because it's ... you know? So I find that people maybe cling on to more their other background that they have because I find that ... being Canadian is not being Canadian.

Positive answers to the question of Canadian culture indicated a broad acceptance of what one might call public mythic characteristics, such as that Canadian culture was tolerant, polite, understated, peaceable, and symbolized through corresponding elements such as (especially!) hockey, maple syrup, the beaver, health care, Mounties, a predilection for the particle, "eh!," and not infrequently Tim Horton's and the "I am Canadian" Molson's commercial. Or, here is another version:

> Well, there are some things that I identify with Canada and I'm kind of a little bit proud of. I mean CBC is Canadian and then we have some really nice shows too that were strictly Canadian: Royal Canadian Air Farce and Bob and Doug Mackenzie ... things that were actually quite good and Canadian. (Edmonton Mixed Group 4)

Behind these varying attitudes, one senses an implicit debate about what "counts" as culture. As one participant in an Edmonton mixed group put it:

> I don't know. I think Canadian culture is not so much a matter of – culture for a lot of the cultures of the world is very much centred on religious tradition, or cuisine, or a form of dress and traditions within the family; where Canadian culture is not any one of those things. It's based on a set of ideals and principles, like tolerance, respect for diversity, respect for justice, striving for peace. I think that's how you should define Canadian culture.

Religious Freedom and Religious Equality

It is a commonplace that religion and culture are not the same thing, but that they are nonetheless intimately related. While the participants in this project on the whole did not disagree with this proposition, their responses to the questions about religion had a rather different flavour when compared to those they gave with respect to culture. Religion as a category, one might say, operated differently than did the category of culture. Thus, most of the groups considered that there existed a high degree of religious freedom in Canada, even though there were some problems in this regard. Almost all the non-Christian groups, including the mixed and control groups, considered that there were no significant barriers to the practice of their religion, whatever that might be, if they identified with one at all. That includes the two Tamil Hindu groups, the somewhat Buddhist Southeast Asian group, and the two Muslim groups, Somali and Turkish; it also includes the four Sikh groups. In the Toronto Sikh group, for instance, when asked if they were free to practise their religion without constraint, the general opinion was that, yes, they could, although that may not have been the case twenty years ago. The same question asked of the Turkish Muslim group elicited a chorus of agreement: "I think there is"; "definitely"; "you can practice your religion wherever you are, doesn't matter"; and "it works." And from among the Southeast Asians, one participant responded, "Moi, je dirais qu'en général, je trouve qu'on a une grande liberté religieuse."

This is not to say that these groups reported no discrimination on a religious basis; both Muslims and Sikhs discussed difficulties attendant upon wearing what French law calls "ostentatious religious symbols" like hijab and kirpans. In the same Sikh group just cited, after the general agreement that religious freedom existed in Canada, one participant added this qualifier: "I think there's still some limitations, though. I know my husband went to a Brampton court ... and I don't think he was allowed to wear his kirpan. He had to take it off. So there are." The restrictions on the wearing of the kirpan came up in other Sikh groups as well, pointing to its symbolic role in concretizing limits on religious freedom. Interestingly enough, the turban did not arise in a similar way among the Sikhs, even though it, too, has been controversial in the Canadian context (cf. Gualtieri 1995). Similarly, the issue of hijab arose several times in the Somali Muslim group in Ottawa; participants reported a number of relatively negative experiences associated with wearing the hijab. Here is one such report:

> I ... wear hijab, I'm visibly Muslim. So, I was working with another Muslim and she was wearing hijab too, and you know we went to the washroom together, we were just fixing our hijab and the lady walked in. And, she was just, you know, asking us questions about it. But, it wasn't really from a curiosity perspective it was more from an assumption – like, "Why do you wear it?" Like, she was asking us, "Oh, who made you wear it?" or like, "Do your parents, did your parents make you wear it?" And, she also had that whole feeling of like, you know, male domination like, your father made you put it on, or you know "there must be a strong male influence in your ... you know."

The participants interpreted such incidents, and others such as the difficulty in finding prayer space in some situations, as rendering it more difficult to practise their religion, but not truly as a lack of religious freedom. This freedom they felt was present in Canada, especially when compared to other countries like France, Belgium, or even Egypt.

Attitudes toward religious freedom were remarkably similar among most of the Christian groups, something that may be seen as surprising given that almost everyone, regardless of which group one is considering, acknowledged the dominant position of Christianity in Canada. A typical example comes from the Vancouver Korean Christian group. There, the general answer to the question about whether there was religious freedom in Canada was "definitely," but with the qualifier that Christianity held a privileged position, which may or may not continue. As one participant put it:

> I think Christians are way more recommended [sic] than the other religions, maybe because of Canadian culture; it used to be Christians from back in Europe ... but since our culture is multiculturalism, people are trying to equalize the status of the religions – like even back ten years ago, people look differently to other religions, like Sikhism or even Muslims. But since the population of immigrants are growing – status is definitely becoming equalized.

Alongside such declarations of Christian dominance and even privilege, however, were attitudes that pointed somewhat in the opposite direction: Christianity was neither privileged nor dominant, but it should be. In several instances, most clearly in the African/Caribbean group from Toronto and in the Haitian Protestant group in Montréal, participants protested that they could not practise their Christian faith fully, that they in fact did not enjoy religious freedom, especially in that they could not openly demonstrate their faith without negative repercussions. A couple reported losing jobs because they engaged in what they felt was Christian activity; several declared themselves hesitant about taking out their bibles in public or of even mentioning their faith to strangers in public. A member of the Haitian Protestant group related his negative experience, linking it explicitly to the question of freedom to practise his religion:

> Moi, je travaillais à [une entreprise à Montréal], ... Pis, un de mes superviseurs était homosexuel ... Mais la Bible condamne l'homosexualité pis

il y a des versets très clairs que la Bible dit ça, mais tu peux pas dire ça. Mais c'est quoi la liberté religieuse? C'est pour cette raison que je dis qu'il n'y en a pas. J'ai dis ça à un de mes collègues ...: "Ils me mettent à la porte justement parce que j'ai dit un commentaire homophobe." C'est Romain chapitre premier qui nous dit très clairement que l'homosexualité c'est mal. Mais tu peux pas dire ... il y a pas de liberté de religion ... On parle pas des vraies affaires. On parle pas des religions, on va dire, "Ce gars là c'est un protestant!" J'ai perdu ma job. J'ai été barré de [l'entreprise] pour un commentaire homophobe tandis que la Bible dit clairement que l'homosexualité c'est mal.

A participant in the African/Caribbean group in Toronto gave a parallel account involving her bible-reading:

I lost a job because of the fact that I was a Christian and I read my Bible. And I had an email from my employer saying that that's offensive reading material and I need to do it on my own time ... she said, oh, they had several complaints about me reading it. And I said, it's ok that you guys can read your magazines of witchcraft and, you know, your Harry Potter. And I'm supposed to just say it's not offensive to me, but as soon as you hear about Jesus, as soon as you see the Holy Bible, it's offensive. ... and in the email it said, you know, "we need to be respectful about other people's beliefs and religion." I thought, "Ok, well what about mine?" You know? So I kind of paused for a second. I said, you know, I find Canada's more accepting of every other God that, you know, from different cultures and different backgrounds than the one that from the beginning, who was here!

Some members of several of the other Christian groups in Toronto and Vancouver shared a more muted version of this opinion. Here the occasional response to the religious freedom and equality questions was that the policy of multiculturalism sometimes had the effect of expecting Christians to be more tolerant than others because theirs was the majority religion. As a participant in the Vancouver Filipino group put it, "if you think about it, ... as a Christian we're expected to be the religion to accept everyone, but for other religions, ... they don't have that expectation on them." A stronger version of this attitude was expressed by a participant in the Vancouver South Asian Christian group:

I think Christianity – it was so major and was so huge in Canada that now, anything to do with Christianity ... is no, no, no, we can't talk about that in school, can't say the Lord's Prayer, can't say merry Christmas, can't host bible studies, but okay yeah, it's okay if you wear your turban, that's fine. I'm not saying that's bad – I'm just saying that's the general perspective. It's okay if you bring your dagger to school, yeah, it's okay if we set up a room for you to pray once or twice a day, that's fine, but, no, you can't say merry Christmas, because that will be offending people, the humanists, because they don't want to hear that.

In this regard, it should be noted that, in Toronto, we felt obliged to organize a separate focus group for devout Chinese Christians because in our first Chinese Christian focus group held in that city, the more devout were clearly made to feel uncomfortable about expressing their opinions by those for whom religion was not all that important.

Corresponding to the Christian complaints from certain groups, there was also the occasionally expressed opinion that Canada should be a Christian society, dominated publicly by Christianity and Christian precepts, that Canada was regrettably not or no longer such a society, and that Christianity was the clearly superior religion to all others. Two members of the African/Caribbean group were not the only ones to lean in this direction, but they did say it most directly. In the words of one of them:

And I just kind of feel like ... we're dropping what we've grown up in our personal lives to learn because we want to take on this Canadian [multicultural thing] ... I thought it was so great – and I still do – it's so great that Canada's loving and accepting. And this is the Christian way, we're supposed to be accepting and loving and peaceful. But [it's] going too far. If our Canadian leaders are not Christian, they're leading us astray. And that's the problem. I feel like I was being led astray ... Canada is a blessed nation. Because even when we were formed, um, like obviously we were formed with Christian values. But like, the thing about it, like now we're starting to step away from ... those values that made Canada.

Parallel to this sort of understanding, however, a much larger number of participants from a great variety of focus groups were quite averse to any sort of religious dominance – while accepting a certain de facto privileging of Christianity for historical and demographic reasons – judging that religions should be treated equally, to a large degree were so treated in Canada, and, moreover that certain limits on religion were justified when issues of public safety and the rights of others came into play. In this respect, the attitudes of non-Muslims about the place of Islam in Canadian society were illustrative. On the one hand, a number of participants from a variety of the focus groups averred that Islam was one religion in Canada against which there was overt discrimination. From the Vancouver Filipino group, for example, in which participants complained about Christian disadvantage, we also hear this relatively complex message:

> I don't think Christianity is the only thing targeted, though. I have Muslim friends from back home who, because of 9/11 for example, they feel targeted; she says at the airports people stop her every time, just because she wears a headscarf. I think for them it's worse. I don't know if it's a cultural thing or the media portrays them as villainized. My friends are Iranian; every time they pass through the border, they have to get out of their car, be checked, be asked questions, gotta get their fingerprints – it's pathetic … I think the dominant religions – not just Christianity – get the bad end of the stick – when something bad happens, there is a lot more coverage on them, the image on them is bad – Muslims also get it bad.

On the other hand, there were those who directly or by implication indicated that they felt that Islam could be somewhat problematic and would have to be limited, but only in its "extreme" forms. To illustrate, toward the end of a long exchange among members of the Vancouver Korean Christian group about whether Islam should be limited, one hears this intervention:

> I think the bottom line is that if you allow freedom of religion, as long as it doesn't violate the laws and the values of Canadian society – because you can allow freedom of religion, but I think a nation's number one priority is to ensure the health and safety of its own culture and its own people. So freedom of religion should definitely be there, but if it gets too extremist or radical or anything, regardless of the religion, there should be measures in place to … counteract that – and to make sure that everyone has an equal footing.

In other words, it was not uncommon to hear that there was a need in Canada to establish limits to religious freedom. Much like in the larger public debate, a number of the participants in the focus group saw few problems in the expression of cultural diversity in Canada, but definitely some potential problems in the expression of religious diversity. Religion, quite a number declared, had to be prepared to make compromises; unfettered religious freedom was not so much impossible as undesirable. The clearest expression of this attitude came from the Orthodox Christian group in Montréal:

> Je suis absolument d'accord avec [deux autres participants]. Il faut dire, c'est bien beau d'avoir sa propre religion et d'avoir la liberté de la pratiquer mais il faut s'arrêter. Il faut décider de ce qu'est la culture québécoise ... Quelles sont les valeurs auxquelles nous nous attachons tous? Nous sommes multiculturels, oui. Il y a plusieurs cultures qui nous ont façonnés, oui. Mais à un moment, il faut se dire qu'est-ce qu'on choisit?

Broadening these considerations a bit, the majority of participants, while espousing religious freedom and opining that it existed for the most part in Canada, were also of the opinion that true religious equality probably was impossible and certainly didn't exist in Canada. The prevailing reason given for this was that Canada was historically and in certain respects still a country where Christianity dominated, both because of the Christian majority that still existed and because of the past influence of Christianity in making Canadian and Québec society what they were. Some in Montréal even suggested that to truly integrate into Québécois society it really helped to be at least nominally Christian because of this historic influence. Many others pointed to the existence of Christian holidays – from Easter and Christmas to Sundays – as evidence of this dominance, while also admitting that these were not really religious holidays anymore; it was just that Christians could still make them Christian holidays. Another way of understanding the unlikelihood of religious equality was that the exclusivist nature of some religions made it very difficult for a situation to develop in which one religion would not try to unsettle any equality that might exist or be developing. This was part of the fairly widespread opinion that there had to be limits to the freedom that religions had.

The Control and Mixed Groups

If we expected sharp differences between the "experimental" groups and the "control" groups, we didn't get them. Actually, in designing the project and on the basis of the previous research project, we thought it more likely that there would be some, but relatively few and that those differences might not be that important. This expectation was therefore more or less confirmed, but with some important qualifications. The first of these stems from the fact that the mixed and the control groups tended to attract a disproportionate number of people who were non-religious or were only nominally religious. Put differently, in leaving religious identity qualifiers out of our advertisements for participants, in this age group the result was a majority of participants for whom religion was personally not that important. This contrasted sharply with the groups where we did ask explicitly for specific religious iden-tities. One consequence of this different composition that one might have expected is that members of the mixed and control groups could have been more suspicious of religion, to expect it to be kept within "appropriate" limits, and to be worried about religious "excesses." Yet this was not the case. Although some participants in these groups, for instance, worried about Sikhs wearing kirpans or Muslim women wearing niqab ("masks"), this opinion was not overly strong and in any case was challenged by other participants. And such differences of opinion did, as noted, arise occasionally in some of the religiously iden-tified groups as well. Moreover, the mixed and control groups were not appreciably different from the "experimental" groups in their atti-tudes to the possibility of religious "free exercise," to use the American term, and to the nature and value of Canadian multiculturalism (none of these groups was held in Montréal). They felt, with the qualifica-tions already discussed, that there was freedom of religion in Canada. They also had as much trouble with the question of Canadian culture as any of the other groups and gave similar answers. In addition, they were similarly "critically positive" about multiculturalism, stressing as much as the rest that this was much more a phenomenon of the large urban centres than it was of smaller cities, towns, and the rural areas.

This, however, brings us to one of those peculiarities that one really ought to expect from a project like this, and that is this: the two "con-trol" groups we conducted in Sydney, NS, were culturally among the most "ethnic" of all the groups, as "ethnic," for instance, as the Serbian or the Turkish groups. Unsurprisingly, given the location, the "ethnic-ity" in this case was a Cape Breton identity. The vast majority of the participants who composed the two control groups in Sydney were Cape Bretoners. They were acutely aware of the specificity of Cape Breton identity and culture – sometimes expanded to a sense of "Mar-itime" (including Newfoundland) culture – and realized the degree to which Cape Bretoners "kept to themselves" and were thus as silo-and enclave-forming as any urban immigrant group. The difference, of course, was that they were not a minority but a majority ethnic group, much like the Québécois in Montréal. This sense of cultural solidarity, recognized as having "Celtic" roots, was clearly expressed in both Cape Breton groups, for example in the following excerpts:

> *Group 1:* Yeah, the Cape Breton identity still has very deep roots in its Celtic ancestry. And like, what J [another participant] was saying with the, ah the clan mentality and the work hard all day party hard all night kind of, um, family community that you know, if someone's in need, the neighbours will come over and help out. Um … and it's [a] very strong sense of community, so much so that when you do go away to these places and you're out West or you're in BC or you're down in the States and you do meet up with other fellow Cape Bretoners or even like Nova Scotians, you guys stick together like glue! And it's like, there's this magic … magnetic connection that draws people together; because I've been in the most random of places and then all of sudden have a bunch of, like, Cape Bretoners and Newfs just converge on each other and realize where they're all from, and then be inseparable for the rest of the time spent on that trip.
>
> *Group 2: P1:* [Laughs]. When you're in that place, and they'll talk to you for like hours and you'll go get something to drink or something. Like it doesn't matter where you are, if you find another Cape Bretoner, you're friends right away.
>
> *P2:* 'Cause, like, even, like, people who work out West and stuff are all, like "Oh, you're from Cape Breton" and they all, like, you know, even if you don't know them from here you're just, like, oh they feel like they know them; … that they're from the same place.
>
> *P1:* Yeah, yeah that's the one funny thing about Cape Bretoners.
>
> *P2:* Yeah.
>
> *P1:* As soon as you go someplace else, if you meet another Cape Bretoner, they're instantly you're best friend.

When asked whether this sense of "clannishness" did not also exclude, for instance, native Black and Aboriginal people in Cape Breton, the members of these groups either averred that this was just natural, as like associated with like, or that this was more something the older people did and that their generation was more open to cultural mixing and the acceptance of cultural diversity. They were, disapprovingly, very aware of the degree to which Aboriginal and Black populations in their region were "kept apart." In this way, therefore, our control groups confirmed what we found in our "experimental" groups: cultures are diverse in Canada; they consist of new cultures that have arrived

with immigration, and of old cultures that are often highly regional-
ized; and overall Canadian culture is either that mélange or something
that can be identified only superficially or with great difficulty. Interestingly enough, in this regard, the third control group, conducted in
Edmonton, was itself just the sort of mélange that many participants
talked about. That was likely an accident of recruitment venue, but it
does show that, in the large cities of Canada, when one advertises for
a group to talk about culture and religion, there is at least a good possibility that the people who show up are going to be culturally and religiously mixed; and that is not the case in the "non-multicultural" areas
of Canada.

Conclusions

What, then, might we conclude from these results regarding the question of the place of religion and culture in Canadian society, including
Québec, Alberta, Vancouver, Toronto, and Cape Breton societies (and
that is what not a few participants thought existed in Canada)? The
first conclusion is that, if these groups are anything to go by, then at
least in the large urban centres of Canada, the fact of multiculturalism as well as the ideal has been internalized by a great many people,
especially among the sort of subpopulations that we examined. In that
light, the display and public face of this cultural plurality is unproblematic and is expected to be displayed and lived publically, and increasingly so. Multicultural realities are to be lived and enacted "in public."
By contrast, religious diversity is somewhat more suspect and is to be
kept largely "in private," at least in the sense of not being or appearing to be "imposed" on others. Here the complaints of the conservative
Christians that felt that they were restricted in their practice and that
Canada had, as it were, gone to the dogs of secularism, or the expectation that was most explicit in the Eastern Christian Montréal group to
the effect that religion should not be in the public sphere (whatever that
may mean more precisely), are perhaps particularly illustrative. This
would explain why the "flashpoint" issues with regard to diversity in
Canada are so much more frequently "religious" issues, and only very
rarely "cultural" ones. Everyone, it seems, loves the dizzying variety of
restaurants, the colourful display of cultural differences at urban multicultural fairs and festivals, and most people expect to see the variety
inscribed in the faces of public figures from politicians to media per-
sonalities. To the degree that these public displays are deemed to be

inadequately present and *insufficiently* manifest in their interactions and mutual influence, multiculturalism is itself a sham or inadequate. Discrimination, silos, enclaving, or the manifest and persistent domination of some cultures over others are unacceptable and, difficult though it may be, they ought to be overcome. Again, only some of the members of the Eastern Christian group in Montréal were hesitant in this regard, and this was because they felt that multiculturalism carried within it the danger of making Québécois culture just one among the rest, and therefore inevitably threatening it.

Somewhat different is the attitude to the public display of religious difference, even if few participants could be all that precise about where exactly the line between culture and religion was to be drawn. While the majority of our participants also expected this to be unproblematic and even celebrated – especially among those who were the carriers of these religious differences – there was also a significant minority who expressed some degree of reservation in this regard. Freedom of religion was fine, but there had to be limits; religions, unlike cultures, could be dangerous and disturbing, and above all, they should not be aggressively or, for some, even noticeably public. Religion, one might conclude, was by and large good, but best kept to oneself and for one's group, that is to say, in private. Culture, by contrast, should and could be publically displayed and celebrated, the more the better perhaps. In other words, there seems to be a strong tendency in Canada – including very definitely Québec – for a kind of soft secularism, a *laïcité ouverte* perhaps, to adopt the language used by the Bouchard-Taylor Commission Report (Bouchard and Taylor 2008a, 2008b), one that is understated, polite, and tolerant, and religion should be the same. Intriguingly, while some participants implied this to be a feature of Canadian culture and identity, and not a few declared that part of that identity was to be "not American," no one pointed to contrasting secularities as being an expression of that non-American character. Between Canada and Québec, yes, but not between Canada/Québec and the United States. In this regard, while it is a bit speculative thus far, it does seem that the "problem" with religion is only for some that it challenges what is supposed to be a dominant secularism. The other diagnosis is twofold: first is that religion, left without restraining limits "won't mix," that the supposed exclusivism of religions makes inevitable the constant danger of clashing diversities, of one religion seeking to become dominant over the others, such as was desired by members of at least two or three of the Christian groups. In other words, unlike culture perhaps, religion can present a danger to precisely the sort of "mixing" that is at the heart of what is deemed to be valuable and proper multiculturalism or inter-culturalism. Second, however, religion for some has the potential for contradicting other, superordinate values, including not only (multicul-tural) inclusion, but also that of public safety and security (represented by "daggers" and "masks") and that of gender equality.

   An equally significant conclusion, however, is that, with some exceptions – the Turkish Muslim group dominated by much more recent immigrants and the Serbian Orthodox group are representative – the vast majority of members of the second generation and 1.5 genera-tion of recent immigration, irrespective of what part of the country one is talking about, consider themselves to be integral parts of this coun-try, to belong here, even and especially when not a few of them still have occasional or frequent experiences of discrimination on the part of segments of the hitherto-dominant population. There is the expec-tation that Canada is to some degree and should become more and more in the future a "multicultural" society in the sense of incorporat-ing and including within itself multiple different identities, both cul-tural and religious. They are perhaps no clearer than others on exactly how one enacts that combination of "living one's differences" in a way that "integrates," "includes," "accommodates," and "accepts" them in a harmonious, peaceable, and mutually edifying way. Yet that expec-tation is strong, even among the "controls": the "rest of the world" belongs here. With respect to the opening question about the assess-ment of multiculturalism and religious diversity, the participants in this research, with few exceptions, would side with those that valorize the ideal of ongoing and increased diversity as a positive and, in many respects, typically Canadian value, and against those that would see it as problematic. Their answer to the latter might in fact be that the way to address the problems of diversity is to value it more and increase it, not the other way around.

NOTES

1 The data set analysed for this chapter is therefore different than that which Rubina Ramji has used for her chapter in this volume. Although both of us were members of the research team for both projects, her data are taken from a similar project carried out in 2004–2006 that included 200 interviews with participants from Muslim, Hindu, and Buddhist backgrounds.

2 A program on the French-language Québec network, TVA.
3 A French-language version of the Weather Network.
4 A city that is part of greater Vancouver and has a heavy concentration of
   Punjabi Sikhs, the heaviest in Canada. In the current Canadian House of
   Commons, this area is represented entirely by members of parliament
   of Punjabi Sikh origin, from across the political spectrum. For a map of the
   religious concentration of Sikhs in Surrey, see Beyer and Martin (2010, 96).

REFERENCES

Beyer, Peter, and W. K. Martin. 2010. "The Future of Religious Diversity in
    Canada." Ottawa: Citizenship and Immigration Canada.
Beyer, Peter, and Rubina Ramji, eds. 2013. *Growing Up Canadian: Muslims, Hin-
    dus, Buddhists.* Kingston and Montréal: McGill-Queen's University Press.
Bissoondath, Neil. 1994. *Selling Illusions: The Cult of Multiculturalism in Canada.*
    Toronto: Penguin.
Bouchard, Gérard, and Charles Taylor. 2008a. "Building the Future: A Time for
    Reconciliation." *Commission de Consultation sur les pratiques d'accommodement
    reliées aux différences culturelles.* Québec: Québec Government Printing
    Office, 22 May.
Bouchard, Gérard, and CharlesTaylor. 2008b. "Fonder l'avenir. Le temps de
    la conciliation." Québec: Commission de Consultation sur les pratiques
    d'accommodement reliées aux différences culturelles.
Castles, Stephen, and Mark J. Miller. 2003. *The Age of Migration: International Pop-
    ulation Movements in the Modern World* (3rd ed.). New York: Guilford Press.
Citizenship and Immigration Canada. 2011. "Promoting Integration. Annual
    Report on the Operation of the Canadian Multiculturalism Act, 2009–2010."
    Ottawa: Citizenship and Immigration Canada. Available at www.cic.gc.ca/
    english/resources/publications/multi-report2010/index.asp
Dib, Kamal, Ian Donaldson, and Brittany Turcotte. 2009. "Integration and
    Identity in Canada: The Importance of Multicultural Common Spaces."
    Canadian Ethnic Studies/Études ethniques au Canada 40(1): 161–87.
Foner, Nancy, and Richard Alba. 2008. "Immigrant Religion in the US and
    Western Europe: Bridge or Barrier to Inclusion?" *International Migration
    Review* 42(2): 360–92.
Gualtieri, Antonio R. 1995. "Multiculturalism and Modernity: The Sikh Tur-
    ban and the RCMP." *Policy Options/Options politiques* 16(2): 27–31.
Jupp, James. 2002. *From White Australia to Woomera: The Story of Australian
    Immigration.* New York: Cambridge University Press.

Karim, Karim H. 2009. "Press, Public Sphere and Pluralism: Multiculturalism Debates in Canadian English-Language Newspapers." *Canadian Ethnic
Studies/Études ethniques au Canada* 40(1): 57–78.

Kymlicka, Will. 2010. "The Current State of Multiculturalism in Canada and
Research Themes on Canadian Multiculturalism 2008." Ottawa: Citizenship
and Immigration Canada.

Lucassen, Leo, David Feldman, and Jochen Oltmer, eds. 2006. *Paths of Integration: Migrants in Western Europe (1880–2004)*. Amsterdam: Amsterdam University Press.

Metcalf, Barbara D., ed. 1996. *Making Muslim Space in North America and
Europe*. Berkeley: University of California Press.

Portes, Alenjandro, and Ruben G. Rumbaut. 2001. *Legacies: The Story of the
Immigrant Second Generation*. Berkeley: University of California Press.

Robertson, Roland. 1992. *Globalization: Social Theory and Global Culture*. London: Sage.

Ryan, Phil. 2010. *Multicultiphobia*. Toronto: University of Toronto Press.

Sibley, Robert. 2008. "Intolerable." *Ottawa Citizen*, 19 May.

Steyn, Mark. 2006. "The Future Belongs to Islam." *Maclean's*, 20 October. Available at www.macleans.ca.

PART II

Private Life

4 Maintaining and Nurturing an Islamic Identity in Canada – Online and Offline

RUBINA RAMJI

As Islam becomes increasingly transnational, the "authoritative use of the symbolic language of Islam" has become fragmented and contested (Eickelman and Anderson 2003, 1). Although many Muslims explain their lives through the normative language of Islam, we know that being Muslim does not have the same meaning for all followers of the faith. Muslim identity politics take on many forms, including class interests, nationalism, and family networks; furthermore, these identity formations differ vastly between Muslim-majority states and populations in which Muslims form a minority.

This chapter examines how second-generation Canadian Muslims perceive Islam, live their faith, and how they develop and facilitate their religious knowledge through an intensive yet individualized use of the internet. Cyber-Islam has taken on many manifestations. Multiple Muslim worldviews "present a reference point of identity within a conceptualization of Islam" (Bunt 2009, 1). These online forms of Islam offer religious instruction, religious knowledge, marginal and alternate beliefs, peer-to-peer networking, and a sense of community. The Islamic world online has become open-sourced, and this openness of knowledge and scholarship has created a cyberspace where individuals can be exposed to "new influences outside of traditional spheres of knowledge and authority" (Bunt 2009, 3). This study explores how second-generation Muslim youth living in Canada are using public cyber-interactions and resources to maintain and transform their private religious identity offline.

Islamic Youth Growing up in Canada

Although Canadian society remains largely Christian, other religions have taken a foothold in Canada. Between 1991 and 2001 the Muslim,

Hindu, Sikh, and Buddhist communities in Canada have nearly, if not already, doubled in size (Bramadat 2005, 24). Therefore religion continues to be important in relation to the creation of identities, boundaries, and group solidarities in Canada. In reality, research being conducted in Canada has revealed that recent immigrant children and youth are twice as likely to attend religious services in comparison to their Canadian-born complement (Biles and Ibrahim 2005, 165).

Muslims have been immigrating to Canada for decades, and so the population of Canadian-born Muslim youth has grown substantially. These younger Muslims, referred to as the second generation, have no direct ethnic connection to their parents' homeland, and therefore have to define Islam and its practices for themselves without any ethnic influence, in juxtaposition to the ethnic cultural values they have received from their parents.[1]

Even though European studies have found that migrant Muslims living there tend to turn to a Muslim identity because of their contact with different cultures from their homeland, this research deals with a different cohort of immigrants (there is little research on second-generation immigrants). This research project[2] examines the involvement of second-generation immigrant[3] Muslim youth, aged 18–27, who have at least one immigrant parent and were either born in Canada or who arrived in Canada before the age of ten. Those interviewed came from Muslim backgrounds, and were living or studying in the Canadian urban areas of Toronto, Ottawa, and Montréal. The interviews were conducted over a two-year period, from September 2004 to April 2006.

The research project's aim was to investigate participant involvement in the Islamic tradition, whether it was personal, communal, or institutional, as well as their attitudes towards religion. The question of their religious identity or lack thereof was central to the investigation. Interviewees were asked about their upbringing within their inherited religious identity, their own involvement in the religion in which they were brought up, the adoption of any religious practices, and unconventional practices they may have acquired. They discussed how their own views and practices differed from the parental generation (the first generation of immigrants), and how they situated themselves within Canada and the wider world. The focal point of this research was to find out how this generation was or was not reconstructing their overall and specifically religious worldviews, practices, and identities. Our organizing assumption was that these youth are "caught between two worlds," meaning in between the religious and cultural identities and experiences of their parents and those of mainstream Canadian culture.

The second-generation Muslims in this study are not being confronted by a new culture, but rather have been raised in, and feel completely at ease in Canadian culture. They have been raised to contend with a variety of identity dimensions in their lives, those of their Islamic faith, their parents' ethnic cultural heritage and their exposure to the values and practices of Canadian culture through school, politics, and the media.

For this particular study, the interviewees' own self-definitions about their religious involvement was utilized in the classification (Ramji 2008, 197). By examining orthopraxis (actions of obligation), intentions, familial, and institutional influences, as well as levels of belief,[4] participants provided us with a rich tapestry of identity-formation and-maintenance tools. The participants, using their own self-definitions about belief and practice, were eventually separated into a ten category system. Ninety-three people were interviewed who considered themselves to have Muslim backgrounds. Of the 93 participants, 58 were female and 35 were male.

The ten categories fashioned from the 93 participants' own perceptions were further grouped together to illustrate everything from little or no involvement in the faith to orthodox practices of Islam: those in categories 1 to 3 define themselves as atheists or non-followers of a religion but are Muslim by culture and family. Those in categories 4 to 6 are moderately involved in their faith and do not consider Islam to have a central place in their lives. They have a general knowledge of Islam and participate in some aspects of the faith. Those in categories 7 to 9 are considered highly involved Muslims, following the five core pillars of the Islamic tradition but have internal variations in the way they construct their Islamic identity. Those in category 10 support the necessity of adhering to five pillars but also insist that only the Qur'an and ahadith are valid sources for living and practicing Islam. Any other sources are considered innovative and therefore not permitted within the true following of the faith. They espouse forms of Islamic Sunni ideology (the only legitimate sources are the Qur'an and the Sunna, the traditions of the Prophet Muhammad and the early community) and practice that they considered to be "pure" or "original" forms of Islam. In comparison to the highly involved Muslims (category 7–9), those in the highest category (10) are not only putting Islam at the centre of their lives but they put a highly demanding and conservative form of Islam there.

While we must be careful in our interpretations across categories, one conclusion seems clearly justified: a significant number, perhaps even a majority, of second-generation Muslims in Canada are at least highly involved in their religion. Second-generation Muslims are not being lost in significant numbers to the secularism of the majority of the Canadian population.[5]

Transnational Islam Online

Online networking can be transformational in that it can affect relationships, affect personal and communal worldviews, and engender social change. But this technology can also act to "mirror" one's offline religious expression and experience rather than providing a new articulation of faith (Bunt 2004, 123). Islam online varies from the orthodox to the esoteric and the marginalized. Although many of these sites are designed specifically to propagate the faith (including computer programs that offer prayer direction and time, as well as Qur'anic recitations), others claim to offer specific authoritative religious perspectives about the religion (dispensing commentaries, sermons, advice and opinions, or fatwas). More and more websites are trying to develop a more sympathetic way of comprehending Islam, directed toward non-Muslims or those Muslims living outside Muslim countries, through a "specific set of interpretative and culture values" (Bunt 2004, 124).

An internet search for the word "Islam" yields links to hundreds of thousands of sites featuring everything from shopping to sermons to "Web-muftis" who provide answers to theological and legal questions. The Web allows almost anyone to air a broad range of views and perspectives. Many of these views and perspectives result in discussion and debate within the numerous forums and chat rooms found online.

Some say the internet has also altered consensus-building among the ummah, or major Islamic forces. What used to take decades, even centuries to agree on – interpretations in the Qur'an, for example – has been accelerated by the internet's ability to give instant access to the teachings and thoughts of distant Islamic scholars and to original texts. Practices, laws, and beliefs, once bound by geography, are evolving into a mainstream Muslim identity – on internet time (NPR.org).

In terms of popular Islamic sites, the Web offers resources for daily religious life – festivals, rites of passage, and materials related to specific cultural, religious, political and/or linguistic interests. "It is possible to

Figure 4.1. Islam.com

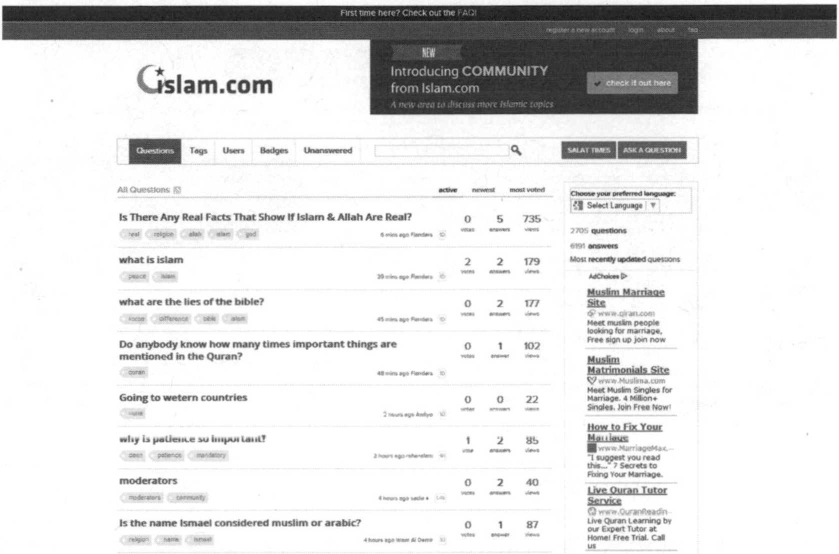

link up with other members of a religious affiliation online or enter into e-mail or chat room dialogue with a religious scholar" (Bunt 2004, 126). And now, many Islamic sites offer the possibility of connecting with potential Muslim partners for marriage. The three main sites (as of 2013) that appear on Google are Islam.com, IslamiCity.com, and IslamOnline.net. All three are portal sites, in that they each serve as a point of entry for services or sites related by geography, industry, or topic; in this case, Islam. Islam.com is a site that offers both an introduction to Islam for those who are searching for answers about the faith, and also caters to the practitioner. The site has articles on Islam (information about Islam, Allah, and Muslim festivals) and also has the Qur'an and surahs online. It proffers a variety of discussion forums ranging in subject matter from politics, business, science, education, and teaching Islam to literature and recipe exchanges. It also provides many utilities so that surfers have reason to return to the site regularly. These utilities include Eid and hajj cards, request for prayers, the Islamic calendar, and Islamic wallpapers. Furthermore, as a portal site, it offers links to newspapers around the world. It also sells, through Amazon, a digital Qur'an that can be translated into seven languages.

Figure 4.2. IslamiCity

IslamiCity.com has two sections: for the surfer, it provides access to feature news articles and multimedia, special sections on science and finance, and an introduction section to Islam (pillars, prayers, history, a Qur'an search and glossary, and even an Islamic quiz). But for those who have membership, the site offers access to discussion forums, radio, CyberTV that has various channels of Islamic content, live television from Mecca and Medina, marriage connections, a gift store, and the ability to make online donations. Membership also allows a person to convert to Islam over the telephone. The site claims its authenticity by stating that a new person visits IslamiCity.com every three seconds and that one person converts over the phone every 50 hours. In fact, it illustrates how, through their own outreach projects, people have come to experience the faith for themselves. On the homepage scroll the names of those who have taken the shahadah and the site also provides audio recordings of those who have called in to proclaim their conversion to Islam. It also offers a question-and-answer service so that one can pose questions to "experts" on religious topics. IslamOnline.net also offers membership, discussion forums, e-cards, matrimonial connections, a date converter, and a newsletter. It appears as a news site in that it offers "top news" stories at the beginning of the homepage. Of note in all three sites is that "membership" does not require members to profess their Muslim identity in order to join in the discussions taking place in the forums and chat rooms. In fact, anyone can become a member of these sites, and often one can see that these sites cater to the non-Muslim in order to encourage further entrance into the portal and conversion.

People are doing online what they do offline, but in innovative ways. This swing to the online world has two critical consequences: "a crisis of authority and a crisis of authenticity" (Dawson and Cowan 2004, 2). Information that is posted online does not need to be examined or evaluated by others, thus making anyone online an "instant expert" on anything. This unique feature of the internet has changed the way people approach their faith through the use of this medium. Unorthodox and nonconformist views, found side by side with those that espouse orthodox views, do not reduce the so-called "truth" of a religion online, but instead add to the constructed and pluralistic character of religious expressions found among many people who hold the same faith. The internet, in affecting religious life, can make small changes that "expand and enhance our religious sensibilities and levels of satisfaction" by presenting new and diverse experiences and possibilities to religion (Dawson and Cowan 2004, 12).

Larsen (2004) has found that "religion surfers" (those who get religious and spiritual information on the net and connect with others on their spiritual journey) use the internet as a supplemental tool to enhance an already deep commitment to their beliefs and their churches, synagogues, or mosques (p. 18). Many use the internet to make themselves feel more committed to their faith. Religion surfers "take their faith seriously in the offline world and use online tools to enrich their knowledge of their faith and to practice their devotions" (Larsen 2004, 19). The Pew Internet and American Life Project found that more than 74 per cent of religion surfers attended religious services weekly, if not more often. In fact, 86 per cent of these surfers acknowledged that they prayed or meditated at least once a day.

Just as Islam itself is being shaped through technology, Muslims are shaping themselves through cyberspace: creating "notions of Muslim identity and authority that echo and intersect with similar notions in the nondigital real world" (Bunt 2009, 13). What does this mean for second-generation Muslims living their faith in a country where they are a minority? In our research study, we found that the internet accommodated individuals who were being religious outside the control or influence of an organized religious institution. This private act of identity construction is done through public exploration. In this way, the internet serves to accentuate the bricolage form of religion being constructed by these Muslim youth.

How Muslim Youth Negotiate Islam in the Public Sphere

Within this study, a separation between notions of ethnicity and religion was made clear amongst many of the highly involved Muslims (categories 7 to 10). These Muslims tend to separate the notion of ethnicity from their practice of Islam. Participants often criticize what they consider to be their parents' cultural practices, such as extravagant weddings, listening to music, and encouraging career over marriage (it is important to remember that many did not argue with their parents about their faith). The culture/religion distinction is critical for those who consider themselves as better practitioners of the faith than their parents. They felt that their parents often indulged in ethnically acceptable behaviour that the participants felt was in fact contrary to their understanding of the faith. They have undertaken their own personal searches to better understand Islam. Their sources of authority are often the internet, electronic chat rooms, and personal readings. Their parents encouraged this kind of personal search for knowledge. Correspondingly, they do not consider the mosque an important source of counsel. The two participants who fall into category 10 are women, so it is of note that they do not attend Friday *jum'ah* services as it is not required of them, yet they practise their faith at the highest level. Thus, the mosque itself does not play a role in their lives. They are both involved in their local Muslim Student Associations. They deny the validity of intra-Islamic distinctions like Sunni versus Shi'a, and consider the non-Sunnis as not authentically Muslim. In either case, their Islam is a Sunni Islam. They conscientiously make all aspects of their lives as Islamic as possible. They do not feel alienated from Canadian society in the sense of feeling that they belong somewhere else. This is part of the culture/religion distinction. They are highly critical of various aspects of the dominant culture in Canada (for example, when the topic came up, they were opposed to the recent federal legislation that puts gay and lesbian marriages on an equal footing with male/female marriages).

As this research focuses on an internet-literate generation, it can easily be understood that the second generation are nurturing their concepts of self-identity and authority through online formats as well. Studies illustrate that Muslims "seek out specific truths and affiliations online when they cannot be accessed in the local mosque or community context" (Bunt 2009, 32). Our study of second-generation Muslims in Canada takes this theory one step further, in that the majority do not turn to the mosque or local community for guidance and understanding about their faith. More than 50 per cent of the sample in this project searched the internet for specific authorities, answers, and communities in which to nurture their faith. Of the 93 participants who were interviewed in this project (58 females and 35 males), more than half of the highly involved used the internet to understand their faith. In total more than 40 per cent of the involved participants turned to online resources as a way of finding knowledgeable sources of authority.

The two Muslim participants, both Sunni, who were in the top category of the ten-point scale acknowledged that they used the internet in order to find sources of authority when they couldn't find the answers that they sought in the Qur'an or hadith. They both knew exactly what sources they wanted to find on the internet and did not spend time chatting or acting in "unIslamic" ways. The first participant (Muslim Female 13, age 20) (Beyer and Ramji 2013) began to "academically" study Islam in high school by going onto the internet and listening to lectures by scholars and reading the Qur'an – she did not go to the local imam (Beyer and Ramji 2013). When asked if there were people who were authorities in Islam, her response was that the imams from past times (near the time of the Prophet) were authentic as they were "consistent with the Qur'an and hadith" (Muslim Female 13, age 20). Although she frequented Islamic internet sites, she did not feel the need to pose questions in forums or chat rooms as she believed that those who did ask questions in these venues had no belief. It illustrated their "lack of knowledge" and she considered herself "knowledgeable" as to where to seek her answers (Muslim Female 13, age 20).

The other category 10 participant (Muslim Female 09, age 21) insisted that Western values and thoughts have corrupted some people who claim to be Muslims on the internet, and therefore have compromised the true teachings of the religion. She herself uses the internet to read a lot of lectures and speeches, but she is very precise in who she listens to:

> Like before I was just "oh, he's Muslim whatever" and just listen to it, but now I'm like, okay I have to listen to the one that I know will not lead me to any other path, you know; that will lead me you know, to pure, the way Islam, pure Islam basically. So there's only certain speakers I listen to, you know, and what not. (Muslim Female 09, age 21)

When concepts fall outside the realm of the Qur'an and hadith for answers – such as societal innovations like using the internet – she only focuses on scholars who are based in Saudi Arabia as she considers them authentic. When examining how contemporary Muslim scholars approach the concept of the internet, it has been found that they find "no incompatibility between Islam as a religion and its representation on the internet" (Bunt 2009, 25). Although the participant believes that the internet as a concept has a lot of negative elements to it which could be considered anti-Islamic, focusing on certain scholars helps her negotiate the hazards of surfing:

> They would make such rules like the internet is okay as long as, you know, you do not go on these things that are not allowed in Islam. Like things that people would not be sure, you know, 'is it against our religion' and whatnot. You know, things that are modern day things that people just wouldn't know how to handle, they wouldn't know how to connect it with Islam. They would tell them how to connect to it. (Muslim Female 09, age 21)

At the same time, this same participant favours the teachings of Abu Tasneem, an American who converted to Islam about thirty years ago and learned Arabic by himself. "Like the way he talks is really amazing and like, just, when I hear him talk, I'm like: this is the way Islam is. Like the way he talks, I wish more people listened to him" (Muslim Female 09, age 21). What she considers the voice of authority regarding uses of innovation does not correlate to her concept of authority about the Qur'an and hadith. She chooses the person who she believes espouses what she believes Islam to be. This is a clear trend amongst all participants who formed their own religious identity: they do not rely on parental influences (as their parents encourage them to search for their own answers) or institutional influences (as they do regularly attend mosque and when they do, they do not see the imam as an expert), and what they consider authentic on the internet is highly individualized (also seen in Helland 2004). Although they felt that there was a global sense of Islamic community on the internet, they do not hold to one particular way of defining or living it.

More than half of the highly involved Muslims used the internet as an important source for finding answers, but more than half also considered the imam at the mosque a reliable source of information. This correlation aligns with the fact that many of the highly involved Muslims, male and female, were involved in one way or another with their local mosques. At the same time, many did not maintain a sense of community with members of their mosques in their daily lives and also critiqued the culture of their parents in relation to their practice of Islam. Additionally, seven of the highly involved Muslims were members in their local Muslim Student Association.

One highly-involved Sunni female (Muslim Female 04, age 22), who used the internet often, said that she used it specifically to better understand the Qur'an and hadith so she spent much of her time on Sunni websites as that was their focus (maintaining the idea that authority lies only with a certain understanding of Islam). She also did not find it necessary to follow just one particular authority on the internet as she herself found they deviated from each other.

> Um, there's just difference of interpretations and there's different scholars that they go by and, for me personally, I'm against going like following one scholar and just being like, 'OK, whatever he says goes'. Because I don't – I like looking into things and I think it's better to get the whole realm of opinion rather than just like following this one thing. (Muslim Female 04, age 22)

In terms of her daily life, this particular highly involved Muslim female did not like what she was learning in university about certain practices (in particular the teachings about wearing the veil), so she turned to the internet to better understand the arguments that existed "out there." In a university class she was taking on women and Islam, she found that the professor was offering proofs for not veiling:

> ... and saying, 'oh you know we're just supposed to cover, like the thing is supposed to be modesty, you not supposed to wear hijab.' And I almost kind of fell into that until I really – and again, it goes to the whole superficially knowing something vs. going in depth and really looking into something. (Muslim Female 04, age 22)

Going against the academic understanding of Islam she was receiving in university, this participant found other explanations through the internet to give her a better understanding of the teachings of her faith. For this reason, she decided to start wearing the hijab.

> And once I was convinced and I really like *really* looked into it, I was like 'okay, I need to do it' because I can't pick and choose God's commands. Like whatever is said, I have to do it. There's no leeway for it ... I was pretty content with like the way I was living. I was fine. I was like, I had

no issues, I had no like problems with how I looked and how I was living and stuff like that. But then like with the whole God consciousness, and like whole like actually obeying God's command, then it goes with – like I have to follow, right? (Muslim Female 04, age 22)

After examining "every single opinion" on the internet, she then had to examine what was appropriate in terms of covering oneself to maintain modesty. She studied the Qur'anic verses but found them vague, so once she decided to wear the hijab, the question of how to wear it appropriately became a question. Rather than turning to a member of her family, she again turned to the internet to determine how much to cover. She found, through her online searches of hadith, that the hijab and the jilbab (loose fitting coat) are mandatory but the niqab (face covering) is not mandatory and therefore should not be worn by Muslim women. She surmised this interpretation of covering from a hadith she found on the internet that claims that the Prophet said "nothing from a woman should be showing of her except her face and her hands" (Muslim Female 04, age 22).

A highly involved Shi'a Muslim female (Muslim Female 24, age 22) began searching for a deeper understanding of her faith through friends and then the internet, because her parents did not practise the faith. She turned to an Orthodox Christian friend to compare how Islam differed from the faith of her friend. She saw the internet as a wonderful tool to learn about Islam.

I was using the internet searching articles all the time. I was getting kind of obsessive at times. And then just reading a lot, and I think I was getting most of my information from books and the internet and then anything I would kind of like, any information I may have read off the internet, I would kind of maybe go to whether it was a Christian concept, I would maybe bring it up nonchalantly with someone at church and: "oh what do you think about – I read this … what do you think about it, and what're your views on that," and then that's kind of how it built and it went on for a bit. (Muslim Female 24, age 22)

She did not religiously discriminate with whom she discussed her faith. Through Yahoo she joined different religious chat rooms (such as the Jewish and Hindu chat rooms) because she enjoyed the perspectives of people from around the world: illustrating the general acceptance of the diversity of religious traditions in Canada. Canada's multiculturalism was held in high regard by the participants in this project. In terms of belonging to a public religious community, our interviewee (Muslim Female 24) said that she found a strong sense of it on the internet even though it was an anonymous way of communicating with others.

> Interviewer: Right, did you find a sense of community on the internet?
> Interviewee: Yeah, actually, because I dunno, I dunno if it's because it's so anonymous but yet so intimate at the same time that … yeah, I did, like it's weird because I mean these people, like there's some people like I knew everything about. (Muslim Female 24, age 22)

One highly involved Sunni female (Muslim Female 26, age 20) used the internet "all the time" to research areas that were pertinent to her life at the moment, in this instance marriage and children: she admitted that she was currently "shopping around" for a husband online. She also enjoyed the discussion forums as they offered her a variety of perspectives on various topics. She did not search for one authority, but conducted her own research on topics that were of interest to her.

A highly involved Shi'a Muslim female (Muslim Female 42, age 21) used the internet to send letters to the twelve imams on their birthdays. She thought it unfortunate that the main authorities of Islam, for her, were not educated in Western countries as Muslims living in Western countries could not access them and vice versa. But at the same time, she would not appreciate answers from authorities that did not make sense to those living in Western countries. When asked about her views on the imams in their local mosques as voices of authority in Islam, she stated:

> I wouldn't go to the imam in the mosque or anything in my mosque because I've heard him speak and I don't agree with the half the things he says. I suppose if I did have any questions, I love the internet, so I'd probably look it up or you can email a scholar like some scholar at a university or an academic. (Muslim Female 42, age 21)

Another highly involved female Sunni Muslim (Muslim Female 05, age 19) had a Somali Muslim friend who insisted that wearing the hijab was mandatory in Islam, and rather than taking her word on it as an authority, she turned to the internet as well as the imam of her mosque even though she was initially reluctant to ask the imam:

I've heard stories about where they're [imams] stern and everything, stern and restrictive. But he wasn't. He was really friendly. And he liked how I was curious, so he just talked to me more. And then he told me to do my own ... research ... So he was just like, "if you don't believe me, you should look it up yourself." (Muslim Female 05, age 19)

This sanctioned approval by Muslim figures of authority to access the internet as a way of seeking religious knowledge has been highlighted by various Islamic scholars (Bunt 2004, 125). Rather than being led to a particular discourse online, this participant was free to explore multiple discourses in order to form her own interpretation on Islamic regulations. "And then I looked it up on the internet cause I was interested to know what others had to say about it. So I looked up scholars ... I wanted to know what, why people thought so and how I could refute it [oppressive views of women in Islam]" (Muslim Female 05, age 19).

Although a previous participant found that wearing the hijab (head scarf) and jilbab (long, loose fitting coat which covers the entire body) were mandatory in Islam through her own research on the internet, this Muslim woman came to the conclusion that the concept of modesty in Islam did not mandate the wearing the hijab:

I think it's a really commendable thing to do because it shows that you have enough confidence in yourself to not have to rely on other characteristics, but your own personality. And the women I've met who wear hijab are really secure and healthy human beings as opposed to some more insecure women I've met who don't wear hijab.

I don't think it's imperative as in you, you're sinning if you don't wear hijab. I think it's the concept of hijab which is very encouraged. And it's not just the physical scarf that is hijab. It's more the concept as in, of modesty, as in you don't just go and flirt just for the sake of flirting. You have to like have a certain control over yourself which shows respect and dignity in yourself. (Muslim Female 05, age 19)

This project found that Muslim men were equally individualistic in their undertaking to better understand Islam. One highly involved male (Muslim Male 09, age 27), in trying to understand his faith, felt that what he saw of Islam was strange – at first he thought that the meaning of being religious meant:

Just staying in your room and praying and having a big beard and wearing a long dress. That's what, and I started thinking, gee, I really didn't want to … I don't want that, right? 'Cause that's the only thing I saw … the religious people were the ones that did that. That's something that didn't make sense. I stayed away from it. (Muslim Male 09, age 27)

He felt that many Islamic "scholars" were stuck in the past (for instance wearing robes and having long beards, while maintaining an archaic language – Arabic). For this particular young man, the goal of Islam was to make sure the world runs properly and to keep advancing: this included fashion. He believed the religion itself had changed: the main goal of Islam in its infancy was to spread the word of Islam. With the advent of the internet, he believed that this goal had been met. So he was in search of someone who was "current with the times." In fact, this participant considered the Arabic language impossible to truly comprehend because it was an old language and so his search was to find a scholar to whom he could relate. By conducting his own research online, he found a particular "scholar" online, one that reflected his own values, which gave him answers about his faith.

What I started to learn was … I ran into a guy on the internet who basically is very religious, but was in a suit. That intrigued me, as to, is he actually religious or is he a new breed? [chuckles] Like where is this coming from? Anyways, I started understanding from him basically a bit more about the religion, like he started explaining things that I had memorized, right? So he started explaining to me, like ok this … well, not to me, but I mean he's a fairly famous guy. His name is Amr Khaled. I think he's currently residing in Britain or Lebanon. He's an Egyptian fellow, he's not even a preacher – for us an imam – he's not an imam. But he's just … I think he's an accountant actually. But he just studies a lot, and he's very good with people. (Muslim Male 09, age 27)

This online scholar gave him the answers to the questions he couldn't find anywhere else; this made him a reliable source. His website offered both English and Arabic translations, making it easier to access. This participant found that what Amr Khaled was teaching online was consistent "with the truth as far as I've seen it. So I'll take that for granted" (Male Muslim 09, age 27). There were times when he didn't understand the explanations but was willing to accept them because this person was a "reliable source." He even went so far as to engage in online career counselling with this scholar so that he could do his best at what he was good at. Through the use of modern technology such as algorithms and psychological testing, Amr Khaled was helping young Muslim youth be the "best" they could be in this world: what Islam expects of Muslims. This participant found out that he was a "computer guy." For this participant, being religious meant regular prayers and following the mandated rituals of Islam. Yet, it also included a deeper understanding of how to run the world properly. It could not just be about prayer and spreading the word of Islam:

> But also there's the part of life that you have to ask "why are we here?" ... I mean, that's fairly well defined for us. We're here to just carry on and do ... advance in ourselves and make sure the world runs properly. We're not here just to pray, because, like, that's what angels are for [chuckles]. That's all they do, so ... We can do that, but we also take care of other things. We have rules that we have to put down on the earth and have people go by them. So that's what I believe. Um, your main thing in Islam back then was to spread the word. Right now there's internet – done! [chuckles] Alright, people already know about it. (Male Muslim 09, age 27)

In fact, it is important to note that Amr Khaled is an educated alim – a scholar who chose not to wear the clerical robe, donning a suit and sporting a trim moustache (no beard) to reach out to a global audience online as a secular preacher, while being financially sustained by religious groups (Roy 2004). It is difficult to know what political and financial support many of these Islamic internet sites receive, as they appear non-affiliated. Roy (2004) also observes that many Islamic movements utilize the internet in ways that are "perfectly adapted to a basic dimension of contemporary globalization: that of turning human behaviour into codes, and patterns of consumption and communication, delinked from any specific culture" (258). By trying to disassociate culture and politics from these sites, they align themselves well to the demographic we studied, who do not feel any specific attachment to the cultures of their parents. Of interest in our study was that both Sunni and Shi'a participants frequented IslamOnline.com as it offered a variety of services, from chat rooms to prayer times. Some participants joined the chat rooms with keen interest while others shied away from them, searching for their own answers on Islam. The major portals offered discussions and readings in English, which was of critical importance to the majority of our participants as English was the language of choice (very few could actually read Arabic even though they read the prayers of the Qur'an in Arabic).

The way that many of these online sites and portals have constructed themselves, by not being culturally associated, and by using English as the main language, allows them to attract Muslims living in the diaspora, thereby becoming transnational. These sites reach out globally to connect Muslims. The concept of the global "ummah" or Muslim community via the internet represents "the perfect place for individuals to express themselves while claiming to belong to a community to whose enactment they contribute to the enacting of, rather than being passive members of" (Roy 2004, 183). Even though a majority of male participants attended Friday jumah prayers at their mosque or on campus, they did not feel directly connected to the local Muslim community surrounding them. Many turned to the internet to find an online global Muslim community to which they could belong. One highly involved male (Muslim Male 28, age 22) had an Indian background and both the mosque and Muslim Student Association he was involved with in Ottawa were Arab-based. Although they gave him rides and invited him over for dinners, they didn't truly understand his Indian cultural background and therefore didn't "know" him. Whereas online, he was able to find a religious community:

> The community I feel, the Shi'a community is more of a broad thing, like world-wide, like on the internet right? I read these forums and stuff like that. On there, I feel that community, like there are people out there that agree with me and they're my type I guess. (Muslim Male 28, age 22)

Interestingly, the forum that he frequented was set up by a Pakistani person and Arab person and he noted that the two communities often clashed on the forum. He felt limited as to which Muslim forums he could participate in as he found that there was a lot of anti-Shi'a sentiment on the internet. He tends to only join sites that have points of view which he agrees with:

> Basically, a lot of sites out there that are really like ... they're very anti-Shi'a, like they're very ... they show a lot of hatred. Like, they'll say y'know, Shi'as are non-Muslims, they're this, they're that whatever right and there's this one site that goes to all of them and takes their articles and like kind of like analyses them and like makes rebuttals to them. So ... that site is really good. I really read it a lot because like ... anytime I have a doubt about my own thing, my own faith or whatever if I'm questioned by my friends or anything like that, I'll read into this site and I'll find, you know how I was talking a long time ago about the logic behind it and stuff like that? ... That's where I get a lot of that from, the proofs and stuff like that. I read it there and then it's really rewarding to me, you know. And

then other stuff, like various like information sites, if I want to know about
this or that or Muharram or this area of practice or like the madras and
what they say about different issues that I go back to, that's where I find a
lot of stuff. (Muslim Male 28, age 22)

In many cases within this study, the internet can be seen as an outlet
for finding diverse perspectives and authorities within Islam: the internet offers an authentic global community for the minority Shi'a followers, who often are not recognized by the "orthodox" schools of Islam
as well as for the Sunni who hold divergent views on what it means
to be a Muslim (Lawrence 2002, 245). There are many dedicated sites
just for the Sunni majority that were regularly accessed by participants
who were moderately to highly involved in the practice of their faith.
Both Sunnipath.com and Islamicity.com were accessed by Sunni Muslims, to watch religious programs or to just listen to the recitation of the
Qur'an. Yet our participants showed a willingness to research as many
opinions as possible, not relying on one particular authority or scholar
on the internet. This diversity lends itself well to the way in which they
are constructing their various Muslim identities – individualistic and
without pressure from family or friends.

Many Muslims felt challenged to justify their faith after the events
of 9/11. Many of our participants also felt a need to better understand
their faith in order to explain why they continued to follow Islam; a
few who were non-believers also studied Islam to better understand
the problems they felt lay within the faith. A majority of the moderately to highly involved participants, who were just entering their teens
in 2001, went online to comprehend the truths and falsehoods being
spread through the media about Islam. A moderately involved Muslim
male (Muslim Male 29, age 19) was in grade 9 when the events of 9/11
occurred, and he stated that it was a wake-up call for him to truly comprehend the faith he had been following since childhood. He claimed
that searching Islam on the internet actually made him more religious
because he was now thinking about religion on his own, rather than following what he had learned:

   … then it was sort of like a wakeup call, then I started realizing that, I have
   to start reading, and I have … sort of … I have to grow on my own, I have
   to mature and I have to become independent and realize why I do things,
   and not just do them because someone else is telling me to. (Muslim Male
   29, age 19)

He did not turn to his father because he acknowledged that there was both a generation gap and a cultural difference between them: he felt his father didn't see religion in the same way as the participant. Although his older brother was a source of inspiration when he was younger (and they could relate to each other), he would generally go online to comprehend why he did what he did as a Muslim. This, in turn, made him a stronger follower and practitioner of the faith. He would never turn to an imam "for any questions or anything" (Muslim Male 29, age 19).

Although a few of the highly involved Muslim participants were critical of various aspects of Canadian society, they also showed a greater tendency to mesh their Islam with dominant Canadian values and orientations. For them, to be Muslim was to be modern, kind and peaceful: it was their role to make the world a better place. The vast majority of our participants are very comfortable as Muslims and as Canadians. Accessing Islam online added to their sense of identity but did not affect their sense of "citizenship." While they are engaging in unique constructions of their faith, they do not distinguish between being Muslim and being Canadian, between Islam and the West, or between homeland and diaspora (Beyer 2007, 58–61).

The participants who fell into the moderately involved categories also turned to the internet as a way to search for answers about their faith. They also did not feel the need to turn to the imams of their mosques, but for different reasons. Many shied away from organized associations and scholars because they perceived themselves to be different in their practice of Islam: for instance they didn't dress modestly enough (they didn't wear a hijab or concealing clothing) or considered themselves to be too culturally oriented. They dated, drank alcohol, or smoked: all the things that better Muslims would not do.

One moderately involved female stated that, in terms of meeting the needs of youth, the mosque and the imam were only for the very, very religious youth, not like herself. She felt that the imam would give her a hard time for not wearing a headscarf, and therefore turned to the internet to better understand the rituals and practices of Islam (usually when someone else would ask her about it – for instance what is Eid and how many Eid festivals are there every year?). Another moderate female said that, because of her unfamiliarity with the faith, she would not approach the imam but rather look up her faith on the internet. In fact, she was currently reading an English translation of the Qur'an online.

As for the category of non-believers, they did not find religion to be of significance in their lives, while a few felt estranged by their religious heritage. For the non-believers, religion of any kind was simply not very important. They were raised in homes where religion was not stressed or they had gradually left the religion over time and without any backlash. The one non-believer who did research religion online actually created his own blog to challenge religious beliefs.

Conclusion

Our study has found that the majority of second-generation Muslims in the sample are clearly highly involved in their faith: very few seem to be drifting away from their faith, especially if they began their involvement as children. Their Islam is for the most part individualistic rather than community-oriented, although many feel that they are part of a non-descript global community of Muslims, a public space found in cyberspace. Only a small minority relies on a particular authority, and never the same one. Their Islam is also highly varied in its details: with the exception of the two participants in category 10, the rest could not really be classified neatly along "liberal/conservative" lines, although on personal moral issues, the general trend was definitely in a conservative direction.

The vast majority, including especially the highly devout, feel comfortable in Canada. They see themselves as part of the public religious landscape of Canada. There is a strong emphasis on humility, kindness, compassion, and peace as central concepts to their Islam – a unique understanding of their faith, which in many instances was far more important than the five pillars of Islam: in this way, quite distinctive to these Canadian Muslims, and for them, truly genuine to their understanding of the faith. They are utilizing a logical approach to create a judicious understanding of their religion, rather than just carrying on parental influences and understandings of their faith. Their approach utilizes the internet for their knowledge about being Muslim, which is, in turn, leading them to a distinctive (re)construction of Islam. What is considered "authentic" Islam is not being discussed here as it does not "reflect the reality" of what these youth are doing both on and offline: all definitions are legitimate.

Canadian Muslims seem to be displaying certain similarities to second-generation European Muslims (primarily in Great Britain, Germany, France, Denmark, and the Netherlands). They draw the same religious and cultural distinctions, display a desire to create their own religious self-consciousness through personal analyses of scripture and sources of knowledge rather than relying on parents, elders, or the local mosque, and many use internet experts and online chat groups to "push the frontiers" of their Muslim values and practices (Vertovec and Rogers 1998, 10–14). In comparison to their European counterparts, the majority of the Canadian Muslim youth in this project tend to live their religious lives privately and do not focus on religious mobilization in the Canadian cities in which they live. They do not seem to have a fear of marginalization as many European Muslim youth feel. Also, there is no sign of a strong "civil religious" national ideology "if it is not multiculturalism itself, even in Québec with its strong nationalist traditions" (Beyer, Ramji, and Saha 2005, 23). One major element that separates them from American and European Muslims is their lack of immersion in popular youth culture. Consumerism and fashion, modes of local language expression and music were found to be a large part of American and European Muslim youth life (Vertovec and Rogers 1998, 10–14). In comparison, the Canadian youth did not show a strong inclination towards this immersion. Many claim to have successfully avoided such pressures and maintain a critical attitude towards youth culture in Canada. They strongly believe that they can be Muslim and Canadian, but do not have to give in to the temptations of secular youth culture.

It is impossible to measure how much the internet has nurtured their Canadian Muslim identities, but it is clear that they avail themselves of the transnational resources available to them online and that their religiosity is being constructed, and even enhanced, online, in the public sphere. They do not search out support from their local Muslim communities, associations, or mosques as sources of knowledge. Their understanding of Islam is uniquely modeled on the "five pillars" (shahadah, salat, sawm, zakat, and hajj), a strong moral compass, and a desire to make the world a better place. Although they are individually searching for their own ways of being a good/"real" Muslim, they also embody the ideal image of a member of a global ummah, connected to other Muslims throughout the world. They espouse an "authentic" or "real" Islam by venturing away from familial and cultural interpretations of the faith, while at the same time displaying their diversity in the way they choose authoritative voices in Islam. They define "Islam" independently and follow it devoutly, globally, online.

NOTES

1 The research in this chapter is part of a larger investigation about second-generation Muslims. Information on all three immigrant groups studied, Muslims, Hindus, and Buddhists, can be found in Beyer (2007, 2008) and Beyer and Ramji (2013).
2 "Religion among Immigrant Youth in Canada" is a research project funded by the Social Sciences and Humanities Research Council of Canada. The author collaborated with Peter Beyer (principal investigator), Shandip Saha, and Leslie Laczko at the University of Ottawa; Nancy Nason-Clark at the University of New Brunswick; Lori G. Beaman and Marie-Paule Martel Reny at Concordia University in Montréal; and John H. Simpson, Arlene Macdonald, and Carolyn Reimer at the University of Toronto. This research study on Muslims is part of a larger study that focuses on second-generation immigrants from Buddhist, Hindu, and Muslim backgrounds who were residing or studying in the urban regions of Toronto, ON, Montréal, QC, and Ottawa-Gatineau.
3 By definition, the phrase "second-generation immigrant" implies that that an individual is not a "Canadian." As a second-generation Canadian myself, I am a Canadian citizen and do not consider myself an immigrant. The phrase is used in the context of the larger research project, and therefore will be used in this chapter (with restraint).
4 Muslims who see themselves as Salafists tend to look at the level of one's Muslimness (see Roald 2001).
5 No significant variation was found in the three different cities in which the research was undertaken.

REFERENCES

Beyer, Peter. 2007. "Can the Tail Wag the Dog? Diaspora Reconstructions of Religion in a Globalized Society." *Nordic Journal of Religion and Society* 20(1): 41–63.
Beyer, Peter. 2008. "From Far and Wide: Canadian Religious and Cultural Diversity in Global/Local Context." In *Religious Diversity in Canada*, edited by Lori G. Beaman and Peter Beyer, 9–40. Leiden: Brill.
Beyer, Peter, and Rubina Ramji, eds. 2013. *Growing Up Canadian: Muslims, Hindus, Buddhists*. Kingston and Montreal: McGill-Queen's University Press.

Beyer, Peter, Rubina Ramji, and Shandip Saha. 2005. "Religion Among Immigrant Youth of the Second Generations in Canada and Europe: Muslims & Buddhists." Paper presented at the Society for the Scientific Study of Religion, Rochester, New York, November.

Biles, John, and Humera Ibrahim. 2005. "Religion and Public Policy: Immigration, Citizenship, and Multiculturalism – Guess Who's Coming to Dinner?" In *Religion and Ethnicity in Canada*, edited by Paul Bramadat and David Seljak, 154–77. Toronto: Pearson Longman.

Bramadat, Paul. 2005. "Beyond Christian Canada: Religion and Ethnicity in Multicultural Canada." In *Religion and Ethnicity in Canada*, edited by Paul Bramadat and David Seljak, 1–29. Toronto: Pearson Longman.

Bunt, Gary R. 2004. "Rip. Burn. Pray.: Islamic Expression Online." In *Religion Online: Finding Faith on the Internet*, edited by Lorne L. Dawson and Douglas E. Cowan, 123–34. New York: Routledge.

Bunt, Gary R. 2009. *iMuslims: Rewiring the House of Islam*. Chapel Hill: University of North Carolina Press.

Dawson Lorne L., and Douglas E. Cowan. 2004. "Introduction." In *Religion Online: Finding Faith on the Internet*, edited by Lorne L. Dawson and Douglas E. Cowan, 1–15. New York: Routledge.

Eickelman, Dale F., and Jon W. Anderson. 2003. "Redefining Muslim Publics." In *New Media in the Muslim World: The Emerging Public Sphere* (2nd ed.), edited by Dale Eickelman and Jon W. Anderson, 1–18. Bloomington: Indiana University Press.

Helland, Christopher. 2004. "Popular Religions and the World Wide Web: A Match Made in (Cyber) Heaven." In *Religion Online: Finding Faith on the Internet*, edited by Lorne L. Dawson and Douglas E. Cowan, 21–33. New York: Routledge.

Larsen, Elena. 2004. "Cyberfaith: How Americans Pursue Religion Online." In *Religion Online: Finding Faith on the Internet*, edited by Lorne L. Dawson and Douglas E. Cowan, 16–19. New York: Routledge.

Lawrence, B. B. (2002). "Allah On-Line: The Practice of Global Islam in the Information Age." In *Practicing Religion in the Age of the Media: Explorations in Media, Religion and Culture*, edited by Stewart M. Hoover and Lynn Schofield Clark, 237–53. New York: Columbia University Press.

NPR.org. 2012. "Islam on the Internet: A Special Report." *National Public Radio Website*. Available at http://www.npr.org/programs/watc/cyberislam/

Ramji, Rubina. 2008. "Being Muslim and Being Canadian: How Second Generation Muslim Women Create Religious Identities in Two Worlds." In *Women and Religion in the West: Challenging Secularization*, edited by Kristin Aune, Sonya Sharma, and Giselle Vincett, 195–206. Aldershot: Ashgate Publishing.

Roald, Anne-Sofie. 2001. *Women in Islam: The Western Experience*. London: Routledge.

Roy, Olivier. 2004. *Globalised Islam: The Search for a New Ummah*. London: Hurst and Company.

Vertovec, Steven, and Alisdair Rogers, eds. 1998. *Muslim European Youth: Reproducing Religion, Ethnicity and Culture*. Aldershot: Avebury.

5 Maghrebi Jewish Migrations and Religious Marriage in Paris and Montréal, 1954–1980

YOLANDE COHEN AND YANN SCIOLDO-ZÜRCHER

Responding to Nancy Green's invitation that migratory trajectories should be examined from a comparative perspective, this study examines, in both space and time, the religious marital practices among Sephardic Jews settled in Paris and Montréal who, in the post-colonial context, had been leaving their countries of birth (Green 2002, 23).[1] The statistical study of these religious marriages not only analyses relocation patterns, but also more broadly, reveals the repercussions of these migrations among host communities.[2] It demonstrates that both migrants and members of host social structures underwent wide-reaching cultural reconfiguration.

The early post-colonial period saw the almost complete disappearance of North African Jewish communities, be it in a brutal fashion as in Algeria, or in a more diffuse, yet just as an irreversible manner, as in the cases of Tunisia and Morocco. In 1954, about 500,000 Jews lived in North African French possessions; that number had shrunk to about 62,000 by the end of 1967 (Bensimon 1971, 1).[3] Only a few thousand currently reside in North Africa. Because in Algeria these communities maintained a long-standing French citizenship, and had acquired the national "habitus," the vast majority of Algerian Jews relocated in France, where they benefitted from legislation designed to facilitate the economic and social reintegration of repatriated colonials (Scioldo-Zürcher 2010). Tunisian and Moroccan Jews who had French citizenship were entitled to the same rights as the French. For their part, non-French citizens were considered by the national administration as regular migrants, as were "Muslims" who came to France in search of job opportunities during that era. A policy entailing quicker naturalization procedures for some Jews was established with the support of the local French Jewry.

Nonetheless, the paths to France and the permanent resettling of these migrants were neither automatic nor even obvious. Significant numbers relocated to Israel and Canada. More than 80 per cent of Moroccan Jews immigrated to Israel; 8,000 crossed the Atlantic to North America, where conditions of reception and citizenship were facilitated by the local Jewish communities.

This study relies on a cross-data comparison between, on the one hand, data taken from a quantitative study of *kétoubot* (religious marriage contracts), and on the other hand, marriage preparation records from synagogues in France and in Québec (in the latter case, including the publication of banns). This data provides a snapshot of a section of the North African Jewish community, which consisted largely of young adults, as it underwent its migrating process.[4] Similarly, the comparison between the French and the Canadian contexts illuminates the diverse perspectives of these new communities with which the host countries had to deal. Even though the "Jewish marriage" has been a favoured topic in Jewish studies, comparing these marriages in migration remains a marginal subject of research and one that this chapter attempts to address. In the following pages, we will show the importance of those migration movements for the redefinition of the Jewish communities in diaspora. We will also explore how the migrants' relations to public and private spaces have been modified by their rooting in a new environment. We want to show the importance of those migrants' contribution to the renewal and even to the survival of the Jewish communities in both Paris and Montréal.

Comparing Community Organizations: Toward a Comparative Analysis of Jewish Practices

The proposed comparison is timeline-based. Both periods we chose to study correspond to the strong influx of North African Jewish populations. The scrutiny of French marriage records focuses on the 1954–1970 period.[5] This period covers the era that saw the independence of both North Africa French protectorates (Tunisia and Morocco) and Algeria, as well as the anti-Jewish backlash in the same countries resulting from the 1967 Israel-Palestine conflict. In the case of Québec, the data covers the 1970s, a pivotal period in Canadian Jewish immigration. With 7,995 Moroccan Jews arriving between 1960 and 1991 (according to the 1991 Census), they rapidly constituted the most compact subgroup of the

Montréal Jewish community. The synagogues included in this study were selected to demonstrate, as widely as possible, the multifarious character of Judaism. Since 1808, mainstream Judaism in France – often qualified as "consistorial" Judaism (*judaisme consistorial*) due to its administrative structure which contoured the institution of the consistory – had acted as the Jewish community's traditional representative before the French state, though it coexisted with a minority liberal Judaism well-ensconced in the French capital. Both traditions have their own institutions.

Inaugurated in 1876, the monumental and prestigious *Synagogue des Tournelles* is located in Paris' fourth *arrondissement*, within the *Pletzl*, the city's historic Jewish neighbourhood and traditional destination for the Ashkenazi immigration (Jarassé 2003, 77–81). In 1958, consistorial authorities proposed, not without controversy, to make this temple available to all Jewish migrants from North Africa. This took place in the aftermath of the Second World War, when the reconstruction of the French Jewish community made it essential to integrate North African Judaism by granting it a symbolic place in one of Paris Judaism's most elevated grounds. The temple became not only the focal point for Jews of Constantine (Algeria), Rabbi Feuerwerker having been replaced by Rabbi Chekroun, but also the focal point for all North African Jews, regardless of the cultural traditions they had left behind – at least until the building of synagogues specifically designed for their former regional rites, from the mid-1960s on (Scioldo-Zürcher and Bahoken 2009).

The ULIF Copernic, *Union Libérale Israélite* de France (hereinafter *Synagogue de l'Union libérale israélite*) had a different kind of background. Created in 1907, this hub of liberal Judaism never had a rabbi under consistorial authority. A world unto itself within French Judaism, this institution was, from the outset, accused of permissiveness by its detractors. However, this synagogue succeeded in imposing a modernized Jewish practice on the Parisian landscape, thus fulfilling the wishes of its founders to fashion a Judaism "adapted to the needs of the times" (Poujol 2007). The "liberal adventure" continued in the post-Second World War period, and the synagogue rapidly gathered an important number of adherents. They went from 125 in 1945 to more than 600 as the 1960s began (Meyer 1988, 347). Nonetheless, Rabbi Zaoui, a native of Oran and present at the *téba* (chair) since 1946, imposed a return to the Hebraic language and, for the religious celebration of marriages, requested the conversion of non-Jewish spouses.

Finally, the *Spanish and Portuguese synagogue (SPS)* was founded in Montréal in 1777 by British descendants of Spanish and Portuguese Jews. Canada's oldest synagogue, this Sephardic institution today practises modern Sephardic orthodox rituals.[6] Its building moved on several instances before settling in the Snowdon-Côte-des-Neiges neighbourhood in 1947. This area, where most new migrants settled, rapidly became a "Jewish neighbourhood." Since the 1990s, it has housed the new "Jewish campus," where all of Montréal's major Jewish institutions are located (the YM-YWHA Jewish community centre, the Gelber Conference Centre, the Segal Theatre, etc.). During the 1960s, this synagogue, of which 80 per cent of members were English-speaking Ashkenazi, also became a centre for numerous Moroccan Jews attracted by its Sephardic name.[7]

A Significant Community Renewal

From 1955 to 1970, a total of 8,910 weddings were registered in Paris's consistorial synagogues, of which 2,151 took place at the *Synagogue des Tournelles*.[8] Between 1963 and 1970, 706 weddings were celebrated at

Figure 5.1. Number of annual weddings held in the *Synagogue des Tournelles*, the *Synagogue de l'Union libérale israélite*, and the *Spanish and Portuguese Synagogue* in Montréal, 1954–1980

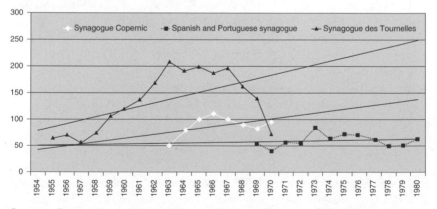

Sources: *Consistoire central* (central consistory), marriage preparation records of Paris synagogues; Archives de l'*Union libérale de France*, *Synagogue de l'Union libérale israélite;* publication of banns, *Spanish and Portuguese Synagogue*, Montréal

the liberal *Synagogue de l'Union libérale israélite*. For its part, Montréal's *Spanish and Portuguese Synagogue* saw 725 couples marrying between 1970 and 1981. From 1955 to 1969, the number of consistorial marriages in Paris increased annually by 6.14 per cent, while the *Synagogue des Tournelles* saw an annual increase of 5.31 per cent for the same period of time.[9] Between 1963 and 1970, the number of weddings celebrated at the *Synagogue de l'Union libérale israélite* grew at the even faster pace of 8.23 per cent annually. For its part, with an average rate of only 1.14 per cent, Montréal's *Spanish and Portuguese Synagogue* had a weaker annual growth, though this temple remained significant to the renewal of Québec Judaism.

As seen here, weddings increased substantially in all three synagogues with the arrival of new migrants from North Africa. The 1965–1966 crest in the number of weddings held in both Paris synagogues, respectively

Table 5.1: Number of total consistorial weddings in Paris and number of weddings held at the *Synagogue des Tournelles* in Paris, 1954–1970

Year	Total number of consistorial weddings	Total number of weddings held at the *Synagogue des Tournelles*	Percentage of weddings held at the *Synagogue des Tournelles*	Indexed fluctuation of consistorial weddings	Indexed fluctuation of weddings held at the *Synagogue des Tournelles*
1955	332	64	19%	100	100
1956	317	70	22%	95	109
1957	387	55	14%	117	86
1958	405	74	18%	122	116
1959	411	106	26%	124	166
1960	443	121	27%	133	189
1961	508	137	27%	153	214
1962	556	169	30%	167	264
1963	710	208	29%	214	325
1964	675	191	28%	203	298
1965	669	199	30%	202	311
1966	Missing data	187	Missing data	Missing data	292
1967	Missing data	197	Missing data	Missing data	308
1968	824	162	20%	248	253
1969	849	139	16%	256	217
1970	812	72	9%	245	113
Total	8910	2151	24%		

Source: *Kétoubot* and marriage preparation records, Paris Consistory Archives, 1954–1970

Table 5.2. Number of weddings held at the *Synagogue de l'Union libérale israélite*, Copernic Street, Paris, 1963–1970

Year	Number of weddings	Annual percentage of weddings held	Annual growth rate	Indexed fluctuation
1963	51	7%		100
1964	76	11%	49%	149
1965	100	14%	32%	196
1966	111	16%	11%	218
1967	99	14%	−11%	194
1968	90	13%	−9%	176
1969	83	12%	−8%	163
1970	96	14%	16%	188
Total	706	100%		

Source: Marriage preparation records, *Synagogue de l'Union libérale israélite*

Table 5.3. Number of weddings held at the *Spanish and Portuguese Synagogue*, Montréal, 1970–1981

Year	Number of weddings	Annual percentage of weddings held	Annual growth rate	Indexed related fluctuation
1969	55	8%		100
1970	40	6%	−27%	73
1971	57	8%	43%	104
1972	55	8%	−4%	100
1973	85	12%	55%	155
1974	63	9%	−26%	115
1975	72	10%	14%	131
1976	70	10%	−3%	127
1977	63	9%	−10%	115
1978	49	7%	−22%	89
1979	51	7%	4%	93
1980	63	9%	24%	115
1981	2	0.3%		
Total	725	100%		

Source: Publications of banns, *Spanish and Portuguese Synagogue*, 1970–1980

311 for the *Synagogue des Tournelles* and 111 for the *Synagogue de l'Union libérale israélite*, shows the impact of a demographic reality, that is, that of baby-boom children coming to the age of marriage. Considering the impact of the Second World War genocide on the Ashkenazi population, the number of weddings was considerably cut back

by the demographic slump it caused.[10] Thus, the increase was due to Jewish immigration and, in the specific case of the *Synagogue des Tournelles*, the arrival of North African Jews. Finally, in the case of the Montréal synagogue, the peak was reached in 1973, when 155 weddings were held. Still, the average age for marriage did not change. It was 27 years in 1955 and oscillated between 25 and 26 years in the following years.

In other words, all three synagogues underwent a major replenishment of their members, be they due-paying or not. Regardless of specific ritual practices and religious traditions, immigration accounted for the increase of their congregants and, indirectly, for the perpetuation of Judaism. This was the primary impact of post-colonial Jewish immigration; it repopulated French synagogues and prevented those of Montréal from emptying. It put together a new Judaism, blurring the ritual and ethnic frontiers which, until this time, were divisive, at least within the territorialized *imaginaires* of the colonial spaces and of the Jewish diaspora. The Sephardi and Ashkenazi spaces became similar. With this development, Jewish identity was led to redefine itself within the matrimonial context.

The Space and Time of Religious Marriages: A Considerable Jewish Maghrebi Migration

The figures below tabulate the birthplaces of spouses. They show the wide variability in the points of convergence among spouses-to-be in these three synagogues. The *Synagogue des Tournelles* quickly became a reference point for Paris' Maghrebi identity, which consisted of 17 per cent non-colonial French adherents. The *Synagogue de l'Union libérale israélite* and the *Spanish and Portuguese Synagogue* in Montréal did not experience any change in ritual practices, and thus identity references, and drew more than two-fifths of Jews born respectively in France, Québec, or elsewhere in Canada. However, both institutions faced the task of integrating a large foreign-born population, the majority of which consisted of North African Jews. The countries of *Machrek*, which includes Israel and Egypt, are unrepresented, or, in the Canadian case, sparsely represented. Algeria, Tunisia, and Morocco account for more than 78 per cent of the spouses brought together in matrimony at the *Synagogue des Tournelles* and 30 per cent of those who married at the two other synagogues. Moreover, all three synagogues were compelled not only to welcome the newcomers, but also to "open" their structures to them, a process which was made official by consistorial authorities themselves in the case of the *Synagogue des Tournelles*.

Beyond the issue of ritual practices, this process involved granting "political" responsibilities to new migrants who welcomed the opportunity to exercise them. For instance, the *Spanish and Portuguese Synagogue* saw both a renewal of its Administrative Council – several key positions were quickly filled by Iraqi Jews, who were among the first to arrive and settle – and the infusion in the rituals of Judeo-Moroccan cantillations. These changes are well-illustrated by the appointment, at the *Spanish and Portuguese Synagogue*, of the *hazzan* (cantor) Samy El Maghribi, a popular Moroccan singer also known as Salomon Amzallag,[11] and by the Ashkenazi Rabbi Howard Joseph in 1968.

It is noteworthy that these three synagogues welcomed people from a culturally varied Judaism that is as European and North American as North African, and mostly urban. However, the "Maghrebization" of all three synagogues took different forms: while both French synagogues regrouped people from various North African backgrounds, the *Spanish and Portuguese Synagogue* became mostly a gathering point for Moroccan Jews.

Marriage Types

While the evidence indicates that all three synagogues established themselves as hubs for a vast Sephardic Judaism, the dynamics whereby various Jewish subcultures, local and Maghrebi, mixed with each other remained to be examined. To achieve this, several different "types" of marriages were identified according to the birthplaces of spouses. The marriage hereby categorized as "Maghrebi" involves the union of two persons born in North Africa. A Metropolitan marriage involves two people originating from mainland, non-colonial France. In this context, a "European" marriage denotes two fiancés from other countries of continental Europe, Russia included. These categories can be overlapped in order to reflect marriages between people of different origins. For instance, a "Metropolitan/European" marriage means the union of a person from France and a person from another continental European country. Furthermore, the intent is not to invest individuals with a static cultural essence, nor to claim that being born in Algeria or Tunisia turns a person into a representative of an entire Sephardic culture. On the contrary, the intent is simply to outline the geohistoric characteristics of unions.

Table 5.4. Main birthplaces of spouses marrying at the *Synagogue des Tournelles*, the *Synagogue de l'Union libérale israélite*, Copernic Street, Paris, and the *Spanish and Portuguese Synagogue*, Montréal, 1954–1980

Country of birth	Spouses married at the *Synagogue des Tournelles*	Share of country of birth (percentage)	Spouses married at the *Synagogue de l'Union libérale israélite*	Share of country of birth (percentage)	Spouses married at the *Spanish and Portuguese Synagogue*	Share of country of birth (percentage)
Algeria	1712	41.4%	194	13.8%	8	0.5%
Belgium	17	0.41%	18	1.3%	6	0.4%
Canada	0	/	0	/	568	39%
Egypt	36	0.9%	51	3.6%	39	2.7%
United States	4	0.1%	16	1.1%	57	3.9%
France	722	17.4%	669	47.4%	35	2.4%
Iraq	1	0.02%	0	0%	32	2.2%
Israel	11	0.3%	6	0.4%	55	3.8%
Lebanon	0	0	1	0.07%	26	2.8%
Morocco	337	8.1%	87	6.2%	413	28.4%
Poland	45	1.1%	9	0.6%	30	2.1%
Rumania	15	0.4%	11	0.8%	22	1.5%
Tunisia	1185	28.6%	143	10.1%	5	0.3%
USSR	5	0.1	7	0.5%	24	2.8%
Other	49	1.2%	197	14.1%	135	9.3%
Total	4139	100%	1410	100%	1455	100%

Sources: *Consistoire central* (central consistory), marriage preparation records of Paris synagogues; Archives de l'*Union libérale de France*, *Synagogue de l'Union libérale israélite*; publication of banns, *Spanish and Portuguese Synagogue*, Montréal

Table 5.5. Main types of marriages, *Synagogue des Tournelles*, 1954–1970

Type of marriage	Number	Percentage
Maghrebi	1447	67%
Mainlander/Maghrebi	237	11%
Mainlander	204	9%
Maghrebi / European	48	2%
Maghrebi / Israeli	11	1%
European	11	1%
Other	5	0.2%
No indication	151	7%
Total	2151	100%

Table 5.6. Main types of marriages, *Synagogue de l'Union libérale israélite*, Copernic Street, Paris, 1963–1970

Type of marriages	Number	Percentage
Maghrebi / Mainlander	259	37%
Mainlander	174	25%
Maghrebi	75	11%
Mainlander / European	71	10%

Source: dossiers de préparation au mariage, *Synagogue de l'Union libérale israélite*, 1963–1970

Table 5.7. Main types of marriage, *Spanish and Portuguese Synagogue*, 1970–1980

Type of marriages	Number	Percentage
Maghrebi	134	18%
Canadian / Canadian	156	15%
Maghrebi / Canadian	113	15%
Canadian / European	51	7%
Maghrebi / Europeans	51	7%

Source: Publication of banns, *Spanish and Portuguese Synagogue*, Montréal

It can be clearly seen here that the transmission of the Sephardic identity passes through various geographic and cultural spheres. While the "Maghrebi" marriage accounts for 67 per cent of all unions at the *Synagogue des Tournelles*, it respectively represents only 11 and 18 per cent of those in the two other synagogues. Eleven per cent of marriages celebrated at the *Synagogue des Tournelles*, 15 per cent of those held at the *Spanish and Portuguese Synagogue*, and 37 per cent of those at the *Synagogue de l'Union libérale israélite*, involved a North African native and one from the host country. Also noticeable, at least in France, is the importance of "inter-Maghrebi" marriages, that is, involving spouses from two different North African countries. The specific case of Moroccan natives illustrates this phenomenon quite well.

The Case of Moroccan Natives

If one studies marriages between Moroccan natives and natives from another North African country, it clearly appears that the "Moroccan community" did not turn in on itself in terms of its national identity.

Table 5.8. Marriages involving Moroccan natives and other Maghrebi natives at the *Synagogue des Tournelles* (1954–1970), the *Synagogue de l'Union libérale israélite* (1963–1970), Copernic Street, Paris, and the *Spanish and Portuguese Synagogue*, Montréal (1970–1980)

Country of birth	*Synagogue des Tournelles*	*Synagogue de l'Union libérale israélite* (1963–1970), Copernic Street	*Spanish and Portuguese Synagogue*
Morocco / Morocco	25%	63%	91%
Morocco / Algeria	57%	31%	3%
Morocco / Tunisia	16%	6%	3%
Morocco / Egypt	2%	/	3%
Total	100%	100%	100%

Of all the "Maghrebi weddings" held at the *Synagogue des Tournelles*, more than 75 per cent involved Moroccan natives marrying a person from Algeria or Tunisia, with, however, a very strong predominance from Algeria. At the *Union Libérale* on Copernic Street, which is not a synagogue following Algerian rituals, one notes an openness to weddings involving Jewish Moroccan natives with Jewish natives of Algeria and Tunisia in almost the two-fifths of the cases. In Montréal, in the absence of Tunisian and Algerian Jews, marriages between two Maghrebi natives involved only Moroccans, apart from a few rare cases.

Intermarriages and Conversions to Judaism

In all three synagogues, marriage preparation records also contain information pertaining to the spouses' religion and include, when necessary, the request for the conversion of one spouse. The *Spanish and Portuguese Synagogue* and the *Union libérale* on Copernic Street offered accelerated conversions. Candidates needed to acquire elementary knowledge of Judaism, which came down to the basic rules of *Cacherout* (ritual alimentary rules) and some knowledge of Jewish religious history. The *Synagogue de l'Union libérale israélite* sometimes accepted a mere promise of conversion.[12] Conversely, consistorial Judaism was far stricter on this issue. Conversions necessitated many years of preparation and were considerably more demanding in terms of knowledge requirements.[13] We can find in these administrative and religious procedures the central role of women in Judaism. All transmission of Judaism passes through women, and must be in conformity with religious rules: in the case of conversion or remarriage, the rabbi notes precisely the occasion at the *Mikvé*. When all this has been done, he grants the religious union. In addition, in order to tabulate all of the mixed marriages celebrated by the consistory, it was necessary to study the marriages in all the synagogues in order to extract cases in which one of the spouses, man or woman, was not of Jewish faith. Left aside were marriages in which the spouses, even if Jewish, were either divorced or widowed.

The data gathered on the three synagogues highlights an important religious divergence: the tendency to religious endogamy can be seen within consistorial Judaism, the proportion of mixed marriages not increasing with the arrival of North African Jews. However, the two other synagogues display a very marked tendency toward religious exogamy (that is a liaison with a non-Jewish person, even if she or he intends to convert to Judaism to get married). Intermarriages involving conversion to the Jewish religion of the non-Jewish spouse reveal that exogamy was practised by a third of those who married at the *Spanish and Portuguese Synagogue*, and half at the *Synagogue de l'Union libérale israélite* (respectively 30 per cent and 50 per cent of unions). Knowing that the conversion of the spouse was voluntary and that it marks his or her more-or-less exclusive commitment to the new religion, the authors wished to know more about what we perceived to be a genuine phenomenon.

Table 5.9. Number of marriages involving at least one converted spouse, Jewish central consistory, *Synagogue de l'Union libérale israélite* (1963–1970), Copernic Street, Paris, and the *Spanish and Portuguese Synagogue*, Montréal, 1954–1980

	Number of converted women	Number of converted men	Total number of conversions
Paris Consistory 1954–1970	345 (4%)	41 (0.5%)	386 (4%)
Union libérale israélite, Synagogue de l'Union libérale israélite, 1963–1970	317 (45%)	47 (6.7%)	364 (51%)
Spanish and Portuguese Synagogue, 1969–1980	182 (25%)	37 (5%)	219 (30%)

Sources: *Consistoire central* (central consistory), marriage preparation records of Paris synagogues; Archives de l'*Union libérale de France*, *Synagogue de l'Union libérale israélite*; publication of banns, *Spanish and Portuguese Synagogue*, Montréal

A Religious Exogamy "Compensated" by Conversion to Judaism, Mainly by Women

In this context, we hypothesized that the initial stages of immigration were perhaps experienced as a unique moment of freedom leading some migrants to transgress the family and religious taboos to permit romantic love (*l'amour romantique*) (Berdugo-Cohen, Cohen, and Lévy 1987, 40). Or perhaps, more prosaically, exogamy simply accompanied migration. Life stories show that religious exogamy is tempered by conversion to Judaism, when permitted and authorized by rabbis. The gender of the individuals continues to be of fundamental importance in reference to the practice of conversion to the Jewish religion. As already noted by Sébastien Tank-Storper (2007, 31), the converted population was largely female, in a proportion oscillating between 70 per cent and 85 per cent.[14] We found this female predominance in the data from both the *Spanish and Portuguese Synagogue* and the *Synagogue de l'Union libérale israélite*. In the former case, among 740 marriages, 219 involved a conversion to the Jewish religion, thus 30 per cent of couples, with women being the ones mostly undergoing conversion: we counted 182 instances (84 per cent of couples involving a conversion) of which 50 per cent were born in Canada (the remainder being divided among 13 countries). Among these women, four converted with one or more children. Among 37 men (5 per cent) who converted to Judaism for their marriage, 25 (66 per cent) were born in Canada, the remainder coming from France, Great Britain, or the United States.

At the *Synagogue de l'Union libérale israélite*, 317 (45 per cent) women converted to Judaism upon their marriage with a Jewish man. Among these, 71 per cent were born in mainland France, the others coming from thirty different countries. As to the men, 7 per cent converted (47 persons out of 705) to Judaism and 77 per cent among them were born in mainland France (from a total of five countries represented). Proportions of women born in the host country who had converted to Judaism upon marrying were thus very important in both synagogues. Through migration we note a marked change in the marriage market: almost half of the men married spouses born in the host country. This went beyond the traditional explanation which attempts to link female conversion to the important traditional role women held in the transmission of Judaism.

The most common case involved a man born in Morocco who married a non-Jewish Québec woman, or a North African man who married a non-Jewish French woman as in the case of the *Synagogue de l'Union libérale israélite*. The general pattern was that these young men married as soon as they arrived in Montréal and Paris with (most often) young Catholic women, and that they were eager to convert them to Judaism in order to get married. This appears to confirm the hypothesis of marriage structured by social homogamy rather than religion, even if the conversion indicated the wish of spouses to remain within Judaism. Recent studies in demography demonstrate that the matrimonial choices of couples increasingly tend to bring together partners from diverse geographical origins, creating marriages that are socially diverse (Bozon and Héran 2006, 16–17). In this context, conversion permits the reestablishment of a balance. As Sébastien Tank-Storper writes:

> conversions within the marriage setting should be understood as a means of reconciling the two conflicting matrimonial lines of thought: social homogamy and religious endogamy. The conversion appears as a "gift" made to the Jewish spouse in response to the sacrifice which constitutes the exogamic marriage, a gift which is often the result of the constraints which Jewish institutions force upon mixed couples.[15] (Tank-Storper 2007, 32)

We can suppose that, attracted by the ease with which they established relationships with young women they met in public places or at work, and charmed by the prospect of following their inclination rather than tradition or the wishes of their parents, these young men chose to marry young women, with little consideration for the woman's social-economic or familial background. This type of marriage reinforced their idea of fitting into their new host country. They later attempted to compensate for what could appear as a transgression from their community by resorting to conversion. Whereas it remains difficult to know whether they lived in the context of secular Judaism, which would have predisposed them to marrying a non-Jew,[16] the fact remains that they saw as possible the idea of marrying for love all the while remaining within the community and within Judaism. An interview that we conducted with two male respondents who married fiancées who had converted, and with the rabbi who presided over the conversions and the marriages, revealed that in the first years after arriving, the men felt relatively sheltered from a sense of transgression since the marriages were celebrated at a synagogue, with the rabbi's blessing. Their marriages of love became, through the ritual consecration by the rabbi, marriages of reason, in conformity with the idea they had of themselves, and which permitted them *de facto* to remain within the Jewish community. In interviews conducted during the 1980s by Marie Berdugo-Cohen, a Moroccan Jew tells how he met his future wife (a non-Jewish French woman) in Montréal and the difficulties which this marriage, celebrated at the *Spanish and Portuguese Synagogue*, entailed for his family:

> When I arrived in Canada, I met friends, mostly boys. I did not know Moroccan girls, or very few. Everything changed the day when I met a young lady who was about twenty years old, and who, like me, was also from another country, from France. She was in Montréal for a very short stay, two or three months to improve her English, and then was to return to her parents. Of Catholic background, she was single daughter and worked au pair. Her father worked in aviation, and she was thinking of becoming an air hostess. She was very pretty and I liked her a lot. She had everything to please me, nice with a good education. ... How was it that a guy like me, brought up in Jewish traditions, could decide on his own to marry a non-Jew? I always had a high regard for religion and I lived in a very Jewish house, as we all did in Morocco. I knew that marrying a non-Jew was the thing you shouldn't do, and I still believe this to be true. Finally, I decided that she was the girl who suited me more than all others. That she wasn't Jewish was a big hassle, I did not know how to tell my parents, my family. I introduced the idea little by little ... For a year, I repeated to my future wife that I would not marry her, since she wasn't Jewish ... what I found the most consoling was that she didn't have any relative here. She was alone, she was a single daughter. Her conversion was therefore total. (quoted in Berdugo-Cohen, Cohen, and Lévy 1987, 146–50)

We can see in this interview how this man, who met a non-Jewish French woman in a context where he did not socialize with Moroccan Jewish women of his age, outlines the constraints that their marriage constituted for him and his family. It is also interesting to see that the constraint of this marriage with a convert was somehow compensated by the fact that this woman did not have a Catholic religious loyalty and was far from her family. Therefore we can see, in this interview excerpt, the assertion by this young man of his individuality through the choice of a young woman who suited him as a future spouse; we also note that this assertion derives from a generational behaviour common among many young people who wish to embrace modernity, even though traditional family requirements weighed strongly on them. But does this appeal of modernity play itself out in the same manner for young girls?

It is difficult to know with certainty, since these young girls could also choose to marry non-Jews: very few among them did so in the three synagogues here studied, but we cannot gauge this phenomenon for those who married in a civil celebration. The contrast between genders is noticeable, and one could affirm that the predominance of converted women constitutes one of the effects of the masculine domination that imposes the religion of the men (migrants) onto the women (natives) who wish to marry. In this regard, the modernity of the men's behaviour is a screen covering traditional and unequal attitudes in gender relationships. This double bind seems to be at the heart of the Jewish community reconfiguration in Montréal.

Jewish and Francophone in Québec

French language proficiency constituted an important factor in migratory projects as well as in the selection of potential migrants by the Canadian and Québec state administrations. Most of those whom we interviewed were men and women who studied in the French language, either in the schools of *l'Alliance israélite universelle*, or in the lyceums and schools of the *Mission française*. Their parents tended to speak Judeo-Arabic or Judeo-Spanish, sometimes French but not always. They had the opportunity to migrate due to family reuniting policies sustained at the time by the Canadian government. As a result, the bond with French, the language of colonization but also of their emancipation, found an echo in Québec, where it determined to a large degree Québec identity, which at the time, was being strongly asserted. We clearly see the extent to which the studies that have been devoted to this new wave of Jewish immigration used to their own ends the arrival of these newcomers, who were thrown from the outset into the linguistic battle. After a first wave of studies dedicated to the socio-economic integration of those migrants within the mainly English-speaking Jewish community,[17] a second wave of studies in contrast tried to assimilate them into the francophone majority,[18] which eventually led to genuine studies of their presence in Québec and in the Jewish diaspora.[19]

In a context where French was establishing itself as the main language of Québécois "citizenship," the fact that these new immigrants were mostly French-speaking contributed to changing the terms in the relation between Jews and non-Jews, but also the relationship of these newcomers with the mostly English-speaking Ashkenazi majority.

The linguistic cohesion of Québec's various Jewish Ashkenazi groups around English – Yiddish being little more than a reminiscence – seemed compromised. Hence, the arrival of Sephardic Jews reinforced the multinational and plural character of Montréal's Jewish community by adding totally new linguistic and cultural characteristics, all the while laying out new parameters for Judaism. As a result, language and ethnic origin, as well as religious practice, were to become powerful markers of a recomposed identity.

This identity was to crystallize around the way Sephardic Jews presented themselves both to the Jewish community and the Québec society at large. Processes of identity reconstruction which implied a return to former references, references sometimes mythic (the Sephardic Golden Age), grouped themselves around a reinterpretation of Sephardic traditions in light of new Québécois identity parameters, of which language was the main vector. Thus there came to be an equation between Sephardic and francophone. Due to the quick economic integration of some Sephardics, and the community commitment of others, they were to contribute to the renewal of community structures through the creation of new institutional apparatuses around Sephardic identity (the *Communauté Sépharade du Québec*, which became the *Communauté sépharade unifiée du Québec*, the Maimonides Schools, the publishing of the journal *La voix sépharade*, etc.).[20] This complex identification with Sephardic Judaism has been, in all, beneficial for Moroccan Jews in Montréal. On the one hand, it blurred in part the post-colonial character of this immigration and instituted a not-always fortunate confrontation with the mostly-Anglophone Jewish Ashkenazi community. On the other hand, it allowed those Jewish Moroccans who appropriated this identification to constitute themselves into an interest group and a cultural community. In this sense, it fit into the Québec political landscape that favoured belonging to the francophone cultural world, all the while benefiting from policies – and state sponsorship – which favoured the emergence of Canadian multiculturalism in a cosmopolitan city such as Montréal. As newcomers, they found in Montréal enough space to establish themselves within the traditional Jewish quarters, as well as to create enclaves in the general francophone culture (the *festival sefarad* being one case in point). In effect, the Sephardic's geographic, religious, and social outlook placed them from the beginning at the heart of the wider Jewish community of Montréal, even if the practices of some of them diverged from traditional endogamic expectations placed upon them. The community therefore became increasingly diverse.

The Use of Public Spaces by Jewish Moroccans

The Moroccan Jewish migration flow deeply marked Montréal's Jewish Community through the incorporation of new religious and linguistic practices, and *in fine*, a new social restructuration of Québec's Jewry. Upon their arrival, these migrants mainly settled in the Anglophone, middle-class area of Snowdon, in Montréal, where Jews already made up a significant part of the population and where communitarian structures had already been established (social centres, hospitals, Anglophone schools which were, before the late laicization of teaching, the only ones who accepted Jewish children).

The Jewish Moroccan population became an integral part of the Jewish community. The spatial distribution of married couples attending the *Spanish and Portuguese Synagogue* during the seventies clearly showed that more than 50 per cent of the population originating from Morocco used to live within a 1.6 kilometer radius of the synagogue. Many migrants saw this site as a meeting place, where they could reunite with other Moroccan families.

Nevertheless, more than 30 years later, it is interesting to note that the area of Snowdon is no longer a place where cultural and ethnic Jewish heterogeneity is visible. Modern, non-distinct, semi-detached buildings now take precedence. There is nothing unusual to see, except a few discreet *mezouzot*, showing that the area is now occupied by a few practicing Jewish families.[21] Only a few community and religious shops are located in the area. On the streets lining Mackenzie Park, where the *Spanish and Portuguese Synagogue* is located, Montréal's Jewish public mise en scène clearly appears: a Jewish campus, including the Gelber Centre, the Segal Cultural Complex, and the Jewish Community Centre with its various sport and education associations. All of these are located not far from the imposing Jewish General Hospital. The Jewish Community Centre, previously named the YMHA, groups together a nursery, a primary school, and a *Talmud Torah*. Listed on the front door, in French, English, and Hebrew, is the religious denomination of the place. But, in spite of the signs of appropriation of this space, there are no reminders of the multiple origins of the community and in particular, no mention of the Moroccan origins of the local inhabitants. In other words, if identity is perceived as a "reflecting construction," Grégoire Chelkoff reminds us that visibility in the public space is achieved by revealing oneself to the Other and to oneself (Rozenholc 2010, 22).

Figure 5.2. Map of the Snowdon area, compiled from archives of the *Spanish and Portuguese Synagogue* publications of banns for the marriages of its members

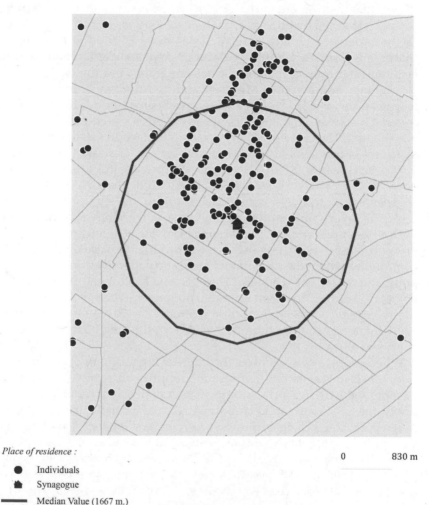

Place of residence :

● Individuals
🏠 Synagogue
▬▬▬ Median Value (1667 m.)

0   830 m

Sources: Publication of banns, *Spanish and Portuguese Synagogue,* 1969–1980, Montréal, Canada. (Céline Bergeron, Yolande Cohen, Linda Guerry, Yann Scioldo-Zürcher, © Migrinter, 2011)

In certain streets, the homogeneous Jewish composition is fore-grounded whilst the diversity of the Montréal Jewish Community is completely overlooked. The geographer Emmanuel Ma Mung has shown that the Chinese in diaspora have created peculiar urban pub-lic spaces, labeled by him as "Own World" ("*monde propre*"), which are easily recognized by any observer (Ma Mung 1999). These symbolic spaces are associated with a genealogy and a shared vision, which facilitates the coming together of new migrants and the descendants of migrants. In downtown Montréal, four red traditional *porticos* have recently been installed.[22] Nonetheless, even before the addition of these covered walkways, the area was already seen as a predominantly Chi-nese quarter. The Chinese are by no means obliged to live there, but the district is both a symbol and a resource for the diaspora to develop a particular type of solidarity. In the case of the Jews, this urban phenom-enon of "Own World" is similar, but more subtle. Just like the Chinese are seen in Montréal as a homogeneous group, the Jews present them-selves as a very uniform entity. The area is therefore constructed as both a "resource space" that gives material and religious means to the group (Godelier 1984), but also as an appropriated place by the Jewish community where the inhabitants are clearly identified by the whole population of the city (Di Méo, Castings, and Ducrounau 1993). Nowa-days, most of the Moroccan migrants no longer live in the district, but the synagogue is still an important reference for the community, espe-cially for family and community celebrations (hosting 120 to 150 events every year).

When taking a closer look at the internal organization of the institu-tion, it becomes apparent that certain identities are firmly established. Except for the two minority groups who organize their ceremonies out-doors, the Loubavitch and Hassidic rituals and a couple of celebrations in the park (the president of the synagogue remembers celebrating the *Chavouaot* festival there), the majority of the celebrations take place inside the synagogue in allocated rooms, thus requiring significant planning. There is a "Sefarad Chapel" in the synagogue which gath-ers together all Moroccans who want to maintain their specific rituals.

Consequently, in the Snowdon district, there is a very specific mise en scène of Montréal's Jewish population. This mise en scène erases all ref-erences to the national origins and the numerous identities of the Sefarad World in the public space to ultimately create a general Jewish reference. Public tensions are thus neutralized, and the area is therefore viewed as a place of national heritage for all Jews in Montréal, regardless of their language, time spent in the country, religious background, generation, and degree of affiliation. The *Spanish and Portuguese Synagogue* therefore underlines its patrimonial function which allegedly encompasses all Jews in Montréal. Its letterhead proclaims that it has been "at the service of the community since 1768," insisting on a shared history conceptualized as a uniting factor. In addition it states that 80 per cent of the celebrations are organized by non-members of the synagogue.

Conversely, in the neighbouring suburbs of Montréal, where an important part of the Moroccan Jewish migration flow has settled since the 1980s, we find a truly public representation of the Moroccan Jewry. Côte-Saint-Luc, Ville-Saint-Laurent, Dollard-des-Ormeaux developed a strong Jewish demographic component after their recent urbanization. This current population exhibits a strong affiliation to both Jewish and Moroccan origins in the public space. This is clearly illustrated by the noticeable Maïmonide School's Mohamed V pavilion (located in 1969 in Côte-Saint-Luc, with a second campus opened later) in Ville-Saint-Laurent, or in the Sephardic synagogues *Ora Haïm* and *Petah Tikva* which still gather the practising Jewish Moroccans of these towns.

Finally, two different Jewish public spaces are recognizable. In Montréal, the Moroccan Jewish origins of some of the inhabitants are not readily discernible to others except for in the semi-private space of a synagogue. A "co-presence" in the Jewish community exists, but it's clearly minimal.

However, in the suburbs, Moroccan influence is much more identifiable and ownership affiliation is proudly claimed. There is thus a truly historic meaning to the place constructed over a long period of time which attributes the idea of a "melting-pot" to the central public space of the city. This idea is characteristic of North American countries with a high rate of immigration. Simultaneously, on the periphery of the town, a Moroccan identity, constructed by a new generation of migrants, is highly visible and easily identifiable. Nonetheless, this does not mean that the places are in competition with one another.

Even though each synagogue is financed by contributions from its members, some of the faithful do not hesitate in using both places, despite directions from the management which opposes this practice. They choose the synagogue based on the type of meaning they wish to attribute to their celebrations. The *Spanish and Portuguese Synagogue* is used to celebrate important events whereas the other synagogues, closer to their places of residence, are generally used for daily or weekly rituals.

In Paris, the same phenomenon is observed. When the history and the prestige of a synagogue is well-known, such as in the case of the *Synagogue des Tournelles*, the general Jewish or Sephardic nature of the rituals is privileged over the origins of particular rituals. In the *Synagogue de l'Union libérale israélite*, the public space is not committed to any specific use. The memory of the bomb attack (on 3 October 1980) is engraved in history and the religious authorities are clearly looking for discretion in the public sphere. On the other hand, like in Montréal's case and in the Parisian suburbs, the number of ethnic synagogues is increasing (in Le Pré-Saint-Gervais, Pantin, Aubervilliers, Les-Lilas) with a much more explicit spatial marking of the origins.

Conclusion

The comparison of the marriages celebrated in these three synagogues reveals two main tendencies in the face of mass migration. The Jewish consistory, reinforced by its position as the representative of French Judaism, consolidated its stranglehold on newcomers, without any significant preoccupation concerning other types of faith. It saw in the arrival of Maghrebi Jews a means of reconstructing the community and, at the same time, felt obliged to keep them within the parameters of Orthodox Judaism, to the point of neglecting the consequences of the weakening of a good number of constraints which weighed on young Jews when they were residing in their home countries. Modern Montréal Orthodox Judaism as well as Liberal Parisian Judaism, have not hesitated to "manufacture Jews," to the point of soliciting conversions, in order to make up for those who were perhaps on the point of leaving Judaism.

These North African Jewish migrations have, without a doubt, had an influence on matrimonial strategies; migrant men and women easily entered into exogamic marriages. Conversions do not seem to be a way to experience upward social mobility. Rather, they are an entrée into "Western modernity," which makes room for the notion of individuality and romantic love.

While host communities and home countries were considerably entangled, this nonetheless remained a short-term phenomenon that immediately followed the migrations. A decade after these arrivals in France and in Québec, international Jewish institutions were eager to redefine who was a Jew; in effect it put an end to the community openness they had previously exhibited. At the same time, during the 1980s, the construction in France and Québec of an independent Sephardic community that granted itself schools (Maimonides in particular) and synagogues or reappropriated old ones, reinforced the religious dimension of endogamic marriage. The arrival of more orthodox rabbis who promoted a traditionalist, or even ultra-orthodox Judaism, similarly found many followers in the Jewish community. Conversions came to be understood as so many ruptures with this tradition, and were closely monitored and limited to a few cases. One can ask oneself if this return to the norm is not due to the fact that Jewish North African migrations toward France and Québec had withered, which entailed a certain return to a matrimonial norm understood as "traditional," but which neglected the role of availability toward the Other which is part of the Jewish tradition as well.

In conclusion, our data pushes us to reflect upon Sephardic identity. If this identity revolves around a Maghrebi reference, it is also in about one-quarter of the cases a synthesis of Jewish Ashkenazi and Sephardic traditions and identities constructed in mainland France and Québec. In other words, whereas the Sephardic imagination sometimes discerns a mythic Neverland in the form of Maghrebi landscapes, the post-colonial Jewish migration, in France and in Canada, has shown capability of opening itself to the world, all the while retaining a sense of its own centre. This illustrates well the manner in which Judaism passes through historical time and the space of migration. It does so by the adaptation of some of its members to the modernity of the host community, all the while keeping in mind a strict Orthodox Judaism. This religious and community referent shows to the group a direction that gives it the illusion of having always remained within the rules of religious orthodoxy.

NOTES

1 This chapter (80 per cent of the content) was previously published as Yolande Cohen and Yann Sciolodo-Zürcher, "Migrations juives maghrébines à Paris et Montréal, approche quantitative du mariage religieux en migration, 1954–1980," in *La bienvenue et l'adieu, migrants juifs et musulmans au Maghreb*, edited by Frédéric Abassis, Karima Dirèche, and Rita Aouad (Paris: La Croisée des chemins à Casablanca et aux éditions Karthala, 2012). A first version of this text was also previously published as Yolande Cohen and Yann Sciolodo-Zürcher, "Migrations juives maghrébines à Paris et Montréal, approche quantitative du mariage religieux en migration, 1954–1980," Collections

électroniques du Centre Jacques Berque (2013, http://cjb.revues.org/). It has been reproduced here with the permission of Frédéric Abessis, scientific editor.

The authors would like to thank Linda Guerry (UQAM) and Jacqueline Sklavos (Université de Poitiers) for their help and advice. Our sincere thanks are addressed to Hubert Villeneuve, who so aptly translated the text from French to English.

2 This study is part of a comparative research on contemporary Jewish immigration in Paris and Montréal conducted by Yolande Cohen and Yann Scioldo-Zürcher. For the Paris case, see Scioldo-Zürcher and Bahoken (2009). For the Spanish and Portuguese Synagogue case, see Cohen and Guerry (2011). See also Cohen (2011).

3 In 1967, 53,000 Jews resided in Morocco, 8,000 in Tunisia, and only 1,000 in Algeria (Bensimon 1971, 1).

4 The *kéboutot* are notarized marriage certificates that have a religious value during that period. However, marriage preparation records have a specific administrative and religious function, as they attest to both spouses' compliance of religious rules pertaining to marriage; notably, they include data on the religion of the engaged couple, be they members of the Jewish community or not. They also include information on the couple's birthplaces (and those of their parents), their profession, and, in some cases, their nationality. In Canada, the publications of banns contain further information. In contrast to France, where only civil marriage acts have legal value in accordance to the principles of Church-State separation, synagogue banns in Canada are sent by the rabbi, who, just like every minister of major religions, also acts as a civil servant, thus making the religious marriage the official civil act. As a result, the rabbi should inform public authorities as to the levels of education and languages spoken among households.

5 Unfortunately, following the loss of many archives, the files from the Synagogue de la rue Copernic that could be studied only covered the years from 1963 to 1970.

6 On this synagogue's history, see Blaustein, Esar, and Miller (1971).

7 During these years, this synagogue was important to Moroccan Jews, though many also married at the Shomrin Laboker congregation, according to Rabbi Joseph, who took office in 1970.

8 Part of the data for the years 1966 and 1967 is missing.

9 The year 1970 was not taken into account in this latter case. The smaller number of weddings resulted from building restoration works and not from any disaffection from the part of congregants.

10 More than 79,000 people were deported from France, including 11,400 children. See Klarsfeld (1985, 180).

11 He kept this position until 1984. Upon his departure, another Morocco-born cantor, Yehuda Abitan, was hired by the synagogue.

12 An examination of a conversion case in one of the synagogue's marriage records clearly reveals the elementary aspect of the procedure. It should be noted that the mention "*à convertir*" ("to be converted") can sometimes be found beside the names of a spouse's parents who were married at the liberal synagogue, but who did not officially completed their Jewish conversion, even after a few decades.

13 Furthermore, the consistorial administration kept in a separate register all unions in which the woman was not officially Jewish (which happened when the mother, or both parents, did not belong to Judaism). The same register also contains a list of marriages involving a divorced or widowed Jewish woman. Conversely, when a man is divorced, widowed, or has non-Jewish mother or parents, the *kétouba* of the marriage will be registered as an endogamic Jewish union.

14 In the stricter orthodox ritual practice, the woman's conversion (often done in a more liberal or modern orthodox ritual) is not always, nor everywhere, recognized. This might result in a difficult situation, including for the children of these converted women.

15 "(…) les conversions par alliance doivent se comprendre comme le moyen de réconcilier deux logiques matrimoniales conflictuelles: l'homogamie sociale et l'endogamie religieuse, et la conversion apparaît comme un « don » fait au conjoint juif en réponse au sacrifice que constitue le mariage exogame, don bien souvent forcé par les contraintes que font peser les institutions juives sur ces couples mixtes." (Tank-Storper 2007, 32).

16 Marylin Bernard noted in her research on Jewish women in Québec City that those who married non-Jews had generally been raised in a secular Jewish context (Bernard 2008, 86).

17 The first works published on Moroccan Jews in Montréal addressed the problems experienced by these migrants pertaining to adaptation and integration. These works came primarily from McGill University's School of Social Work and approached this topic mainly from the Jewish Anglophone perspective, predominant at the time. See Amber and Lipper (1968), Berman, Nahmiash, and Osmer (1970), and Batshaw and Lowe (1971).

18 Then, the very fact that these Moroccan immigrants were French-speaking made them an object of interest (Anctil and Caldwell 1984).

19 Ethno-sociological works came afterward. See notably Filion (1979), Dinelle and Barnette-Dalphond (1985), Berdugo-Cohen, Cohen, and Lévy (1987), and Elbaz (1989, 1993). Finally, the more recent work of Anctil and Robison (2010) attempt to reinterpret their history within Québec's Jewish community.

20 Different models of integration were studied. The successful economic
    integration of North African Jews was demonstrated by economist
    Naomi Moldofsky (1968) and psycho-sociologist Jean-Claude Lasry
    (1989), both of whom showed that members of the community, for the
    most part, managed to reach the same professional status they had in
    their native countries. Several among them found employment oppor-
    tunities in so-called "ethnic" enterprises, either Sephardic or Ashkenazi.
    Moreover, their geographic integration was also attested by their estab-
    lishment in traditionally Jewish neighborhoods (in downtown Montréal),
    or more recently Jewish (Côte-Saint-Luc), and the creation of their own
    points of identity reference at the crossroads of Judaism, *La Francophonie*,
    and Sephardim.
21 The eruv leading to the synagogue are practically invisible. They are small
    signs located in the streets near the synagogue that show the recom-
    mended route that the faithful can take during their rest days, without
    transgressing the religious rules. In Paris, these do not exist.
22 They were installed in 1999 by Beijing's authorities.

REFERENCES

Amber, Phillis, and Irene Lipper. 1968. "Toward an Understanding of Moroccan
    Jewish Family Life." Unpublished MA thesis, McGill University, Montréal.
Anctil, Pierre, and Gary Caldwell. 1984. *Juifs et réalités juives au Québec*. Qué-
    bec: Institut Québécois de Recherche sur la Culture.
Anctil, Pierre, and Ira Robison. 2010. *Les communautés juives au Québec*. Qué-
    bec: Septentrion.
Batshaw, Huguette, and Beverly Lowe. 1971. "The Integration of Moroc-
    can Jewish Immigrants in Montréal (1964–1970)." Unpublished MA thesis,
    McGill University, Montréal.
Bensimon, Doris. 1971. *L'Intégration des Juifs nord-africains en France*. Paris:
    Mouton.
Berdugo-Cohen, Marie, Yolande Cohen, and Joseph Lévy. 1987. *Juifs
    Marocains à Montréal. Témoignages d'une immigration moderne*. Montréal:
    VLB Editeur.
Berman, G., D. M. Nahmiash, and C. H. Osmer. 1970. "A Profile of Moroccan
    Jewish Immigrants in Montréal 1957–1967." Unpublished MA thesis, McGill
    University, Montréal.
Bernard, Marylin. 2008. "Vivre, s'intégrer et interagir en étant minoritaires
    à plusieurs égards: le cas des femmes juives à Québec des années 1940 à
    aujourd'hui." Unpublished MA mémoire, Université Laval, Québec.

Blaustein, Esther I., Rachel A. Esar, and Evelyn Miller. 1971. "Spanish and Por-
    tuguese Synagogue (Shearith Israel), Montréal, 1768–1968." *Jewish Historical
    Society of England: Transactions* 2: 111–42.
Bozon, Michel, and François Héran. 2006. *Le choix du conjoint*. Paris: La
    Découverte.
Cohen, Yolande. 2011. "The Migrations of Moroccan Jews to Montréal: Mem-
    ory, (Oral) History, and Historical Narrative." *Journal of Modern Jewish Stud-
    ies* 10(2): 245–62.
Cohen, Yolande, and Linda Guerry. 2011. "Mariages et parcours migra-
    toires: Juifs nés au Maroc et mariés à la Spanish and Portuguese Syna-
    gogue de Montréal (1969–1981)." *Studies in Religion/Etudes religieuse*,
    40(4): 1–25.
Di Méo, Guy, Jean-Pierre Castingts, and Colette Ducrounau. 1993. "Territoire,
    patrimoine et formation socio-spatiale." *Annales de Géographie* 102(573):
    472–502.
Dinelle, Johanne, and A. Barnette-Dalphond. 1985. "Femmes et judaïsme. Les
    femmes immigrantes sépharades à Montréal." Unpubished MA thesis, Uni-
    versité du Québec à Montréal.
Elbaz, Mikhaël. 1989. "D'immigrants à ethniques: analyse comparée des pra-
    tiques sociales et identitaires des Sépharades et Ashkénazes à Montréal." In
    Les Juifs du Maghreb. Diasporas contemporaine, edited by Jean-Claude Lasry
    and Claude Tapia, 79–101. Montréal/Paris: Presses de l'Université de
    Montréal/L'Harmattan.
Elbaz, Mikhaël. 1993. "Les héritiers. Générations et identités chez les Juifs
    sépharades à Montréal." *Revue européenne des migrations internationales* 9(3):
    13–34.
Filion, Fernand G. 1979. "La Communauté Sépharade de Montréal. Une anal-
    yse ethno-historique des structures communautaires." Unpublished PhD
    dissertation, Université Laval, Québec.
Godelier, Maurice. 1984. *L'idéel et le matériel: pensée, économies, société*. Paris:
    Fayard.
Green, Nancy L. 2002. *Repenser les migrations*. Paris: Puf, Le Nœud Gordien.
Jarassé, Dominique. 2003. *Guide du patrimoine juif parisien*. Paris: Parigramme.
Klarsfeld, Serge. 1985. *Vichy Auschwitz. Le rôle de Vichy dans la solution finale de
    la question juive en France. 1943–1944*. Paris: Fayard.
Lasry, Jean-Claude. 1989. "Essor et tradition. La communauté juive nord-africaine
    au Québec." In *Les Juifs du Maghreb. Diasporas contemporaines*, edited by
    Jean-Claude Lasry and Claude Tapia, 17–54. Montréal/Paris: Presses de
    l'Université de Montréal/L'Harmattan.
Ma Mung, Emmanuel. 1999. "Autonomie, migrations et altérité, Habilita-
    tion à diriger les recherches, Habilitation à diriger les recherches," sous la

direction de Gildas Simon, Université de Poitiers. Unpublished paper as part of an accreditation program to supervise research programme.

Meyer, Michael. 1988. *Response to Modernity: A History of the Reform Movement in Judaism.* New York: Oxford University Press.

Moldofsky, Naomi. 1968. "The Economic Adjustment of North African Jewish Immigrants in Montréal." Unpublished PhD dissertation, McGill University, Montréal.

Poujol, Catherine. 2007. "Les débuts de l'Union libérale israélite (1895–1939). Le pari de moderniser le judaïsme français." *Archives Juives* 40(2): 65–81.

Rozenholc, Caroline. 2010. "Florentin: une mise en perspective d'un quartier de Tel Aviv dans la mondialisation (2005–2009)." Thèse doctorale, Université de Poitiers, 22.

Scioldo-Zürcher, Yann. 2010. *Devenir métropolitain, politique d'accueil et parcours de rapatriés d'Algérie en métropole, 1954–2005.* Paris: Ed. de l'EHESS.

Scioldo-Zürcher, Yann, and Françoise Bahoken. 2009. "Se marier aux Tournelles. Approche sociodémographique du mariage séfarade en France post-coloniale (1954–1970)." *Archives Juives* 42(2): 82–97.

Tank-Storper, Sébastien. 2007. *Juifs d'élection, se convertir au judaïsme.* Paris: CNRS Editions.

6 Talking about Domestic Violence and Communities of Faith in the Public Sphere

Celebrations and Challenges

NANCY NASON-CLARK

Overview

Many religious men, women, teens, and children look to their faith community for guidance and practical assistance in the aftermath of domestic violence.[1] This is true in the Canadian context, where my research began over twenty years ago, but it is also the case in the United States, and in other countries around the world – in cultures and places where my expanding research agenda has taken me. Whether someone is helped first by their congregation (through a pastor, priest, or other religious leader) or a community-based agency (through a social worker, domestic violence advocate, or legal counsel), those who respond need to understand both the issue of domestic violence and the nature of religious faith. Building bridges of common language, perspective, respect, and understanding between sacred and secular sources of help presents both opportunities to be mined and challenges to be overcome. Such collaboration has the potential to impact religious victims, survivors and perpetrators of domestic violence and their families, as one might suspect, but also the professionals who walk alongside them on the journey to healing, justice, accountability, and wholeness. In this way, the collaborative community table has a public dimension. The problems of domestic violence, as well as the solutions to it, extend beyond the individual people who are part of naming it and framing a response. Here it reaches the public square, building cooperation and partnerships between people working from different constituencies – including religious ones – where the lessons learned can help us to understand, and shape, the debate on moving beyond tolerance and accommodation to religious minorities (and majorities) in our society.

Throughout this volume, individual chapters address religion in the public sphere. My contribution to this discussion is both theoretical and practical. Our[2] research on domestic violence and communities of faith highlights the unique information and spiritual needs of religious clients in an increasingly diverse and pluralistic cultural and religious context (Nason-Clark 1997, 2000a, 2004, 2009; Beaman-Hall and Nason-Clark 1997; Kroeger and Nason-Clark 2010). But our work in translating the findings of social science studies[3] to social action initiatives at the local, national, and international level offers the perspective of a demonstration project, helping scholars and activists alike to contextualize what happens in specific cultural and geographical spaces when the community response to domestic violence includes those informed by a religious perspective (Nason-Clark 2005; Nason-Clark, Fisher-Townsend, Holtmann, McMullin, and Ruff 2009).

Since this chapter offers a specific example of observing – and understanding – religion in the public sphere related to one social issue, that of domestic violence, it begins with an exploration of that social issue first. It then moves to consider international examples of the intersection of domestic violence and religion in the public arena, and then focuses on Canada, and Atlantic Canada in particular. Explicating the relationship between domestic violence and religious faith involves relatively uncharted waters – fraught with obstacles such as reservations within the public sphere about discussing the issue generally, and then more specifically to discussing the issue with those whose perspective is, in part, informed by religious convictions and commitment. Talking about domestic violence often makes people feel uneasy. Talking about religion and abuse makes it that much more uncomfortable. There is the persistent reluctance amongst those who are religious to acknowledge and respond to domestic violence as a problem both within and beyond communities espousing strong religious convictions. For others it is simply the subject of abuse – it is too painful, or too close to home.

As the chapter unfolds, I attempt to offer an analysis of this complicated relationship by employing various narratives – including the criminal justice narrative, the therapeutic narrative, the advocacy narrative, and the religious narrative – to concretize how the connections between religious faith and violence amongst intimates unfold in various jurisdictions where our research has taken us: in Atlantic Canada, in western Canada, throughout the United States, and in other countries of the world. Since I believe that Atlantic Canada is a unique observational field, I conclude with an explication of the ways that religion and violence are framed in the public sphere here and how that is similar to – and different from – other jurisdictions. But we need to be clear, the context of forging a relationship between communities of faith and those responding to domestic violence has its own unique challenges and to understand that, even in part, is where the chapter begins.

Introduction

Domestic violence is a pervasive reality that knows no boundaries of class, color, country, or faith perspective (Stirling, Cameron, Nason-Clark, and Miedema 2004). Its prevalence around the world has been documented through statistics collected by government agencies, the World Health Organization, the United Nations Secretariat, and large numbers of academic researchers (Kroeger and Nason-Clark 2010). Published research and academic writing on domestic violence developed rapidly throughout the 1970s and 1980s (DeKeseredy and MacLeod 1998; Dobash and Dobash 1979; Martin 1981; Straus and Gelles 1986; Straus, Gelles, and Steinmetz 1980). Its scope expanded in the 1990s as advocates and survivors mobilized and declared a call for action to permeate all sectors of society (Loseke 1992; Thorne-Finch 1992; Timmins 1995; Walker 1990). By 2000, domestic violence had reached the radar screen of physicians, mental health professionals, criminal justice personnel, educators, researchers, and government bureaucrats. Yet, religious voices were often silenced, or sidelined, and a *holy hush*[4] still operated in many congregational or religious circles.

From the earliest days of the battered-women's movement, there was a reluctance to see any perspective informed by religious language or passion as part of the *solution* to abuse (Brown and Bohn 1989). Yet, it was undeniable that a woman's religious faith might shape her experience and disclosure of battery and the road she would choose to travel in her quest for wholeness in its aftermath (Clarke 1986; Fiorenza and Copeland 1994; Fortune 1991; Halsey 1984). There was mounting evidence that some abused women were turning to their religious leaders for assistance (Giesbrecht and Sevcik 2000; Horton and Williamson 1988; Weaver 1993). But the story of what happened when men, women, and children looked to their faith community after violence at home was yet to be told.

For almost twenty years, we have been learning that some religious survivors claim their faith sustains them through the protracted, ugly reality of domestic abuse: it empowers them, through spiritual and practical resources, to flee the abuse and seek safety and solace in a context free from the violence of the past. Others are consumed by the *sacred silence*, fighting demons both within and without. They are ultimately prevented from leaving behind the fear or reality of abuse. For most of my career I have been interested in exploring the intersection of religious faith, gender, and domestic violence. Together with graduate students and research colleagues, I have conducted studies that focus on religious leaders, congregations, women's organizations within faith communities, transition houses, professionals and advocates who work with the abused or abusers, abused religious women, religious men who are perpetrators, and the variety of programs and services that are offered to families impacted by domestic violence. We have explored these relationships through quantitative research projects and qualitative studies – using surveys, interviews, focus groups, participant observation, and case file analysis. More recently, I have become involved in translating social science research for a broader public, through speaking engagements, consultations, articles, books, and the creation of a web-based series of training modules and resources.[5]

What I have learned in the process of data collection and dissemination is that the problem of domestic violence is widespread, its frequency and severity touch all communities – including those that are religious – and that for those of deep religious faith the journey towards accountability, justice, healing, and wholeness requires the resources of our secular culture, nuanced by the *language of the spirit*. In the discussion to follow, I will attempt to illustrate the necessity and complexity of this challenge if we as a society are to respond with compassion and best practices to all of our citizens – those with, and those without, religious faith and spiritual practices.

Talking about Domestic Violence and Religion

The Criminal Justice Narrative

At first blush, one might sense that there is little to say about the relationship between domestic violence and religion from the perspective of police, parole, probation, the courts, or judges. Yet, such is not so. Interwoven through the interviews with probation and parole officers, the stories told by police and judges, and our research with religious men who act abusively, are threads of religious language, the adoption of concepts infused with religious meaning, and many examples of religious practices and beliefs that interface with domestic violence as it relates to the criminal justice system. I wish to draw attention to three: harnessing the potential of religious language for change; building bridges for increased accountability; and recognizing the impotency of any one discipline alone to affect change in the lives of families impacted by domestic violence.

In order to illustrate this point, I offer the story of Skip[6] (Nason-Clark and Fisher-Townsend forthcoming), one of almost 100 men, most of whom we were able to interview every six months for a period of four years in the aftermath of his involvement with the criminal justice system for domestic violence and his mandated attendance at a 52-week, state-certified batterer intervention program. Skip has worked for almost 20 years in grounds care on a large university campus. He grew up in a middle class home and as a result of extensive childhood travel and social capital acquired from his parents he is more adept than many of his peers at articulating his views. This explains how he found his way to the faith-based STOP program we are studying because he refused to return to a secular program in the local area after a worker in the agency there accused him of having a ghostwriter prepare his written assignment. Skip's parole officer outlined the options in the area, indicating that STOP was one of the choices. Drinking to excess by the time he was 13, involved in several robberies to finance his drinking habit by the time he turned 15, Skip is unfamiliar neither with the criminal justice system nor intervention services. Yet, the STOP program was able to engage Skip and hold him accountable for at least the four years we were involved in following his therapeutic progress. Here, he learned early on that he had something to gain by participating in the program – a message that was communicated through the language of consumer choice by the group facilitators, office staff, and other men in the program at STOP. Once he was motivated to engage in the program, accountability became part of the process to help him achieve HIS goal of change. The coordinated efforts of the agency and the criminal justice system – mediated in large measure, but not exclusively, by his parole officer and the group facilitator at STOP – kept him accountable. Reconnecting with the faith of his grandmother, which he made his own during adolescence, the STOP program offered Skip another language to talk about his new start. Workers in the criminal justice system harnessed this language in their work to ensure both his continued nonviolence and compliance with the court's demands of him. Interagency cooperation also offered the criminal justice employee a bridge to connect the secular and the spiritual. Chris, the probation officer, was able to employ elements of therapeutic accountability (steeped in religious language) as he worked with Skip.

The reputation of the agency within the criminal justice, therapeutic, and advocacy communities is solid. While some do not personally endorse their faith-added approach, of course, there was no sense that their work was compromised by religious persuasion, nor any evidence that the agency was proselytizing clients or pushing a faith-based agency, nor were they reluctant to accept clients from a variety of faiths or no expressed faith. While several very religious men we interviewed at the agency were quite annoyed that group facilitators at STOP did not express more openly a faith-based perspective on their lives or journey after violence, many men referred to how well group facilitators were able to call religious men to accountability. Regularly they did so by refusing to accept the men's attempts at justifying their abusive acts using the language of the Scriptures, or their varied faith traditions.

Building bridges of collaborative action between faith-based community agencies and the criminal justice system is an enormous challenge. While recent years have witnessed many innovative projects that involve selected features of a coordinated community response, such as specialized domestic violence courts, or law enforcement officers who are uniquely trained to respond to cases of domestic violence and work in a multi-disciplinary context, most community-enhanced efforts to combat domestic violence or respond to its victims do not recognize any role for either spiritual leaders or agencies that have a faith-based or faith-enriched mission statement. However, religious leaders and professionals with a faith-based or faith-enriched perspective play a critical role in calling religious men to accountability and offering spiritual and practical support to religious women and children who have been victimized by male aggression in the family context.

Of course, there is also a dark side, a reality check, as it were, in any collaborative efforts with faith communities. This needs to be recognized. One example illustrates the challenge. Several judges we interviewed, or met, in the course of fieldwork noted that the only time they witness faith leaders in the courtroom is in support of the accused – while the victim sits alone with a court-appointed advocate. Sometimes, this is a result of the fact that the abusive man has sought the help of a religious leader after a 911 call, or when his female partner has sought refuge in a transition house for battered women. Sometimes, the man has a long-standing relationship with the church, or both the violated and the violator are part of the larger church community. Irrespective of whom initiates contact – victim or aggressor – the bond between a male church leader, male church lay leadership, and a man accused of harming his family is a resource that can aid in the struggle to assist religious families after violence strikes home.

The Therapeutic Narrative

While some come voluntarily, most men who attend batterer intervention classes do so because they have little or no choice in the matter. They have been mandated by the courts as a result of a conviction for abuse, or they have been referred by wives, therapists and/or religious leaders as a final gasp before the relationship is considered dead. Religious women, in particular, hold out great hope that such intervention will change the violent men with whom they are in relationship and at whose hands they have suffered. Over the last five years, we have sought to explore whether there is any basis on which to hold out such hope. Since many women of faith do not want to terminate their relationships with the abusers – either temporarily or forever – they cling to a notion that if only their partners would seek help in a program specifically designed for men who act abusively that the violence would cease and their physical and emotional safety would be restored.

In the first attempt ever to examine empirically the characteristics of men who attended a faith-based batterers' intervention program in the northwest quadrant of the United States, we analysed over 1,000 closed case files. Compared to men in secular programs, this data revealed that men attending a batterers group in a faith-based context were more likely to have witnessed or experienced abuse in their childhood homes, while rates of alcohol abuse and criminal histories were similar (Nason-Clark, Murphy, Fisher-Townsend, and Ruff 2003). Men who were clergy-referred were more likely to complete (and graduate from) the program than those who had been mandated by a judge alone, and when the criminal justice mandate was reinforced by a religious leader completion rates were highest. In fact, the moral authority of a religious leader was a significant factor in raising completion rates, even though non-compliance of a court order could result in further legal sanctions. It appears that sharing a religious worldview with other men in a program for batterers may actually provide a *safe place* for abusive religious men to challenge themselves and others – preparing for a day when their abusive pasts will no longer be replicated in current acts of violence.

Our fieldwork in faith-based batterer intervention programs, where many, but not all, men were raised in homes that were explicitly religious, reveals that staff are able to hold men accountable employing both the language of secular culture – through their professional credentials, training, and experience – and the language of the spirit – through their knowledge of sacred texts, rituals, beliefs, and everyday practices. For men of faith this has a profound impact. Erroneous religious thinking is challenged and an abuser's religious ideology is harnessed in ways that have the potential to nurture, monitor, and reinforce a violence-free future.

In a faith-based agency, spiritual overtones can be woven into the curriculum to direct positive benefit (Fisher-Townsend, Nason-Clark, Ruff, and Murphy 2008). Many men who are controlling in intimate relationships – exercising abuse to reinforce submission or their own needs and wants – both justify the abuse they have meted out to their partner and blame her for the abuse with subtle or not-so-subtle references to their religious tradition. Chris Sollows's story (Kroeger and Nason-Clark, 2010) illustrates this point. He had just switched careers and recently changed marriage partners when we first met him. He was 39 years old, a teacher of science in a junior high school, and lived with his wife – a physiotherapist – and seven children in a blended family situation. After the first 911 call, his wife insisted that he attend the STOP program we are studying. Chris was not happy with the agency because they challenged directly his belief that he was "in charge" and that the Bible gave him authority to be the unrestrained leader in his home. When he would claim in group that the curriculum was not right "according to the Bible," group facilitators would actually read the relevant Bible passages in response to his disruption. They were able to use their knowledge of the religious traditions and texts to deflate and counteract the erroneous claims of a religious abuser.

In some of our fieldwork in western Canada, we observed that this sometimes happened when a faith-enriched group facilitator or therapist would challenge a religious man in a secular intervention group. By faith-enriched we are referring to those with secular credentials and secular employment but personal religious faith that they have made known in the work context. Obviously there are people of diverse religious faiths who are employed in therapeutic contexts who never reveal to their clients or co-workers their own personal religious or spiritual journeys. There are others who share with clients or co-workers a religious or spiritual awareness yet are unable or unwilling to harness their tradition, or the tradition of others, as it relates to the work that they do. But there are those in many contexts where we have conducted fieldwork or interviews and learned of their ability *and* willingness to challenge religious thinking that thwarts the therapeutic progress towards enhanced accountability or change in the aftermath of domestic violence.

The Advocacy Narrative

Providing shelter, information, and support to women and children who flee their homes in the aftermath of domestic violence is the work of transition houses and their staffs across Canada, the United States, and many other parts of the world. The stress of the work and its concomitant emotional demands is ever present upon shelter workers and their directors, as are the financial insecurity and tight budgets under which shelters are forced to operate. Through extensive experience in working with those in the advocacy community, and in interviews with directors and staff in many locations, it became very clear that workers are caught between the demands of the work, their training stressing the importance of boundaries, and their knowledge of the value of the services they provide for those whose lives are in turmoil.

In many urban areas, where the transition houses are often located, there are growing numbers of immigrant families and the diversity of women seeking refuge at the shelter reflects these societal realities. Offering services and support to women from a wide range of religious and cultural backgrounds is very challenging at a practical level. While an executive director of a transition house may want the facilities to be respectful of all women's cultural and religious experiences and choices, most staff have little specific knowledge or life events that would enable them to talk with understanding and empathy to Muslim or Jewish women, or Mormons or Pentecostals. In point of fact, highly religious women of any tradition pose some challenges for workers at the shelter (Beaman-Hall and Nason-Clark 1997; Nason-Clark 1996). Sometimes workers blame the woman's religious background for her troubles; other times they believe if she were less religious, it would be easier to find solutions to the violence that permeates her life. Sometimes workers do not know how to assist a highly religious woman as she journeys towards healing and wholeness after domestic violence strikes at home.

There are often specific religious contours on the road from victim to survivor (Nason-Clark 1999). To be blunt: highly religious women can be especially vulnerable *when* abused. They are likely to hold the intact family in high regard, to consider separation and divorce as unsatisfactory options, and to be especially optimistic concerning intervention (therapeutic or legal) in the life of the partner who perpetrated the violence. They may also be especially prone to blame themselves, experience high levels of shame, and believe that they have disappointed their faith community, its leaders, and even God. To be sure, they require practical help but they also often require spiritual assistance.

Since many religious leaders are ill-equipped to offer this assistance, a coordinated effort is the option of choice for providing both emotional and practical help. Our research with religious leaders reveals that only 8 per cent believe that they are well-prepared to respond to the needs of families impacted by abuse – despite the fact that most are called upon several times a year to do so. Since so many faith traditions celebrate "family values," it is imperative that they are part of any community-wide response to or dialogue on abuse in the domestic context.

Many workers in secular therapeutic contexts do not feel comfortable addressing a client's spiritual needs, even when the woman herself raises this as an essential component of her life experience. Without spiritual credentials, these workers find it hard to know how to intervene when a woman or a man believes that his or her faith tradition gives license to abuse. Our research reveals that a cultural language that is devoid of religious symbols, meanings, and legitimacy is relatively powerless to alter a religious victim's resolve to stay or return to a marriage – no matter what the cost to her physical or emotional health. But spiritual language alone may not ensure that a victim's need for safety, security, and financial resources to care for herself and the children will be met.

Sometimes, the language of the caregivers drowns out the language of those impacted most by domestic violence – women and children. Talking about violence in the public square involves negotiating the delicate terrain of egos, values, disciplinary boundaries, and divergent practical and emotional strategies for health and safety. The conversation is replete with challenges – steeped in place, and time.

Region-Specific Responses or Solutions

I would like to draw attention to a variety of strategies that are employed in various regions to respond to this type of dialogue as it has been introduced above. First, in our work in Atlantic Canada, we have observed religious leaders building awareness and response capacity to enter the public dialogue on domestic violence and religion. While there are many factors that support such a conclusion, allow me to offer five: the frequency with which religious leaders' assistance is sought; the reluctance of clergy to refer abused women and other family members to community-based agencies; the strong support of women-only networks within congregational life; the training challenges facing religious leaders; and women's call for spiritual resources. The majority of clergy in Atlantic Canada are called upon several times a year to respond to a woman who is being abused by her current partner, a man who has acted abusively towards his partner, or adults who are coping with issues of abuse from their past. Most religious leaders we have surveyed or interviewed perceive that they are not prepared to respond to situations involving domestic violence and yet many are reluctant to make referrals to those resources or personnel in community-based agencies who do have the expertise.[7] Resistance to referring parishioners to other professionals is highest amongst the most poorly equipped pastors (those reporting little or no training). Thus where it is needed most, it is least likely to occur. It is not surprising, then, that we have learned through interviews and focus groups with church women that those who look to their pastors for help are often disappointed to find that there is limited understanding of the dynamics of domestic violence by those leaders, a modest knowledge of the resources that are available in the community, and a lack of ability (or willingness) to offer help of an explicitly religious nature. Yet, when clergy do speak out (over 30 per cent of pastors report they have preached a message condemning family violence), discuss violence in their premarital counselling (40 per cent of pastors say they include this in one or more of their counselling sessions), offer referrals or encouragement for a woman to seek community-based expertise, or hold those who are abusive accountable for their actions, its impact is profound.

In a series of studies linked to a broader initiative in Alberta, we found that sustaining momentum and maintaining critical players is an ongoing challenge in keeping religion and violence in the public sphere. Worker burn-out is high. Turnover in many agencies and churches is an ongoing challenge. The emotional strength needed to carry on as a first responder in situations of domestic or sexual violence must be sustained by varied forms of community and religious support. The domestic violence advocacy community in Calgary is a case in point. FaithLink is a unique faith-based organization that developed several years ago with the mandate to promote sacred/secular collaborations and dialogue on issues of violence in the family context.[8] The heightened awareness in Calgary of the need to include faith communities and their leaders in the struggle to end domestic violence and to respond with best practices to those impacted by it was the result of several initiatives at the community level – the Sheriff-King Shelter, specialized domestic violence courts, and Home-Front, a centrally organized collection of systems and services that make up a research-validated integrated community response to domestic violence.

Even in a context where religious leaders are welcomed in principle to the collaborative community table, there are enormous challenges. And often it is particular clergy in particular traditions who are invited to join the collaborative work, while other co-religionists are not. The demands of the work of responding to families impacted by domestic violence are intense and when coupled with the demands of ministry to the sick, the dying, and others whose needs can place leaders on call at inconvenient times and places, it takes a toll on the religious leader to be a religious spokesperson within the domestic violence community. Sometimes also it can take a toll on the religious community because of the time commitments that can be required of the religious leader, making him or her unavailable for other congregational needs. Personnel changes threaten tenuous alliances, shifting economic times and altering resource allocations mean that groups can never take for granted continued support for their efforts, and population expansion bringing even greater religious and cultural diversity means that the collaborative table must be ever-expanding. Thus, the addition of new people representing religious and cultural constituencies that may not have participated before in any collaborative venture on domestic violence seems to necessitate that collaborative dialogue always revert back to a discussion fixated on a rather elementary level. This is frustrating for seasoned professionals and makes it very difficult to bring newcomers on board with those who have been working together for some time. Newcomers can be easily discouraged by what they see as established partnerships and veterans of the collaborative process can feel like they are wasting their time. Thus, maintaining momentum creates challenges that must be identified, and discussed, even as strategies to respond to them are generated and implemented. It takes enormous effort to maintain dialogue at the community level, and gains that are made can be very easily lost.

Over the past five years I have conducted fieldwork and worked collaboratively on issues of domestic violence and religious faith with women and men involved in the advocacy community, the criminal justice system, the religious community, and the therapeutic community in several US sites – Eugene, Oregon; Charlotte, North Carolina; and Columbia, Missouri. Working in each of these very diverse cultural contexts has highlighted some of the opportunities and challenges of working within a multi-disciplinary context to create and sustain a dialogue about domestic violence around the collaborative table at the community level. The collaborative dynamics are very similar on both sides of the border, but in Canada there is much less enthusiasm for faith-based initiatives, far fewer experiments, and a reluctance for workers in the advocacy, criminal justice, and therapeutic communities to identify as "people of faith." What this means, then, is that attempts in Canada to forge collaborative ventures with religious leaders are more difficult to establish and maintain in the area of domestic violence, and there is less support for any such initiatives despite our interest in religious diversity. But, arguably, like the context of the United States, differences will be observed in various regional contexts.

Eugene, Oregon is a small city within a state with a very high proportion of religiously-unaffiliated and self-identified "non-religious" people.[9] The state has more than twice the national average (17 per cent vs. 7 per cent) of those who self-classify as religious "nones." In this context, the Eugene Domestic Violence Council brings together representatives from various sectors of the community that interface with the issue of violence in the family. Home to one of the largest faith-based batterer intervention programs in the United States, Eugene is an ideal location to consider dialogue between the sacred and the secular regarding violence in the family. Eugene is also home to WomenSpace, an umbrella organization offering services and drop-in facilities for victims/survivors, a women's shelter, legal aid and advocacy services, and a broad range of programs providing education and support. In this context, community dialogue concerning domestic violence brings into the conversation the faith community primarily through the executive director and staff of Christians As Family Advocates (CAFA), a faith-based agency with a series of professional programs related to abuse. The reputation of CAFA, along with its executive director (who founded it many years ago), within the criminal justice, advocacy, and religious communities is pervasive and strong. There was no sense that its work was compromised by religious persuasion, nor any evidence that the agency was proselytizing clients, or reluctant to accept clients from a variety of faiths (or no expressed faith). Without exception, those in the criminal justice and advocacy communities were supportive – indeed enthusiastic – of the work of CAFA and comfortable making referrals to its many programs. The bidirectional referral network in Eugene between CAFA and other secular agencies attempted to offer a seamless set of services for those whose families had been impacted by domestic violence. However, even in this context, fiscal realities – especially for those working in the criminal justice system as judges, and parole and probation officers – meant that there was far too much work and far too few staff. Dialogue in the public square, in Eugene, was augmented by respect for a faith-based agency and its credentialed and competent staff. Despite all these advantages, however, it was still difficult to bring religious leaders of any faith perspective to the collaborative table. In informal conversations we learned that this was often because they simply wished to defer to the agency – metaphorically washing their hands of direct involvement – so that they would not be confronted directly with the impact of violence in families of faith.

In Charlotte, North Carolina, the African American churches – or rather women within the African American churches – have taken the lead in establishing and supporting the collaborative community response as far as the faith community is concerned. Charlotte, known as the "City of Churches," is an ideal location to explore the intersection of gender, race, religion, and domestic violence. While many congregations and their leaders have been reticent to speak out against domestic violence or respond compassionately to those impacted by it, women within the African American churches have a long history of looking out for one another when obstacles are faced by their "sisters." Because so many African American women here are deeply committed to their faiths and to the struggle to eradicate abuse, it would be hard to imagine how conversation in the public square could occur without reference to religion. Even in meetings of the North Carolina Coalition Against Domestic Violence – with its strong feminist underpinnings – and the local advocacy committees, issues of spirituality and faith are discussed openly and often. At times this relationship between religion and domestic violence is mediated by African American women clergy, but often it is lay women within the African American churches that pioneer the dialogue. Given the religious landscape in Charlotte, many workers in the criminal justice and therapeutic communities are also people of faith, working in a secular context, but adding a spiritual dimension to their work or religious faith to the conversation. While their work is not "faith-based," it is "faith-enriched" since issues of spirituality and religion are raised frequently within all the sectors of the domestic violence community. It is not uncommon to hear police officers, court advocates, social workers, and the full range of community-based service providers refer to the role of spirituality and religion in matters involving abuse in the family. Yet, in this context too, bringing male religious leaders to the collaborative table is a challenge – they defer to the women in their congregations, or others within their churches who respond to abuse from the vantage point of their professional work.

In contrast to Charlotte and Eugene, Columbia (Missouri) represents "America's heartland." Amidst the rural landscape, and with less cultural diversity, Columbia is home to some mega-churches and the full range of both conservative and liberal Protestants. In this university town, there is an array of services that are provided by either the university or professional schools within the academy. The shelter has several connections with local congregations, mediated by relationships between staff and their churches or connections within those churches. The women clergy here also are an important feature of understanding the public dialogue between abuse and religion, though in this context there are few African Americans.

Across the United States, dialogue at the local level on the issue of domestic violence cannot ignore the role of religious leaders or their congregations. These are important allies in providing services and offering a prophetic voice to condemn violence in the family context. Yet, within the United States there are distinct differences in *how* the discussion is framed, *who* is invited to the collaborative community table and *what* is expected of the various constituents. Faith-based services and faith-enriched workers in community-based agencies offer critical mediating roles in the public dialogue. Sometimes it is their credentials that bring them to the table, or their work experiences. Sometimes it is their religious perspective, or the delicate relationship of negotiating multiple identities – such as a survivor and advocate.

In smaller studies, we have considered the Jamaican or Croatian contexts. In the Caribbean country of Jamaica, the interface between religion and domestic violence can be found at almost every turn. Advocates in Kingston, the capital city, work closely with agencies where most or all of their professional staff are people who are strongly affiliated with their churches. By far most of the social workers, advocates,

and health workers with whom we had conversations were men and
women with deep faith commitments. They saw no discord between
their work and their religious identities. Secular agencies, in fact, were
dependent on churches and their leaders to assist in the struggle to
respond to those impacted by domestic violence and to try to model
violence-free family living. While pastors reported some reluctance to
speak out about the issue from the pulpit, they were deeply involved with
men who were violent and women who were their victims. Under very challenging conditions, with so much poverty and so much violence, religious
leaders and congregations were involved in dialogue about domestic
violence and their role in working together with community agencies.

In contemporary Croatia, our studies of religious leaders and social
workers revealed that there is virtually no dialogue about domestic violence and religion, and no optimism that such conversations would ever
occur. Workers in secular agencies say little about their faith or personal
life circumstances, fearing that it would bring great condemnation from
their superiors. Religious leaders appear to have little interest in any
dialogue with those who work in the helping professions – regarding
their work to be a potential challenge to the missions of the churches.
There are few shelters in the country and in interviews with some of
those involved in the advocacy community we learned that they were
rather hostile to the involvement of any people who were religiously
inclined, fearing that they would offer advice or assistance that would
undermine women's physical or emotional safety.

The Relationship between Religion and Domestic Violence in the Public Square: Where Does Atlantic Canada Fit?

Twenty years ago when I first began a series of studies investigating
how religious leaders in New Brunswick, Nova Scotia, Prince Edward
Island, and Newfoundland responded to women, children, and men
in the aftermath of domestic violence, many in the academy and the
secular community raised an eyebrow to question my judgment. They
felt that there was no role for religious voices at the collaborative community table and they were not shy is saying so. From this perspective,
religion was part of the problem undergirding why domestic violence
was rampant in the community; few could envision how it could be part
of the solution. In part this is an example of some of the themes identified in Paul Bowlby's chapter in this collection – it was a reaction to the
failed Victorian social imaginary of a Christian nation. The influence

of secularization fuelled a desire to separate completely talk of human rights from any language with religious overtones. The struggle to get domestic violence on the secular agenda had been in large measure a feminist project and this constituency in particular was not at all enthusiastic about incorporating voices informed by religion into the debate. Yet, religion was still thriving in many parts of Atlantic Canada – especially in rural communities. And with a paucity of trained workers in domestic violence outside the smaller cities and urban areas, pastors, priests, and other religious leaders continued to be one of the very few resources available when there was crisis in the family context.

Another factor worth noting is the lack of cultural diversity in most rural communities in Atlantic Canada, in part a reflection of the unwillingness of many immigrant families to stay in the region for a protracted period of time. Whereas notions of cultural competence in the advocacy community outside Atlantic Canada often surfaced in debates about how transition houses might meet the needs of the women who sought help there, these issues were slower in coming to the fore in the Atlantic region. And through our early fieldwork we learned that many women of strong religious convictions in Atlantic Canada chose to seek help first within their religious congregation or its leadership. Our very high response rate to surveys and interview requests in eastern Canada amongst clergy (often over 75 per cent) is a further indicator that the issue was impacting their work, whether they wanted it to or not. Throughout Canada, and in particular in Atlantic Canada, there was a reluctance on the part of many workers in community-based agencies to declare – or even acknowledge – their own personal religious backgrounds or persuasions. This reluctance differentiated criminal justice, advocacy, and therapeutic staff here from many that we interviewed in the United States and in the Caribbean. In David Lyon and Marguerite Van Die's book, *Rethinking Church, State and Modernity: Canada between Europe and America* (2000), I wrote a chapter in which I argued that the data I had been collecting on domestic violence was evidence that religious faith was a resource that many victims or survivors of domestic violence called upon at their point of need, and that religious professionals were part of the solution to any collaborative community response to reducing violence. The rapidly changing nature of religious and cultural diversity in the Canadian context over the last ten years has impacted my work in that fewer scholars or activists now raise an eyebrow when it is suggested that religious leaders collaborate with others in the community to respond to victims, abusers, or their families.

Notions around best practices for cultural competence, interestingly, have opened the dialogue for divergent religious voices to be present – in western Canada first, but now also in the Atlantic region. One further point to be raised involves the degree to which a social system of women helping women operates within congregational life in Atlantic Canada. Informal support structures within communities – especially religious ones – are aided in the Atlantic region by a less mobile population and smaller church and residential communities. Women run into each other in the neighbourhood, at the grocery store, and at church, and the support they offer those in need is the safety net that many depend upon when violence strikes at home. In our research, many women of faith in Atlantic Canada bemoan how poorly informed their pastors are about issues involving abuse, and clergy's limited understanding of community-based resources. Yet, while they may be disappointed with church leadership, it does not stop them individually from reaching out to another woman at her point of need or looking for help themselves within the faith community when abuse threatens their physical or emotional health.

Conclusion

Religious faith and domestic violence are comingled. The story of what happens when religious people look for help in the aftermath of domestic violence is replete with spiritual overtones, as it is with practical and emotional issues. Whether the abused or those who abuse others are helped first by their church or a secular agency, it is critical that those who respond understand both the issue of domestic violence and the nature of religious faith. When domestic violence is discussed in the public area, it is critical that there is a place in the collaborative community dialogue for those who understand the specific vulnerabilities and specific needs of highly religious people. Perspectives informed by religious faith are not only part of the problem associated with domestic violence, they must be part of the solution to it. For this to happen – for bridges to be built between secular and sacred frameworks – and for movement between these perspectives to be bidirectional, there must be mutual respect and understanding, built on a foundational belief that ending domestic violence involves the entire community. In no small measure the success of such true collaboration involves the valuing of credentials, including emotional, experiential, and religious currency that various players bring to the collaborative table; negotiating the delicate terrain of faith-enriched, faith-based, faith-hostile and faith-neutral responses to domestic violence; and a sincere belief that a failure to understand religious diversity compromises best practices and increases risk in any community responses (criminal justice, therapeutic, advocacy) to domestic violence.

NOTES

1 Nancy Nason-Clark would like to acknowledge with gratefulness the agencies that have funded her research program over the past twenty years, including the Louisville Institute for the Study of Protestantism and American Culture, the Social Sciences and Humanities Research Council, the Lawson Foundation, and most recently the Lilly Endowment, which provided a five-year grant to enable the development of the RAVE Project.

2 Over the years I have had the privilege of working with a wonderful group of men and women, some of whom began their academic careers as graduate students under my supervision. As well the RAVE Project enabled me to work with colleagues from a variety of disciplines, located in various places in Canada and the United States.

3 Several manuscripts based on my research program are referenced throughout this article. Over the years some of the research is quantitative, whereas other studies are qualitative in nature; some has involved victims, survivors, and perpetrators, while other projects have focussed on those who work with individuals and families affected by violence.

4 *Holy hush* and *sacred silence* are phrases I use to draw attention to the spiritual and practical motivations and implications of religious leaders failing to respond adequately to domestic violence in families of faith (Nason-Clark 1999).

5 See www.theraveproject.org

6 The names of people and the agencies are fictitious; the stories, however, are based on interview transcripts.

7 This is true within the evangelical community, but also within mainstream denominations (Nason-Clark 2000b, 2004, 2005). We have collected data from Baptist, Wesleyan, United, Anglican, and Salvation Army personnel in Atlantic Canada, but in other jurisdictions I have worked with Roman Catholic, Jewish, and Pentecostal communities as well, and their leaders believe the results would be similar there. In a project in western Canada (Sevcik, Nason-Clark, Rothery, and Pynn 2011) results were similar – to be specific, religious leaders did not believe they were equipped to respond

to situations involving domestic violence, despite the fact that congregants continued to seek the leaders' help in these matters. As a result,
women of faith are often disappointed with the assistance religious leaders provide.

8 As of 2011, the funding to FaithLink is in jeopardy and there is no succession planning in the aftermath of the retirement of its leadership core. It
will likely not continue and so the collaborative work there with religious
organizations and religious leadership is threatened.

9 Data found on Adherents.com (2002).

REFERENCES

Beaman-Hall, Lori, and Nancy Nason-Clark. 1997. "Partners or Protagonists?
The Transition House Movement and Conservative Churches." *Affilia: Journal of Women and Social Work* 12(2): 176–96.

Brown, Joanne, and Carole Bohn, eds. 1989. *Christianity, Patriarchy and Abuse:
A Feminist Critique.* Cleveland: The Pilgrim Press.

Clarke, Rita-Lou. 1986. *Pastoral Care of Battered Women.* Philadelphia: Westminster Press.

DeKeseredy, Walter, and Linda MacLeod. 1998. *Woman Abuse: A Sociological
Story.* Toronto: Harcourt Brace.

Dobash, Russell P., and Emerson R. Dobash. 1979. *Violence Against Wives:
A Case Against the Patriarchy.* New York: Free Press.

Fiorenza, Elisabeth S., and Shawn M. Copeland, eds. 1994. *Violence Against
Women.* London: SCM Press.

Fisher-Townsend, Barbara. 2008. "Searching for the Missing Puzzle Piece: The
Potential of Faith in Changing Violent Behavior." In *Beyond Abuse in the Chris-
tian Home: Raising Voices for Change,* edited by Catherine C. Kroeger, Nancy
Nason-Clark, and Barbara Fisher-Townsend, 100–20. Eugene: Wipf and Stock.

Fisher-Townsend, Barbara, Nancy Nason-Clark, Lanette Ruff, and Nancy
Murphy. 2008. "I Am Not Violent: Men's Experience in Group." In *Beyond
Abuse in the Christian Home: Raising Voices for Change,* edited by Catherine
C. Kroeger, Nancy Nason-Clark, and Barbara Fisher-Townsend, 78–99.
Eugene: Wipf and Stock.

Fortune, Marie. 1991. *Violence in the Family: A Workshop Curriculum for Clergy
and Other Helpers.* Cleveland: The Pilgrim Press.

Giesbrecht, Norman, and Irene Sevcik. 2000. "The Process of Recovery and
Rebuilding Among Abused Women in Conservative Evangelical Subculture." *Journal of Family Violence* 15(3): 229–48.

Halsey, Peggy. 1984. *Abuse in the Family: Breaking the Church's Silence*. New York: Office of Ministries with Women in Crisis, General Board of Global Ministries, United Methodist Church.

Horton, Anne, and Judith Williamson, eds. 1988. *Abuse and Religion: When Praying Isn't Enough*. New York: D.C. Heath and Company.

Kroeger, Catherine, and Nancy Nason-Clark. 2010. *No Place for Abuse: Biblical and Practical Resources to Counteract Domestic Violence* (rev. ed). Downers Grove: InterVarsity Press.

Loseke, Donileen R. 1992. *The Battered Woman and Shelters: The Social Construction of Wife Abuse*. Albany: State University of New York Press.

Lyon, David, and Marguerite Van Die. 2000. *Rethinking Church, State and Modernity: Canada between Europe and America*. Toronto: University of Toronto Press.

Martin, Del. 1981. *Battered Wives*. San Francisco: New Glide.

Nason-Clark, Nancy. 1996. "Religion and Violence Against Women: Exploring the Rhetoric and the Response of Evangelical Churches in Canada." *Social Compass* 43(4): 515–36.

Nason-Clark, Nancy. 1997. *The Battered Wife: How Christians Confront Family Violence*. Louisville: Westminster John Knox Press.

Nason-Clark, Nancy. 1999. "Shattered Silence or Holy Hush: Emerging Definitions of Violence Against Women." *Journal of Family Ministry* 13(1): 39–56.

Nason-Clark, Nancy. 2000a. "The Steeple and the Shelter: Secularization and Resacralization in Contemporary Canada." In *Religion, Secularization and Modernity in Canada*, edited by David Lyon and Marguerite Van Die, 249–62. Toronto: University of Toronto Press.

Nason-Clark, Nancy. 2000b. "Making the Sacred Safe: Woman Abuse and Communities of Faith." *Sociology of Religion* 61(4): 349–68.

Nason-Clark, Nancy. 2004. "When Terror Strikes at Home: The Interface Between Religion and Domestic Violence." *Journal for the Scientific Study of Religion* 42(3): 303–10.

Nason-Clark, Nancy. 2005. "Linking Research and Social Action: Violence, Religion and the Family. A Case for Public Sociology." *Review of Religious Research* 46(3): 221–34.

Nason-Clark, Nancy. 2009. "Christianity and the Experience of Domestic Violence: What Does Faith Have to do With it?" *Social Work and Christianity* 36(4): 379–93.

Nason-Clark, Nancy, and Barbara Fisher-Townsend. forthcoming. *Men Who Abuse*. Under contract with Oxford University Press.

Nason-Clark, Nancy, Barbara Fisher-Townsend, Cathy Holtmann, Steve McMullin, and Lanette Ruff. 2009. "The RAVE Project: Developing

Web-Based Religious Resources for Social Action on Domestic Violence." *Critical Social Work* 10(1): 1–12.

Nason-Clark, Nancy, Nancy Murphy, Barbara Fisher-Townsend, and Lanette Ruff. 2003. "An Overview of the Characteristics of the Clients at a Faith-based Batterers' Intervention Program." *Journal of Religion and Abuse* 5(4): 51–72.

Sevcik, Irene, Nancy Nason-Clark, Michael Rothery, and Robert Pynn. 2011. "Finding their Voices and Speaking Out: Research Among Women of Faith in Western Canada." In *Responding to Abuse in Christian Homes*, edited by Nancy Nason-Clark, Catherine Clark Kroeger, and Barbara Fisher-Townsend, 169–89. Eugene: Wipf and Stock.

Stirling, Mary L, Catherine A. Cameron, Nancy Nason-Clark, and Baukje Miedema, eds. 2004. *Understanding Abuse: Partnering for Change*. Toronto: University of Toronto Press.

Straus, Murray A., and Richard J. Gelles. 1986. "Societal Change and Change in Family Violence from 1975 to 1985 as Revealed by Two National Surveys." *Journal of Marriage & Family* 48(3): 465–79.

Straus, Murray A., Richard J. Gelles, and Suzanne K. Steinmetz. 1980. *Behind Closed Doors: Domestic Violence in the American Family*. New Brunswick: Transaction.

Thorne-Finch, Ron. 1992. *Ending the Silence: The Origins and Treatment of Male Violence against Women*. Toronto: University of Toronto Press.

Timmins, Leslie, ed. 1995. *Listening to the Thunder: Advocates Talk About the Battered Women's Movement*. Vancouver: Women's Research Centre.

Walker, Gillian A. 1990. *Family Violence and the Women's Movement: The Conceptual Politics of Struggle*. Toronto: University of Toronto Press.

Weaver, Andrew J. 1993. "Psychological Trauma: What Clergy Need to Know." *Pastoral Psychology* 41: 385–408.

PART III

The Public/Private Continuum

7 Beyond Religious Accommodation in the Workplace

A Philosophy of Diversity

SOLANGE LEFEBVRE

The private sector has not received enough attention in the debate on reasonable accommodations in Canada.[1] This circumstance represents quite a paradox, since the 1985 Canadian case in which the concept of "reasonable accommodations" was first applied to religion precisely concerned the private sector (*Ontario Human Rights Commission and O'Malley v. Simpsons-Sears Ltd.*). A woman working for a big department store, having converted to the Adventist Church, complained to the Ontario Human Rights Commission that her employer refused to arrange a work schedule allowing her to obey the Adventist Church's strict observance of the Sabbath from sundown Friday to sundown Saturday. In its summary, the Ontario Human Rights Commission concluded that "the employer did not discharge the onus of showing that it had taken reasonable steps to accommodate the complainant." That same year, the Supreme Court, ruling on another case, also in the private sector (*R. v. Big M Drug Mart Ltd*), handed down a groundbreaking decision that reshaped the fundamental definition of religious freedom. At issue was Alberta's law forbidding Sunday shopping. In this case, upon a re-examination of the *Lord's Day Act* and Sunday Observance, the Court concluded that "Any law, purely religious in purpose, which denies non-Christians the right to work on Sunday denies them the right to practise their religion and infringes their religious freedom."

In the new millennium, more cases involving public schools and health care institutions were brought to court, especially in the province of Québec. By that time, religion had, so to speak, become a "public" issue, and many cases came to be debated in the public arena, especially those concerning public and semi-public institutions and community organizations. In Montréal's public schools, the kirpan worn by young

Multani was a source of controversy, as were many other cases around some Jewish and Muslim symbols and practices (*Syndicat Northcrest v. Amselem 2004*; *Multani v. Commission scolaire Marguerite-Bourgeoys* 2006). But what was happening in the private sector?

At least in the Québec context, would it come as a surprise that private firms might not wish to find themselves in the spotlight of public controversy? Perhaps this motivating force could explain why the private sector generally became increasingly tight-lipped on the topic. After the Bouchard-Taylor Commission, in 2009 and 2010, to test this hunch, and to find out what was actually being done in the private sector, I conducted a study of the private sector's strategies for adapting to religious diversity and a number of training sessions on this theme for a few private firms.[2] The qualitative research itself included 15 companies (11 in the Montréal area and 4 in remote areas), where 25 interviews with executives, vice-presidents of human resources, and employees were carried out.[3] Three focus group sessions with employees also took place in the manufacturing and financial sectors. In addition, results based on a preliminary analysis were presented at a discussion session with 25 business leaders. While these numbers may appear small, quantitatively speaking, they are nonetheless rather significant for the purposes of qualitative research. A semi-structured interview framework was used throughout. How do private businesses manage cultural and religious diversity? We know very little about this question, except for a few cases made public because they have ended up in court. It was in the aftershock of the Bouchard-Taylor public inquiry, which focused primarily on issues of cultural and religious accommodations in public and semi-public institutions and community organizations, that the lack of research on these issues, to my view, fully emerged.

Before presenting a few findings from this research, and in order to better understand and situate them, the first section analyses the way the Bouchard-Taylor Commission addressed or did not address the private sector on the reasonable accommodations issue. The second looks at the main dimensions of the legal context guiding the strategies used in Québec and at the federal level to handle diversity in the workplace and how management addresses cultural and religious diversity in some companies. In the second section, a few results from the qualitative research are presented. The first section outlines some of the main findings; the second and third sections present a selection of the empirical data obtained from the private firms that agreed to be part of the research. The key finding of the research is the following: instead of accommodating, private businesses who are explicitly managing diversity, have chosen to pursue what I have termed a global "philosophy of diversity." It involves a vision of diversity that, instead of focusing on religion as the sole source of tension and burden on the enterprises, situates religion as one among many issues.

Part I – Context

The Bouchard-Taylor Commission and the Private Sector

In the spring of 2007, historian and sociologist Gérard Bouchard and philosopher Charles Taylor were given a mandate by the Government of Québec to investigate a number of issues related to the reasonable accommodation of religious practices, which were generating controversies across the province (Bouchard and Taylor 2008). Among its fundamental orientations, the final report recommends supporting instances of concerted adjustments in all the environments concerned, in order to avoid a systematic recourse to litigation. It cites the "citizen route" as the preferred way to adequately respond to reasonable accommodation requests. In fact, the latter already seems to be the case. According to the report, very few accommodation cases make their way into the legal system, whereas, on the ground, many adjustments are being negotiated on a daily basis (Bouchard and Taylor 2008, 162). That is precisely what I was looking for in my research on the private sector.

As mentioned in the introduction, after a very detailed analysis, the search for references to the private sector in the documents published by the Bouchard-Taylor Commission – final reports, research reports, briefs – revealed (to my great surprise) that this sector receives almost no attention in the Commission's work. Very few private sector briefs were submitted. In the section on the interpretation of their mandate, the co-chairs write the following:

> Given the range and complexity of the questions to be analysed, we decided to concentrate our efforts on the question of accommodation in public institutions, where most of the problem cases arose that fuelled the crisis. Consequently, we will focus to a limited extent on businesses, despite the difficulties that they are experiencing, as in any other pluricultural milieu. We must also point out that the business community, which submitted only one brief and participated very little in the public debate, had little contact with the Commission (Bouchard and Taylor 2008, 33–4).

Was this scenario also the case during the consultation process that preceded the development of the final report? I found that the commissioners, in fact, included private companies in the initial consultation document in several ways that focused on work-related issues and discussed integration and language issues (Bouchard and Taylor 2007). It touches on what is fully developed in the final report: the alleged manipulation or twisting of facts by the media in a number of heated debates, including the "Mont-Saint-Grégoire sugarhouse" incident. Although "a representative of Astrolabe, a Muslim association, [had] met with the sugarhouse's owners to discuss certain changes to the menu, which would apply solely to the members of the group," an article in a local paper, "Accommodating Sugarhouses: Pork-free Pea Soup and Prayers in the Dance Hall," contributed to a sensationalist response (Bouchard and Taylor 2008, 57, 72). A "sugarhouse" is, of course, a private-sector business, like the YMCA, which was also involved in a similar incident. In this case, a private agreement between the gymnasium and Yetev Lev synagogue next door led to the public perception that because of "the duty of accommodation, the management of the YMCA was obliged to acquiesce to the demand from Orthodox Jews to change the gymnasium windows to prevent young Jews in the area from seeing women in training sweat suits" (Bouchard and Taylor 2008, 70). The report also presented the feelings of some citizens that the kinds of exaggerated perceptions and various exemptions requested and obtained in the workplace (religious holidays, in particular) represented "trivial incidents" through which "our society's core values are being undermined" (Bouchard and Taylor 2008, 68, 72). Moreover, the consultation document often provides private sector examples when inviting citizens to imagine solutions to problems.

This imbalance raises the question of why the private sector failed to respond to the Commission's invitation. As previously stated, it is certainly a matter of confidentiality and fear of public opinion. But, despite the private sector's limited participation, careful analysis of the documentation nevertheless provides glimpses of a few private-sector views. More than 900 briefs were submitted to the Commission. The final report indicates that only one brief was received from the private sector. It is difficult to determine what type of brief would necessarily be specifically linked to the private sector. My analysis found a dozen or so documents that could be linked to the private sector, if the briefs from various professional associations (notably the Interprofessional Council, Conseil des métiers de la construction, Ordre des comptables, etc.) are included.

These briefs primarily discuss very broad issues and contain very lit-tle information on the concrete management of accommodations. They nonetheless present a number of interesting ideas. I shall touch on two of them. First, the Canadian Italian Business and Professional Associa-tion brief points out that the integration of Italian immigrants at the beginning of the century was not easy, but that it improved over time, thanks to the fact that these immigrants took an active stance (CIBPA 2007). Second, the Foundation of Enterprises for the Recruitment of For-eign Agricultural Workers (Fondation des entreprises en recrutement de main-d'oeuvre agricole étrangère) states that labour in this sector is largely dependent on seasonal immigrant workers and that in a num-ber of situations things have worked out well for workers and employ-ers alike, especially when work groups are homogenous, that is, the individuals are from the same country, religion, and/or culture (Fon-dation 2007). The Foundation's brief presents the example of a group composed of devout Catholics from South America, who freely display their images and statues of the Virgin Mary in the workplace.

More generally, a keyword search of all documents related to the Commission shows that the private sector is mentioned several times in various briefs and documents. The main findings include:

- High unemployment among certain minority groups is often men-tioned and integration is highlighted as a priority;
- The briefs call for more recognition of immigrants' training and skills, to facilitate their integration;
- Muslims are often mentioned as an example to illustrate the dis-crimination certain immigrants are subject to as well as to point out the diversity among them.

In my opinion, one of the most relevant briefs on these matters was prepared by the Québec Bar. The following statement clearly reflects one of the key findings of the research that will be elaborated in a fur-ther section:

> Many jurisprudence examples show that reasonable accommodation is part of Québec culture and that the technique developed by labour law courts can be adapted to other milieus ... Thus, the duty of accommoda-tion is a day-to-day reality in workplaces. The Québec government should draw inspiration from them, since they so effectively managed diversity by creating tools or policies meeting the demands of their employees ... But it is interesting to go beyond the legal debate to see that the goal of

reasonable accommodations is increasingly being outstripped by diversity practices, resulting in several fruitful initiatives.[4] (Barreau du Québec 2007; my translation)

The Bar strongly advocates such diversity practices and it is true that, as I will explain later in this chapter, this philosophy of diversity is one of the most original and refreshing ideas put forward by the private sector. In the following sections, we refer to key ideas included in the Bouchard-Taylor Report and weigh them against our findings.

The Legal Context

The legal context shaping the management of cultural and religious diversity has four main underpinnings: the Québec *Charter of Human Rights and Freedoms*, the *Canadian Charter of Rights and Freedoms*, the Provincial Equal Access Employment Programs, and the *Federal Employment Equity Act*. First, Québec firms are primarily required to comply with the Québec *Charter of Human Rights and Freedoms* and the *Canadian Charter of Rights and Freedoms*, most particularly with the provisions against discrimination related to sex, age, ethnic, and religious affiliation, as well as those related to respect for freedom of conscience and religion. Second, they must comply with Québec's *Act Respecting Equal Access to Employment in Public Bodies*.[5] This legislation seeks to protect groups that may be discriminated against, such as: women, persons with disabilities, Aboriginal people, people who are part of a visible minority, and those whose maternal language is neither French nor English and who belong to a group other than Aboriginal or a visible minority. This law applies in the case of public bodies with more than 100 employees. In addition, equal access employment programs must be implemented when a "contract compliance program" is in place.[6] Third, federal employers with over 100 employees and financial institutions, particularly banks, are subject to the *Employment Equity Act* and to the *Canadian Charter of Rights and Freedoms*. It is important to note that this Act does not mention religion, religious freedom, or freedom of conscience. As in the case of the Québec contract compliance program, the designated groups are women, Aboriginal people, persons with disabilities, and persons who are part of a visible minority. Employers subject to the Act must report annually on their activities (including demographic data on their employees) and maintain tools to monitor their application of the Act.

My results seem to indicate that the *Employment Equity Act* as well as mandatory programs promoting equal access to employment are quite effective. In fact, the best diversity practices were found in two firms subject to the Federal Act. A third firm subject to Québec's equal access employment programs also seemed to manage diversity issues well, although its employees refused to give us access to this firm's internal reports. Among the businesses included in the research, there were two daycare centres. While considered private firms, such businesses are also subject to public regulation. The findings show that, owing to the clear guidelines provided by the Government of Québec (which is also their main source of funding), these businesses emerge as above average in their management of diversity. Firms that explicitly manage diversity have developed a philosophy of diversity in harmony with equity legislation. But these firms first organized their diversity management policies and strategies in response to issues linked to discrimination against women, thereby creating a framework for handling other types of diversity as well. Note, however, that religion is often implicit in this approach, and that it remains marginal compared to what are recognized as the real challenges of responding to diversity, in particular, those related to accommodations for persons with disabilities. Finally, the notion of reasonable accommodations is central for handling diversity in the private sector. It would seem that most of the literature on this issue concerns those aspects covered by equity laws.[7] In fact, a careful look at some of the research and publications in Québec shows that religion is considered more explicitly as a factor in the research on the public sector.[8]

Part II – Research Findings on the Private Sector in Québec

This section introduces the main findings of my qualitative research conducted among 15 Québec firms. The key finding is as follows. In the management field, the guiding principle would be akin to a "philosophy of diversity." First inspired by gender issues, this approach now appears to be the logic applied to all other types of diversity management (Kossek and Lobel 1996; Wilson and Sayers 1996; Özbilgin 2009). This finding was reflected in the interviews conducted in the few firms that showed the most significant diversity management strategies. Religion would thus be just "one more" diversity among many others, such as: gender, sexual orientation, disabilities, ethnicity, age, generation, and so on. The larger firms all have diversity management departments or an office of diversity, and, in Canada, as was previously explained, they must comply with certain equity laws. It is worth noting that, in my review of the literature on management and diversity, I have noticed that the religious factor itself is currently receiving less attention in the private sector. Religion may be one of the most recent diversity factors to enter public debate, but perhaps not the last.

Main Conclusions

A Specific Approach to "The Reasonable"

Despite this philosophy of diversity, the diverse data collected left me with a contradictory impression. The interviewees demonstrated openness to diversity, but even those with much experience in the diversity arena mention only a few examples of significant religious accommodations. Underlying what informants say is a conviction that the response to any request will be considerably limited by concerns about the firm's productivity and sensitivity to its customers.

Private ... and Confidential

It was crucial throughout the interviewing process to ensure confidentiality in regard to the identity of both the firms and the employees participating in the research. This assurance was necessary for legal, ethical, and simply business reasons. Even firms known as diversity "champions" expected strict confidentiality. In the Québec context and beyond, models of openness to diversity, especially when it comes to religion, run the risk of alienating the more secularist segments of the population who oppose any accommodation of religious diversity.

Lack of Resources, Eagerness for Immigrant Workers in Remote Areas

There exists a factor challenging some businesses in Québec today: a labour shortage. This problem seems to be most evident in remote areas. Interviewees from regions far removed from major urban centres have serious problems attracting immigrant labour, despite the efforts made to date. But companies that want to provide potential employees from visible or religious minorities with greater opportunities for mobility within the province are calling for more effective strategies to improve the readiness (and, at times, to counteract the discriminatory attitudes) of traditionally homogenous communities.

In this regard, I cite here an eloquent remark from a Québec manager of French-Canadian origin: "I have a marvelous Muslim employee who wears a veil; how can I make her work in a rural branch? It's impossible; she would be subject to too much prejudice ... and it would not be good for business." He appreciated his female Muslim employee, and he was also facing a labour force shortage in remote areas. This manager told us he was expecting some support from the state (like training tools, awareness campaigns, clear governmental statements) to help change mentalities and help develop a greater openness to diverse religious symbols and practices.

Yet in my interviews with other representatives from various companies, the conventional "racist" image of homogenous communities was not the dominant one; quite the contrary. Instead, I heard sad stories about huge efforts made to welcome immigrants, but without success. To the question: "Around religious diversity, can you think of issues you are currently facing or anticipating?" One female consultant working for a human resources consulting firm established in several Québec towns, with about 80 employees across the provincial territory and about 40 in the regional urban centres, answered:

> In human resources, occurrences are likely to be less frequent in rural areas, for obvious reasons. But in general, even consultants from Toronto sometimes complain about the complexity of managing diversity. In rural areas, the thought of attracting immigrants has moved to the back burner because of multiple failures in the past. For example, the community worked hard to take in a few refugee families, but because of a lack of other members from the same community, services and specific resources, these people quickly left for larger cities after their "probation" period. The term used is "defeatism." In all areas, the main issue is the lack of resources and the struggle to retain workers, to the extent that firms are now investing in the youngest members of the diverse rural communities, to attract and retain them, instead of trying to attract immigrants.

This characteristic aspect is of great significance towards understanding the philosophy of diversity at work in regions that are situated away from large urban centres. Often portrayed as xenophobic, in some compelling cases, they instead seemed impotent in the act of trying to maintain a population and work force stemming from recent immigrants.

A Fear of Religious Diversity

After the "reasonable accommodations debate," there was a great fear of the complexities that diverse religions would bring to some firms, expressed especially among our interviewees in the Greater Montréal Area. To the question: "Over the past few years, the media has often raised issues related to cultural, ethnic and religious diversity in society (for example, in relation to the activities of the Bouchard-Taylor Commission). Are these issues reflected in your business?" A Montréal account manager from a provincial employment agency with 35 permanent employees and 600 external employees answered: "Yes and no. Diversity is an issue, since many firms are requiring our services to recruit, and saying they just want to hire some 'Tremblays' [a very common name among 'old stock' French-Canadians]. So, yes, we find stereotypes in certain companies."[9] This response confirms the fact that a number of companies maintain a fearful disposition towards recruiting anybody who is likely to ask for certain accommodations of a religious nature. We ought to remind ourselves that the climate surrounding the Bouchard-Taylor Commission was characterized by hyperbolic media coverage with regard to certain accommodations. Additionally, since many public opinions had critiqued religious accommodation practices, it follows that these voices of dissent influenced the manners in which certain companies have perceived such requests. When employees recommend hiring only "Tremblays," it reveals that certain companies prefer hiring employees of French-Canadian origin. But the sentiment also reveals the frequent conflation between accommodations and recent immigration that arose in those debates. In fact, a number of accommodation requests have been submitted by Canadians whose families have been settled in the country for several generations, notably from French-Canadian origins (Bouchard and Taylor 2008, 41, 50).

Statistical Background

The fact that employment equity legislation and equal access employment programs do not explicitly address religion, as explained in the first section, has important consequences. Few statistical surveys of the labour force include religion. From an analysis of Canadian Statistics 2001, one can conclude that Muslims and Sikhs are highly affected by unemployment (Beyer 2010). The jobs they tend to find are concentrated in sectors such as retail, manufacturing, and the food industry. My research findings flag these sectors as sometimes resistant to individual requests for religious accommodations. A careful analysis of the statistics also reveals evidence of considerable differences, across towns and regions, in the proportion of those new immigrants whose religions (Islam, Buddhism, Hinduism, Sikhism) are likely to call for accommodations when their numbers are compared to the general population. The proportions are as follows: all of Québec, 2 per cent; City of Montréal, 4 per cent; Québec City, 0.5 per cent; Saguenay (remote region), 0.1 per cent. The small proportion found in the Saguenay region is typical of all rural regions in Québec.

A Great Variety of Challenges

In the diversity management field, there are at least three different approaches that can be taken: ethno-management, intercultural management, and diversity management (Chevrier 2003; Schneider and Barsoux 2003; Mutabazi and Pierre 2008). There seems to be a relationship between a firm's economic sector, demographic profile of employees and customers, location, and how it approaches diversity management. In this regard, a particular pattern seems to emerge, but our data were not sufficient to demonstrate it extensively; I can however mention a particular example to help illustrate. The composition of the workforce seems to create very different conditions, problems, questions, and solutions. For instance: I conducted some training sessions for a big company established in both Ontario and Québec. In Montréal, the approach was more about ethno-cultural management, since the immigrants, chosen for their francophone linguistic background, represented only a few countries. The challenges faced by the company were thus limited to a few specific ethnic and religious groups. This circumstance was also the case in Ottawa, where the line was drawn between Anglo-Canadians and French-Canadians that led to the adoption of an intercultural approach, in order to support the harmonization of these two significant groups. In Toronto, some teams from the greater urban area were so diverse that ethno-cultural or intercultural approaches were not at all relevant. What was clearly required was a vision based on a philosophy embracing all kinds of diversities. Depending on the composition of the workforce and its location, any of the three approaches could be dominant, or they could be combined.

Methodological Limitations

It is important to note that I can only report on what was said about specific cases. The team never had the opportunity to observe how events played out in reality. Moreover, it is interesting to note that most of the people interviewed at the larger firms were either vice-presidents or managers of human resources. When we asked about religious diversity, we were specifically directed to the organization's human resources department. The nature of the obtained data limits the findings to those individuals in charge of the personnel and activities of such departments. While a few of the employees we spoke with knew very little about diversity in general, one should not overlook the fact that interviewing executives also poses a serious problem: in some cases, we felt we were only allowed to see the corporate image that the firm wishes to project. Only a few employees we could interview sounded like they were candidly representing their opinions. Given the fact that field work on religious diversity is quite rare in the private sector, at least in Québec, our results are nevertheless quite telling. In the context of the current public debates, the importance of confidentiality, as previously exposed, rendered the recruitment of the individuals and groups quite demanding. About one in three companies approached responded to our initial request for their participation in this study.

Oddly enough, among the 25 managers and few employees interviewed, no one had read the Bouchard-Taylor Commission's Report. In their opinion, despite all the debates it sparked, nothing specific seems to have come out of the consultation. They also thought there had been no real follow-up. Most individuals in the firms we visited said they already had an ethics code related to diversity management that they are required to uphold. This trend reminds us that one of the Commission's recommendations for private businesses concerned the need for the government to develop a simple and practical tool to help manage requests for accommodation.

The following sections will provide a few examples and narratives showing how this philosophy has been applied in some of the private companies my team and I visited during the research project. From among our qualitative results and with reference to our interviews, I have chosen to present three examples of positive diversity management and two examples of the kinds of difficulties that businesses encounter today.

Three Examples of Sound Diversity Management

This section presents a number of fruitful solutions to diversity management issues. Although the various companies face everyday challenges, sometimes the simplest solutions seem to be the most effective. We will also see how businesses have developed a philosophy of diversity to address the real world needs of the employees and clientele, while mostly trying to find ways to avoid exacerbating concerns pertaining to religious diversity.

Daycare Centres

We visited two daycare centres to conduct research. The first was a cooperative centre in a small town located in a remote region, with a staff of about 20 employees, all women and French-Canadians. Their clientele was made up of 65 children, the families of which included a few Africans, and previously, one Muslim. The second, in Greater Montréal, comprised 72 regular employees that generally reflected the diversity of the city. The majority of employees were women, including two Muslims who wore distinctive religious symbols. In both cases, a female manager was interviewed.

One interviewee explained that the daycare centre in the remote region is making significant efforts to welcome the very few immigrant clients. Internal documents include regulations regarding specific dietary needs (drawn from information prepared by a Montréal umbrella group) as well as a code of ethics. One example of sensitivity to diversity is the offering of a vegetarian meal option. The following quotation from the manager expresses a realistic view of diversity in that context:

> On a personal level, I have not heard many comments or expressions of interest regarding the Bouchard-Taylor Commission, which is seen as far from us. People in the area are open and like all that is exotic. I am myself fascinated by Montréal's Hasidic Jews. We travel a lot, you know! ... However, if the few immigrants in my region were Arabs with beards, I would maybe associate them with terrorism.

The statement at once expresses a curiosity about visible religious differences, even a fascination or sense of exoticism that is situated in a generally homogenous demographic where few people apart from

French-Canadians live. An expression of Islamophobia nevertheless remains present in the image of the "Arab terrorist with a beard," one that echoes the fears about Islamic fanaticism that were expressed during the reasonable accommodations debates and after 9/11.

The Montréal-area daycare is, on the other hand, very multicultural. Two main findings emerged. First, facing a large number of specific dietary requests, the daycare started serving only vegetarian meals. Second, the daycare noted that requests for accommodations had only increased since the Bouchard-Taylor Commission:

> In our enterprise, there is great diversity ... Out of 72 employees, 40 are from different cultures. They manage as best as possible because it's their bread and butter to work with people from all over the world ... I don't see any other way. Accommodations must be made. It's as simple as that ... and it is managed this way: they meet as a team and handle situations case by case.

This comment is emblematic of the philosophy of diversity that many companies have developed over their years of experience as a simultaneous reflection of the reality of diversity and the desire for economic production within that complex social network.

As a business model, moreover, daycares possess a number of particular traits. Although they are privately operated, they are nonetheless subject to provincial rules and regulations regarding their operation. As a result, they have ready access to a number of useful diversity management tools. On the other hand, daycares are largely concerned with providing services to families and their children and therefore seem more willing to recognize their accommodation requests, whether related to clothing or diets. With regard to the latter, simply offering a vegetarian meal option seems a frequent solution to many of the requests. The daycare in the remote area also offered a diverse variety of menus in this regard. The frequency of requests has also influenced the types of solutions implemented.

Financial Sector

The two firms visited in the financial sector seem quite advanced in their diversity management, in terms of both employee and client profiles. Both a business and a legal reason account for this tendency. In one case, the resources for handling diversity include: several internal documents, calendars of employees' religious holidays, focus group reports on diversity, and information on the location of multipurpose accommodation rooms. Demonstrating the importance of the Employment Equity Act, reports are made each year on the development of measures taken to hire Aboriginal and disabled individuals, and the advancement of visible minorities and women. This firm is a national financial institution with international offices and thousands of employees in Canada, with a minimum of 15 per local office. In Québec, this firm has over 150 branches and thousands of employees. Overall, 64.3 per cent of its employees are women, 31.1 per cent are visible minorities, including Aboriginal people, who account for 1.5 per cent of employees, and 2.8 per cent are people with disabilities. This enterprise was the only one that provided us with internal statistics, based on their annual report on equity law. Asked to react to the Bouchard-Taylor Commission, one female manager spontaneously said: "That is old stuff for us, we are way beyond … the enterprise has already been managing accommodations for a long time. Its experience is so advanced that it can now anticipate almost anything." She went on to explain how the company already had designated multifunctional rooms that could be reserved for prayer and other functions and internal calendars to inform employees about major religious holidays.

The other firm, a supra-regional financial institution, primarily located in Québec, but with national and international offices, did not make internal statistics available to us. It is also subject to the Employment Equity Act. Four executives were interviewed: one female human resources manager responsible for diversity and one male diversity advisor (both at the head office of the company), and two branch managers located in multiethnic neighbourhoods, one male and one female. A focus group was carried out with the employees of one of the branches. Goals exist for developing awareness of diversity among the staff, as a top female human resources manager based at the head office explains:

> Diversity in general is managed by the means of specialized services. For several years, some training tools have been carefully developed but in brief formats. There is an awareness-raising video and a facilitation kit in the format of small cards that can be read and discussed [in a] few minutes at the beginning of meetings. These tools concern diversity in all its forms.

This female manager was very well trained in diversity management, exposing quite clearly the "philosophy of diversity" previously mentioned as a key approach to accommodation requests in the private sector. When asked about the possibility of specific training on religious diversity, she said: "A document about religion would be good. But we must not get into generalizations like 'Jews are like this,' 'Muslims are like that,' and so on. Nowadays, there are too many factors to consider." Her comments demonstrate her sensitivity to stereotyping; she understands that we cannot fit each religion into "a box."

We also visited two branches that were located in very multicultural areas of Montréal. The respective managers interviewed reported that the majority of employees were of diverse nationalities. The following represents the opinion of one of the two managers, a female vice-president of human resources: "Religious diversity is already being managed, in the same way that any other accommodation request is managed. It is in the private domain, so it is managed like any private request." The other manager said:

Diversity is a necessity faced by the company, which adapts to all nationalities. Some clients want to be served by people of the same nationality. Some clients speak neither French nor English. Some speak Russian, for example, so the company must ensure that there is someone who can answer them in Russian.

Despite this discourse on diversity, one could see that there were certain limits to the acceptance of religious diversity. One of the local managers said:

Arrangements can always be made between co-workers, but a cultural or religious reason for leave would not take precedence over any other request. There was one case where an employee requested time off for Ramadan, but he made his request on Friday for the following Monday. The manager could not respond in such a short time, so the employee chose to leave, knowing he would not be able to keep his work hours.

While many protocols are being developed by companies in the private sector, there nonetheless remains a reciprocal nature to reasonable accommodation.

More generally, in the context of the Bouchard-Taylor Commission, average employees were presented as not being favourable to reasonable accommodations for religious reasons. But they may have been reacting to the distorted facts reported in numerous media:

> These issues reflect the day-to-day reality of life in the enterprise, and are often discussed among employees during lunch break. Their customers are very diverse. Employees are hired also to respond to the needs of customers. Although opinions, at the time of the Bouchard-Taylor Commission, diverged, everyone was able to take part in the dialogue on the subject of reasonable accommodation. The majority of employees found that the majority of accommodation requests appeared to be exaggerated.

Many of the people working in these situations were also able to detect a disconnection between what the media had been reporting and what they were actually witnessing in the workplace.

High-tech Sector

We were able to interview only a few employees from one multinational firm with thousands of employees engaged in technological manufacturing. Clearly obliged to deal with diversity in all its forms and also subject to the *Employment Equity Act*, this firm did not, however, provide us with any statistics. Its complaint cases are classified as confidential, so we were unable to access them. We interviewed four executives, including two vice-presidents, one human resources manager, and one union official, plus one Muslim employee.

The four executives interviewed showed curiosity about our research findings. They were not familiar with religious diversity and provided only anecdotal examples. Again, in general, it seems that in very large companies, contentious issues are seldom brought to the attention of senior management; instead, immediate supervisors manage them on a case-by-case basis. A human resources manager explained:

> The person responsible for company ethics may receive complaints, but nothing is planned ahead. So, there is an ethics and compliance manager. This person receives anonymous complaints about harassment, promotion issues, etc. There is a complaint file and a database, but everything remains anonymous.

Despite their lack of concrete examples, some executives told us without reserve that their company was not exempt from various types of prejudice, especially in the context of the reasonable accommodation debate. As a human resources manager puts it:

> Cultural differences "sometimes cause problems" (for the past two to three years, mainly – which meant, at the time of the interview, since 2006). It is important for French Canadian employees to maintain their Québec values in relation to immigrants. Old prejudices are present at all levels of the hierarchical pyramid. Following Bouchard-Taylor, there were a lot of discussions within the company. It is mainly whites, "old boys," who run other companies throughout the world. Examples of Québeckers' thoughts upon meeting with other foreign business people: "communist Swedes," "damned French." There are prejudices. A dose of sensitivity would be welcome.

The union official told us a little bit more about some issues around diversity management:

> We knew of one case in which offensive expressions were used to refer to a black person, but the employees involved apologized and it was resolved. Some time ago, there was a specific request for religious reasons, concerning the fact that an employee did not want to take mandatory holidays because they originated in a religion other than his own. Since the request pertained to holidays, I handled it without taking it to management. But that person no longer works in the company. Nevertheless, the enterprise keeps an "accommodations" binder, but it contains mainly requests to arrange working hours in relation to childcare needs. If I had to manage more accommodation cases for religious reasons, I would have to see the request, because each request is handled depending on its importance. Even so, there needs to be a major reason for changing our schedule, even though work-hours are flexible.

One manager told us that there had been a number of accommodation cases that did not work out, such as the request for use of a prayer room by a Muslim employee at certain times of the day. The company refused to make a specific room or space available for prayer simply because they did not have the extra space. This particular point related to the interview we conducted with a Muslim employee. He reported being extremely satisfied with diversity management in his department. His interview is worth quoting in greater detail:

Diversity is not "managed" in the company, rather it is integrated; it goes without saying. We had a potluck meal in my department; of the 60 people who attended, 30 were of different ethnic origins ...

We serve clients from several countries around the world and we have to adapt. If Muslims want to observe a holiday or pray, it's all very discreet and consistent with company norms ...

For example, sometimes I use my sick days or family leave for religious reasons, but I give advanced notice and I'm discreet about it. If the company needs me that day, I'm flexible and make myself available ...

Colleagues reserve a meeting room to pray without necessarily telling everyone. It's a matter of courtesy. We're happy and grateful to be recognized for our skills, and we're conscious of respectfully adapting to the norms of the environment.

This excerpt is quite telling. This international business firm has gained extensive knowledge about facilitating cultural and religious integration. Relations seem to be generally harmonious, except when differences among national cultures are involved.[10] But the employee is very flexible in the way he lives his religious practices, putting them after the employer's requirements. More generally, it is interesting to note that the prejudices the managers talked about as well as the tone of this interview seem to point to the same sources of tensions. Employees are accustomed to managing differences on a daily basis. But by carefully hearing what has been said in the above excerpts, one also catches overtones that tell us the company is quite inflexible on very specific requests. The Muslim employee would not ask for a prayer room and would be very flexible when it comes to his religious practices. The needs of the company's performance come first.[11] I will quote him again below, in response to an excerpt from a focus group session read to him, on the subject of Muslim employees in another company.

Two Examples of Difficulties

Some difficulties were reported with more precision in visits to two other companies. It is perhaps because they are smaller, that our team could get a clear and explicit sense of the way they feel and how they deal with the issue.

Local Manufacturing Firm

This firm is engaged in manufacturing technical materials for construction. Its workforce varies from 125 to 200 employees, depending on annual sales. One human resources manager and one shop supervisor were interviewed, and we were able to conduct a focus group with some employees. The manager explained that employees are very diverse in terms of ethnic origin and citizenship status. The firm is unable to keep these types of statistics up-to-date however. This firm must deal with broad diversity and like other firms in this situation (as discerned in the interviews), it seeks management assistance from human resources networks rather than academic experts or government authorities. The human resources manager explains the situation frankly:

> We recruit a lot more immigrants than "old stock" Québeckers ["*Québécois de souche*"]. So, because of this, there are always Québeckers who are less able to accept people, people of colour. Everything boils down to knowing oneself and knowing others. We think that others are different, but if we look closely, they are not that different after all. Tolerance and intolerance are as prevalent here as everywhere else. But with the law, we don't have a choice. Once, an employee said something nasty to a person of colour, and was then suspended for three days.

Thus, if someone utters slurs related to colour, race, or sex, the person is suspended. In the company, human resources manages the issue of diversity. When there are complicated situations, information is shared between the human resources departments of various companies similar to this one. External training has provided a better understanding of communication between certain cultures. Since receiving this training, the human resources manager has changed the way he greets his employees and he better understands why some people in his company do not get along for cultural reasons.

The supervisor notes that there have been more requests since the Bouchard-Taylor Commission. For a barbecue, there was a request for something other than meat, but nothing else. These managers let us set up focus groups with their employees. Here are excerpts from a focus group session with French-Canadian employees:

> Reasonable religious accommodation ... is a hot button issue. What first comes to mind is the sugarhouse situation and the accommodation made for Jewish schools on the weekend.

We accommodate because we don't know what to do about this any-more. We need immigrants, but what do we do with them? The reason for accepting immigrants is work.

They come to work at this company and they stick together, not like' Québeckers. They also tend to treat Québeckers as racists as soon we ask them for something.

Québec is soft and this goes way too far, to the point that soon this won't be our home anymore ... reasonable accommodation is a problem that mainly affects Muslims who want Québeckers to submit to their religion.

People don't understand why we go somewhere else without wanting to change everything, while, when they come, they want to change every-thing ... One employee said to me that, one day, he tripped over a Muslim person who was praying between two machines.

The other employees reacted loudly to the mention of this incident, saying:

Oh yes, the one who washes his feet in the sink; it's disgusting ... because the business only employs two Muslims, the situation is manageable.

But as one employee points out:

If we had to hire a lot of people and there were more of these types of employees, the company would have problems.

Here one can see the problem of managing religious diversity when a firm has few resources and little experience with which to broach the issue. Presented with this excerpt, the Muslim employee from the firm cited earlier (see "High-tech" section) reacted strongly: "These Muslim workers showed such a lack of respect, praying like that!" While the act of washing feet in the office lavatory can be easily construed as dis-tasteful in today's corporate context, such "unusual" behaviours need to be decoded for employees in the context of larger post-colonial issues and dealt with appropriately so the necessary steps of prayer, for exam-ple, can be managed in a way that does not inconvenience other work-ers. The statement, "When they come, they want to change everything," demonstrates a lack of sensitivity to post-colonial issues on the part of the speaker, potentially detrimental to office relations in a context where an Aboriginal person, for example, might one day become a colleague.

These comments reveal that the subject of accommodations remains challenging due to religious intolerance and perhaps mismanagement of diversity among staff. Moreover, it should be noted that these opinions were provided during the only focus group session with employees that we were able to conduct without the presence of a manager. It nevertheless confirms what was previously stated. Day-to-day conversations in any company will reflect society at large, the same prejudices, the same fears.

Provincial Employment Agency

In a provincial employment agency with 35 permanent employees and 600 external employees, all internal employees are "old stock" Québecers of French-Canadian origin. There are numerous immigrants among the people that the agency places in firms, especially companies engaged in manufacturing and skilled trades. Skilled labour shortages account for the large number of immigrants placed by the agency. Paradoxically, several companies using the agency's services asked explicitly that only "old stock" Québecers be selected for interviews, for fear of the legal complications that might arise from cultural or religious differences. Legally, under the *Charter of Rights and Freedoms*, the agency is not permitted to accept these types of requests, but it does anyway. An accounts manager was interviewed and explains: "Legally, under the *Charter of Rights and Freedoms*, our company cannot accept these kinds of requests, but our clients make them anyway." This example reveals the current extent of the problem in Québec. This point was confirmed by a large focus group we carried out with executives. For fear of complications, many companies chose their employees at the beginning of the process, thus anticipating the religious factor, without explicitly mentioning it.

Conclusion

In this chapter we presented only a few examples from our results, but based on the analysis of our full body of data, we have found that location, business connections, business sectors, employee and client profiles as well as the more or less restrictive policies and legislation governing private enterprises seem to have a structuring effect on diversity management. Given the limitations of this research sample, the conclusions are only preliminary:

1. Despite the challenges and problems faced by many companies, the philosophy of diversity found in the private sector is inspiring. It is related to the notion of equality that first emerged in the struggle for

gender rights many years ago. Businesses subject to the federal *Employment Equity Act* and Québec's equal access employment programs have had to develop explicit approaches that foster diversity. However, the groups affected by this Act and these programs are primarily women, Aboriginal people, disabled individuals, and visible minorities. As religion is not explicitly mentioned, it is still not taken into account as a relevant issue. The comment we got from a manager of a large enterprise resounds: "Religious diversity is already being managed, in the same way that any other accommodation request is managed. It is in the private domain, so it is managed like any private request." In this simple sentence, one can understand that, for some managers in the private sector, there is no such thing as "religious freedom" as distinct from other rights or needs. And the Muslim engineer's thinking seems to go in the same direction:

> [S]ometimes I use my sick days or family leave for religious reasons, but I give advanced notice and I'm discreet about it. If the company needs me that day, I'm flexible and make myself available ... We're happy and grateful to be recognized for our skills, and we're conscious of respectfully adapting to the norms of the environment ...

Several remarks implied that accommodations of a religious nature would not be acceptable if they harmed the productivity of the company in some way.[12] In certain cases, managers refused to treat the issue of religious freedom in a targeted manner. One manager at a financial institution said: "A cultural or religious reason for leave would not take precedence over any other request" (See section titled "Three Examples of Sound Diversity – Financial Sector").

2. The largest enterprises provided a wider range of examples of management practices. Their international scale seems to foster openness and flexibility among employees. However, the areas in which these companies are located seem to be an important factor as well, at least in the perceptions of employers. Some would say there exists a greater likelihood of racist reactions or discriminatory attitudes in the branches that are located in homogeneous towns or neighbourhoods. Still, the interviews in the rural regions revealed a more nuanced reading of the challenges, as even when branches in remote areas try to attract recent immigrants as employees, the expatriates generally display a preference towards living within the more diverse demographics of larger cities.

3. The private sector seems, somewhat predictably, to be a parallel image of the public sector. But this portrait bears a number of interesting implications. First, most of the enterprises interviewed would rather seek the assistance of a private firm, rather than an academic institution, to deal with diversity. Second, no interviewees had read the Bouchard-Taylor Commission's Report, either in its condensed or complete version. An undeniable gap exists between the work of the Commission and the private sector. Keep in mind that the main feature of the internal tools the private sector has developed, when they do exist, is their brevity. On the other hand, academic researchers have no access to the resources developed by a number of firms for one key reason. Developed at a cost, the resources belong to the firms in question. The firms that developed these resources met us with the same restrictions.

4. Although our sampling is not exhaustive, the research shows that when firms deal with a diverse clientele, they are more likely to respond to these issues by developing a consistent vision and practical tools, essentially for economic reasons. This finding is equally true for daycare centres, financial institutions, and retail businesses. The smallest or most unstable companies have fewer resources to address these issues and are less interested in doing so. It is also important to note that sectors experiencing a labour shortage recruit many immigrants, and this can result in tensions across various cultures and religions, tensions that are more or less well managed.

5. The personnel who manage diversity issues tend to be restricted to a specific department designated by the firm. These individuals have usually received specific training and/or have benefited from extensive experience in diversity issues. But their confinement to this specialized service does not necessarily foster the dissemination of a corporate vision of diversity throughout the entire organization.

Beyond these strengths and limitations, one must be reminded that the private sector is often on the front line in matters of diversity. It is there that the interactions between first- and second-generation adult immigrants and the host society are most intense. It is there that younger and older adults interact on a daily basis, learning to live and work together within the frameworks of their different values, beliefs, and world visions. For that reason, the private sector remains one of the most fascinating, yet understudied research fields in diversity today.

NOTES

1   Thank you to Lori G. Beaman. The title of this chapter, and the vision
    behind it, were inspired by the problematic at the heart of Beaman's
    "Religious Diversity and Its Limits: Moving Beyond Tolerance and Accom-
    modation" SSHRC-funded MCRI (*Religion and Diversity Project*, religion-
    anddiversity.ca).
2   This research was carried out from October 2009 to April 2010 by mem-
    bers of the Chair of Religion, Culture, and Society. I conducted several
    interviews, developed the final analyses, and drafted the report. I was
    assisted by Ludovic Robert and Marie-Ève Garand, doctoral students, who
    conducted several interviews and developed pre-analyses. Benoit Dostaler,
    Chair coordinator, also contributed at several stages of the research. Louis-
    Charles Gagnon-Tessier and K. Gandhar Chakravarty, doctoral students,
    also prepared reports based on their qualitative analysis of the numer-
    ous documents, reports, and briefs issuing from the Bouchard-Taylor
    Commission.
3   As planned, various types of enterprises in various sectors were
    included: two financial, one local to Québec and the other national and
    international; one multinational high technology firm; five small and
    medium firms in Greater Montréal; one large retail firm; and four firms in
    remote areas (small and medium). Unfortunately, no enterprises in Qué-
    bec City agreed to participate, citing lack of time. The four enterprises
    in a town far from major urban centres cooperated fully, helped by the
    fact that they were approached by a colleague of Solange Lefebvre with
    previous contacts in the area. It should be noted that two-thirds of the
    enterprises cooperating with this research had previous connections with
    someone in the research team. The need to resort to previous contacts
    helps understand the difficulties we faced finding private sector organi-
    zations willing to cooperate with this research. In this article, Lefebvre
    also includes few data obtained from a big high technology firm installed
    in few Canadian provinces, where she conducted few training sessions
    on diversity.
4   Translation of: De nombreux exemples jurisprudentiels démontrent que
    les accommodements raisonnables font partie de la culture québécoise
    et que la technique élaborée par les tribunaux dans le domaine du droit
    du travail peut être transposée dans d'autres milieux. … L'obligation
    d'accommodement est une réalité quotidienne dans les milieux de travail.
    Le gouvernement du Québec devrait s'inspirer de ces derniers qui ont su

efficacement gérer la question de la diversité en créant des outils ou politiques répondant aux demandes de leurs employés (2007, 21–2).... Mais il est intéressant de dépasser le débat juridique pour constater que les accommodements raisonnables cède nt de plus en plus le pas aux enjeux de la diversité, port d'attache de plusieurs initiatives fructueuses (2007, 25).

5 See Programmes d'accès à l'égalité, http://www.cdpdj.qc.ca/Pages/Default.aspx

6 An explanation is available on the website of the Human Rights Commission, http://www.cdpdj.qc.ca/en. See the section related to Affirmative Action Programs (under Publications). Detailed information related to these programs can only be found on the French version of the website; see http://www2.cdpdj.qc.ca/PAE/Pages/default.aspx. A list of enterprises subject to the contract compliance program can be found at http://www.cdpdj.qc.ca/fr/publications/docs/pae_obc.pdf

7 On these matters, see Brunelle (2001).

8 For instance, see Jézéquel (2007), who in the section of her book about the workplace offers no contribution on religion, although it is discussed in the section on schools and health care system.

9 See also Bouchard and Taylor (2008, 232).

10 One employee, for example, expressed the following: "There are clashes with international clients for cultural reasons, such as differences related to relationships with authority. In Montréal, people get impatient when foreign partners take too long to consult their superiors."

11 A recent ethnographic study on the integration of African and Caribbean Rastafari immigrants in Montréal revealed more about the difficulties related to reasonable accommodation (Chakravarty 2008). In addition to being Black, participants discussed the prejudices they encountered at workplaces in the education, medical, and construction sectors due to stereotypes that equated dreadlocks (a symbol of faith) and marijuana addiction. One interviewee reported being terminated from a medical clinic for refusing to cut his hair.

12 In a way, it could relate to Beaman's (2012) recent analysis of Supreme Court judgments on reasonable accommodation, basing their argument more on cost-benefit than harm, as was the case before.

REFERENCES

Barreau du Québec. 2007. "Les droits fondamentaux: une protection pour toutes et tous." Mémoire présenté à La Commission de consultation sur les pratiques d'accommodement reliées aux différences culturelles. Montreal, Québec.

Beaman, Lori. 2012. "Religious Freedom and Neoliberalism: From Harm to Cost-Benefit." In *Religion in the Neoliberal Age: Political Economy and Modes of Governance,* edited by François Gauthier and Tuomas Martikainen, 193–210. Farmham: Ashgate Publishing.

Beyer, Peter. 2010. "The Difference that a Religion Makes: Variations in Socio-Economic Conditions for Different Non-Christian Religions in Canada." Paper presented at National Metropolis Conference, Montréal, Québec, March 18–21.

Bouchard Gérard, and Charles Taylor. 2007. "Accommodation and Differences. Seeking Common Ground," edited by Commission de consultation sur les pratiques d'accomodement reliées aux différences culturelles. Québec: Québec Government.

Bouchard, Gérard, and Charles Taylor. 2008. "Building the Future: A Time for Reconciliation." Commission de consultation sur les pratiques d'accommodement reliées aux différences culturelles. Québec: Québec Government Printing Office.

Brunelle, Christian. 2001. *Discrimination et obligation d'accommodement en milieu de travail syndiqué.* Cowansville: Éditions Y. Blais.

Chakravarty, K. G. 2008. "Double Others: the Marginalization of Secular-Spiritual Rastafari Immigrants in Montréal." *Scriptura* 10(2): 57–74.

Chevrier, Sylvie. 2003. *Le management interculturel.* Paris: Presses Universitaires de France.

Canadian-Italian Business and Professional Association (CIBPA). 2007. Brief presented to La Commission de consultation sur les pratiques d'accommodement reliées aux différences culturelles. Montréal, Québec.

Fondation des entreprises en recrutement de main-d'œuvre agricole étrangère (FREME). 2007. "Mémoire de FERME a la commission de consultation sur les pratiques d'accommodements religieux reliées aux différence culturelles." Montréal, Québec.

Jézéquel, Myriam. 2007. *Les accommodements raisonnables: quoi, comment, jusqu'où?: des outils pour tous.* Cowansville: Éditions Y. Blais.

Kossek, Ellen E., and Sharon A. Lobel. 1996. *Managing Diversity: Human Resource Strategies for Transforming the Workplace.* Blackwell HRM Series. Cambridge: Blackwell Business.

Mutabazi, Evalde, and Philippe Pierre. 2008. *Pour un management interculturel: de la diversité à la reconnaissance en entreprise, Diversité culturelle et dynamique des organisations.* Paris: L'Harmattan.

Özbilgin, Mustafa. 2009. *Equality, Diversity and Inclusion at Work. A Research Companion.* Cheltenham, Northampton: Edward Elgar.

Schneider, Susan C., and Jean Louis Barsoux. 2003. *Management interculturel*. Paris: Pearson Education.
Wilson, Trevor, and Mary Ann Sayers. 1996. *Diversity at Work: A Business Case for Equity*. New York, Toronto: J. Wiley.

CASES

Multani v. Commission scolaire Marguerite-Bourgeoys, [2006] 1 R.C.S. 256.
Syndicat Northcrest v. Amselem, [2004] 2 S.C.R. 551.
Ontario Human Rights Commission and O'Malley v. Simpsons-Sears Ltd., [1985] 2 S.C.R. 536
R. v. Big M Drug Mart Ltd., [1985] 1 R.C.S. 295.

LEGISLATION

An Act Respecting Equal Access to Employment in Public Bodies. R.S.Q., chapter A-2.01
Canadian Charter of Rights and Freedoms, R.S.C, 1985 Appendix II, No. 44. *see also* Part I (ss. 1 to 34) of the *Constitution Act, 1982*.
Charter of Human Rights and Freedoms. R.S.Q., chapter C-12.
Employment Equity Act (S.C. 1995, c. 44)
Lord's Day Act, 1906 (Can.), c. 27.

8 Religion and the Incorporation of Haitian Migrants in Montréal

MARGARITA A. MOONEY

Introduction

In November 2009, I attended Mass at Notre-Dame d'Haïti Catholic Mission in Montréal, where I had conducted fieldwork several years prior.[1] Drawing on the Gospel readings from Mass that day,[2] the priest exhorted the Haitian faithful in attendance to respond to God's call to give of themselves and to trust that God will give back even more. He further warned them to be sure not to treat others like dogs just because they are poor. For this community of mostly poor Haitian immigrants whose daily needs for food, housing, and work may go unmet, this simple message carries a profound meaning. Time and again, Haitians told me that despite their worldly poverty, they desired to also respond to God's call to give of themselves. When they do humbly ask for assistance, they feared being looked down upon as helpless. To assist Haitians' incorporation in Montréal, in the 1970s, Catholic clergy and engaged lay leaders in Montréal founded a social service agency, the Bureau of the Haitian Christian Community of Montréal.[3] Even though many Haitians today still encounter economic hardship, and even as prejudice against Haitians has risen, the Québec government reduced its cooperation with mediating institutions like the Bureau that for so many years had successfully provided a bridge between Haitians and the new home society institutions.

In this chapter, I will first review the different stages of Haitian migration to Montréal, which began with the migration of mostly highly educated Haitians in the 1960s but changed to include mostly working-class Haitians by the late 1970s. In response to the difficult path to inclusion for lower-skilled Haitians, Haitian Catholic intellectuals and clergy founded a Catholic mission to welcome Haitians, Notre-Dame d'Haïti, and the Bureau. Although these organizations played a central role in the successful integration of Haitians in Montréal in the 1980s and 1990s, debates about Québec's national identity and ambivalence about the place of religion in the public square led to the increasing marginalization of these organizations and has slowed the integration of Haitians in Montréal.

This chapter draws on ethnographic observations and interviews conducted at Notre-Dame d'Haïti Catholic Mission in Montréal during 2002, as well as follow-up visits to Notre-Dame in 2008 and 2009. During those visits, I participated in regular church services, attended prayer groups, and sang in the choir. I also conducted in-depth interviews with twenty members of Notre-Dame, including clergy and lay leaders, and asked about the spiritual and social mission of Notre-Dame. Furthermore, I interviewed ten leaders of Haitian associations in Montréal, both those with ties to the Catholic Church, like the Bureau, as well as organizations like Maison d'Haïti, without ties to any religious group.[4] In those interviews with leaders, I inquired about the principal challenges Haitians face to their incorporation in Montréal, what programs their organizations run to address those problems, how they acquired private and government funding for their programs, and about the quantity and quality of their cooperation with government agencies. In order to understand how government officials viewed Haitians' inclusion in Montréal overall and to learn whether government agencies cooperated with Haitians' religious and civic institutions to overcome those challenges, I interviewed several government officials who work on immigration and interculturalism in Québec. Although the government leaders I spoke to may not represent the entire breadth of views about the public role of religious organizations in Québec, the quotes presented in this chapter nonetheless illustrate one important narrative around religion in the public sphere in Québec, namely that the state should not cooperate with organizations that have any ties to a religious community.

Studying Haitian immigrants in Québec provides important insights into the larger debates about ethnic and religious pluralism in Canada, and interculturalism in Québec specifically, which this volume addresses. As mentioned in the introductory chapter, Québec receives sustained attention in this volume due to its complex ethnic and religious identity. Although many voices advocate for greater secularization of the public sphere in Québec, my chapter shows that Haitian immigrants to Québec do not always accept that religion must be kept in the private sphere. Whereas the chapter by Connor and Koenig in this volume does not find many significant differences in how religion influences immigrant integration in Québec compared to the rest of Canada, my comparison of Haitians in Québec with Haitians in the United States and France yields different findings. Through my comparison of the Haitian communities in Miami, Montréal, and Paris, I show how including religion in the public sphere could benefit the inclusion of newcomers to Québec in part because Haitian migrants in Montréal look to the religious communities to mediate for them in the public sphere. Although Québec's practice of inter-culturalism acknowledges the importance of ethnicity to how people participate in the public sphere, in practice, Québec's interculturalism marginalizes religion to the private sphere.

Haitian Migration to Montréal

In the 1960s, the Québec government recruited Haitian professionals to work at the newly created French-language government bureaucracies created during the Quiet Revolution. Because of both their lower educational backgrounds relative to earlier Haitian migrants and an economic recession in Québec, the rapid and successful adaptation of Haitian professionals and students from the 1960s was not matched by subsequent waves of Haitian immigrants who arrived in Québec in the 1970s (Dejean 1978; Labelle, Larose, and Piché 1983). Beginning in the 1970s, Québec underwent an economic recession that disproportionately affected new Haitian migrants with low levels of human capital (Labelle, Larose and Piché 1983). For example, in the late 1970s and early 1980s, unemployment among Montréal's blue-collar workers – including employees in the manufacturing sector that included many Haitians – rose to 30 per cent. High unemployment hit Haitians particularly hard. Consider that, in the 1990s, Québec's overall unemployment rate varied from 9 to 12 per cent, but it rose to as high as 27 per cent for Haitians (Labelle, Salée, and Frenette 2001).

These newer Haitian migrants also differed from earlier migrants in that many more of them arrived in Québec alone rather than with their families. Prior to 1972, Haitians could enter Canada as tourists and apply for a work visa after their arrival. However, because of an economic downturn and growing unemployment, in 1972 the Canadian government changed its laws to require all potential immigrants to apply for visas in their home countries (Dejean 1978; Labelle, Larose, and Piché 1983). These changes did not prevent low-skilled Haitian migrants from seeking a brighter future in Québec, but they frequently lacked enough money or legal status to move with their families and thus often began their journeys alone.

Although many middle-class Haitians settled in areas of Montréal such as Laval, and are relatively well integrated into Québécois society, many more working class Haitians have stagnated in the impoverished conditions of North Montréal and Saint Michel (Torczyner 2001). Unlike their predecessors, these working-class Haitians generally do not all speak French fluently, many have not finished high school, and their households are often headed by women. As a result of increasing numbers of low-skilled Haitians migrating to Québec, both Haitian leaders in Montréal and the Québécois government realized that the rapid adaptation of professional Haitians would not be matched by those working class Haitians who, partially as an unintended consequence of the Québec government's own recruitment policies, followed the path of earlier compatriots seeking to escape political repression and a weak economy in Haiti.

Haitians' Mediating Institutions

Haitian migrants in Montréal faced both symbolic and structural hurdles in their incorporation. As mentioned previously, many working-class Haitian migrants entered under family reunification or entered as tourists and then adjusted to residency status – but because they were not recruited, there were initially no programs to help them find jobs, apply for asylum, and learn French, among other things. Haitian migrants to Montréal included many Haitian members of religious orders such as the Jesuits and the Spiritains,[5] who have their provincial headquarters in Québec. Once in Montréal, these Haitian Catholic clergy and other lay leaders easily formed networks with local church leaders to build social programs and advocate for Haitians' legal status and social support.

In the 1970s, a group of Haitian Catholic clergy and lay leaders, led by Father Paul Dejean, working at the Bureau, wrote letters to the Québec government on behalf of undocumented Haitians in Montréal and even met personally with government officials, arguing that, because of the poor conditions in Haiti, Haitians should qualify for humanitarian visas to Québec. During two legalization campaigns orchestrated by the Bureau, personal connections between Haitian Catholic clergy and Québec Catholic clergy proved crucial in legitimizing the claims of Haitian asylum-seekers who feared political repression in Haiti. Organizations like the Bureau and the Centre for Social Aid to Immigrants, a social outreach branch of the Sisters of Bon Secours that first began working with immigrants and refugees after the Second World War, provided the Montréal Haitian community with skilled leadership and financial resources to start social programs. Hence, Haitian leaders drew on their own experiences in Haiti as well as the experience of Catholic religious orders and their affiliated social service agencies, like the Centre for Social Aid to Immigrants, which helped the Bureau write its initial charter, to build programs for Haitians.

One common narrative about the Quiet Revolution is that the state took over all social services, such as hospitals and schools, from the church. Despite the fact that some Catholic clergy and lay leaders opposed the reforms of the Quiet Revolution, many other Catholic clergy, lay leaders, and intellectuals were inspired by Vatican II's calls for an opening to modernity and respect for democracy and participated actively in transforming Catholic education and hospitals into state-run institutions. In fact, the name "Quiet" Revolution indicates that, unlike the more contentious French Revolution, many members of the Catholic hierarchy and lay leadership supported the development of a modern welfare state in Québec. In fact, some Catholic clergy directly participated in the creation or functioning of state agencies. In the 1960s, Monsignor Alphonse-Marie Parent presided over an educational reform commission (Balthazar 2009). As another example, during one of the Bureau's legalization campaigns in the 1980s, Québec's Minister of Immigration was a Jesuit priest, Jacques Couteau, who had many personal connections to Haitian clergy. Hence, Haitians' early experiences in Montréal indicate that even after the Quiet Revolution, Catholic leaders and organizations nonetheless were often central in secular institutions serving the poor and immigrants, such as Haitians.

By around 2000, however, the situation began to change. As described in the Bouchard-Taylor Report (Bouchard and Taylor 2008), there are many people in Québec who began to think that they were accommodating too much to immigrants' ethnic and religious identities. In part to reinforce Québec's identity as a secular and inter-cultural society, government agencies asserted their preference to work with multi-ethnic and secular organizations in 2003. As both an ethnic organization and one with ties to the Catholic Church, this change affected the Bureau's ability to work with government agencies, leading its leaders to remove the word "Christian" from its name. Similarly, in hopes of continuing to receive government funding, the religious sisters who run the Centre for Social Aid to Immigrants also removed any reference to Christianity from their charter.

When asked whether government agencies in Québec work with religious institutions that are concerned about immigrant integration and whether he coordinated efforts with Haitians' religious institutions, Pierre Anctil, director of the Québec government's Council of Intercultural Relations, said "Churches only work with the poor in the US because the state is absent. In Québec, the state has replaced the church." Such comments express a narrative held by many secular elites according to which the Quiet Revolution replaced, once and for all, private institutions (most of them Catholic) that promoted social welfare. However, this narrative overlooks the substantial Catholic contributions to the bureaucracies and institutions of the modern Québécois state, including organizations like Centre for Social Aid to Immigrants. Other Black immigrant groups to Québec similarly rely on religious organizations to assist their inclusion, a fact often ignored and invisible to many Québécois government officials (Ives 2010; Ives and Sinha 2010). Even if some Québécois intellectuals and government officials may be open to collaborating with immigrants' religious institutions, others are ambivalent and still others are decidedly hostile. But the perception amongst Haitian organizations was that in order to work with the government, they were better off covering up their religious origins or ties.

Moreover, given the poverty, unemployment, and school dropout rates of Haitians in Montréal, Haitian leaders expressed concern that reducing government cooperation with the same institutions that supported earlier Haitian migrants would only make things more difficult for Haitians now. The well-publicized debates during the Bouchard-Taylor Commission and Report further demonstrated that, for many Québécois, religious belief should be merely symbolic and religious practices should be strictly private. Pious acts that are common among working-class Haitian Catholics in Montréal, such as attending a Charismatic prayer service and Mass to ask the Blessed Virgin Mary to intercede for one's family, or invoking the Holy Spirit's healing powers to save one's children from gangs or drugs, clash with the demystified and largely cultural Catholicism of other residents of Montréal. Going up the hundreds of stairs in front of St. Joseph's Oratory on one's knees as a sign of penance publicly demonstrates a vigorous faith shared by few native Québécois today. The disdain Haitians sense towards their private piety and their often public demonstrations of faith leads them to feel that their strong Catholic identity presents a barrier to their symbolic incorporation in Montréal.

The Haitian Catholic Mission of Montréal

In the following section, I draw from interviews conducted at Notre-Dame d'Haïti Mission in order to illustrate several recurring themes from my interviews with Haitian Catholics in Montréal. Haitian migrants often mentioned their many economic hardships and perceived increasingly prejudiced attitudes towards them. The Haitians' prayer reinforced their dignity as "children of God" and their participation in religious activities provided meaning and agency.

"A Child of God"

During my participant observation at Notre-Dame, one of the lay leaders I interacted with frequently was named Jacques.[6] One evening after a Friday night choir rehearsal, we sat down for an in-depth interview. Jacques told me that he migrated to Montréal as a teenager with all of his brothers, sisters, and parents. He has a steady job as a factory manager, and he has earned the respect of his bosses. Most of all, he feels blessed to have a strong faith. Although he works six days a week, is married, and has two children, Jacques spends all of his free time leading church activities. In addition to Sunday Mass, he participates in a Wednesday evening prayer group that meets at different people's homes across Montréal. On Saturdays, after he gets off work at noon, he attends a prayer group at Notre-Dame and then goes to choir rehearsal.

Although he is well settled in Montréal, Jacques is poignantly aware how many other Haitians have not adapted as successfully as he has. In addition to Haitians' low human capital, Jacques described how Haitians' adaptation in Montréal is further complicated by growing negative stereotypes of them. Jacques laments that all the news on the radio and television about Haitians repeat stories about poverty in Haiti and the lack of Haitians' social integration in Montréal. As a result of these negative stereotypes, Jacques feared that, "Some of our youth here don't respect themselves anymore, and they contribute to the bad image of Haitians by forming gangs. We Haitians have to come together to show that we can do something for ourselves." In contrast to many images of Québec as welcoming to all immigrants, Jacques clearly perceived that, "In this country we suffer humiliations, we have to work hard. We are also a minority, what they call a visible minority. When one of our group does something wrong, they stigmatize us all." Hence, despite having a stable job and leading a life of work, family, and prayer, Jacques commented that he and many other Haitians in Montréal have to work "four times as hard" to get ahead.

The difference between himself and some other Haitians, Jacques believes, comes from his ability to deflect stereotypes by holding on to a positive self-image rooted in his faith. Rather than letting Québécois negative stereotypes about Haitians affect his self-image, Jacques insisted that since he believes each person is "a child of God," all people are therefore equal. Because he believes firmly that he is a "child of God," he has great self-respect, which helps him get along with Québécois people, even those who may initially not treat him well. "If you want people to respect you, you have to respect yourself first."

Because he perceives prejudice against Haitians in Montréal, Jacques dedicates his free time to leadership at Notre-Dame in order to teach others, especially the youth who attend choir rehearsal on weekends, that they too are "children of God" and that they do not have to internalize negative opinions about Haitians. At the beginning of choir rehearsal or prayer group, Jacques often referred directly to events about Haitians being covered in the news, and insisted that Haitians have to maintain their pride despite the real or exaggerated problems being portrayed in the media. First and foremost, Jacques exhorted other member of Notre-Dame not to stray from their relationship with God, which he insisted ultimately should be the basis of their self-image.

"Building the Kingdom Together"

One stereotype Haitians face is that, as poor immigrants, they contribute little to Québec society yet expect to receive handouts. One Catholic lay leader in Montréal I interviewed in her home near Boulevard Pie IX, Marie, eloquently described how her persona and group prayer helped her become a *giver* and not just a *receiver*. Two decades prior, Marie moved to Québec as a young 20-year-old mother. When she first arrived in Québec, she always felt lonely when people she encountered in public would intentionally avoid eye contact with her. Like so many other Haitians in Montréal, Marie commented on how cold it is in Québec, by which she means both the weather and human relations.

To fight her feelings of solitude, Marie joined a small prayer group of eight to ten people. In contrast to the meaninglessness she felt as just one more immigrant working mother in Montréal, Marie's small prayer group lifted her up by providing a sense that others care for her and that her actions did matter.

Like many other Haitians, Marie insisted that she did not simply want to receive charity, but rather desired reciprocal relationships of mutual support. However, migrating to Montréal breaks many social ties that take time and effort to rebuild. By meeting with others on a regular basis for prayer, she was able to build the trust needed to work with others on their own problems or societal problems. Quite similar to Jacques, she pointed to teaching each person to see himself or herself as a dignified "daughter" or "son of God" as the first step in dealing with Haitians' problems. Because so many Haitians who migrate to Montréal feel isolated and frustrated, she explained, first they have to learn to see their own dignity and only then will they be able to help build a better society.

Part of helping people see their own dignity, she further elaborated, is teaching them that they can contribute something to the group. Joining and eventually leading a prayer group made Marie feel like she "belongs somewhere." She added that believing that "you belong somewhere means that your idea is important, your contribution is important in the construction of [God's] kingdom. When you feel that you are somebody, [that] you are a person, [that] you are important, you can move mountains, and that is faith." In contrast to the isolation and powerlessness one can feel, Marie further explained that:

> Faith is what gives us the confidence that we can build together the kingdom. The kingdom isn't my kingdom, it is the kingdom of all. That's why we have to build it together. Suddenly, you feel important, and when you feel important, you feel like you have something to give to others. Often, one has the impression that the poor ask incessantly, but suddenly someone asks you to contribute, because you have something to give, too. Things change when suddenly I see I have something to give.

Marie's comments illustrate how immigrants who move to a new home are not just interested in attaining material benefits, but also seek to become "givers" of something. If they are unable to give something material, they are always able to give others moral encouragement through their prayer. For Marie and many others, the ability to give encouragement through prayer provides a feeling of dignity and inspires them to come forward and work with others to solve larger social problems. In the absence of these social ties that foster dignity and hope, Marie, Jacques, and many other Haitian leaders in Montréal feared many members of their community would not be able to face problems such as unemployment and school failure.

Comparing Haitians in Montréal, Miami, and Paris

How do Haitians' experiences in Montréal compare with two other important cities of the Haitian diaspora? By 2000, Haitian communities in Miami, Montréal, and Paris had large working classes and small upper and middle classes, but the origins of the three communities are nonetheless quite different. Because of Haiti's proximity to Miami, the Haitian community there initially grew due to a large influx of boat people starting in the late 1970s. Haitians faced greater prejudice in Miami compared to Montréal or Paris; for example, Haitian boat people were reported to be spreading tuberculosis and AIDS in South Florida, further contributing to their negative image in Miami and to discrimination as well as prejudice against them (Stepick 1992, 1998). Census data from 1980 and 1990 clearly indicates that Haitians were not only poorer than non-immigrants in Miami but were the poorest amongst all of Miami's numerous immigrant groups. As new Haitian migrants in Miami settled in Little Haiti, the impoverished conditions of Little Haiti's residents had not improved greatly compared to previous decades. However, by 2000, Miami-Dade County had the largest population of the Haitian diaspora, surpassing New York, it had also developed a sizeable middle class in areas like North Miami. Several Haitian-Americans won local political office, including the office of the mayor of North Miami.[7] Hence, despite their disadvantageous starting positions, Haitians in Miami developed a sizable middle-class community with strong community institutions and local political representation. Despite some similar socio-economic indicators for Haitians in Miami, Montréal, and Paris, Haitians in Miami undoubtedly have the strongest institutional base of support for their incorporation. For example, even though Haitians had the lowest parental human capital and income of any national-origin group in the Children of Immigrants Longitudinal Study, they also had the highest levels of religious participation, which led to their greater educational attainment and labor market integration among second-generation Haitians (Portes and Rumbaut 2006, 323).

Interviews with government officials and religious leaders in Miami further illustrate how the receiving context can recognize and enhance the positive influence of religion on immigrant inclusion. As one government official in Miami, Dr. Lumane Claude, explained, both because of political repression in Haiti and their negative reception in Miami, Haitians are more likely to trust the church than the government. As Dr. Claude explained, "The church is the only place people can really trust … You see the priest if you don't have food. Hey, you're not going to the government, you're not going to the social services. It's a shame to go to those places, but it's okay to tell the church that you have a problem. They're [Haitians] not thinking of social services, they're thinking of the church."

For their part, the leaders of Miami's Toussaint Center, a social service centre founded by Catholic clergy and lay leaders, and the Haitian Catholic mission that goes by the same name as its counterpart in Montréal – Notre-Dame d'Haïti – did not try to incorporate Haitians without state assistance, but rather first tried to mobilize community resources and then seek additional support from state resources. The history of the Toussaint Center – which started off as a volunteer effort in space borrowed from the church and grew to have a budget of millions of dollars in local, state, and federal funding to support Haitians' integration – exemplifies how government officials in Miami cooperate with religious leaders to promote common goals. Government officials in Miami acknowledge that the Toussaint Center was able to successfully serve the Haitian population, with its volunteer efforts, community resources, and trust, beyond what the state could have done. To acknowledge the civic importance of the religious and social activities of Notre-Dame and the Toussaint Center, white, Hispanic, and Haitian civic leaders often fill the first few rows of Notre-Dame during three-hour special Masses in Haitian Creole given on religious or civic holidays.

In Paris, despite efforts of Catholic lay leaders to support Haitians' incorporation, the association most trusted and recognized by Haitians – Haiti Development – never received much government recognition or funding. The dominant trend among French intellectuals and government officials is to hold to an assertive secularism which essentially posits that state vigilance and control over religious institutions is necessary for social progress (Cesari 2007; Kuru 2007). The logic of assertive secularism reasons that the state may justifiably intervene in matters of religious practice in order to ensure that individuals are not coerced into a practice deemed incompatible with French identity. At best, therefore, immigrant religion in France is to be ignored, but at worst it must be marginalized in order to achieve successful immigrant inclusion.

Despite the promises of equality in French Republicanism, the 2005 riots in the largely immigrant-inhabited *banlieues* where nearly all Haitians live highlighted the structural and symbolic exclusion of many immigrants in France. During several weeks of rioting, first- and second-generation immigrant youth – most of them North African or sub-Saharan African in origin – burned thousands of vehicles and defaced symbols of the French Republic. Scholars, politicians, and the French public continue to debate the causes and solutions of this failed immigrant integration. Some point to the lack of good education and jobs, whereas others argue that some immigrants are just too culturally different to be integrated into the French nation. Although Haitian youth in the Parisian *banlieues* were not reported to be among the protagonists of the riots, nearly all Haitians in Paris live in the often-dangerous *banlieues* where they lack social networks that would help them get jobs and where they must avoid danger on the streets.

Working-class Haitians in Paris are aware that their pious religious beliefs separate them from secular French society and from most highly educated Haitians in Paris. Whereas Haitian parents believe that successful inclusion requires both hard work and a strong community of faith, they express concern that the general secular climate in French society militates against their children's faith. Without a protective barrier of faith, Haitian parents fear that their children will join the downwardly mobile sector of the immigrant *banlieues* where they live. In addition, the Haitian elite in Paris generally follow the secular expectations of Republicanism and *laïcité* whereas lower-income Haitians maintain their vibrant religious faith and practice. As the French model of immigrant incorporation discourages in discourse and practice the formation of "durable" ethnic and religious communities, immigrants to France, including many Haitians, who face structural constraints on their integration – unemployment, discrimination, etc. – have fewer community organizations to support their successful inclusion.

Hence, of the three Haitian communities – those of Miami, Montréal, and Paris – only Haitians in Miami encountered a context where government and religious agencies cooperate to support their integration. Although French secularism is the more rigid than that of Québec, with regard to Haitian migrants, Québec's practice of secularism falls short of the goal of open secularism laid out in the Bouchard-Taylor Report. As a consequence of an understanding of secularism that relegates religious belief to the private sphere and avoids cooperating with religious agencies, Haitians in Montréal face increasing economic and symbolic challenges to their incorporation without the support of mediating institutions that their counterparts in Miami, but not in Paris, rely on for their inclusion.

Conclusions

Haitians' low human capital and economic problems in Québec have led to much socio-economic stagnation. Despite the contributions of religious organizations to immigrant incorporation, many government officials in Québec interpret secularism to mean noncooperation with these institutions. The government regulations that had resulted in funding cuts to the Bureau and to the Centre for Social Aid to Immigrants were later revised to specify that while dioceses and parishes could not receive government funding, service organizations with ties to a particular faith tradition could still receive funding. But, the ideology of secularism in Québec is so strong that some government officials behave in practice as if the state will not cooperate with religious institutions. Québec's practice of secularism has marginalized Haitians' mediating institutions and hence likely slowed their successful integration.

Concerns about immigrant inclusion in Québec are interpreted in relation to a historical narrative in which religion retards progress and in which the state needs to preserve Québécois national identity. Even though private religious belief and practice are tolerated, public religious expressions and service institutions with ties to religious institutions are suspected of conflicting with Québécois national identity and secularity. Despite the historical influence of Catholicism on Québécois identity and the active participation of some Catholic leaders and organizations in the political modernization and liberation achieved during the Quiet Revolution, strong religious beliefs and vibrant religious institutions working in social programs are more often seen as a problem rather than a part of the solution to challenges immigrants face in their incorporation. Ethnographic, interview, and census data on Haitians presented here illustrate that the Québec model of immigrant integration has not worked for many Haitians, who face significant economic and symbolic barriers to their inclusion. Greater ethnographic work on immigrants' religious lives and the contributions of religious organizations to immigrant integration may alter the dominant narrative of religion as necessarily a barrier to social progress rather than a step towards solving social problems.

Although some scholars argue that the Quiet Revolution directly built on modernizing efforts begun by the Catholic Church (Balthazar 2009), the consensus viewpoint in Québec is that the Catholic Church was an obstacle to modernization and progress in Québec. Positive contributions of religious institutions and ideals to the modern state in Québec are generally overshadowed by a narrative of religion-state conflict (Van Die 2001). The architects of the Quiet Revolution and a generation of Québécois scholars constructed a narrative in which Catholicism kept people attached to traditional ways of life and thus contributed to their oppression under the powerful Anglophones in Québec.

As David Lyon wrote, rather than presuming secularization will lead to the disappearance of religion it Canada, it is important to ask how belief has been relocated (Lyon 2000). Ethnographic studies that take religion seriously and document religious practices, such as the one I completed for *Faith Makes Us Live: Surviving and Thriving in the Haitian Diaspora* (Mooney 2009), are crucial to move the debate beyond just theories or perceptions not based on rigorous research. The ethnography I conducted highlights how, in contrast to some understandings of religion as oppressive, Haitian migrants rely on their faith to construct meaning and belonging, which then leads them into social action to resolve their incorporation challenges.

Despite the historical influence of Catholicism in Québécois identity and the active participation of some Catholic leaders and organizations in the political modernization and liberation achieved during the Quiet Revolution, for many Québécois intellectuals and government officials, public religious expressions and faith-based service institutions are suspected of conflicting with Québécois secular identity. Although the public role of religion in Québec is still being debated, and some government officials may seek to accommodate religious expressions or groups in their work, for the government officials I interviewed, immigrants' strong religious expressions – such as those described above – are more often seen as a problem for their integration rather than a part of the solution to challenges faced in that incorporation. Even though not all Québécois intellectuals or government officials may see religion as a problem for Haitians' inclusion, the Haitian immigrants I interviewed all agreed that their religious piety constitutes a symbolic barrier to their incorporation into what they see as an extremely secular society. Furthermore, leaders of Haitian organizations remarked that their institutions have lost legitimacy with the government and support from the government because of their religious identity.

Similarly, Peter Beyer's and Solange Lefebvre's work on second-generation Haitians in Montréal (presented in Beyer's chapter, this volume) illustrates that some Haitian youth (both Catholic and Protestant) have internalized the expectation that their religion should be private. Some Haitian youth resented having to keep their religion private, and they feared that talking about their faith at work or school would produce negative repercussions. At the same time, the fervent religiosity of many immigrants to Québec could gradually reconfigure the boundaries of religion and state in Québec and shape new understandings of how religious belief adapts to modernity.

More generally, Canadian multiculturalism policy and Québec's inter-culturalism policy recognize that ethnic identity, but not religious identity, is an important source of community bonds. Immigrants such as many Haitians question this assumption, and claims made by religious groups may lead to a new understanding of religion in the public sphere in Canada and Québec. As Fournier and See point out in their chapter for this volume, the public sphere is supposed to include multiple perspectives. However, I have shown that Québec's secularism seeks to privatize religious identities and organizations while actively incorporating ethnic identities and organizations into public policies and discussions. Hence, while a less rigid form of secularism than that of France, Québec's secularism is not neutral in practice.

NOTES

1 This chapter is based on research I conducted in the Haitian communities of Miami, Montréal, and Paris. See Mooney (2009).
2 First Kings 17:10–16, and the Gospel parable of the widow's mite (Mark 12:41–44).
3 In French, *le Bureau de la communauté chrétienne des Haïtiens à Montréal*.
4 The interviews were conducted in either French or Haitian Creole by the author (Mooney), and the translations in the text were also done by the author.
5 The Congregation of the Holy Spirit, commonly known as the Spiritains.
6 I have changed the names of people I interviewed at Notre-Dame.

7 For greater detail on Haitians' socio-economic incorporation in Miami, see
   Mooney (2009) and Stepick, Dutton Stepick, Eugene, Teed, and Labissiere
   (2001).

REFERENCES

Balthazar, Louis. 2009. "La nationalité québécoise et l'Église catholique." In
   La nation sans religion? Le défi des ancrages au Québec, edited by Louis-André
   Richard, 131–54. Québec: Presses de l'Université Laval.
Bouchard, Gérard, and Charles Taylor. 2008. "Building the Future: A Time
   for Reconciliation." Commission de consultation sur les pratiques
   d'accommodement reliées aux différences culturelles. Québec: Québec Gov-
   ernment Printing Office, 22 May.
Cesari, Jocelyne. 2007. "The Muslim Presence in the United States and France:
   Its Consequences for Secularism." *French Politics, Culture, & Society* 25(2):
   34–45.
Dejean, Paul. 1978. *Les Haïtiens au Québec*. Montréal: Les Presses de l'Université
   du Québec.
Ives, Nicole. 2010. "Outreach to Immigrants and Refugees as Ministry: A
   Descriptive Summary of Ways in which a Sample of Churches Support
   Immigrants and Refugees in Montréal's Black Communities." Final report
   for faith-based dossier of the Black Communities Demographic Project,
   2006–2009. Montréal, Québec.
Ives, Nicole, and Jill Witmer Sinha. 2010. "The Religious Congregation as
   Community Partner in Refugee Resettlement: An Overview of Theory and
   Practice for Social Workers." *Canadian Social Work Review* 12(1): 210–17.
Kuru, Ahmet T. 2007. "Historical Conditions, Ideological Struggles, and State
   Policies Toward Religion." *World Politics* 59(4): 568–94.
Labelle, Micheline, Serge Larose, and Victor Piché. 1983. "Émigration et immi-
   gration: les Haïtiens au Québec." *Sociologie et sociétés* 15(2): 73–88.
Labelle, Micheline, Daniel Salée, and Yolande Frenette. 2001. "Incorporation
   citoyenne et/ou exclusion? La deuxième génération issue de l'immigration
   haïtienne et jamaïcaine." Unpublished report. Rapport de recherche soumis
   à la Fondation canadienne des relations raciales, Montréal, Québec.
Lyon, David. 2000. "Introduction." In *Rethinking Church, State, and Modernity:
   Canada between Europe and America*, edited by David Lyon and Marguerite
   Van Die, 1–19. Toronto: University of Toronto Press.
Mooney, Margarita A. 2009. *Faith Makes Us Live: Surviving and Thriving in the
   Haitian Diaspora*. Berkeley: University of California Press.

Portes, Alejandro, and Ruben G. Rumbaut. 2006. *Immigrant America: A Portrait*. Berkeley: University of California Press.

Stepick, Alex. 1992. "The Refugees Nobody Wants: Haitians in Miami." In *Miami Now!: Immigration, Ethnicity and Social Change*, edited by Guillermo Grenier and Alex Stepick, 57–8. Gainesville: University Press of Florida.

Stepick, Alex. 1998. *Pride against Prejudice: Haitians in the United States*. Boston: Allyn & Bacon.

Stepick, Alex, Carole Dutton Stepick, Emmanuel Eugene, Deborah Teed, and Yves Labissiere. 2001. "Shifting Identities and Intergenerational Conflict: Growing up Haitian in Miami." In *Ethnicities: Children of Immigrants in America*, edited by Ruben Rumbaut and Alejandro Portes, 220–66. Berkeley: University of California Press.

Torczyner, Jim L. 2001. "The Evolution of the Black Community of Montréal: Change and Challenge." McGill Consortium for Ethnicity and Strategic Social Planning, Montréal, Québec.

Van Die, Marguerite. 2001. *Religion and Public Life in Canada: Historical and Comparative Perspectives*. Toronto: University of Toronto Press.

9 The Intersection of Religious Identity and Visible Minority Status

The Case of Sikh Youth in British Columbia

KAMALA ELIZABETH NAYAR

British Columbia has witnessed a tremendous growth in religious and ethnic diversity, especially after Canada made changes to its immigration law in 1967 and instituted the Multiculturalism Policy in 1971.[1] Given British Columbia's close proximity to Asia, the province has drawn and continues to draw in many Asians. The Chinese currently comprise the largest visible minority group in British Columbia. However, since many members of the Chinese community practise the Christian faith, the Sikh community has emerged as the largest non-Christian group in the BC Lower Mainland (Statistics Canada 2005).

Sikhs follow a 500-year-old tradition that originated in the geographic region of the Punjab in present-day India and Pakistan. The foundations of Sikhism were laid by Guru Nanak (1469–1539), the first of a succession of 10 Sikh gurus.[2] Sikhism grew in the struggle against Mughal rule. In the course of that struggle, the Sikhs developed a martial tradition of fighting against social injustice and for the protection of human rights. Following the martyrdom of the fifth guru, Guru Arjan Dev, in 1595, the sixth guru, Guru Hargobind, adopted the symbolism of two swords to represent *miri-piri*, the temporal and spiritual realms. Later, for his defence of the religious freedom of the Hindus, the ninth guru, Guru Tegh Bahadur, was beheaded in Delhi in 1675. Subsequent to Guru Tegh Bahadur's martyrdom, Guru Gobind Singh, the tenth guru, established the Khalsa Order or Sikh Brotherhood to fight against Mughal oppression and aggression (1699).

Sikhs who receive baptism or initiation into the Khalsa Order are required to maintain the five emblems of the Sikh faith: (1) comb (*kanga*), (2) dagger (*kirpan*), (3) undershorts (*kacchera*), (4) cast iron bangle (*kara*), and (5) unshorn hair (*kes*) covered with a turban or headscarf

(Grewal 1991, 41).[3] Men initiated into the Khalsa Order are to take Singh (Lion) as a surname, while women are to take Kaur (Lioness or Princess) as their surname. Although the Khalsa Order established by Guru Gobind Singh encompasses the baptized (*amritdhari*) or orthodox Sikh, not all Sikhs bear the five articles of faith. Since the late 1800s, as a result of the Singh Sabha movement, recognition has been accorded to Sikhs as *kesdharis* (bearer of unshorn hair), who – while not baptized – follow the principal requirement of unshorn hair (*kes*) covered by a turban or headscarf. Sikhs who do not follow this chief requirement but still believe in the spiritual teachings of the gurus are called *sahajdharis* (gradual adopters) (Singh 2008, 146).

Though its roots in Canada go back to the first decade of the twentieth century, the Sikh community did not become a significant immigrant group until the post-war period (Nayar 2004, 17–18). With the large influx of Sikh immigrants beginning in the 1970s, the Sikh community has grown in diversity, including a number of Sikhs who choose to uphold their religious identity. While there have been some legal cases relating to amendments to school policies with respect to Sikh students and teachers wearing the *kirpan* (dagger) in Ontario and Québec, there has not been any legal issue over the *kirpan* in British Columbia even as the province has allowed for the establishment of private Sikh schools. Notwithstanding the BC government's initiatives in accommodating Sikhs, there still exists a cohort of Sikh youth in British Columbia that encounters a lack of intercultural understanding in the public education system. Although religious affiliation is primarily seen as an individual or private choice, religious and ethnic identity construction occurs and may even be played out in the public sphere. It is therefore critical for educational institutions to comprehend intercultural dynamics so that these institutions can effectively respond to a body of students from ethnic and religious minority backgrounds.

Drawing on a case study of students wearing controversial Khalistan[4] t-shirts at a public high school in Surrey, this chapter analyses how Sikh youth as individuals relate to the public sphere. The chapter consists of three parts: the first part locates the Sikh community in British Columbia's Asian religious landscape. The second part provides a case study of the controversial Khalistan t-shirt incident at a BC public high school.[5] Lastly, the third part analyses the issue that some Sikh youth face in negotiating their identities both as Sikh and a visible minority Canadian. In doing so, the case study sheds light on (1) the influence of the media's portrayal of the Khalistan issue, (2) Sikh youths' expression of marginalization through the "rap-ization" of the Sikh tradition, and (3) the value of genuine cultural validation in the public education system.

British Columbia's Asian Religious Landscape

British Columbia's diverse Asian religious landscape has become more visible over the last four decades, even though the Chinese first set foot on BC soil in the mid-1800s, the Japanese began arriving in the province in the 1880s and the Punjabis in the early 1900s. At that time, BC attracted Asians seeking greater economic opportunity based on the province's earlier need of manual or semi-skilled labour for railway construction, natural resource extraction, and production. In spite of BC's labour needs, the province was unreceptive to visible minority groups. The federal government imposed various discriminatory measures in immigration law, like the head-tax on the Chinese (1885–1923) (Roy 1989, 2003; Ward 2002), the continuous journey clause for "East Indians"[6] (1908–1947) (Johnston 1979; Nayar 2013), and the internment of the Japanese during the Second World War (Roy 2003; Ward 2002). Moreover, BC took away the right to vote from the Chinese in 1874, the Japanese in 1895, and the East Indians in 1908, as a manoeuvre to restrict their ability to exercise power (Nayar 2013). Although no federal legislation disenfranchised these groups, federal disenfranchisement also took place because the federal voters list was made up from the provincial lists.

Despite Canada's history of exclusion of visible minorities and BC's hostile sociopolitical environment, Asians became Canadian citizens on 1 January 1947 when the federal government instituted the *Canadian Citizenship Act*. It was, however, not until 1967, with Canada's institution of the point system as part of the *Immigration Act* that the doors widened for non-European – including Asian – immigrants (Pendakur 2000, 78–82). Subsequently, Asian communities grew substantially, with a large majority of them established in BC. According to the 2006 census, such communities in British Columbia were comprised of 432,435 Chinese, 274,205 South Asians (including 232,370 "East Indians," 7,975 Pakistanis, 4,150 Sri Lankans and 570 Nepalese), 94,250 Filipinos, 51,860 Koreans, 41,585 Japanese, 30,835 Vietnamese, and 10,565 Taiwanese, along with some Malaysians, Mongolians, and Tibetans (Statistics Canada 2006b).

Besides the changes to Canadian immigration law, the country's introduction of the Multiculturalism Policy in 1971 provided better opportunities for immigrants to retain their traditions, in contrast to the previous environment of immense pressure to assimilate into Canada's dominant Anglo society. Since the BC Lower Mainland has been the major locus of Canadian Asian settlement, the area now manifests a rich Asian religious landscape. For instance, in the municipality of Richmond, the agricultural reserved land developed between Blundell Road and Williams Road on No. 5 Road (apart from the residential areas) opens up to a variety of Asian religious places of worship: Ling Yen Mountain Temple for Chinese Buddhists, the Ram Krishna Mandir Vedic Cultural Society for Hindus, the Az-Zahraa Islamic Centre for Shia'a Muslims, Indian Cultural Centre Gurdwara for the Sikhs and the Chinese Evangelical Church for Chinese Christians. Moreover, just off No. 5 Road sits the Jami'a Mosque for Sunni Muslims and a Fujian Evangelical Church. While some may call the No. 5 Road in Richmond the "Highway to Heaven," many Asians and non-Asians alike now also refer to Richmond as "Little China."

Since the 1980s and 1990s, ethnic enclaves have emerged in the suburbs of BC's Lower Mainland. In fact, 43.6 per cent of Richmond is comprised of Chinese people, while there is also a growing Chinese presence in Vancouver (30 per cent) and Burnaby (30 per cent) (Statistics Canada 2006a). South Asians (predominantly Sikhs), who were once concentrated in South Vancouver and Burnaby during the late 1970s and 1980s, have since primarily shifted to Surrey; even so, the South Asian presence in Vancouver has increased to 9.9 per cent of the city's total population. Meanwhile, Surrey has the second-largest proportion of South Asians in a single Canadian municipality, with over 27.5 per cent of its population now comprised of South Asians even though many have moved to Abbotsford in the Fraser Valley, where South Asians comprise 16.3 per cent (25,600) of the city's total population (Statistics Canada 2006a).

The BC Sikh Community

As a result of the establishment of the sponsorship system as part of Canadian immigration policy and the marked increase in migration during the post-war period, the Sikh community has emerged as the largest non-Christian group in BC's Lower Mainland. The sponsorship system worked in favour of Sikh immigrants since most of the earlier "East Indian" immigrants had been Sikh (Nayar 2004, 17). From the time the Sikhs first migrated to British Columbia in the early 1900s up to the present, the *gurdwara* (Sikh temple) has proven to be the primary medium through which the Sikh community has been able to successfully establish itself in a province with now over 135,310 Sikhs (Nayar

2010, 44; Statistics Canada 2006b).[7] Despite the many different challenges that the community has faced with regard to immigration, the
Sikhs asserted their religious and cultural identity by building *gurdwaras*, which have also served as an essential place from where Sikhs
have lobbied for social justice and political rights (Nayar 2010, 53).

There is a broad spectrum both of religious affiliations within the BC
Sikh community and of political affiliations with various *gurdwaras*.
These extend to connections with federal, provincial, and municipal
political parties. Moreover, unlike the earlier generations of Sikhs,
who tended to give up many of their customs in order to fit in with
"white" society, some of the more recent immigrants have chosen to
maintain the orthodox practices that they brought with them from the
Punjab. The growth in numbers of Sikhs who are vocal about maintaining Sikh orthodox customs has resulted in an increase in tensions
between the earlier and the more recent immigrants, between the
orthodox and the more assimilated Sikhs. Besides, during the 1980s,
some Canadian Sikhs felt that the Indian government was marginal-
izing their compatriots in the Punjab. In response to armed separatist
activity inside the Golden Temple complex at Amritsar – the Sikhs'
most holy place of worship – the Indian military launched Operation Bluestar on 3 June 1984. This attack spurred some non-orthodox
Sikhs in Canada to take their religion more seriously and to become
baptized, while other non-orthodox Sikhs sympathized with the creation of a Sikh state because they identified with the ethno-nationalist
movement for greater autonomy for the Punjab (Nayar 2004, 139, 185).
Operation Bluestar and the Khalistan movement resulted in tensions
between Sikhs and Hindus living in the BC Lower Mainland for about
fifteen to twenty years.

There were three main international groups that involved themselves in anti-India protests: Babbar Khalsa International (1981–2003),
the International Sikh Youth Federation (ISYF, 1984–2003), and the
World Sikh Organization (1984–present). Some of the Lower Mainland *gurdwaras* had been taken over by pro-Khalistan organizations,
because of the earlier voter apathy and subsequent outpouring of
emotion in response to Operation Bluestar. These *gurdwaras* raised
funds for the Khalistan movement in the Punjab and lobbied Western governments concerning human rights violations there (Tatla 1999,
151–81). Despite concerns raised over national security with respect
to a couple of these organizations since their inception, especially
after their alleged connection with the Air India tragedy in 1985, the

Babbar Khalsa and ISYF were banned as terrorist organizations only in 2003, following the new security measures undertaken by the Canadian government in the aftermath of the 9/11 attacks on the United States. (Nayar 2004, 162–3; 2008, 17–32). All the while, there has also been a "silent majority" within the community that has remained uninvolved in such activities. While the Khalistan movement dissipated in the early 1990s, some Canadian orthodox and *kesdhari* Sikhs continue – from the perspective of human rights – to concern themselves with economic issues faced by marginalized farmers in the Punjab and global Sikh identity.[8]

Along with the shift towards issues concerning a "global" diasporic Sikh identity, it is noteworthy that Sikh immigrants are familiar with secular law as practised in India, and therefore they (a) are comfortable with the secular legal framework under the Canadian state, (b) use the system to appeal rulings that do not accommodate their religious practices, and (c) lobby elected officials to help their cause (Nayar 2011). Given the Sikh historical experience of Mughal and British oppression, the Sikhs possess a tradition of standing up against any violation of their religious freedoms. As a result, issues around the turban (*dastar*) and *kirpan* have emerged in which Sikhs have proved to be a challenge in the Canadian public sphere (Nayar 2011).

In various provinces of Canada, Sikhs have been successful in persuading school districts to allow them to attend schools with their *kirpans*. Although the issue emerged in Ontario in 1990,[9] the most recent case has been in Québec.[10] While the *kirpan* has been a controversial issue in such provinces and has required "institutional accommodation," interestingly there has never been any legal action over the issue in the BC education system. The long-standing history of Sikhs living in the province may account for the lack of legal controversy over the *kirpan*. In fact, with respect to education, the BC Sikh community has benefitted from Canada's policy of multiculturalism (Nayar 2004, 190). In 1986, the Sikh private school called Khalsa School – a full-time school that follows the provincial curriculum from kindergarten to grade ten and at the same time provides instruction in the Sikh religion and Punjabi language – was established in Vancouver. A second Khalsa School (Newton campus, Surrey) was opened in 1992; and a third Khalsa School (Old Yale Road campus, Surrey) in 2008. In the same year, the Sikh Academy began as a private school offering pre-kindergarten to grade seven in Surrey. In addition, since 1996, several BC public high schools have been offering Punjabi language instruction in the regular curriculum. Despite these multicultural initiatives, controversy erupted at a public high school in Surrey over a group of Sikh youth wearing Khalistan t-shirts.

Case Study: Khalistan T-Shirts in the Public Education System

On 18 April 2008, around twenty students wearing Khalistan t-shirts went to their local high school in Surrey, which is situated in a neighbourhood that has a large South Asian population. In reaction to the "violent" nature of the Khalistan t-shirts – bearing an image of a popular Khalistan militant leader holding a spear and a revolver strapped to his side – the students were advised both that the t-shirts were inappropriate and that they were forbidden from wearing them at school. School administrators banned the Khalistan t-shirts on the ground that there was a range of negative reactions to the clothing. The School District communications manager explained: "I think it's safe to say that even within the Indo-Canadian community, Khalistan, and the pursuit of it, is something that is controversial in that community. Whether that is political or the violence related to that, there were some concerns expressed" (CBC News 2008c).

A critical question that arises from this incident, however, is as to whether or not the wearing of these t-shirts was really about Khalistan politics by Sikh militants as portrayed by the media. Significantly, the twenty students, who wore the Khalistan t-shirts, were primarily *not* "Khalsa" (orthodox) Sikhs. Moreover, the incident occurred one week after the media-driven attention given to the Surrey Vaisakhi parade[11] on 12 April 2008, which some "politicians were reluctant" to participate in because of some controversial Khalistan-related photographs (CBC News 2008b). The Vaisakhi parade received much media attention because Premier Gordon Campbell and many other politicians, who attended the parade in 2007, faced political embarrassment after it was revealed that one float had displayed a photograph of alleged Air India bombing mastermind Talwinder Singh Parmar (CBC News 2008a). In response to both Sikh and non-Sikh disapproval, the organizers of Surrey's Vaisakhi parade in 2008 set up a tent which discretely displayed photographs of victims of human rights violations in the Punjab, along with pictures of militants whom Khalistan sympathizers revere as Sikh martyrs. While the media sensationalized the display of

Khalistan-related photographs and the potential for violence, the Vaisakhi parade and festivities – with over 100,000 attendees – proceeded without any incidents of violence (CBC News 2008b).

Due to the media coverage surrounding the violent pursuit of Khalistan, the school district in its handling of the t-shirts incident appears to have looked at the incident from the perspective of Sikh militancy rather than to have responded to the students' personal circumstances. Given the fact that the t-shirts included the image of swords, the students did cross a boundary at the public institution, especially since they were familiar with the school district policy of no imagery or replicas of firearms on school grounds. And, indeed, school districts impose such policies in order to mitigate situations of violence. In doing so, the school district appears to have overlooked other issues relating to the action of these predominantly non-orthodox Sikh students wearing Khalistan t-shirts. Rebellion typically associated with adolescence converging with cultural memory that visible minorities often possess – along with the intercultural dynamics that exist in public institutions within the ethnic enclave context – may be better understood by exploring it as the expression of marginalization through the "rap-ization" of the Sikh tradition.

The "Rap-ization" of the Sikh Tradition

The Khalistan t-shirts worn by the cohort of twenty students consisted of a popular image of the militant leader Jarnail Singh Brar (Bhindranwale) holding a metal spear and a revolver strapped to his side. Along with the depiction of Jarnail Singh, there was also the following slogan on the t-shirts: "A physical death I don't fear, a death of consciousness is a sure death." This is a popular slogan that Jarnail Singh used in his speeches until his death in 1984. Although the slogan was used in the context of a cohort of Sikhs challenging the central Indian government during the 1980s, some Sikh youth have, in fact, fused it with African American style conscious rap; that is, Sikh rappers now use the slogan during their stage performances. Consistent with African-American conscious rap, many themes are incorporated in order to raise awareness about social and cultural issues. For example, Saint Soldier in his song entitled "Sister" speaks out against infanticide in a manner to raise awareness about the injustices inflicted on females in the Punjab and the diaspora (Saint Soldier and Deep Mangli 2010, verse 3). Given the Sikh concept of *miri-piri* and the collective memory of oppression at the hands of for- eign invaders, the Sikh tradition easily converges with conscious rap. While conscious rap is a constructive method for speaking out about injustices such as racism or gender inequality, these themes are also often the underlying force bolstering the gangster image (Counsellor 2, personal communication, 15 February 2011). Gangsta rap, a sub-genre of hip-hop that emerged in the mid-1980s, displays the reckless "gangster" lifestyle of inner-city youth, and also includes themes of discrimination and oppression.

In the case of the t-shirt incident, upon hearing that a few students had been given a warning when they appeared at school with Kha-listan t-shirts, more students wearing the t-shirt went to school in pro-test, with the attitude that said "Who is to say I can't wear it? It's my right." The students' approach converges with the rebellion typical of adolescents, and even more so with the destructive attitudes found in gangsta rap.

Prior to this incident, there had also been a case in which a student wore a t-shirt with two guns on each side of a serrated metal ring or quoit (*cakkar*) and the double-edged sword (*khanda*). Following the Bab-bar Khalsa logo with guns, the two guns replaced the two swords of the traditional *khanda* insignia, a sacred Sikh symbol exemplifying *miri-piri* (temporal and spiritual realms) in the context of the universality of humankind.[12] At the same time, the gun has become iconographic in rap culture because it represents the "ghetto" and symbolizes the means of destruction, which is often found in rap lyrics from the perspective of both the perpetrator and the victim; the gun has become symbolic of the rage that visible minorities may feel (Dyson 2007, 91–3). As one blogger has written about the Khalistan t-shirt incident: "The guns of the Babbar Khalsa logo has become 'cool.' It has become the Sikh youth Che Guevare T-Shirt. Find another logo kids" (Langar Hall Blog 2008).

At first blush, one may draw a linear understanding of post-1984 Sikh youth – who have been raised in homes sympathetic to the Kha-listan movement and have grown up hearing about the Sikh past – as part of some "imaginative project of Khalistan" (Shani 2008, 102–5). However, many Sikh youth gravitate towards rap culture because it is "cool," and they strongly identify with the themes of marginaliza-tion and discrimination within the Canadian context. As one Sikh coun-sellor in the BC Lower Mainland notes: "Sikh youth actually identify with rap culture because of their own status as a minority in Canada and the portrayal of discrimination and rebellion is congruent with their own 'perceived' or actual experiences" (Counsellor 2, personal communication, 15 February 2011). It is not a surprise, therefore, that their orientation would combine elements of rap culture with the Sikh tradition. In fact, rap has captured the global attention of many groups, which identify it with rebellion against oppression and discrimination (Dyson 2007, 50).[13]

The media is inseparable from the social process, and the discussion of Khalistan politics as portrayed by even publicly funded media outfits tends to shape the narratives about Sikhs in British Columbia (Nayar 2004, 215–16).[14] Since the events surrounding the Khalistan movement and the Air India tragedy (the largest terrorist attack in Canadian history), the turban has become conflated with terrorism (Nayar 2008). In this case, the media's coverage of the parade appears to have had consequential implications for the school's handling of the Khalistan t-shirt incident. The stereotypes perpetuated by the media regarding Sikh violence and the pursuit of Khalistan stifled other interpretations of the incident and obscured intercultural understanding of some Sikh youth in the public education system. As an alternative, the Sikhs – as a resource – could be included in discussions about issues that occur within the community or matter to it, and a culturally validating approach could be utilized. Note the comment of a Sikh counsellor and educator in the Lower Mainland:

> Shortly after the t-shirt incident, I met with three administrators at the school. I thought I could help them better understand how to engage with these students. Rather than exploring the opportunity to better connect with these Sikh students, the issue simply remained a matter of following school district protocol. Such organizational decision-making only furthers the divide between the education system and students from misunderstood communities. Education is supposed to be a collaborative project. All communities have cultural assets for understanding and resolving issues that disrupt societal wellness. (Counsellor 2, personal communication, 15 February 2011)

In the case of youth combatively asserting their identity, a collaborative approach can be more effective. For instance, the traditional Sikh perspective on maladaptive behaviour exhibited by a young person (*jawan*) is the result of an imbalance between adrenaline (*josh*) and awareness (*hosh*), with the former predominant. Moreover, Sikh scripture (*Guru Granth Sahib*) describes the youth as possessing little knowledge and limited insight into existential issues. As the second stage in life, youthfulness (*jawani*) is regarded as follows:

O merchant friend! In the second watch of the night,
you are intoxicated by the wine of youth and beauty.
O merchant friend! Night and day, you indulge in (sensual desire),
and your consciousness is blind to *nam* [the Divine Essence]).
All other tastes are sweet to you (while) *nam* is not enshrined within
(your heart).
You do not possess wisdom, concentration, virtue or self-discipline.
In falsehood, your life is wasted away.
Pilgrimages, fasts, purification, and self-discipline are meaningless,
along with the acts of piety and rituals.
Nanak says: Liberation is attained through devotion (of *nam*),
and all else leads to duality. (*Guru Granth Sahib*, 75–6; cited in Nayar and
Sandhu 2007, 77–8)

According to the Sikh tradition, a healing resource can consist of elders, who, in nurturing the youth through compassion (*daya*), can help them attain a balance between adrenaline (*josh*) and awareness (*hosh*). Such nurturing involves dialogue (*vichar*), during which the youth may acquire knowledge (*gian*), recognize ethics (*dharam*), experience empowerment (*saram*), and grasp truths (*sach*).

Sikh Youth Seeking Cultural Validation in an Ethnic Enclave

Adolescence, according to Western psychology, is a developmental stage in life during which youth form and re-establish their identities. This developmental stage, between the ages of twelve and eighteen, is marked by conflict over identity and by role confusion. Ideally, the individuation process is said to lead to a more developed sense of the self and personal identity, whereas failure to individuate results in role confusion and a weak sense of the self (Phinney, Ong, and Madden 2000). Building on Erik Erikson's stage of identity formation during adolescence, some psychologists have established models of minority identity development. During the initial phase of ethnic minority identity development, as Phinney describes it, ethnicity is often unexplored until an encounter takes place that serves as a catalyst for exploration (Phinney 1992). It is for this reason that critical attention needs to be given to adjustment at school, since it is the main avenue for the children of immigrants to adapt to different cultural norms and to participate in society (Phinney, Horenczyk, Liebkind, and Vedder 2001). Besides, contrary to popular mainstream misperceptions, ethnic minority citizens are concerned about being included as full or equal members of society (Banting 1999, 116).

Cultural memory also plays a critical role in minority identity development, as discussed by Beyer and Mooney in Chapters 3 and 8 of this volume, respectively. Through their own experiences of being "brown" or "other" along with the memory that has been imparted to them by their parents about the challenges they faced when they first arrived in British Columbia, some Sikh students experience having a visible minority status while living in an ethnic enclave (Counsellor 1, personal communication, 10 February 2011). Moreover, when attending a public school in a so-called Sikh or South Asian enclave, where Sikhs form the majority of the student body, these students function within an administrative structure that is dominated by Anglo-Canadians, who may at times not be prepared to deal with unique intercultural scenarios. While school administrators have the authority to enforce school district policy, the issues that emerged before them, including the sequence of events reported in the media about the Vaisakhi parade that preceded the Khalistan t-shirt incident, could perhaps have been better addressed in order to mitigate the perpetuation of negative and stereotypical images of young people of Sikh background and the societal "panic" about immigrant youth crime (Collins and Reid 2009).

Students with a strong cultural or bi-cultural identity may not feel a sense of belonging in the educational setting if their unique religious or ethnic background is not validated. When ethnic minority students lack validation, they are likely to experience adverse feelings, such as disorientation, stress, anxiety, and self-doubt, and may subsequently engage in maladaptive behaviour. Along with rebellion that is characteristic of adolescence, maladaptive behaviour can also be the result of: (a) the feelings of marginalization and isolation from the family and/or mainstream society; (b) the desire for protection against endemic racism or bullying; and (c) the need for social relationships that impart a sense of identity and respect (Sandhu and Nayar 2008, 40–2). According to Ishiyama, people are motivated to seek validating experiences – "the affirmation of one's sense of self and positive valuing of one's unique and meaningful existence" (Ishiyama 1995, 135) – when interacting with the world. Cultural validation involves acknowledging and understanding not only the religious or cultural traditions, but also validating existential situations that influence identity formation of diverse people. Astin contends that ethnic minority students' positive feelings of fitting in culturally can create a sense of affirmation and belonging, and thus the desire to do well in education (Astin 1982).

The Sikhs do not have a tradition of proselytizing others to become Sikh followers. However, the sentiment exists that others need to be better informed about the Sikh religion, not only to correct the media's distorted portrayal of the Sikhs, but also to educate people about who the Sikhs are (Nayar 2008, 30). At the same time, the practice of multiculturalism in the public sphere should not be reduced to mere institutional accommodation or the "multicultural" celebration of diversity, but could also include initiatives towards enhancing intercultural understanding and validation within the public sphere, such as acknowledging the historical, religious, and cultural backgrounds and contributions of diverse Canadians. More specifically, in order to better engage students of visible minority backgrounds, educational institutions could utilize innovative approaches that incorporate curriculum and activities that are more inclusive and interactive rather than exclusive and isolating. There are hopeful signs among educators, who seem to have greater empathy with questions about identity formation among visible minorities in the school system; however, greater support is still required from their administrators.

Conclusion

Many Asians have made their home in British Columbia. Because BC's Lower Mainland has been the primary place of Canadian Asian settlement, the region has a diverse Asian religious landscape. Christianity as the religion of the "dominant culture" can be a means for some Asians to connect with, or create a sense of belonging to, the "dominant culture." Meanwhile, Asians who practise Buddhism or Hinduism can find validation in terms of either religious iconic figures, such as the Dalai Lama and Deepak Chopra, or of in-vogue practices, like yoga and mindful-meditation. Youth from Sikh homes, on the other hand, run a greater risk of experiencing social alienation, especially given the negative media portrayal of their community, which often reinforces stereotypes.

As is made evident in the case of the Khalistan t-shirt incident, some Sikh youth express their "perceived" or actual experiences of marginalization in Canada through the "rap-ization" of their religious tradition. This configuration reflects the intersection of visible minority status and religious identity, which is quite different in reality from the manner in which these students were understood in the public sphere, both by the media and in the education system. It is for this reason that it is important to understand the underlying intercultural dynamic and to address it appropriately. Indeed, the focus should not be solely geared towards the accommodation of religious diversity and celebration through "multicultural days," but rather towards genuine societal validation and inclusion of visible minority citizens so that they have a greater sense of belonging within the Canadian public sphere.

NOTES

1 The Social Sciences and Humanities Research Council of Canada supported this research, and Kwantlen Polytechnic University provided time release from teaching.
2 The Sikh meaning of the term *guru* is Ultimate Reality or the embodiment of that Reality, such as the Sacred Word. Hence, guru as "the embodiment of Ultimate Reality" also refers to the ten personal gurus, who uttered the Sacred Word, and the scripture (*Guru Granth Sahib*), which contains the Sacred Word.
3 These symbols were maintained by members of the Khalsa even though there may be some dispute about the instituting of the Sikh Code of Conduct (*Sikh Rahit Maryada*), since it occurred during the early twentieth century when the Sikh governing body had as its aim to emphasize a "Khalsa" Sikh identity. See McLeod (2003).
4 Khalistan literally means "land of the Pure" and can refer to a separate Sikh state that a cohort of Sikhs attempted to create after India's independence from British colonial rule.
5 The research methodology for the case study consists of four elements: (1) analysis of mainstream newspapers, Indo-Canadian newspapers, and a popular Sikh blog called "Langar Hall;" (2) listening to various Sikh rap artists (i.e., Saint Soldier, Saint Soulja, and Sikh Knowledge) online; (3) participant-observation by the present author at the annual Surrey Vaisakhi parade in 2007 and 2008; and (4) analysis of two semi-structured interviews with counsellors.
6 The British categorized people from India as "East Indian" in order to distinguish them from the "Native Indian." However, "Hindoo" was the popular term used by Anglo-Canadians to refer to all Hindus, Sikhs, and

Muslims. Although the pioneers were categorized as "East Indian," they were all Punjabi and the majority of them were Punjabi Sikh (80–85 per cent). The remaining 15–20 per cent of the BC "East Indian" population consisted of Punjabi Hindus and Punjabi Muslims.

7 In contrast, BC includes only 31,500 Hindus (Statistics Canada 2006b).

8 For further analysis on Sikh identity in a globalizing world, see Shani (2008, chapter 7).

9 In 1990, the question of a Sikh teacher wearing the *kirpan* to school emerged between the Peel County Board of Education and the Sikh community. In 1991, an Ontario Human Rights Commission adjudicator ruled that the Peel County Board must allow Sikh students and teachers to wear the *kirpan* as long as it is not more than seven inches long and is securely fastened inside the clothing. See *Peel Board of Education v. Pandori* (1991).

10 A Sikh student (Gurbaj Singh Multani) was not permitted to wear his *kirpan* to the Marguerite-Bourgeois School in 2002. While the Québec Superior Court's decision was to allow Gurbaj Singh to wear the *kirpan* to school in 2002, it was overturned by the Québec Court of Appeal in 2004. As a consequence, the decision was taken to the Supreme Court of Canada, which, in 2006, decided to allow Sikh students to wear *kirpans* in public schools on the grounds that it did not pose a safety risk. See *Multani v. Commission Scolaire Marguerite-Bourgeois* (2006), *Commission Scolaire Marguerite-Bourgeois v. Singh Multani* (2004), and *Multani v. Commission Scolaire Marguerite-Bourgeois* (2002).

11 Vaisakhi is the Punjabi festival celebrating the harvest at the advent of the month Vaisakh (between April and May). People in villages participate in Vaisakhi by organizing a local fair and by feasting, singing, and dancing. Although Vaisakhi is a traditional agricultural festival for all Punjabis, it has greater importance for Sikhs. According to Sikh tradition, Guru Gobind Singh created the Khalsa Order on the first day of Vaisakh in 1699. In the Punjab, many Sikhs go on pilgrimage to Anandpur (the place of the birth of the Khalsa) to celebrate the occasion.

   In the Lower Mainland, the Sikhs hold a parade that starts and ends at the *gurdwara*; along the parade route, many Sikhs put up tables and give away food, refreshments, and literature. In 1995, the BC government officially recognized the Vaisakhi parade for the Lower Mainland organized by the Vancouver Khalsa Diwan Society Gurdwara, in which many small-town congregations from other parts of the province also participate. However, since the 1998 divide between "orthodox" and "assimilated" groups, two separate parades have been held. The "orthodox" parade

·begins and ends at the Dasmesh Darbar Gurdwara in Surrey, while the original, and now, "assimilated" parade begins and ends at the Khalsa Diwan Society Gurdwara on Ross Street in South Vancouver (Nayar 2010, 53).

12 The *khanda* insignia consists of a sword on each side of a quoit (*cakkar*) and a double-edged sword (*khanda*) exemplifying the *miri-piri* concept within the context of the universality of humankind. While each of the two swords symbolize the inner battle with the ego and the external battle as the last resort for social and political justice, the quoit signifies the interconnected-ness of the world and the double-edged sword represents oneness in all or the dissolution of divisions.

13 For an in-depth analysis on hip-hop culture among South Asians in the United States, see Sharma (2010).

14 For an examination of the CBC's portrayal of Khalistan politics within the BC Sikh community, see Nayar (2008). For further analysis of the role of the media and the Canadian South Asian community, see Jiwani (2006). Jiwani analyses two case studies, both of which involve Sikhs in British Columbia.

REFERENCES

Astin, Alexander W. 1982. *Minorities in American Higher Education*. San Francisco: Jossey Bass.

Banting, Keith G. 1999. "Social Citizenship and the Multicultural Welfare State." In *Citizenship, Diversity, and Pluralism: Canadian and Comparative Perspectives*, edited by Alan C. Cairns, 108–36. Montréal and Kingston: McGill-Queen's University Press.

CBC News. 2008a. "Politicians Grapple with Attending Controversial Parade." *CBC News*, 11 April. Available at http://www.cbc.ca/canada/british-columbia/story/2008/04/11/bc-watts-vaisakhi-parade.html

CBC News. 2008b. "Controversial Photos Displayed at Surrey's Vaisakhi Parade." *CBC News*, 12 April. Available at http://www.cbc.ca/canada/british-columbia/story/2008/04/12/sikh-parade.html

CBC News. 2008c. "Remove Khalistan T-shirts, Surrey Students Told." *CBC News*, 21 April. Available at http://www.cbc.ca/canada/british-columbia/story/2008/04/21/bc-surrey-tshirts.html

Collins, Jock, and Carol Reid. 2009. "Minority Youth, Crime, Conflict, and Belonging in Australia." *International Journal of Migration and Integration* 10: 377–91.

Dyson, Michael E. 2007. *Know What I Mean? Reflections on Hip Hop*. New York: Basic Civitas Books.

Grewal, J. S. 1991. *Sikhs of the Punjab*. Cambridge: Cambridge University Press.

Ishiyama, Ishu F. 1995. "Use of Validationgram in Counseling: Exploring Sources of Self-validation and Impact of Personal Transition." *Canadian Journal of Counseling* 29(2): 134–46.

Jiwani, Yasmin. 2006. *Discourses of Denial: Mediations of Race, Gender, and Violence*. Vancouver: University of British Columbia Press.

Johnston, Hugh. 1979. *The Voyage of Komagata Maru: The Sikh Challenge to Canada's Colour Bar*. Delhi: Oxford University Press.

Langar Hall Blog. 2008. "Did I Mention I Like Sikh T-shirts?" 21 April. Available at http://thelangarhall.com/general/did-i-mention-i-like-sikh-t-shirts/

McLeod W. H. (2003). *Sikhs of the Khalsa: A History of the Rahit Maryada*. New Delhi: Oxford University Press.

Nayar, Kamala E. 2004. *The Sikh Diaspora in Vancouver: Three Generations amid Tradition, Modernity and Multiculturalism*. Toronto: University of Toronto Press.

Nayar, Kamala E. 2008. "Misunderstood in the Diaspora: The Experience of Orthodox Sikhs in Vancouver." *Sikh Formations* 4(1): 17–32.

Nayar, Kamala E. 2010. "The Making of Sikh Space: The Role of the *Gurdwara*." In *Asian Religions in British Columbia*, edited by David Overmyer, Don Baker, and Larry DeVries, 43–63. Vancouver: University of British Columbia Press.

Nayar, Kamala E. 2011. "The Sikhs: Citizenship and the Canadian Experience." In *Perspectives on Faith and Citizenship: Issues, Challenges and Opportunities*, edited by Paul Bramadat for the Ministry of Immigration and Citizenship, 116–40. Victoria: University of Victoria.

Nayar, Kamala E. 2013. "Religion, Resiliency and Citizenship: The Journey of a Vancouver Sikh Pioneer." In *Sikh Diaspora*, edited by M. Hawley, 103–27. Leiden: Brill Academic Publishers.

Nayar, Kamala E., and Jaswinder S. Sandhu. 2007. *The Socially Involved Renunciate: Guru Nanak's Discourse to the Nath Yogis*. Albany: State University of New York Press.

Pendakur, Ravi. 2000. *Immigrants and the Labour Force: Policy, Regulation, and Impact*. Montréal: McGill-Queen's University Press.

Phinney, Jean S. 1992. "The Multi-Group Ethnic Identity Measure: A New Scale for Use with Adolescents and Young Adults from Diverse Groups." *Journal of Adolescent Research* 7(2): 156–76.

Phinney, Jean S., Gabriel Horenczyk, Karmela Liebkind, and Paul Vedder. 2001. "Ethnic Identity, Immigration, and Well-Being: An Interactional Perspective." *Journal of Social Issues* 57(3): 493–510.

Phinney, Jean S., Anthony Ong, and Tanya Madden. 2000. "Cultural Values and Intergenerational Value Discrepancies in Immigrant and Non-Immigrant Families." *Child Development* 71(2): 528–39.

Roy, Patricia. 1989. *A White Man's Province: British Columbia Politicians and Chinese and Japanese Immigrants, 1858–1914*. Vancouver: University of British Columbia Press.

Roy, Patricia. 2003. *The Oriental Question: Consolidating a White Man's Province, 1914–41*. Vancouver: University of British Columbia Press.

Saint Soldier and Deep Mangli. 2010. "Sister" (featuring Sukhraj) [digital track]. Available at http://saintsoldier.bandcamp.com/track/sister. Vancouver: Azad Records.

Sandhu, Jaswinder S., and Kamala E. Nayar. 2008. "Studying the Sikh Diaspora: First Year University Experience of Punjabi Sikh Students." *Sikh Formations* 4(1): 33–46.

Shani, Giorgio. 2008. *Sikh Nationalism and Identity in a Global Age*. New York: Routledge.

Sharma, Nitasha T. 2010. *Hip Hop Desis: South Asian Americans, Blackness, and a Global Race Consciousness*. Durham: Duke University Press.

Sikh Rahit Maryada. 1982. Amritsar: Shiromani Gurdwara Parbhandak Committee.

Singh, Pashaura. 2008. "Sikh Dharam." In *Religions of South Asia*, edited by Sushil Muttal and Gene Thursbury, 131–84. New York: Routledge.

Statistics Canada. 2005. "Population Projections of Visible Minority Groups, Canada, Provinces, and Regions, 2001 to 2017." Available at http://www5 .statcan.gc.ca/bsolc/olc-cel/olc-cel?catno=91-541-XIE2005001&ISSNOTE= 1&lang=eng

Statistics Canada. 2006a. "Canada's Ethnocultural Mosaic, 2006 Census: Canada's Major Census Metropolitan Areas: Vancouver Four in Ten Belonged to a Visible Minority Group." Available at https://www12.statcan.gc.ca/ census-recensement/2006/as-sa/97-562/p24-eng.cfm

Statistics Canada. 2006b. "Population by Religion by Province and Territory (2001 Census)." Available at http://www.statcan.gc.ca/tables-tableaux/ sum-som/l01/cst01/demo30a-eng.htm

Tatla, Darshan S. 1999. *The Sikh Diaspora: The Search for Statehood*. Seattle: University of Washington Press.

Ward, Peter W. 2002. *White Canada Forever: Popular Attitudes and Public Policy toward Orientals in British Columbia* (3rd ed.). Montréal and Kingston: McGill-Queen's University Press.

CASES

Commission Scolaire Marguerite-Bourgeois v. Singh Multani [2004] J.Q. No. 1904
Multani v. Commission Scolaire Marguerite-Bourgeois [2006] 1 S.C.R. 256, 2006
  SCC 6
Multani v. Commission Scolaire Marguerite-Bourgeois [2002] Q.J. No. 619 (QL)
Peel Board of Education v. Pandori [1991] 3 O.R. (3d) 531 (Div. Ct.)

10 Curricular Heresy

Theological Religious Studies and the Assessment of Religious Pluralism in Canada

PAUL ALLEN

In her recent book *Nomad*, Ayan Hirsi Ali, the Somali-born writer and former Dutch parliamentarian, states with unambiguous certitude that *"All human beings are equal, but all cultures and religions are not"* (Hirsi Ali 2010, 212). Such expressions of liberal individualism, of which this is but one instance, are in the ascendant. Like Hirsi Ali, many in the West have called multiculturalism into question in recent years. Implied in this renewed scepticism is a fear of the equality of religions that is part of a multicultural ethos. But, assessing the virtues and vices of religions is a very treacherous exercise, especially for professional scholars of religion, and we are rightly averse to doing so. But how might we address public anxieties over the role of theologically driven worldviews in our pluralistic society?

Over the past century, with the rise of Religious Studies departments and the intellectual turn toward the phenomenological study of religion, judgments concerning religion have become more circumspect, tolerant, and descriptive. "Thick description," to use the anthropologist Clifford Geertz's famous term, is the common perspective among scholars of religion in academic programs in Canada and elsewhere. This perspective has much to commend it. The shift to Religious Studies is positive for its instinctive appreciation of diversity in Canadian society and other societies that practise tolerance and safeguard religious freedom.

In a political context that requires a deep assessment of religion and religious pluralism, however, I would claim that the academic discipline of Religious Studies is insufficient to sustain and deepen our understanding of religious traditions – at least by itself, it is insufficient for this task. Nor does it seem able to help ward off more recent threats to religious freedom in Canadian society and elsewhere. I am convinced that a more prominent role should be accorded to a nuanced theological approach in the scholarship on religion. This is so that diversity and religious pluralism do not become a prescriptive orthodoxy that proscribes the capacity for (secular) self-criticism. A secular scholarly milieu should not be above criticism in the way that historic theological orthodoxies tended to be protected by ecclesiastical privilege.

However, this call for a complementary theological approach to Religious Studies comes at a time when institutions of theological education are not always able to retain a visible and vibrant status in Canadian culture in the way they once did. The decline of theological education's institutional links reflects the diminished standing of some Christian churches in Canada, particularly the once-dominant liberal Protestant denominations. Yet the need and evident desire for more opportunities in theological education and spiritual formation appears to be strong. In this paper, I will describe the intellectual outlook of what I term "theological religious studies" with attention to the capacities that such a perspective offers for dealing with religious pluralism in Canada.

One perception pertaining to theological education is that, due to its tradition-bound character, it is biased. But, the allegation of bias only holds true if its relation to a particular tradition means that it is therefore a form of private knowledge or is oriented exclusively to doctrine. Rather, in complementing Religious Studies, theology is a form of public knowledge that pertains to competing traditions and their respective sets of beliefs and practices. In fact, this is why theology can claim an epistemology and an interdisciplinary scope that justifies its place in the public academy, and therefore, a place within many Canadian universities. From a geo-political or sociological perspective, moreover, it is the case that only "good theology beats bad theology." If a particular religious tradition abuses the civic obligations that come with a pluralistic social context, the only way to really understand the theological problem that is probably responsible is to regard that tradition through a serious theological lens, especially for the benefit of those whose interpretation of the tradition has led to extremist attitudes and beliefs.

In order to assess how well Canadian universities are suited to a theological, humanistic assessment of religious pluralism instead of an exclusively social-scientific assessment, I will draw on four issues. First, I will summarize briefly the state of theological and religious studies education in Canada. Second, I will contextualize this state of affairs with respect to a humanities-based understanding of diverse cultures and religions. Third, I will note how such aspirations compare with other situations internationally, and fourth, I will identify the significance of the theology of world religions as a field that warrants greater promotion in academic treatments of religious pluralism. I would like the academy to shift attention away from the phenomena of visible diversity by moving toward an understanding of "invisible" *religious belief* that pertains more directly to the academic study of religious pluralism.

Religious Studies and Theology in Canada

The state of religious education in Canada is in great flux. The steady decline and elimination of some nominally Christian educational institutions over the past two decades have taken place at both the grade school and at the post-secondary levels of education. Gone are many of the provincially mandated religiously based educational systems. Notably, the Catholic and Protestant school systems in Québec and Newfoundland have been dismantled. Rumours exist that the same fate awaits Ontario's Catholic system. Such institutional changes are thought to reflect the wider secularization that has taken place in Canadian society over the past forty years. Many theological schools, especially the established divinity colleges at large urban universities and some of the smaller affiliated colleges in the regions have experienced diminished enrolments and financial strain. Yet, paradoxically, the rise of Christian practice among many immigrant groups to Canada alters a straightforward portrait of religious pluralism conceived on the basis of the secularization thesis as evident in such instances of decline (Beyer 2005, 165–96). So, we are witness to certain contradictory trends in Canadian society concerning religion, especially Christianity. The contrast between thriving immigrant churches and the wilting influence of older mainline theological schools is one of those contradictions.

Many religious institutions today actively resist secularization, especially those schools which are tied to immigrant groups and to some extent, Christian theological schools. At the grade school level, private Jewish, Muslim, and Christian schools that express a strong commitment to their religious traditions continue to thrive. Based on a more longstanding history and despite accreditation struggles as well as a hostile campaign launched against some of them by the Canadian Association of University Teachers, Christian colleges and small universities continue to attract students in significant numbers.[1] These institutions do not typically engage the issue of religious pluralism.

However, such is not the case with the theological colleges of various Catholic seminaries and Protestant divinity schools in Canada. Historically influential schools in the federation of colleges that now make up the Toronto School of Theology, the Vancouver School of Theology, and the Atlantic School of Theology along with notable other schools in Montréal, Edmonton, and Saskatoon, and seminaries located in London (Ontario), Winnipeg, Ottawa, and elsewhere have trained large numbers of Christian clergy historically. These centres of theological education have been a mainstay of Canadian theological literacy, and their engagement with religious pluralism is typically strong and clear. And, one of the changes in the make-up of these institutions is the cultural and ethnic diversity of the larger student body, particularly in Vancouver, Toronto, and to some extent, Montréal. Courses in the theology of world religions are commonplace in these institutions, which reflects to some extent the presence of Religious Studies departments on or near their campuses. The ethos of these schools is far less defensive and apologetic than 50 years ago and they are thus far more open and culturally diverse. There seems to be a strong reliance upon the sheer good will of faculty members and their institutions for interpreting and responding to religious pluralism. Yet, because of their diminished influence, these schools do not have the capacity to translate this good will into a solid intellectual current that would flow into the broader streams of Canadian society. Neither do theological schools influence Religious Studies departments any more as was the case 30 years ago. Institutions of theological education do not typically have qualms about their own cultural diversity in an age of stronger immigration flows, but they do face the strong rhetoric maintained by Religious Studies scholars, whose advocacy of neutrality and strict disciplinary separation contributes, to some extent, to the isolation of theological scholarship. Theologians, at least in universities and established divinity schools, are typically more open in principle to the contribution of Religious Studies, on questions having to do with pluralism, than vice versa.

Theology and religious studies are practised, taught, and reflected in scholarship by those in universities. Apart from studies and consultations conducted by government agencies such as Québec's Secretariat for Religious Affairs (est. 2000) and Statistics Canada, the preponderant form of reflection on religious diversity emanates from universities. In turn, universities influence profoundly the shaping of Canadian polity and culture through research centres such as the University of

Victoria's Centre for Studies in Religion and Society. By 2008–09, over 1,100,000 students were enrolled in Canadian universities (Statistics Canada 2010a). This figure represents roughly 24 per cent of the population of young adults aged eighteen to twenty-four (HRSDC 2010). But, what types of programs are these students pursuing in their post-secondary education? Evidence points to a slow decline in enrolment in humanities programs, demonstrating that more students are at university for job training purposes, a task that the university in its original form was not designed for. In 1992, according to Statistics Canada, 12.8 per cent of university graduates earned degrees in the humanities, declining significantly to 11.3 per cent by 2007 (Giles and Drewes 2001; Statistics Canada 2010b). Until 9/11, fewer students were enrolling in courses dedicated to the study of religion. Anecdotal evidence suggests that the attention given to religion, and Islam in particular, shifted somewhat after 2001, but it is questionable whether overall religious literacy among graduates with undergraduate degrees in the liberal arts has improved.

So, let us imagine then a scenario where universities should play a lead role in the development of a "theological religious studies" in Canada. In so doing, a university would still garner the expertise of social scientists, but would benefit from the humanities approach of theologians, whose attention to the interpretation of texts and traditions is the condition for the possibility of a discussion of religious pluralism. That is, if we are to understand religious pluralism better, it is incumbent on the scholarly community to enhance religious literacy through a twinning of the distinctive approaches of theological experts and Religious Studies scholars. The academic study of religious pluralism should not presume the virtue of the current situation in which Religious Studies influences theology without a reciprocal influence.

One recent example that demonstrates both the benefits and the risks of twinning these disciplines is Queen's University in Kingston Ontario, where the theology school has recently been subsumed into a larger School of Religion, alongside Religious Studies. The risks seem apparent on the face of things. In this case, it is unclear whether historical ties between Queen's University and the United Church of Canada will suffice to provide for future hires and robust scholarly work in theology. In a press release announcing that the United Church will no longer fund any of the new school's programs, there is the following claim: "Theology programs at Queen's School of Religion address a post-Christendom era, take seriously changing demographics in

Canada, and prepare leaders for a religiously diverse context" (Queen's University 2010a). Yet, there is also this claim:

> The Queen's School of Religion is responding to the need to increase understanding of and engagement with religious difference. The QSR offers the best opportunity to respond to the growing student interest in religious studies, while continuing to preserve the school's original purpose of providing graduate and professional theological programs. (Queen's University 2010b)

It is not entirely reassuring to see theology being "preserved" while Religious Studies is growing on account of perceived student interest. It should be noted that student interest is often a function of clear and creative faculty research agendas, as is the case with many active theologians. If the work of theologians is not appreciated, or quietly ignored as an intellectual embarrassment, or carried out with undue deference to Religious Studies, it does not surprise me to see the contrast between theology and religious studies being described in this way. Yet, we should take solace in the acknowledgment that theology is afforded stature in the university, as opposed to being segregated in a separate college.

A benefit of such a twinned approach is that it allows for theological scholarship that is fostered toward other non-Christian traditions as well as between traditions. One researcher associated with the Queen's School of Religion is the recent recipient of a Lilly Theological Research Grant for a study titled "The Theological Aspect of Reformed Islam." This is an example of the kind of inquiry that carries out a "theological religious studies" in a context where both theology and religious studies are pursued (Queen's University 2010c). Elsewhere, at McGill University, the maintenance of theological programming is fostered by equally formal yet more longstanding arrangements made between the renamed Faculty of Religious Studies (formerly before 1970, the Faculty of Divinity) and the three church colleges with which it is affiliated. Theological Studies at Concordia University has grown, despite the gradual withdrawal of the Jesuits after the 1974 union of the former Loyola College with Sir George Williams College. At the Université de Montréal, the Faculty of Theology has evolved to incorporate Religious Studies, and this is the trend in other universities, although it remains a question in my mind as to whether Religious Studies scholars value the humanities perspective offered by theological inquiry. Inasmuch as this scepticism is warranted, it is incumbent on social scientists to reconceive inquiry into religion in a way that better takes the humanistic perspective of theology into account. This process might begin with a revitalization of the humanities in the university that I outline in the following section and which would mightily benefit an understanding of religious pluralism.

Diversity and the Humanities: Nurturing Democracy

In her recent book *Not for Profit: Why Democracy Needs the Humanities* (2010), Martha Nussbaum argues for the retention of the liberal arts curriculum in order to sustain the model of human flourishing that has sustained democracy in Western societies. Focusing on changes in both the American and the Indian networks of higher education, Nussbaum bemoans the shift away from an understanding of the university as an agent for personal development and enrichment toward an understanding of the university driven by the demands of economic development. She argues that the shift toward an economic *raison d'être* implies the long-run abandonment of democracy. Her critique implicitly questions the research ideal of the contemporary university, which was born in 1810 with Wilhelm von Humboldt's vision for the University of Berlin.

Nussbaum's call for greater attention to the humanities in a university education might suggest a widening of the standard sociological scope available for treating subjects such as religious pluralism. While sociology of religion provides necessary data and theoretical insights for measuring the impact of religious diversity on Canadian society, it cannot cultivate evaluative, imaginative, and empathic capacities regarding religion by itself. For the intellectual setting of those traditions that make up a pluralistic society, the humanities are necessary. A humanities education, as Nussbaum emphasizes, fosters as a matter of habit imagining ourselves in the place of others. A Religious Studies viewpoint that presumes scientific neutrality does not permit such a perspective to take hold. But, if literary, historical, and theological elements of meaning are brought to light, one can begin to imagine another religious narrative grounded in a different history and tradition. The narratives of plural identities require mutual understanding, and examples are unlimited. For instance, can Catholic social teaching inform liberal democracy or vice versa? Can a Hindu re-interpretation of the role of "caste" in the diaspora constitute a philosophical crisis or an opportunity for a reformed Hinduism? Is a contemporary historiography of Quranic texts amenable to the traditional interpretation of God's revelation for Muslims? Understanding a pluralistic, diverse society without an awareness of explicit theological narratives of the world would leave us unable to answer such questions. We would fall short of the goal of true understanding. In contrast, a true understanding of religious pluralism would imply the inclusion of theology.

Studied in the context of the humanities, religious pluralism is not the manageable phenomenon that social scientists sometimes assume. Alasdair MacIntyre (1984) has been a leading sceptical voice concerning the scope of authority that is exercised by the social sciences. Human nature, he maintains, is simply too unpredictable:

> It is necessary, if life is to be meaningful, for us to be able to engage in long-term projects, and this requires predictability; it is necessary, if life is to be meaningful, for us to be in possession of ourselves and not merely to be the creations of other people's projects, intentions and desires, and this requires unpredictability. We are thus involved in a world in which we are simultaneously trying to render the rest of society predictable and ourselves unpredictable, to devise generalizations which will capture the generalizations of others and to cast our own behaviour into forms which will elude the generalizations which others frame. (MacIntyre 1984, 104)

This is an intriguing comment on the unpredictable element of meaning, and it is also why the social management of religious diversity is an elusive goal. So that we are not frustrated by the limits of social science, we should recognize the contribution of the humanities – with their more forgiving attitude toward the sheer paradoxes of life. Therefore, without a genuinely theological complementary perspective, social management goals frame religious pluralism without an understanding of the plausibility structures of religious belief. But, to test plausibility implies the testing of theological claims against reason. Historically, this testing has come under the purview of philosophical or systematic theology. The history and scope of this field is therefore a key aspect to the analysis of speech about God. The limits and paradoxes of this kind of speech undergird the notion of what it means to believe in God or the divine.

What a complementary relationship between the humanities and social sciences also suggests is the importance of epistemology, which is too often left to specialist philosophers in the contemporary university. Anthony Kronman, in *Education's End: Why Our Colleges and Universities Have Given Up on the Meaning of Life* (2007), believes that a form of libertarianism combined with a "constructivist" theory of knowledge have inflicted fatal wounds on the liberal arts. Moreover, according to Kronman, a prescriptive ideology of diversity has:

... undermined the notion of an old and ongoing conversation that gives each entrant a weighted and responsible sense of connection to the past, and substituted the egotistic presumption that we can start a new and freer conversation on our own, engaging all the works of all the world's great civilizations in a colloquy we invent for ourselves ... It has wrecked the humanities' claim to be able to provide organized guidance in the exploration of the question of the meaning of life. (Kronman 2007, 194–95)

I would take from Kronman's caution that Canadian universities with theological faculties and colleges stand to provide a more substantial education by virtue of their connection to the past. Students with a theological background are rooted in the traditions of the historical past, and consequently may foster a greater understanding of what it takes to cultivate authentic religious pluralism, in comparison with those students whose only perspective is contemporary sociological theory or conflict management.

In a Canadian context, the lack of constitutionally interpreted church/state separation jurisprudence does not prohibit theologically informed humanities curricula as in the United States. In the United States, as Robert Wuthnow suggests, there is a widespread promotion of diversity in terms of perspectives that inform the great questions of a classical education. Yet, there is also a functional exclusion of students' religiously based narratives of meaning and value in the very classroom where the promotion of diversity is in full force (Wuthnow 2008). Formally speaking, this contradiction does not hamper Canadian universities. Informally however, the impulses of secularism militate against the maintenance and establishment of theologically oriented programs in Canadian universities. In the end, to the extent that theological programs are still too isolated from the mainstream, there is an insufficient engagement with pluralism, as a function of differences of belief.

International Comparisons on Theology and Pluralism

In Britain and other European countries where ties between universities and state churches (or with the Catholic Church in central and southern Europe) are rooted in centuries rather than decades of tradition, the way that religious studies and theology handle religious pluralism is more complex. In some cases in the UK, Religious Studies programs were introduced to the detriment of theology.[2] In other cases, Religious Studies programs have emerged alongside a continuing vibrant study of Christian theology. By contrast, in the United States, the divide between religious studies and theology has straddled the divide that exists between private and public or state universities. This neat division has not held however, as private universities have expanded religion programs and in some cases, such as Princeton University, maintained its religion program in separation from the (Reformed) Princeton seminary while also hiring theologians in the religion department. But, as Religious Studies programs have evolved in public universities, it is not clear whether this development has translated into a nuanced humanistic perspective on religion. The evidence is mixed and the story is complex. At the outset therefore, there is not an obvious precedent elsewhere along the lines of a theological religious studies for Canada.

However, in Europe, there are some partial models for initiating more theological programming in public institutions for the benefit of an understanding of religious pluralism. The following examples are by no means comprehensive in scope, but they provide some markers for judging how religious diversity can be understood in terms of a theologically oriented humanities education with attention to diversity:

1   The University of Leiden in the Netherlands has initiated programming in Islamic theology, including a three year program that incorporates study of the *Hadith* and primary texts on *sharia* law.[3]
2   The German government has commissioned a report on the state and future direction of theological education in Germany (German Council 2010). This report, while it focuses on the nature and the responsibility of promoting Religious Studies, also includes a number of neutral to positive references to theology. Recently, the thrust of this assessment of studies in religion at the level of higher education has received renewed interest. Reflecting a growing European unease with multiculturalism and religious pluralism, German Chancellor Angela Merkel expressed disappointment in Germany's decades-long official policies of multiculturalism in 2010 with remarks that were widely quoted. In response, the German government is following up Spain's lead by establishing state-sanctioned imam education in Muslim theology, in order to head off what it sees as the sanctioning of extremist theological politics.[4] While the model of a *state*-mandated theological education is questionable, at least it has the virtue of promoting the public good of theological education for better understanding of Islam. The German example also has the additional virtue of being directly supervised within a university setting, at the University of Osnabrück.

3 The Swedish government's academic research funding organization, Högskoleverket (Swedish National Agency for Higher Education), is a state regulatory agency that includes in its purview the ongoing funding for faculties of theology within Swedish universities, a most remarkable fact given the secular character of Swedish society. It is also responsible for the patronage of research that specifically includes theological research.[5] There has also been an explicit turn in neighbouring Denmark in recent years toward research and public explorations of the Lutheran character of Danish culture. The specifically Lutheran traditions cited include human freedom, the role of law, personal privacy, and the qualified theological justification for the state. These are matters about which Danes and other Scandinavians are in great consternation, given their current debates over immigration, the religious identity of minorities, and national identity.

4 Despite the determining interests of the historic British state church, the colleges and universities of the UK provide some opportunities for theological education rooted in a liberal arts epistemology. Yet, the maintenance of theology in these settings, has, until recently, uniformly followed the norms of liberal modernity. A secular model of theological education meant that in the UK, until the dissenting voice of Colin Gunton and several other scholars in the 1980s, British theological education was premised on the need to absorb secularization and Religious Studies curricula rather than assert itself. This history is narrated ably by Gavin D'Costa who draws the startling conclusion that theology should withdraw from the public university (D'Costa 2005, 38–76).

These European anecdotes provide some perspective on the way that theological education may fit in the contemporary university. Much depends on the way that theological scholarship is carried out. That is, these examples do not make the case on their own for the state support of theological education along the lines of some unreformed status quo. While being more ambiguous, the coexistence of theology within the modern public university embodies a connection of the humanities to Religious Studies. The public role for theology serves the goal of intellectual diversity within universities and academies that are otherwise in thrall to an empiricist model of knowledge acquisition. So, theology can serve what Paul Murray (2007) calls "ideology critique." At a time of empiricist dominance in epistemological presuppositions, theology's aspirations to articulate knowledge about God is an implicit critique of those disciplines that are under pressure from a technological and utilitarian mindset. Theologians thus play a central role in assessing religious diversity and pluralism as academics who can offer a different perspective on diversity in a secularized academy and culture from that of their social scientist colleagues.

The Theology of Religions

The last component of this sketch of the argument for a theological religious studies is the significance of the theology of world religions. This field has become a vital and theoretically rich intellectual and theological feast. It emerged as a way of understanding other religious accounts of God or transcendence without stepping necessarily outside of the tradition within which one has chosen to understand God. Or, in certain cases, a theology of religions has allowed new hybrid theologies to develop in the light of two or more religious traditions. In a sense, this field has been incubated by Gadamer's (2004) insight concerning the fusion of horizons. This is the claim that it is impossible to bypass the textual, historical tradition of the interpreter in a proper understanding of a text. For dialogue to be authentic, religious traditions require an openness, that is an openness from somewhere, not an openness that falsely pretends to absolute neutrality. Gadamer articulates this hermeneutic of understanding in terms of the value of the question, which always proceeds from an individual's "pre-judgment." Now, the implicit value that is cultivated by sociologists of religion is that of dialogue between the religious traditions. But no dialogue can take place if theological convictions are deliberately set to one side, which is what Gadamer points out in a general way.

So, the theology of world religions has pointed up the impossibility of pure objectivity. It has focused attention on the complexities that mark the internal diversity of religious traditions as well as the complexities that configure the relations between each of the traditions. The literature is replete with surprises.[6] Paul Knitter's (1995) fourfold typology of interreligious relations (replacement, fulfillment, mutuality, and acceptance) is a development of earlier typologies, notably Alan Race's well-known typology of exclusivism, inclusivism, and pluralism. Instances of dialogue formulated in line with a theology of world religions abound, such as Gregory Baum's reportage of Tariq Ramadan's Muslim theology (Baum 2009). Attempts to communicate relationships between theological and legal rationales for Islamic ethics in modernity are related to this field, but not reducible to it (Fadel 2008).

There is a need to reconceptualize studies of religious diversity in light of the theologies of world religions rather than the standard comparative study of religion. Typically, the latter proceeds from a "functionalist" interpretation of religion. In contrast, the theology of world religions retains a focus on the internal logic of and relationship between the practices and beliefs of each tradition. With a theology of religions, no overriding ideological perspective is necessarily being superimposed upon the subject matter from the outset, unlike the explanatory scope that is sometimes surreptitiously evident in comparative religion.

Admittedly, some theologies of world religions, such as John Hick's pluralism, are more metaphysically determinative, something which has been attributed to his Kantian epistemology. In Hick's (1982) interpretation of Kant's "thing-in-itself," God is monistically identical across religious traditions, with pluralism being merely a pluralism of religious languages. Hick's proposal carries a bluntness that many reject, yet on the whole, the theology of world religions intensifies the search for commonalities and divergences that would be otherwise missed in the study of religious diversity.

Conclusion

In light of the current state of theological education and Religious Studies in Canada, the prospects for a "theological religious studies" is mixed. There is not at the present time a clear way forward to see how education will serve the goal of understanding religious pluralism without a thorough twinning of theology with Religious Studies in a way that would be mutually respectful. Perhaps the instigator for a "theological religious studies" will come from outside the university. Despite its understandable reluctance to engage in theological analysis, the Bouchard-Taylor Commission Report does a very good job in anticipating a different approach to religious pluralism, an approach that parallels the theological religious studies that I've discussed with respect to university curricula.

The managerial reflex continues to be strong in societies that are influenced especially by the instincts of the social democratic political tradition. Indeed, the very existence of the Bouchard-Taylor Commission in Québec is rooted in this managerial reflex. Yet in the end, the Commission's co-chairs adopted some refreshing conclusions, such as the adoption of the language of "open secularism," interpreted to be a modest engagement of liberal democracy for a religiously and ethnically diverse population. The subtitle of the report, "A Time for Reconciliation," is a choice of words that cannot easily be reconciled with a strictly procedural or quasi-legal application of lessons learned. The report upholds what it calls "concerted adjustments," which are those personal stances, actions, and habits that are distinct from the legal avenues by which the "reasonable accommodations" are made. The report states, "From a sociological standpoint, these forms of adjustment precede, in actual fact, reasonable accommodation and go beyond it." (Bouchard and Taylor 2008, 66)

Bypassing a strictly managerial route, the Commission's report points out the more flexible and vital role that individuals play as persons capable of imagining the life of different persons to make adjustments in their social intercourse. "Concerted adjustment" despite the unfortunate jargon, is precisely the kind of approach to diversity that takes seriously the longstanding civilizational and personal loci of religion. Complementary to this approach and possibly even underlying it (if we take Taylor's contribution to be instrumental) is the humanities which stress the human imagination and the allegiance of religious tradition over both the enforcement of norms of social organization and the allegiance of persons to the state.

In conclusion, with evidence suggesting that religious diversity needs a better academic mechanism for understanding its breadth and depth, this paper has argued that there are elements of Canada's traditional avenues of theological education that are pertinent to addressing religious pluralism constructively today. These elements complement the still-dominant social sciences perspective. A reorientation of the discussion toward the humanities, and especially through the theologies of world religions, would be a way forward in appraisals of religious diversity. Some aspects of this approach are evident in European precedents for retaining scholarly theological inquiry. My proposal assumes a positive role for religious traditions in the public square, but there is much about the current perception and preconception of religion that would prevent religious traditions having an active public role to play.

Canada is in need of a discussion about religious diversity that does not settle for a relativist epistemology wherein claims about God and the world – of all kinds – are regarded as off limits for public discussion. As heretical as this proposal may appear, the refusal to engage in debates over the plausibility of religious claims and the aversion to metaphysics that characterizes large swaths of university programming inadvertently affect the analysis of religious diversity. Moreover, a public that has been prepared to hear only bad news when it comes to religion will be unable to probe the raising of questions about God, morality, society, and religion while being more than ready to manage religious pluralism. A university education that sees religious pluralism as a subset of this greater question of meaning is a superior kind of post-secondary education that better serves Canada's pluralistic society. In Canada, Europe, and the United States, as the mixed picture of theological institutions with Religious Studies attests, religious pluralism and a robust academic theology are far from being mutually exclusive perspectives.

NOTES

1 See Lewis (2011) for more on the CAUT campaign.
2 The comparative study of religion can be traced to the thought of Max Müller and his study titled *Introduction to the Science of Religion* (1882 [1870]). Also see Sharpe (1986) and Capps (1995).
3 For more information, see Universiteit Leiden (2010).
4 See Reinmann (2010) and Hockenos (2010). The German Chancellor has remarked: "the tendency had been to say, 'let's adopt the multicultural concept and live happily side by side, and be happy to be living with each other.' But this concept has failed, and failed utterly" (Quoted in Connolly 2010). Note that Merkel's diagnosis is of failed living arrangements, specifically the lack of friendships between native-born Germans and immigrant families. The failure is primarily at this level but it suggests a failure of state policies that were supposedly designed to avoid social fracture. So, this candid diagnosis of Merkel's may pertain, in the end, to a failure of state administration, rather than the ability of people from different cultures to live together.
5 See Swedish National Agency for Higher Education (2011) for general indicators on the scope of research funded. Anecdotal evidence suggests an ongoing level of research support for theology, including funding for the 2008 European Society for the Study of Science and Theology in Sigtuna, Sweden, and a mention of theology in a list of possible disciplines from which nominations for prestigious chairs can be nominated.
6 John Cobb, for instance, does not conform to the image of the liberal protestant when he advocates dialogue in non-pluralist terms: he maintains that as the *Logos* of God, Christ is the creative transformation principle in all world religions. For the most frequently cited survey of theologies of world

religions from a Christian perspective, see Knitter (1995). John Hick (1995) is another theologian closely associated with this field. For an account of religious diversity in terms of a wider psychic and ontology of diversity, see some comments in Suchocki (2003, chapter 2).

REFERENCES

Baum, Gregory. 2009. *The Theology of Tariq Ramadan: A Catholic Perspective*. Notre Dame: University of Notre Dame Press.

Beyer, Peter. 2005. "The Future of Non-Christian Religions in Canada: Patterns of Religious Identification Among Recent Immigrants and Their Second Generation, 1981–2001." *Studies in Religion* 34(2): 165–96.

Bouchard, Gérard, and Charles Taylor. 2008. "Building the Future: A Time for Reconciliation." Commission de consultation sur les pratiques d'accommodement reliées aux différences culturelles. Québec: Québec Government Printing Office, May 22.

Capps, Walter. 1995. *Religious Studies: The Making of a Discipline*. Minneapolis: Fortress Press.

Connolly, Kate. 2010. "Angela Merkel Declares Death of German Multiculturalism." *The Guardian*, 17 October. Available at http://www.guardian.co.uk/world/2010/oct/17/angela-merkel-germany-multiculturalism-failures?intcmp=239

D'Costa, Gavin. 2005. *Theology in the Public Square*. Oxford: Blackwell.

Fadel, Mohammad. 2008. "The True, the Good and the Reasonable: The Theological and Ethical Roots of Public Reason in Islamic Law." *Canadian Journal of Law and Jurisprudence* 21(1): 5–69.

Gadamer, Hans G. 2004. *Truth and Method* (2nd rev. ed.). New York: Continuum.

German Council of Science and Humanities (German Council). 2010. "Recommendations on the Advancement of Theologies and Sciences concerned with Religions at German Universities." 29 January. Available at http://www.wissenschaftsrat.de/download/archiv/9678-10_engl.pdf

Giles, Philip, and Torben Drewes. 2001. "Liberal Arts Degrees and the Labour Market." *Perspectives on Labour and Income*. Available at http://www.statcan.gc.ca/pub/75-001-x/00701/5883-eng.html

Hick, John. 1982. *God Has Many Names*. Louisville: Westminster John Knox Press.

Hick, John. 1995. *A Christian Theology of Religions: A Rainbow of Faiths*. Louisville: Westminster John Knox Press.

Hirsi Ali A. 2010. *Nomad*. Toronto: Vintage Canada.

Hockenos, Paul. 2010. "Educating Imams in Germany: The Battle for a European Islam." *Chronicle for Higher Education*, 18 July. Available at http://chronicle.com/article/Educating-Imams-in-Germany-/66282/

Human Resources and Skills Development Canada (HRSDC). 2010. "Learning – University Participation." Available at http://www4.hrsdc.gc.ca/.3ndic.1t .4r@-eng.jsp?iid=56

Knitter, Paul. 1995. *No Other Name: A Critical Survey of Christian Attitudes Toward the World Religions*. Maryknoll: Orbis.

Kronman, Anthony. 2007. *Education's End: Why Our Colleges and Universities Have Given Up on the Meaning of Life*. New Haven: Yale University Press.

Lewis, Charles. 2011. "Petition Backs Christian Universities in Academic Freedom Dispute." *National Post*, 7 February. Available at http://life .nationalpost.com/2011/02/07/academics-back-christian-universities-in-academic-freedom-dispute/

MacIntyre, Alasdair. 1984. *After Virtue* (2nd ed.). Notre Dame: University of Notre Dame Press.

Müller, Max F. 1882 (1870). "Introduction to the Science of Religion: Four Lectures." London: Longmans, Green, and Co. Available at http://archive.org/details/introductiontoth014888mbp

Murray, Paul D. 2007. "Theology 'Under the Lash': Theology as Idolatry Critique in the Work of Nicholas Lash." *New Blackfriars* 88: 4–24.

Nussbaum, Martha. 2010. *Not for Profit: Why Democracy Needs the Humanities*. Princeton: Princeton University Press.

Queen's University. 2010a. "Changes to Theological Schools." Available at http://www.queensu.ca/religion/news/changetheoschools.html

Queen's University. 2010b. "Queen's School of Religion Officially Launched." Available at http://www.queensu.ca/religion/news/launchstory.html

Queen's University. 2010c. "ATS Grant Awarded to Queen's Professor." Available at http://www.queensu.ca/religion/news.html

Reimann, Anna. 2010. "German University Starts Seminars for Imams." *Der Spiegel*. Available at http://www.spiegel.de/international/germany/0,1518,721818,00.html

Sharpe, Eric. 1986. *Comparative Religion: A History* (2nd ed.). London: Duckworth.

Suchocki, Marjorie H. 2003. *Divinity and Diversity: A Christian Affirmation of Religious Pluralism*. Nashville: Abingdon Press.

Statistics Canada. 2010a. "University Enrolments by Registration Status and Sex, by Province." Available at http://www.statcan.gc.ca/tables-tableaux/sum-som/l01/cst01/educ53a-eng.htm

Statistics Canada. 2010b. "Trends in University Graduation, 1992–2007." Available at http://www.statcan.gc.ca/pub/81-004-x/2009005/article/11050-eng.htm#d

Swedish National Agency for Higher Education (Högskoleverket). 2011. "Higher Education in Sweden." Available at http://www.hsv.se/higher ducationinsweden.4.28afa2dc11bdcdc55748 0002000.html

Universiteit Leiden. 2010. "Islamic Theology." Available at http://www.hum .leiden.edu/education/bachelors-programmes/ba-islamictheology.html

Wuthnow, Robert. 2008. "Can Faith Be More than a Sideshow in the Contemporary Academy?" In *The American University in a Postsecular Age, Religion and the Academy*, edited by Douglas Jacobsen, 31–43. New York: Oxford University Press.

PART IV

Public Life

11 Conservative Christianity, Anti-statism, and Alberta's Public Sphere

The Curious Case of Bill 44

CLARK BANACK

It is well known that Alberta has a unique political history among Canadian provinces. Not only have consecutive conservative political parties ruled the province nearly uncontested since 1935, thirty-three of those years included the premiership of Social Creditors William "Bible Bill" Aberhart (1935–43) and Ernest Manning (1943–68), two devout fundamentalist Christians who moonlighted as the hosts of a religious radio broadcast that drew more than 300,000 listeners at its height (Laycock 1990, 216). That such publically devout men were able to hold political power in Alberta for such a long period obviously tells us something about the importance with which Alberta voters, at least in the mid-twentieth century, viewed a Christian-based message. Indeed, Goa (2011) has noted the pervasive influence of a "Great Plains evangelical Christianity" on mid-twentieth century Albertan society. Yet, despite the gradual transition to a more urban and secular province, complete with the prominent rise of less religious premiers such as Peter Lougheed (1971–85) and Ralph Klein (1992–2006), the province continued to gain notoriety for public-policy stances that seemed to be rooted in conservative Christian belief. The Supreme Court's landmark *Vriend* decision in 1998 was in response to the Alberta government's refusal to include "sexual orientation" as protected ground under the *Alberta Individual Rights Protection Act*. Despite a rebuke from the Supreme Court on this matter, the late 1990s and early 2000s found the province leading the charge against the legal recognition of same-sex partnerships in Canada. This included passage of the *Marriage Act* in March 2000 that reaffirmed the definition of marriage as that "between one man and one woman" and included further provisions to utilize the notwithstanding clause should the courts attempt to impose same-sex marriage on the province. The loud support from evangelical Christian Members of the Legislative Assembly (MLAs) Victor Doerksen, Lorne Taylor, and Stockwell Day seemed to confirm the religious nature of the government's stance against gay marriage (Johnsrude 2000; Geddes and Jeffs 2000; Lloyd and Bonnett 2005; Rayside 2008).

Although same-sex marriages are now permitted in the province, the recent passage of Bill 44, *The Human Rights, Citizenship and Multiculturalism Amendment Act*, by the Alberta Progressive Conservatives (PC) in June of 2009, seemingly fit rather neatly within Alberta's long-running adherence to the demands of conservative Christians. Interestingly, the centerpiece of the act was actually a symbolic gesture that was loudly cheered by the homosexual community. For the first time, "sexual orientation" would be included as protected ground from discrimination under Alberta's human rights legislation. Although sexual orientation had been "read in" to the legislation by the Supreme Court's 1998 *Vriend* decision, the government of the day, who briefly debated invoking the "notwithstanding clause" in order to prevent the Court's decision from influencing their policy with respect to protecting homosexuals from discrimination, made the symbolic decision not to amend their legislation in accordance with the ruling. The decision some eleven years later to change course and formally include "sexual orientation" within the province's human rights legislation was therefore meant to represent a long-overdue act of recognition for the province's homosexual community. However, praise from sexual-diversity activists was quickly muted when it became clear that the bill contained a further change in Section 11. Building upon the province's *School Act*, Bill 44 reaffirmed the right of parents to pull their children from any course of study or educational program that dealt explicitly with religion or sexuality and added sexual orientation to that list. By including such a clause in the *Human Rights Act*, teachers who failed to properly notify parents that such topics would be discussed were now potentially subject to punishment at the hands of the province's Human Rights Commission.

The striking contrast within the bill, which contained both a symbolic recognition of "sexual orientation" and a clause that essentially prevents the introduction of any form of compulsory "gay-friendly" instruction in public schools, was not lost on commentators. As opposition MLA Henry Chase argued, Bill 44

has the potential of turning inclusive, secular schools into bigotry-breeding battlegrounds, with both teachers and students caught in the parental/

religious rights crossfire. While Bill 44 proposes to protect sexual orientation in the workplace and in tenancy, the right to discriminate would be enshrined in the public school classroom. (Legislative Assembly of Alberta 2009, 1469)

Indeed, there was immediate suspicion that the province's religious conservatives, in the form of both lobby groups and individual socially conservative MLAs within the Conservative caucus, had insisted on the inclusion of the "parental rights" clause as a trade-off of sorts, in exchange for consenting to the symbolic recognition of sexual orientation as protected ground within the human rights legislation (Simons 2009a, 18A; 2009b, 14A). Opposition MLAs, the provincial teachers association, sexual diversity advocates and liberal-leaning journalists erupted in a chorus of protest but to no avail. Perhaps most interestingly, despite the commotion raised by gay-rights advocates and progressive journalists, the more sustained criticism from the Alberta public did not centre on the socially conservative connotations of a clause which favoured the rights of religious parents over the responsibility of the state to provide an educational curriculum based upon the principles of tolerance and inclusion. Rather, it was the potential for well-intentioned teachers to be hauled in front of a human rights tribunal that really struck a negative chord with members of the public. After clarifying that teachers would not face prosecution if they inadvertently brought up any of the taboo subjects in the course of general instruction, the government easily passed the bill and the controversy has largely faded from the minds of the electorate (CBC 2009).

This chapter, which draws on substantial archival work and a number of semi-structured interviews with current and recently retired Alberta PC MLAs, revisits both the immediate context around Bill 44 as well as the broader political culture of Alberta in an effort to help explain both the origin of the controversial "parental rights" clause contained in Bill 44 and the lack of any serious public opposition towards it. Although the popular perception of Alberta is that of a province dominated by conservative Christian sentiment that fuels an overt hostility towards homosexuality and any corresponding public policy that appears to legitimize such behaviour, this chapter argues that the actual nature of Alberta's public sphere is far more complicated. Conservative Christianity has strongly influenced the political culture of Alberta but it has done so in a manner that goes far beyond the generation of anti-homosexual attitudes. There is little doubt that such religiously based sentiment exists in pockets of both the PC caucus and Alberta's society at large, and this surely played a role in the origin and acceptance of the parental rights clause. However, a more pervasive product of Alberta's conservative Christian heritage is a particular suspicion of government itself, an anti-statist perspective that favours community and family-level solutions to communal problems while simultaneously demanding a reduction in the size and scope of government-led initiatives. The remainder of this chapter demonstrates the manner by which conservative Christianity both directly and indirectly impacted the debate around the parental rights clause in Bill 44 and, in doing so, offers a fresh perspective on the complicated influence of religion within Alberta's public sphere.

The Immediate Political Context of Bill 44

Over a decade after the Supreme Court's landmark *Vriend* decision, certain members of the Alberta government, in an effort to shed the province's intolerant reputation, decided it was time to formally respond to the Court by adding "sexual orientation" to its human rights legislation. Yet, by harnessing this inclusion to a parental rights clause that essentially prevented the introduction of compulsory instruction on sexual orientation within public schools, the Alberta government left many with the impression that social policy in the province is still crafted in response to the demands made by conservative Christians. Indeed, it is undeniable that a certain degree of Christian-based anti-homosexual sentiment was operating behind the demand for this clause. Parental rights in education have long been demanded by the same religiously conservative voices in Alberta who ridiculed the legislative recognition of same-sex relationships and demanded protection for those who were critical of such relationships in the name of freedom of religion.[1] In fact, the Cabinet Minister responsible for Bill 44 openly admits that parental rights were one of many requests made by a group of Alberta faith-based leaders, including Calgary-based Catholic Bishop Fred Henry, an outspoken critic of same-sex relationships, he met with prior to drafting the bill (L. Blackett, personal communication, 7 March 2011).

For socially conservative MLAs who championed the clause within caucus, a sense of immediacy was provided to this cause by a ground-breaking decision in British Columbia in 2006. Faced with the prospect of a lengthy battle before the BC Human Rights Tribunal against a pair of citizens who argued public schools were guilty of discrimination because they failed to include sexual orientation within the curriculum, the BC government agreed to revise public education courses to ensure homosexuality was presented in a respectful manner while simultaneously placing tougher restrictions on the rights of parents to remove their children from such lessons (Steffenhagen 2006). Two separate Alberta PC Cabinet ministers confirmed to the author that the prospect of an Alberta Human Rights Commission eventually forcing the provincial government to revise its curriculum in a similar manner while preventing parents from removing their children from such "gay-positive" instruction was "maddening" to religiously conservative MLAs suspicious of homosexual behaviour and eager to protect the right of citizens to oppose it based upon the *Charter*'s promise of freedom of religion. The inclusion of parental rights in Bill 44 by the PC caucus is therefore best understood as a necessary compromise with such MLAs who were opposed to the broader purpose of the bill, the symbolic recognition of sexual orientation as protected ground from discrimination.

Of course, the vast majority of PC MLAs, many of whom were not operating from an overtly conservative Christian position, also supported Bill 44. The reasons for this support ranged from overt pressure from more religiously conservative rural constituents (the PC party was victorious in 37 of 38 ridings outside of Edmonton and Calgary in the 2008 election giving the caucus a strong rural flavour), to a general personal preference for parents to be more involved in public education, to the simple pragmatic desire to find the votes in caucus necessary to finally include sexual orientation as grounds for protection from discrimination and move on from this issue. Beyond the reasons behind caucus support for parental rights, however, lies a more pertinent question that begs to be answered: why, despite considerable media attention that largely opposed the bill because of the anti-homosexual connotations of the parental rights clause, did the issue fail to generate much opposition within the citizenry of Alberta? Indeed, this lack of opposition seemed to vindicate PC MLA Rob Anderson's claim in the legislature that "there are thousands and thousands of parents, the silent majority, severely normal Albertans that are extremely happy with this legislation" (Legislative Assembly of Alberta 2009, 1469). This acquiescence is particularly puzzling given the largely uncontroversial embrace of mandatory instruction on homosexuality within public schools by the public of neighbouring British Columbia just a few years prior. Is it simply the case that this "silent majority" of Albertans who supported the legislation were motivated by the same conservative

Christian/anti-homosexual perspective that lay behind certain arguments for parental rights in public education? In other words, can the public acceptance of Bill 44 be explained by the overtly religious nature of the Albertan electorate? Although this is a tempting response, especially given the province's past association with Christian political leadership, it is not nearly this simple.

A brief look at the numbers provided by Statistics Canada suggests the "Alberta as a Bible-Belt" theory does not hold water. Although results from the 2011 census are not yet available, the 2001 census shows Alberta ranking second to only British Columbia among all Canadian provinces with respect to the percentage of citizens who declared they had no religious affiliation whatsoever (Statistics Canada 2001). In addition, only British Columbia and Québec contained a smaller percentage of citizens that regularly attended religious services at least once a month than Alberta (Warren 2003). Obviously these statistics do not provide a conclusive picture of religious activity in Alberta but they certainly contradict the general thesis that Alberta is a Canadian outlier when it comes to religious participation among the electorate. Alberta is not, it seems, a province dominated by the religious. Related to this conclusion is the broader point that anti-homosexual sentiment is not as widespread as one might expect. Surely there are significant pockets of Albertans that are outright opposed to the advancement of homosexual rights, especially in areas outside of Edmonton and Calgary, and polls have consistently shown Alberta citizens to be the least enamored of all Canadians by the relatively recent expansion of rights for same-sex couples, but the notion that there is province-wide agreement on this is fiction. As far back as the late 1990s, the government's own research demonstrated significant variation with respect to views towards the definition of a family and the advancement of homosexual rights within the province. Attitudes on gay adoption, spousal benefits, marriage, and even whether homosexuality should be a topic of discussion within public school curriculums, were canvassed and the findings revealed a polarized electorate with only a very slight majority in opposition to the advancement of the homosexual cause (Alberta Justice 1999). A more recent poll suggests that opposition to homosexual rights has fallen considerably. Albertans opposed to the legal recognition of same-sex marriages stands at 28 per cent in 2011, down sharply from 59 per cent in 1996 (Ellis 2011; Varcoe 2011).

So, if Alberta citizens are not unusually religious or overwhelmingly in opposition to the homosexual rights, what then explains their general acquiescence to Bill 44? No doubt conservative religious perspectives help to explain the support for parental rights of a certain portion of the population, and a more general malaise or lack of engagement with public policy issues within the broader electorate is part of the story as well. However, I want to suggest that, for a large swath of Albertans, the clause was accepted not because they harbour religiously based anti-homosexual sentiment but rather because they have been steeped in a broader populist and anti-statist political culture that frowns upon government control that usurps the rights and responsibilities of the "average" citizen. Indeed, it is instructive to consider the manner by which the parental rights clause was sold to the public by caucus supporters. PC MLA Rob Anderson, responding to criticism from opposition MLAs, argued:

> Every member on that side of the House (the Opposition) has stood up ... and said: we know better, the state knows better what our children should be taught with regard to sexuality and with regard to religion.
>
> That's why we're putting parental rights into this, not because we have to but because it's the right thing to do. We need to recognize a parent's role as the primary educator of their children. We are doing it because it's right. We're doing it because we want to reassert that the family and not the state is the fundamental unit of a successful society. (Legislative Assembly of Alberta 2009, 1468)

Anderson's colleague Thomas Lukaszuk added that the parental rights clause would reassure those parents who worry that their children are learning things they do not approve of. These parents, he continues, "simply don't trust the state. They do not want to give the state the right to have the final decision on what their child learns. They want to make sure that they as a parent of a child have that last choice, and I think most Albertans would agree with that" (Legislative Assembly of Alberta 2009, 1471). Within both sets of comments one finds an unmistakable allusion to an idea that goes far beyond religiously based anti-homosexual sentiment. Rather, both MLAs make explicit reference to the notion that the majority of Albertans are generally suspicious of government-run programs, especially ones like education wherein it is conceivable that regular citizens could play a significant role. I want to suggest that it is by way of this particular anti-statist sentiment that the lack of public opposition to the parental rights clause in Bill 44 makes sense from an electorate that is not unusually religious or opposed to

homosexual rights. The irony, however, is that the origins of such sentiment owe much to the particular conservative religious interpretations
that dominated Alberta's public sphere many decades ago. It is to this
connection this chapter now turns.

Conservative Christianity and Anti-statism in Alberta[2]

The Alberta Social Credit League, founded by fundamentalist Christian radio preacher William Aberhart and his protégé Ernest Manning,
ruled Alberta for 36 formative years, from 1935 until 1971. Surely this
background helps to explain the persistence, especially in rural areas
of Alberta, of a religious-based social conservatism. However, the most
important and lasting influence of Social Credit politics in Alberta is
not, I argue, the continuing validity of the Christian message. Rather,
it is the strong individualistic and anti-statist political sentiment that
grew out of Social Credit's particular Christian perspective that still
guides much of the political policy and discourse in Alberta, including that around Bill 44. Of course, suspicion of the federal government
in Alberta stretches back to its earliest days when farmers and small
business owners faced national policies that were clearly designed to
benefit the large financial and manufacturing sectors based in central
Canada. In response, Alberta agrarians established the United Farmers of Alberta (UFA), a participatory organization that eventually
swept into political office by way of its successful efforts to protect the
financial interests of farmers through the utilization of economic coop-
eratives (Rennie 2000). However, this expression of intense grassroots
participatory democracy generated by a distrust of a distant and largely
unresponsive federal government eventually evolved into a more general distrust of the state during the period of Social Credit rule.[3] To
understand the origins of this more general anti-statism requires a brief
detour through the religious belief and political thought of the religious
belief and political thought of the two central Social Credit premiers.

   Aberhart and Manning were devout Christians who adhered to a
strict literal interpretation of the Bible and a fundamentalist eschatology dubbed "premillennial dispensationalism." Dispensationalism was
a method of scriptural interpretation based on the notion that history
has been divided by God into separate "dispensations."[4] In contrast
to many of the more progressive religious perspectives reverberating
through the prairies at that time that sought to build the kingdom of
God on earth through social reform, as was generally the case within

the UFA, premillennial dispensationalists believed that the kingdom of God was wholly discontinuous with the history of our current "dispensation." The shift to the "millennial" dispensation, wherein Christ would establish His kingdom, would occur solely at the bequest of God, not through the works of Christian individuals committed to social action (Ryrie 2007, 27–51). Therefore, the responsibility of mankind within the current dispensation was not to perfect society, but rather to seek and accept the righteousness that God freely offers to all. This required a personal "rebirth" in Christ, an act that was necessary to rectify one's sinful nature and prepare oneself for the millennial reign of Christ (Aberhart 1932). In fact, it was only through this spiritual rebirth that one could be assured of being "saved" by Christ during the Rapture, the time when true Christians are pulled up to Heaven by Christ prior to the seven-year Tribulation wherein the world is ruled by the Anti-Christ. Following this period, the great Armageddon would take place culminating in Christ's final victory over Satan and the establishment of the kingdom of God.

From this particular Christian perspective, Aberhart and Manning believed it was the duty of believers to help save as many individuals as possible prior to the upcoming Rapture by encouraging their spiritual rebirth. "In other words," Manning said, "we express our Love for Him by being concerned about the people He was concerned about enough to die for," and this expression was made concrete in the efforts of evangelization that could save the souls of their fellows (Semotuk 1982). This was precisely the motivation behind Aberhart's wildly popular radio ministry that preceded his entrance into politics. However, by 1932 Aberhart was beginning to sense a growing obstacle that was impeding his biblical message from reaching the hearts of listeners. This obstacle was the intense poverty of the Depression. Aberhart understood such poverty as an impingement on the freedom of the individual and his development and thus society was in need of a particular earthly reform to end "poverty in the midst of plenty" and for this he turned to social credit economics. As an article from the *Alberta Social Credit Chronicle* argued, "Crushing and demoralizing poverty obscures men's spirituality." The goal of implementing social credit economics was to end this poverty and "only then would it be possible to appreciate completely the message of Him" (Materialistic and Spiritual Blend 1934). In fact, as Manning would later explain, social credit economic theory fit well with their interpretation of Christianity because it was based upon its recognition of "the supremacy of the individual as a divinely created creature, possessing, as a result of divine creation, certain inalienable rights that must be respected and preserved" (Manning 1962). Therefore, the goal of the Social Credit philosophy was "A free society in which the individual would have the maximum opportunity to develop himself." This required addressing the poverty of the Depression because the "attention to the cultural realm of life was limited by the economic conditions of that time" (Semotuk 1978). And from the Christian perspective of Aberhart and Manning, full human development required a personal rebirth in Christ.

Although far more could be said with respect to the relationship between religion and the political thought of Aberhart and Manning, the point I want to draw out for this chapter is simply the political implications inherent in this religious perspective. Surely the devotion to biblical literalism that characterized their Christian fundamentalist perspective promoted a social conservatism based upon the moral laws of God, a sentiment that spread through Alberta by way of their radio evangelism. Beyond this, however, was the simultaneous influence they had on the province's broader political culture with respect to attitudes towards the state. The emphasis Aberhart and Manning placed on individual spiritual rebirth, and especially the conditions such conversion required, committed them to an intense devotion to individual liberty that spread throughout the province. Thus, a certain radical anti-establishmentarianism grew out of their opposition to any institution that impinged on the freedom of the individual required to experience spiritual rebirth. For Aberhart, this meant attacking the "Fifty Big Shots" whom he understood to be withholding credit and thus causing "Poverty in the Midst of Plenty." For Manning, who would preside over very different economic conditions in Alberta, this would eventually morph into unconditional support for the free market in the face of an emerging socialism that threatened to subdue the individual to the collective.[5]

Surely the importance of religion has lessened within the contemporary Alberta electorate, except perhaps in rural constituencies, but the strong desire for individual freedom and corresponding suspicion of the state's role in society that emanates out of this particular Christian fundamentalist perspective remains influential. As I have argued elsewhere, this political sentiment equates to an individual-based "populist" conservatism that traces its lineage back to the broad American evangelical Protestant tradition from which Aberhart's fundamentalist perspective largely emerged. This connection has helped to place

Alberta on a political trajectory much closer to the pattern of American political culture than the rest of Canada, which was influenced by a more communal and hierarchal political culture associated with European Christianity (Banack 2013). Of course, broader structural factors, including the province's quasi-colonial status within the Confederation, its distinct immigration patterns, and its economic dependence on particular resources, are also important when attempting to understand the development of Alberta's political culture. In addition, the victory of Peter Lougheed's PCs over Social Credit in 1971 introduced a period of substantial state-led economic development and a corresponding increase in the size and scope of government programs in Alberta that belies this anti-statist attitude inherent in the religiously based philosophy of Social Credit (Richards and Pratt 1979; Tupper 2004). However, the anti-statism of Social Credit was reawakened in Alberta by the emergence of the Alberta-based federal Reform Party led by Ernest Manning's son Preston who, quite interestingly, abides by much of the same Christian-based concern for the plight of the individual that motivated his father (P. Manning, personal communication, 10 November 2010). It is, in my estimation, no coincidence therefore that a central component of the Reform message, which swept across Alberta with startling speed in the late 1980s and early 1990s, was a strong critique of the government's role in everything from economic development to the administration of social programs to the funding of the arts. Although the Reform Party no longer exists, it is critical to understand the impact that Reform's sudden popularity in Alberta during this period had on provincial politics in the province. Responding to an electorate that was suddenly re-energized by the anti-statist message of Reform, the PC party under Ralph Klein embarked on a deep program of cutbacks that aimed at substantially reducing the size and scope of the provincial government (Taras and Tupper 1994, 66–7; Harrison 1995). Perhaps most tellingly with respect to Alberta's long-standing anti-statist political culture, the provincial government was actually able to maintain, and perhaps even enhance, its support among the electorate while imposing these substantial cutbacks (Archer and Gibbins 1997).

The above obviously represents a substantial compression of a great deal of Alberta's political history but, within the parameters of this chapter, I hope it is sufficient to show the religious-based origins of anti-statism in Alberta. And it is precisely this anti-statist sentiment that operates behind what Jared Wesley has recently described as Alberta's long-running adherence to a "code of freedom." Indeed,

Wesley argues that each of Alberta's most successful premiers have, since the Great Depression, "preached individualism ... personal responsibility, free enterprise, private-sector development, entrepreneurship, a strong work ethic, the evils of socialism, and the protection of individual rights and liberties" (Wesley 2001, 55–6). Surely the majority of Albertan men and women, including many politicians, who today abide by these anti-statist sentiments have managed to disassociate them from their initial religious moorings but to miss the fact that they were initially encouraged by the Christian-based politics of Social Credit is to miss a good deal of the story of Alberta's political development and contemporary political culture. And it is from the perspective of this broader "anti-statist" political culture, derived from this religious foundation, that the lack of public opposition to Bill 44 from a largely secular electorate makes sense.

Conclusion: Religion, Anti-statism and Alberta's Public Sphere

In this brief examination of the context surrounding the passage of the controversial Bill 44 in Alberta I hope to have at least pointed us towards a framework through which more general questions related to the place of religion in the public sphere of this province can be approached. It is often assumed, especially by the national media, that Alberta is an overtly conservative Christian society and that this fact explains the province's tendency towards socially conservative policy. As with most stereotypes, there is an element of truth to this view but, in reality, the explanation is far more complex. Rural Alberta remains a rather religious place and the high number of rural MLAs within the governing PC caucus has ensured both a noteworthy presence of religiously motivated government members and a broader strategic need to placate this segment of the population with socially conservative policies. However, the majority urban population, while shedding much of the religious dogma, has largely remained faithful to an anti-statist sentiment shared by rural folk that has grown out of a fundamentalist Christian perspective encouraged by the long reign of Social Credit in Alberta and recently reawakened by the conservative populist message of Preston Manning's federal Reform Party and replicated by the contemporary PC Party under Ralph Klein.

Applying this framework to the issue of religion in the public sphere in more general terms, it seems that the concerns of Christians are certainly welcome in the public sphere and are bound to be heard by the Alberta government. The acceptance of these religiously based demands by the public at large, however, is dependent on the degree to which they speak to the broader role of government in the lives of citizens. Bill 44's parental rights clause, a demand made initially by the religiously conservative, gained public support because it prioritized the role of the family over that of the state with respect to educating the province's children. Somewhat counter-intuitively, the long-running debate over same-sex marriage within the province took place within a similar context. On the surface, a legislative ban on same-sex marriage, which was introduced into the legislature by evangelical Christian MLA Victor Doerksen in March 2000, seems to require more rather than less government interference in the lives of citizens. Yet, within the broader non-religious Alberta public, much of the opposition to same-sex marriage that made such a bill plausible was centred around firstly, the questionable democratic legitimacy of court-made law being enacted by an unelected judiciary and secondly, the potential for religiously oriented marriage commissioners being forced by the courts to preside over same-sex marriages despite their objections on religious grounds. Both of these objections speak to the broader populist and anti-statist sentiment present within Alberta more so than they do to a simple conservative Christian morality dominating policy.

The essence of this position is captured well by the arguments of conservative academic and recent PC cabinet minister Ted Morton, a longtime critic of "judicial activism" and the anti-democratic nature of court-made law in Canada. Despite being perhaps the most outspoken social conservative, "pro-family" MLA within the PC caucus in recent memory, Morton has never alluded to any particular religious beliefs as the foundation for his position. Yet, in defense of his 2006 private members bill that promised legal protection to those who spoke out against same-sex marriage and to those parents who wanted to exclude their children from "pro-gay" instruction in public schools, he argued:

> I don't give a damn what consenting adults do in the privacy of their own homes ... if some parents want their children taught that the marriage of one man and another man is the same as the marriage of one man and one woman, that's their choice and I respect it. But other parents don't

want their children taught this, and they have an equal right to have their wishes respected. (Morton 2006)[6]

Although recent polls suggest that the majority of Albertans do not agree with much of Morton's personal antipathy towards homosexual rights legislation, his broader point regarding the rights of individual citizens to operate in a manner that is free from an overburdening state remains a cornerstone of Alberta's political culture.

A potentially more interesting case, however, that could challenge the foundation of the unlikely coalition that has formed in Alberta between conservative Christians and the non-religious anti-statist crowd who, together, have advocated policies which have hampered the advance of homosexual rights in the province, would be the demand for the recognition of certain religious rights from a non-Christian group. Think, for example, of a demand to introduce Islamic sharia-based courts to settle family law disputes as was briefly debated in Ontario. It seems to me that the secular anti-statist crowd would have little reason to oppose such a demand for it fits neatly within their goal of reducing the role of government in the lives of citizens and simultaneously empowering common people and the community-level organizations of which they are part. The Christian community however, especially those who operate from a more conservative perspective, seem far less likely to warm to the demands of a religious crowd other than their own. Indeed, as Alberta continues to grow into a more ethnically and religiously diverse province, it will be interesting to watch how claims from non-Christian religious groups are adjudicated by both the government and the broader citizenry within Alberta's public sphere.

NOTES

1 Conservative Christian Ted Byfield, editor of the popular news magazine *Alberta Report*, often utilized his weekly column in the 1980s and 1990s to criticize both same-sex relationships and the secular nature of the public school curriculum. In addition, he demanded a stronger role for religious parents in building an appropriate curriculum. See, for example, Byfield (1993, 37).
2 Certain passages from this section appeared originally in Clark Banack, "American Protestantism and the Roots of 'Populist' Conservatism in

Alberta," in *Conservatism in Canada,* edited by J. Farney and D. Rayside
(Toronto: University of Toronto Press, 2013).
3 David Laycock describes the shift in political thinking from the UFA to
Social Credit as the move from "radical democratic populism" to a "Plebi-
scitarian Populism." See Laycock (1990).
4 Aberhart's adherence to premillennial dispensationalism is explored in
Elliott (1980). A detailed history of premillennial dispensationalism is available in Sandeen (1970) and Weber (1979).
5 Manning's defense of the free market is encapsulated within Manning
(1967). For an insightful examination of the religious beliefs operating
behind Manning's political thought see Groh (1970).
6 Ted Morton sponsored a private members bill that would have protected the
rights of marriage commissioners opposed to gay marriage but, despite having the support of the premier and 75 per cent of the Conservative caucus,
the Opposition was able to stall, and thus kill the motion. See CTV (2006).

REFERENCES

Aberhart, William. 1932. "William Aberhart to J.H. Caldwell." *Walter Norman
and Amelia Turner Smith Fonds.* File M-1157-30. Calgary: Glenbow-Alberta
Museum Archives.
Alberta Justice. 1999. "Report of the Ministerial Task Force." Available at
http://justice.alberta.ca/publications/Publications_Library/Reportofthe
MinisterialTaskForce.aspx/DispForm.aspx?ID=36
Archer, Keith, and Roger Gibbins. 1997. "What Do Albertans Think? The Klein
Agenda and the Public Opinion Landscape." In *A Government Reinvented:
A Study of Alberta's Deficit Elimination Program,* edited by Chris J. Bruce, Ron
D. Kneebone, and Ken J. McKenzie, 462–85. Toronto: Oxford University
Press.
Banack, Clark. 2013. "American Protestantism and the Roots of 'Populist'
Conservatism in Alberta." In *Conservatism in Canada,* edited by James Far-
ney and David Rayside. Toronto: University of Toronto Press.
Byfield, Ted, and Virginia Byfield. 1993. "If There Is No National Moral Con
sensus, Then How Are Our Schools Going to Teach it?" *Alberta Report*
20(13): 37.
CBC. 2009. "Premier to Allow Free Vote on Bill Expanding Parental Rights in
Schools." *CBC News,* 26 May. Available at http://www.cbc.ca/canada/
edmonton/story/2009/05/26/edmonton-amendments-bill-44.html#
ixzz0w8naeTky

CTV. 2006. "Time Runs Out in Alta. for Anti-gay Marriage Bill." *Canadian Television Network*, 10 May. Available at http://www.ctv.ca/CTVNEWS/Canada/20060508/klein_gays_060508

Elliott, David R. 1980. "The Devil and William Aberhart: The Nature and Function of his Eschatology." *Studies in Religion* 9(3): 325–37.

Ellis, Faron. 2011. "Traditional or Progressive: Albertans' Opinion Structure on Six Policy Issues." Lethbridge: Citizen Society Research Lab. Available at http://www.lethbridgecollege.ca/about-us/applied-research-innovation/citizen-society-research-lab/alberta-opinion-studies

Geddes, Ashley, and Allyson Jeffs. 2000. "MLAs Pass Bill Outlawing Same-Sex Marriage: Legislation Commits Province to Use Notwithstanding Clause in Necessary." *The Edmonton Journal*, 16 March, 20A.

Goa, David J. 2011. "Pietism, a Prairie Story: Spiritual Transformation." In *Pietism and the Challenges of Modernity*, David J. Goa, Eugene L. Boe, and Cam Harder, 1–14. Camrose: The Chester Ronning Centre.

Groh, Dennis G. 1970. "The Political Thought of Ernest Manning." Unpublished MA thesis. University of Calgary, Alberta.

Harrison, Trevor. 1995. "The Reform-ation of Alberta Politics." In *The Trojan Horse: Alberta and the Future of Canada*, edited by Gordon Laxer and Trevor Harrison, 47–60. Montréal: Black Rose Books.

Johnsrude, Larry. 2000. "Private Bill Would Block Recognition of Gay Marriage: Minister Downplays Significance of Measure." *Edmonton Journal*, 24 February, 7B.

Laycock, David. 1990. *Populism and Democratic Thought in the Canadian Prairies, 1910 to 1945*. Toronto: University of Toronto Press.

Legislative Assembly of Alberta. 2009. "Alberta Hansard." Edmonton: Alberta Government Printing Office, 1 June.

Lloyd, Julie, and Laura Bonnett. 2005. "The Arrested Development of Queer Rights in Alberta." In *The Return of the Trojan Horse: Alberta and the New World (Dis)Order*, edited by Gordon Laxer and Trevor Harrison, 328–41. Montréal: Black Rose Books.

Manning, Ernest. 1962. "Ernest Manning to G.M. Wilson." *Premier Papers*, 1977.173 file 394b, 18 April. Edmonton: Provincial Archives of Alberta.

Manning, Ernest. 1967. *Political Realignment: A Challenge to Thoughtful Canadians*. Toronto and Montréal: McClelland and Stewart.

"Materialistic and Spiritual Blend in the Social Credit Faith." 1934. *Alberta Social Credit Chronicle* 1, 7 September.

Morton, Ted. 2006. "Same-Sex Marriage: A Human Right?" *Edmonton Journal*, 5 September, A19.

Rayside, David. 2008. *Queer Inclusions, Continental Divisions: Public Recognition of Sexual Diversity in Canada and the United States.* Toronto: University of Toronto Press.

Rennie, Bradford J. 2000. *The Rise of Agrarian Democracy: The United Farmers and Farm Women of Alberta, 1909–1921.* Toronto: University of Toronto Press.

Richards, John, and Larry Pratt. 1979. *Prairie Capitalism: Power and Influence in the New West.* Toronto: McClelland and Stewart.

Ryrie, Charles. 2007. *Dispensationalism.* Chicago: Moody Publishers.

Sandeen, Ernest R. 1970. *The Roots of Fundamentalism: British and American Millenarianism 1800–1930.* Chicago: University of Chicago Press.

Semotuck, Lydia. 1978. "Ernest Manning: Interview 2." *Ernest Manning Fonds,* 18 December. Edmonton: University of Alberta Archives.

Semotuck, Lydia. 1982. "Ernest Manning: Interview 39." *Ernest Manning Fonds,* 17 May. Edmonton: University of Alberta Archives.

Simons, Paula. 2009a. "One Step Forward Two Steps Back; Alberta's Human Right's Legislation Still Being Written by Social Conservatives." *Edmonton Journal,* 30 April, 18A.

Simons, Paula. 2009b. "Bill 44 an Evolutionary Dead End; Amendments Create Whole New Class of Potentially Aggrieved Parties." *Edmonton Journal,* 5 May, 14A.

Statistics Canada. 2001. "Religions in Canada: Highlight Tables." Available at http://www12.statcan.ca/english/census01/products/highlight/Religion/Index.cfm?Lang=E

Steffenhagen, Janet. 2006. "Gay Guarantee for Provincial Curriculum." *Vancouver Sun,* 16 June. Available at http://www.canada.com/vancouversun/news/story.html?id=223d5fea-2e50-4b1d-9678-f37850ca50cb

Taras, David, and Allan Tupper. 1994. "Politics and Deficits: Alberta's Challenge to the Canadian Political Agenda." In *Canada: The State of the Federation, 1994,* edited by Douglas M. Brown and Janet Hiebert, 59–84. Kingston: Institute of Intergovernmental Relations.

Tupper, Allan. 2004. "Peter Lougheed, 1971–1985." In *Alberta Premiers of the Twentieth Century,* edited by Bradford J. Rennie, 203–28. Regina: Canadian Plains Research Centre.

Varcoe, Chris. 2011. "Is Alberta Shifting Left When it Comes to Hard-Line Issues Like Abortion, Same-Sex Marriage?" *Calgary Herald,* 6 November. Available at http://www.edmontonjournal.com/news/politics/Alberta+shifting+left+when+comes+hard+line+issues+like+abortion/5665716/story.html

Warren, Clark. 2003. "Pockets of Belief: Religious Attendance Patterns in Canada." *Canadian Social Trends* 68: 2–5.

Weber, Timothy P. 1979. *Living in the Shadow of the Second Coming: American Premillennialism, 1875–1925*. New York: Oxford University Press.

Wesley, Jared. 2011. *Code Politics: Campaigns and Cultures on the Canadian Prairies*. Vancouver: University of British Columbia Press.

CASES AND LEGISLATION

Individual's Rights Protection Act, R.S.A., 1980

Canadian Charter of Rights and Freedoms, Part I of the Constitution Act, 1982

Vriend v. Alberta [1998] 1 S.C.R. 493

12 The "Naked Face" of Secular Exclusion

Bill 94 and the Privatization of Belief

PASCALE FOURNIER AND ERICA SEE

"Please do not impose on us the manner in which we liberate ourselves."
A young Muslim woman testifying before the Bouchard-
Taylor Commission (Bouchard and Taylor 2008, 234)

Introduction

In the West and in several Middle Eastern countries, states are actively and legally intervening to regulate Muslim women's liberty to wear the niqab, a full veil covering the face and the body.[1] Despite the fact that the actual number of women choosing the niqab is often quite low – Adams (2007) estimates the actual number in Québec to be lower than 100 (Adams 2007, 93) – public reactions to this piece of clothing tend to be vigorous and passionate (Cody 2010). Québec is no exception. Recently, with the drafting of Bill 94 (*An Act to establish guidelines governing accommodation requests within the Administration and certain institutions*, 2010), a woman's right to participate in public life with her niqab is likely to be severely limited. The proposed legislation emphasizes the necessity of "un visage découvert" or "naked face" when giving or receiving a broad range of provincial public services in Québec, including government services, as well as services provided at government-funded childcare centres, hospitals, and health and social service agencies.

The niqab prohibition is said to be justified on the basis of state neutrality and gender equality. Ironically, both proponents and critics of the niqab rely on gender equality to articulate their claims: some portray the niqab as a woman's right to freely express her religious convictions in the public sphere, including Amnesty International (2010), while others, including the Collectif citoyen pour l'égalité et la laïcité (2010), view it as a symbolic act of submission to men which projects the image of women as trapped in what Mackinnon (1983) would call a "false consciousness." Against this backdrop, the place of religion in the public sphere stands as a key factor in the acceptance or rejection of the niqab by institutional structures.

Borrowing from Charles Taylor's *A Secular Age* (2007), this chapter focuses on the importance of Bill 94 in negotiating the relationship between religion and the state in contemporary Québec. In particular, it will evaluate the paradoxical ways in which Taylor's scholarship fails to address the political and ideological alliance between the manifestation of secularism, on the one hand, and the emergence of "governance feminism" (Halley, Kotiswaran, Thomas, and Shamir 2006, 340), on the other. Drawing on legal realist interventions, this chapter will argue that the privatization of belief in Québec goes hand in hand with and is perversely reinforced by a colonial discourse on gender equality, leaving some already marginalized women out of the public gaze. Is this legislated demand for a "naked face" truly the logical outcome of a successful feminist movement (as some have asserted) or is this erasure of religious women in fact the latest veil of patriarchy?

Bill 94 in Context

Comparative Law: A Global Trend towards Banning the Niqab?

Québec's Bill 94 arrives in a political milieu in which veiling is being challenged in many parts of the world and in a variety of legal contexts: legislative, judicial, and in the public eye. France is, at the moment, perhaps the most widely known example of this line of debate. In July 2010, the French National Assembly passed a bill which makes it an offence to wear a full-face veil in any public area in France (Décision no. 2010-613 DC), and this bill received the almost unanimous approval of the French Senate in September, 2010 (Davies 2010). The French Justice Minister Michèle Alliot-Marie proclaimed: "The full veil dissolves a person's identity in that of a community. It calls into question the French model of integration, founded on the acceptance of our society's values" (Davies 2010). A similar piece of legislation has recently passed parliamentary approval in Belgium (Mock and Lichfield 2010) and the Danish government is considering a ban on the "burka" (Warburg,

Johansen, and Østergaard 2013). In Italy, old but previously unen-
forced legislative bans on covering the face (stemming back to a period
of civil unrest in the mid-1970s) have now started to be enforced against
Muslim women who wear the niqab (Owen 2010). In the United States
and in Germany, Muslim women have asked the courts to recognize
their right to wear the niqab in the school context and for purposes
of obtaining a driver's license photo (Kahn 2007, 423). In Spain, several cities have expressed their intentions to ban the niqab in some
public places (Islamic Human Rights Commission 2010; Parker 2010).
Niqab bans are being put in place by smaller-scale institutions, such as
colleges in the United Kingdom (Buaras 2009). In Syria and in Egypt,
niqab bans have been adopted as testaments to the secular nature of
the government or as a symbol of intolerance to religious extremism
(BBC 2010; Kenyon 2009).

Québec is yet another manifestation of this global trend, although in
a different guise. In March 2010, the Québec government introduced
Bill 94 (*An Act to establish guidelines governing accommodation requests
within the Administration and certain institutions*, 2010), legislation which
was deemed necessary to "balance individual freedoms with the values
of Québec society, including the equality between men and women and
secular public institutions" (CBC 2010). Like its counterparts in France
and Belgium, Québec's Bill 94 is neutral on its face. It consciously avoids
words such as "niqab" or "burqa," although these were the exclusive
and explicit raison d'être of the bill (Québec National Assembly 2010a).
In fact, many advocates for the bill within the National Assembly have
stridently argued that religious freedom is not a concern because the
bill merely offers a "code of conduct" for religious people of any persuasion to guide participation in secular society (Québec National
Assembly 2010b, testimony by M. Fortin).

The Ideological Underpinnings of Bill 94 and the
Public Reaction to the Bill

The Foundation of Québec's Bill 94

In his defense of the bill, Québec premier Jean Charest emphasizes the
need to strike a balance between the values of Québec society and the
desire for individual freedoms: "this is not about making our homes
less welcoming, but about stressing the values that unite us ... An
accommodation cannot be granted unless it respects the principle of

equality between men and women, and the religious neutrality of the state" (CBC 2010). Bill 94 heavily relies on "the right to gender equality" and "the principle of religious neutrality of the State" to justify its existence; such mention appears not only in the explanatory notes but in Section 4 as well. It emphasizes the necessity of "un visage découvert" or "naked face" when giving or receiving (Section 6) a broad range of provincial public and publically funded services in Québec, including government services (Section 2(1)), schools (Section 2(2); 2(5); 3(1)), childcare centres (Section 3(3)), hospitals (Section 2(2); 2(5)), and health and social service agencies (Section 3(2)). In addition to denying veiled women access to courts and government buildings, it has the effect of preventing even the most banal activities such as going to the local office of the electric company to enquire about charges or picking up a child from a government-funded daycare. The bill stands not only as a policy for standards around service to the public but also as an employment policy for Québec government employees and employees of institutions that receive funding from the Québec government. According to Section 6 of the bill , any accommodation of the "naked face" principle *must* be denied if "reasons of security, communication or identification warrant it."

Unlike its counterparts in Europe, the Québec bill uses the subtler venue of restrictions on requests for "reasonable accommodation" (as defined in *Multani v. Commission scholaire Marguerite-Bourgeoys* 2006, para. 131). The bill strategically avoids a "ban" on people who wear the niqab but instead severely limits the situations whereby government institutions and several provincially funded bodies can accommodate differences in dress. Although the bill's title suggests the implementation of innocuous "guidance" on accommodation, it is in fact introducing the "naked face" concept as a basic social "truth" into Québécois legislative discourse (Wilton 2010). This juxtaposition of a general social "truth" severely curtails the ability to make a case-by-case "reasonable accommodation" determination, as is normally the practice in this peculiar legal domain.

Ironically, although superficially limiting the situations in which a request for accommodation must be denied, it is difficult to imagine a use of public resources that would not demand communication with someone and/or the confirmation of identity (Des Rosiers 2010). The extremely broad reach of Québec public funding would effectively force the niqab-wearing woman to research and plot out the few public locations where she could possibly receive treatment equal to her "naked-faced" sisters. Ironically, the indirect narrowing of access to "reasonable accommodation" is actually a more comprehensive and insidious means of limiting the practice than a more direct ban of the practice under criminal law legislation. Whereas someone may be able to challenge a criminal conviction or pay a fine, limiting the places one is permitted to enter with a "visage découvert" is a persistent condition rather than the one-time event associated with a criminal sanction. This is not at all to suggest, however, that a criminal sanction against the wearing of the face veil would be a preferable circumstance to a civil action. Indeed, as Janet Halley and colleagues discuss in the context of criminalizing prostitution, criminal sanctions bring another host of problems (Halley, Kotiswaran, Thomas, and Shamir 2006, 337).

Public Reaction to Bill 94

The introduction of Bill 94 was heralded by organizations such as the publically funded Québec Council on the Status of Women, which saluted the actions of the government as avant-garde (Conseil du statut de la femme 2010, 17). The Canadian Muslim Congress also expressed support for the bill, stating the wearing of a full-face veil is not an Islamic religious requirement but, rather, an example of "Saudi-inspired" religious extremism (Canadian Muslim Congress 2009). In a press release regarding reasonable accommodation on religious grounds, le Mouvement laïque québécois situates religion as inherently irrational and therefore not reasonable grounds for accommodation (Mouvement laïque québécois 2010). Many scholars have argued that the bill is not really harming anybody because it does not add to the existing body of legal literature on reasonable accommodation (Leroux and Maclure 2010). Its purpose, in fact, is said to merely list "the conditions under which an accommodation may be made" (Bill 94 "Explanatory Notes").

However, the reaction to Bill 94 was not universally positive. In a brief to the National Assembly, the Canadian Council of Muslim Women argued that a legislated ban would be unnecessary in Québec if a properly worded reasonable accommodation policy were put in place to exclude the narrow set of circumstances where it would be reasonable to expect an individual to show her face to access services (Canadian Council of Muslim Women 2010, 2, 4). The Canadian Council on American-Islamic Relations took the more direct view that the law was designed with specifically discriminatory intent based on stereotypes about Muslims (Canadian Council on American-Islamic

Relations 2010, 3, 9). Kathy Malas, spokeswoman of the Canadian Muslim Forum, stated: "In Québec, people have the right to wear what they want. It's not a question of reasonable accommodation at all" (Canadian Press 2010). The Québec Bar's submission analysed the bill from a legal drafting standpoint, noting its potential for vast application and the vagueness of the wording (Barreau du Québec 2010).

Constitutional Vulnerability

While not the primary focus of this article, it is obvious that Bill 94, with its wide-ranging application to Québec public life, is vulnerable to a constitutional challenge on the basis of the *Canadian Charter of Rights and Freedoms'* Section 7 (overly broad application), as well as Section 2 (violation of freedom of religion). The constitutional vulnerability of the bill has been argued in more detail by several of the organizations who submitted briefs to the National Assembly, including the Canadian Council on American-Islamic Relations (2010).

More specifically, Section 6 of the bill is particularly problematic in the potential breadth of its application. It cites "reasons of security, communication or identification" to justify refusing to accommodate the needs and rights of Muslim women who are giving or receiving state services while wearing the niqab. This may well encompass a broad range of actions and is likely to be considered, in our opinion, as constitutionally overly broad under Section 7 of the *Canadian Charter* (*Ontario Human Rights Commission v. Simpsons-Sears Limited (O'Malley)*; *Re B.C. Motor Vehicle Act*; *R. v. Nova Scotia Pharmaceutical*).

The bill may also be attacked for its unconstitutionality on the basis of freedom of religion under the *Canadian Charter's* Section 2 (*R. v. N.S.*; *Syndicat Northcrest v. Amselem*; *Multani v. Commission scholaire Marguerite-Bourgeoys*) and *Québec Charter of Human Rights and Freedom's* Section 3 due to its disproportionate impact on some Muslim women. The 2004 Supreme Court case of *Syndicat Northcrest v. Amselem* (2004) affirmed that the measure of an allegedly violated religious belief is not whether the belief is held by all members of the religion but, rather, whether the belief is "sincerely held" by the person alleging the breach. The court in *Amselem* found:

> [F]reedom of religion consists of the freedom to undertake practices and harbour beliefs, having a nexus with religion, in which an individual demonstrates he or she sincerely believes or is sincerely undertaking in order

to connect with the divine or as a function of his or her spiritual faith, irrespective of whether a particular practice or belief is required by official religious dogma or is in conformity with the position of religious officials. (*Amselem* 2004, para. 46)

Outlining a subjective rather than an objective analysis of a religious belief or practice is particularly relevant in the present case of the wearing of the niqab, mainly because it puts to rest the assertions that the wearing of the face veil is not drawn from the Quran. A recent decision by the Ontario Court of Appeal (*R. v. N.S*, 2010) illustrates the focus on "sincerely held belief" as a basis for analysis. The case dealt with the right of a woman to testify in a criminal trial, while wearing her niqab, against two men who allegedly sexually assaulted her. Despite arguments that testifying while wearing a face veil would deny the accused the right to "face" his accuser, the court found in favour of the woman. The Court stated:

If a witness establishes that wearing her niqab is a legitimate exercise of her religious freedoms, then the onus moves to the accused to show why the exercise of this constitutionally protected right would compromise his constitutionally protected right to make full answer and defence. (*R v. N.S.* 2010, para. 98)

In its reasoning, the court focused on the exclusionary effect of denial rather than an ideologically driven analysis of whether face coverings are appropriate in public settings. It thus introduced a contextual lens to balance opposite constitutional rights, one which accounts for the fact that the individual behind the niqab is both a woman and a racialized member of society:

N.S. is a Muslim, a minority that many believe is unfairly maligned and stereotyped in contemporary Canada. A failure to give adequate consideration to N.S.'s religious beliefs would reflect and, to some extent, legitimize that negative stereotyping. Allowing her to wear a niqab could be seen as a recognition and acceptance of those minority beliefs and practices and, therefore, a reflection of the multi-cultural heritage of Canada recognized in s. 27 of the *Charter*. Permitting N.S. to wear her niqab would also broaden access to the justice system for those in the position of N.S., by indicating that participation in the justice system would not come at the cost of compromising one's religious beliefs ... Adjusting the process to ameliorate the hardships faced by a complainant like N.S. promotes gender equality. (*R v. N.S.* 2010, para. 79 and 80)

Such contextual analysis is far from the intent or the application of Bill 94, which not only stigmatizes Muslim women as a social and religious group but also puts them at a serious disadvantage in terms of gender equality. Assuming that the bill violates freedom of religion, the government will have to demonstrate under Section 1 of the *Canadian Charter* and Section 9.1 of the *Québec Charter of Human Rights and Freedoms* that the legislation is "justified in a free and democratic society." To be successful, the following elements will need to be shown: the bill has a justifiable purpose; it is proportional (*R. v. Oakes* 1986, para. 69; *Multani* 2006, para. 53); and it only constitutes a "minimal impairment" to religious freedom (*R. v. Nova Scotia Pharmaceuticals* 1992). In our opinion, Bill 94 is unlikely to overcome this high threshold (*R. v. Oakes* 1986, para. 69). Moreover, a state-sanctioned division between religion and the state (similar to the "Establishment Clause" concept in US constitutional law) is absent from the *Canadian Charter of Rights and Freedoms* and *The Québec Charter of Human Rights and Freedoms*. Instead, as mentioned previously, the provisions touching on religion in both of these key documents reinforce the primacy of freedom of religion and the need for the law to treat individuals equally and without discrimination on the basis of religion (*Canadian Charter*, Section 15(1); *Québec Charter*, Section 10).

Charles Taylor and the Privatization of Belief

Contemporary public spaces in the West have been "emptied of God, or any reference to ultimate reality" (Taylor 2007, 2). Charles Taylor's *A Secular Age* investigates how this process of secularization occurred (Taylor 2007, 187). In tracing the circuitous journey of religion in relation to public life in Western societies (Taylor 2007, 187), Taylor outlines three understandings/venues by which the secular and the religious have been framed as sharp dichotomies. The emergence of "a secular age" took place, he argues, with a concurrent shift at an individual level from a position of "theistic construal" to one where "unbelief has become the major default option" (Taylor 2007, 14). In this secularized context, "believers and unbelievers can experience their world very differently" (Taylor 2007, 14).

Once cast out from the public sphere, religion becomes lodged in the private sphere, along with the home and the family. For Taylor, the privatization of religion is a logical outgrowth of a "social imaginary" (Taylor 2007, 147) whereby the social life has shifted from one of a shared religious existence to one giving "unprecedented primacy to the individual." This new "buffered identity" (Taylor 2007, 156), producing the individual as "impervious to the enchanted cosmos" (Taylor 2007, 146), put new focus on personal devotion and discipline.

A Secular Age, with its emphasis on religion as outside of the public sphere, provides key theoretical insights to shed light on Québec's urge to relegate the niqab to the private sphere. Set in a context of a "social imaginary" of a "secular state," the requirement for a "naked face" is in fact revealed as a proxy for a wider discomfort with new forms of public displays of religious devotion. Taylor's text has much to offer to explain how the principle of religious neutrality has grown to be seen as a core legal value despite its absence from the Canadian and Québec Charters. However, it suggests no guidance on how the shift from the "secular public" to the "religious private" is carried out when dealing with the clearly gendered subject matter of the niqab. We are left with no insights, on a philosophical or political level, to help us understand the twinning of gender equality with religious neutrality in laws of this type. To better understand the role of gender in this issue, one must ask how feminism, particularly what Janet Halley terms "governance feminism" (Halley, Kotiswaran, Thomas, and Shamir 2006), conveniently came to be an intimate and powerful ally in the "tool box" of secularism.

The Gendered Subject behind the Veil in Québec

What does gender equality entail under the proposed legislation? What are the distributive consequences of advocating for this particular vision of gender equality? Can one be at once a religious woman and a feminist? Is secularism inclusive of diversity? Can it be? One thing is clear: Bill 94's emphasis on "equality between men and women" is largely driven by a "secular social imaginary" of Québec society in which overt forms of religious belief are sequestered from the public sphere. In this context, the niqab is viewed as a visibly gendered and almost aggressive form of religiosity from which Québec as a whole has decided to move away. For the Muslim women involved, equality is conceptualized as the physical ability to meet the metaphorical demand of a "face-to-face" encounter. In other words, the fact that women who veil their faces are not within the class of people who can greet the "face" of the public sphere in an identical manner to men means that that they fail in a gender equality calculus that non-niqab-wearing women pass. The effect of this positioning is that women who choose to wear the niqab are denuded of their agency and their legitimacy as gendered subjects.

One of the most troubling paradoxes of this discourse is the dialogue around whether veiled women are capable of "choosing" to take off the veil in a given circumstance. Advocates for the bill point out that a woman need only temporarily remove her face veil in order to receive the same level of service enjoyed by her fellow Québécers. If one believes that wearing a face-covering veil is a manifestation of a woman's oppression, then one must also believe the woman is powerless to correct her situation. Co-existing with the belief in the "false consciousness" of this·veiled woman is the ironic belief that she is stubbornly refusing to remove her veil even in the most mundane circumstances. Hence, women who wear the niqab are simultaneously seen as trapped by the limits of deep-set patriarchy and free agents who are failing to make the best choice for themselves and for society. Is there a way out?

Religious Freedom and Gender Equality

Another consequence of the linking of secularity and gender equality is that religion is seen as an inappropriate subject matter for the public sphere. Not only is religion relegated to the private sphere, but so is "the family." Frances E. Olsen's landmark article, "The Family and the Market: A Study of Ideology and Legal Reform," outlines a dichotomous "world view that perceives social life to be divided between market and family" (Olsen 1983, 1501). This is in line with Taylor's descriptions of the public realm as a "marketplace" where ideas are exchanged and discourses of power are played out. Critical legal scholars have long asserted the logical faults of such dichotomous rhetorical structure (Harris 2009, 48–9). Commenting on the dualist treatment of public and private, Angela P. Harris writes: "No dichotomy between the public and the private exists: the state, the market, and the family are each a complex network of institutions and practices governed by both state and non-state forms of power" (Harris 2009, 48–9). As a garment predominantly worn by women and inextricably linked to religiously informed beliefs on modesty, the decision of some Muslim women to wear the niqab in public defies this dichotomy by placing women and religious belief in the public sphere.

This tension between religious freedom and gender equality is part and parcel of the urge to "universalize" women's rights (Brandt and Kaplan 1995–1996, 105), articulated at an international level in the United Nations' *Convention on the Elimination of All Forms of Discrimination against Women* (CEDAW 1979). While laudable in intent, CEDAW employs a language of rights and equality that assumes and relies on a commonality of oppression that is not, in fact, universal. Michelle Brandt and Jeffrey Kaplan describe the Convention as a problematic microcosm of the codification of a Western vision of "universal" women's rights (Brandt and Kaplan 1995–1996, 106). The implied universality of the Convention's understanding of women's rights is belied by the high numbers of states signing it with reservations, many of which are based on religious grounds (Brandt and Kaplan 1995–1996, 106).

The second-wave feminist movement, the version of feminism being institutionalized through structures like CEDAW, has been largely articulated through discourse around the "rights" of women. This notion of "gender equality" is one largely focused on, and driven by, white middle-class women in Western countries who wanted equal rights to pay, legislative non-discrimination, and access to contraceptives (Mohanty 1988, 64). Recent feminist scholarship has critiqued "rights talk" as unable to account for specific political contexts, instead dwelling in an ahistorical and acultural vacuum (Brown 1995, 97). The "gender equality" ideal is neither realistic nor inclusive of the wide array of circumstances of real people.

Bill 94 exists at a crossroads between a "social imaginary" of a secular state paired with a "governance feminist" move to institutionalize the ideal of "gender equality." With its origins in the second wave feminist movement in the West, the idea of "governance feminism" (although not the term itself) is an institutionalization of a Western feminist vision of women's rights. The term "governance feminism" was developed by Janet Halley to describe the "incremental but by now quite noticeable installation of feminists and feminist ideas in actual legal-institutional power" (Halley 2006; Halley, Kotiswaran, Thomas, and Shamir 2006, 340). She uses this phrase to describe the effort on the part of some Western feminists to "download their international law reforms into domestic legal regimes" without being cognizant of divergent national realities (Halley, Kotiswaran, Thomas, and Shamir 2006, 346).

Bill 94's professed grounding in "gender equality between men and women" positions it as an entrenchment of second wave feminist ideals failing to consider the circumstances of all women. Through this grounding, the ideal of the "naked face" is characterized as a Western feminist ideal to which Québec society has signed onto through the Québec *Charter*. When combined with the disparate impact of this legislation on Muslims, the bill takes on an Orientalist (Said 1978) tone that contributes to portraying niqab wearers as the ultimate exotic Other. Unfortunately, institutional efforts to codify women's rights have not kept pace with more recent feminist scholarship in which the concept of feminism and norms of womanhood are seen within an intersectional framework of class, ethnicity, race, religion, and sexual orientation (among others). Bill 94's efforts to institutionalize "gender equality" at a national level mirrors the myopic faults of international efforts such CEDAW, each reflecting a deep lack of intersectional understanding of the circumstances of a largely non-white, non–middle class population of women.

Substantive Equality versus Formal Equality

Part of the difficulty in the bill's understanding of "secularism" and "gender equality" as they relate to issues of religious expression is the conflation of the need for "formal equality" with the need for "substantive equality." In her article analyzing the European Court of Human Rights' recent decisions on Turkey's ban on Islamic headscarves in public places, Rachel Rebouché (2009) discusses the distinction between substantive equality and formal equality and the distributive outcomes each produces. She writes: "In brief, substantive equality is a departure from classic or formal equality (or treating likes alike) and from equal treatment (ensuring that laws or policies apply to everyone in the same way). Substantive equality, by contrast, is concerned that laws and customary practices do not diminish women's access to societal goods or perpetuate discrimination" (Rebouché 2009, 712).

Bill 94 reflects a "formal equality" emphasis on removal of certain religious markers from the public view and attempting to erase differences between men and women in the rendering of services. If men and women appear identically bare-faced before social service providers, so the logic goes, the danger of unequal treatment is diminished. Women who differentiate themselves as distinct and different through a face veil threaten to undermine this goal of "formal equality." As a result, Bill 94 attempts to prevent the need for recognition of certain religiously framed gender differences through a blanket opposition to face veils. Bill 94 would look quite different if "equality between men and women" were understood in the more operational "social equality" sense, that is, espousing access to justice considerations.

Conclusion

The issue of "reasonable accommodation" in Québec has been a political focal point for many years. Prior to the drafting of Bill 94, the 2008 Bouchard-Taylor Report was mandated to explore the practice of reasonable accommodation relating to religious/cultural differences in Québec. It found that "Muslims and, in particular Arab Muslims, are, with Blacks, the group most affected by various forms of discrimination" (Bouchard and Taylor 2008, 84). The Report also affirms that girls and women who wear the Islamic headscarf attach different meaning to it and warns against a blanket prohibition on the practice (Bouchard and Taylor 2008, 234). In its conclusion, the Bouchard-Taylor Commission urges taking measures to foster Muslims' participation in society, rather than furthering measures to exclude segments of the population. The Commissioners write: "In short, the way to overcome Islamophobia is to draw closer to Muslims, not to shun them. In this field, as in others, mistrust engenders mistrust" (2008, 235).

This chapter has outlined the negative distributive consequences for religious women leading from passage of Bill 94. Section 1 places the bill within a wider debate within Western societies on secularism and the place of religion in the public sphere. Section 2 scrutinizes the bill's distributive effects within the context of the *Canadian Charter*'s right to religious freedom. Section 3 looks at the ideological basis of the bill and public reaction to it. Section 4 draws on the insights of Charles Taylor to better comprehend the bill's view of religious practice in the public sphere. Section 5 problematizes the bill's understanding of "gender equality" and whether religious women can ever be considered as gender equals in a political environment where their participation in society is severely curtailed. Despite common roots in an effort to correct systemic discrimination, "gender equality" as a legitimate state goal is being pitted against certain reasonable accommodation requests on the basis of religion in cases involving Muslim women's religious dress. Specifically, Québec's niqab ban is a demonstration of the troubling outcomes resulting from a confluence between secularism and a narrowed understanding of who can be a feminist and what constitutes feminist principles.

The passage of this bill will have immediate and dramatically harmful effects on religious women who wear the niqab. Although not mentioned by name, Muslim women are clearly the target of this piece of legislation and it is they exclusively who will be denied their rightful participation in public services. The result of this denial and its chilling effect is a further marginalization of this population of women. Religious women will likely disappear from the public sphere and be indelibly relegated to the private home, where they might effectively be dependent on male family members to navigate the public realm on their behalf. Is the true legacy of a century of feminist efforts to place women into the public realm a damning of certain religious women back to the shadows of the private realm? With the passage of Bill 94, it seems the answer will be a sad "yes."

NOTE

1 The authors would like to extend their thanks and appreciation to Solange Lefebvre for organizing such a wonderful workshop, to Lori G. Beaman and the "Religion and Diversity Project" (Social Sciences and Humanities Research Council (SSHRC)-funded Major Collaborative Research Initiative (MCRI)) for funding this project, and to Anastaziya Tataryn for her research in the preparation of this article. This chapter was previously published as Pascale Fournier and Erica See(2012), "The 'Naked Face' of Secular Exclusion: Bill-94 and the Privatization of Belief," *Windsor Yearbook of Access to Justice* 30(1): 63–76. It has been reproduced here with the permission of *Windsor Yearbook of Access to Justice*.

REFERENCES

Adams, Michael. 2007. *Unlikely Utopia*. Toronto: Viking Canada.
Amnesty International. 2010. "Belgium Votes to Ban Full-Face Veils." 30 April. Available at http://www.amnesty.org/en/news-and-updates/belgium-votes-ban-full-face-veils-2010-04-30
Barreau du Québec. 2010. "Projet de loi 94 intitulé 'Loi établissant les balises encadrant les demandes d'accommodement dans l'Administration gouvernementale et dans certains établissements.'" Letter addressed to Madame Kathleen Weil, Minister de la Justice du Québec. Available at http://www.barreau.qc.ca/pdf/medias/positions/2010/20100430-projet-loi-94.pdf
BBC. 2010. "Syria bans face veils at universities." *BBC*, 19 July. Available at http://www.bbc.co.uk/news/world-middle-east-10684359
Bouchard, Gérard, and Charles Taylor. 2008. "Building the Future: A Time for Reconciliation." Commission de consultation sur les pratiques

d'accommodement reliées aux différences culturelles. Québec: Québec Government Printing Office, 22 May.

Brandt, Michele, and Jeffrey A. Kaplan. 1995–1996. "Tension between Women's Rights and Religious Rights: Reservations to CEDAW by Egypt, Bangladesh, and Tunisia." *Journal of Law & Religion* 12(1): 105–42.

Brown, Wendy. 1995. *States of Injury: Power and Freedom in Late Modernity.* Princeton: Princeton University Press.

Buaras, Assad E. 2009. "Burnley College Bans Niqab Wearing Teen." *Muslim News,* 27 November. Available at http://www.muslimnews.co.uk/paper/index.php?article=4388

Canadian Council on American-Islamic Relations. 2010. "Brief Concerning Bill 94: An Act to Establish Guidelines Governing Accommodation Requests Within the Administration and Certain Institutions." Ottawa: Canadian Council on American-Islamic Relations.

Canadian Council of Muslim Women. 2010. "Brief to the National Assembly of Québec, Committee on Institutions to provide General Consultation on Bill 94 – An Act to establish guidelines governing accommodation requests within the Administration and certain institutions." Gananoque, Ontario: Canadian Council of Muslim Women.

Canadian Muslim Congress. 2009. "Muslim Canadian Congress Wants Canada to Ban the Burka." 8 October. Available at http://www.muslimcanadian congress.org/20091008.html

Canadian Press. 2010. "Québec Government Forced Egyptian Immigrant from Classroom for Refusing to Remove Face Veil." *Islamization Watch,* 3 March. Available at http://islamizationwatch.blogspot.com/2010/03/Québec-government-forced-egyptian.html

CBC. 2010. "Québec Will Require Bare Face for Service." *CBC News,* 23 March. Available at www.cbc.ca/canada/Montréal/story/2010/03/24/Québec-reasonable-accommodation-law.html

Collectif citoyen pour l'égalité et la laïcité (Cciel). 2010. "Pour une gestion laïque des services publics." Available at http://www.cciel.ca/memoire-du-cciel-pour-le-projet-de-loi-no-94

Cody, Edward. 2010. "France Moves to Fine Muslim Women with Full-Face Islamic Veils." *The Washington Post,* 20 May. Available at http://www.washingtonpost.com/wpdyn/content/story/2010/05/19/ST2010051906212.html?sid=ST2010051906212

Conseil Canadien en Relation Islamo Américaine. 2010. "Déclaration: Le Projet de loi 94 du Québec: institution d'une discrimination publique." Available at http://www.caircan.ca/downloads/Bill_94_CAIR_CAN_fr.pdf

Conseil du statut de la femme. 2010. "Mémoire sur le projet de loi no 94, Loi établissant les balises encadrant les demandes d'accommodement dans l'Administration gouvernementale et dans certains établissements." Québec: Conseil du statut de la femme.

Davies, Lizzy. 2010. "France: Senate Votes for Muslim Face Veil Ban." *The Guardian*, 14 September. Available at http://www.guardian.co.uk/world/2010/sep/14/france-senate-muslim-veil-ban

Des Rosiers, Nathalie. 2010. "Projet de loi 94 – Port du niqab: une loi inutile." *Le Devoir*, 3 April. Available at http://www.ledevoir.com/politique/Québec/286333/projet-de-loi-94-port-du-niqab-une-loi-inutile

Halley, Janet E. 2010. *Split Decisions: How and Why to Take a Break from Feminism*. Princeton: Princeton University Press.

Halley, Janet, Prabha Kotiswaran, Chanta Thomas, and Hila Shamir. 2006. "From the International to the Local in Feminist Legal Responses to Rape, Prostitution/Sex Work and Sex Trafficking: Four Studies in Contemporary Governance Feminism." *Harvard Journal of Law & Gender* 29(2): 335–423.

Harris, Angela P. 2009. "Theorizing Class, Gender, and the Law: Three Approaches." *Law & Contemporary Problems* 72(4): 37–56.

Islamic Human Rights Commission. 2010. "Action Alert: Spain – Barcelona Niqab Ban." Available at http://www.ihrc.org.uk/activities/9339-action-alert-spain-barcelona -niqab-ban

Kahn, Robert A. 2007. "Headscarf as Threat: A Comparison of German and U.S. Legal Discourses." *Vanderbilt Journal of Transnational Law* 40(2): 417–44.

Kenyon, Peter. 2009. "Veil Ban at Islamic School in Egypt Fuels Debate." *National Public Radio News Service* , 20 October. Available at http://www.npr.org/templates/story/story.php?storyId=113888541

Leroux, Georges, and Jocelyn Maclure. 2010. "Enjeux de la laïcité." *Spirale* 234(Autumn): 31–3.

Mackinnon, Catharine. 1983. "Feminism, Marxism, Method, and the State: Toward Feminist Jurisprudence." *Signs* 8(4): 635–58.

Mock, Vanessa, and John Lichfield. 2010. "Belgium Passes Europe's First Ban on Wearing Burka in Public." *Independent News Service*, 1 May. Available at http://www.independent.co.uk/news/world/europe/belgium-passes-europes-first-ban-on-wearing-burka-in-public-1959626.html

Mohanty, Chandra T. 1988. "Under Western Eyes: Feminist Scholarship and Colonial Discourses." *Feminist Review* 30(Autumn): 61–88.

Mouvement laïque québécois. 2010. "Une laïcité interculturelle: le Québec, avenir de la France?" Available at http://www.mlq.qc.ca/vx/6_dossiers/accommodement/accommodement_position_en.html

Olsen, Frances E. 1983. "The Family and the Market: A Study of Ideology and Legal Reform." *Harvard Law Review* 96(7): 1497–578.

Owen, Richard. 2010. "Italian Police Fine Woman for Wearing Burqa in Public. *The Times News Service*, 5 May. Available at http://www.timesonline.co.uk/tol/news/world/europe/article7115756.ece

Parker, Debbie. 2010. "Burqa and Niqab Ban in Spain Increased Political Pressure." *Spanish News*, 25 June. Available at http://www.spanishnews.es/20100625-burqa-and-niqab-ban-in-spain-increases-political-pressure/id=2739

Québec National Assembly. 2010a. *Debates.* 39th legislature, 1st session, 2009–2010, vol. 41, no. 69, 18 May. Québec: Québec Government Publishing.

Québec National Assembly. 2010b. *Debates.* 39th legislature, 1st session, 2010–2011, vol. 41, no. 116, 26 November. Québec: Québec Government Publishing.

Rebouché, Rachel. 2009. "The Substance of Substantive Equality: Gender Equality and Turkey's Headscarf Debate." *American University International Law Review* 24(4): 711–38.

Said, Edward. 1978. *Orientalism.* London: Penguin.

Taylor, Charles. 2007. *A Secular Age.* Cambridge: The Belknap Press of Harvard University Press.

Warburg, Margit, Birgitte Schepelern Johansen, and Kate Østergaard. 2013. "Counting Niqabs and Burqas in Denmark: Methodological Aspects of Quantifying Rare and Elusive Religious Sub-cultures." *Journal of Contemporary Religion* 28(1): 33–48.

Wilton, Katherine. 2010. "Second Niqab-wearing Woman Forced Out of Québec Class." *The Montréal Gazette*, 13 April. Available at http://www.canada.com/life/Second+niqab+wearing+woman+forced+Québec+class/2875421/story.html

CASES

Multani v. Commission scolaire Marguerite-Bourgeoys, [2006] 1 S.C.R. 256.

Reference re Section 94(2) of the Motor Vehicle Act, [1985] 2 S.C.R. 486.

R. v. Nova Scotia Pharmaceuticals, [1992] 2 S.C.R. 606.

R. v. N.S.(2010), ONCA 670, 102 O.R. (3d) 161.

R. v. Oakes, [1986] 1 S.C.R. 103.

Syndicat Northcrest v. Amselem, [2004] 2 S.C.R. 551.

Ontario Human Rights Commission v. Simpsons-Sears Limited (O'Malley), [1985] 2 S.C.R.

LEGISLATION

Canadian Charter of Rights and Freedoms, Part I of The Constitution Act, 1982 being Schedule B to the Canada Act 1982 (U.K.), 1982, c.11.
Québec Charter of Human Rights and Freedoms, R.S.Q. ch. C-12.
Bill 94, An Act to establish guidelines governing accommodation requests within the Administration and certain institutions. 1st Reading, March 24, 2010, 39th Legislature, 1st Session, 2010. Québec: Public Works and Government Services Québec, 2010. Re-instated, February 24, 2011. 39th Legislature, 2nd Session, 2011.
Décision no. 2010-613 DC, Loi interdisant dissumulation du visage dans l'espace public. (passed into law on October 7, 2010 after the September 14, 2010 approval of the French Senate)
United Nations. (1979). Convention on the Elimination of All Forms of Discrimination Against Women. GA res. 34/180, 34 UN GAOR Supp. (No. 46) at 193; UN Doc. A/34/36; 1249 UNTS 13.

13 Religion and the Socio-economic Integration of Immigrants across Canada

PHILLIP CONNOR AND MATTHIAS KOENIG

The reappearance of religion in the public sphere of Western societies is to a large extent related to new forms of religious diversity induced by international migration (for an overview see Bramadat and Koenig 2009). In Canada, new immigration inflows since the 1960s have significantly altered religious demographics with a growing number of Muslims, Buddhists, Hindus, and other non-Christian religious groups appearing on the scene (Beaman and Beyer 2008; Kelley and Trebilcock 1998). As other chapters in this volume forcefully show, this increased religious diversity has prompted policymakers, social activists, and academics to retool the idea of multiculturalism, to rethink the role of religion within state institutions, and more generally to reflect upon the place of religion within the public sphere.

Debates on legal, moral, and political aspects of religion in the Canadian public sphere are often premised on common perceptions of how immigrants of non-Christian backgrounds and their offspring adapt to and integrate into a largely Christian, yet secularizing society. Only recently, however, have these premises been put to robust empirical tests in the scholarly literature (for a review, see Breton 2012). Sociologists of religion have started to examine religious adaptation processes among new immigrants in Canada (Connor 2008, 2009). Studies such as those of Peter Beyer and colleagues in this volume have shown that the religious identities and practices of the second generation

This research was made possible with the generous support of the Pew-Templeton Global Religious Futures project. Appreciation is given to the Munk School of Global Affairs at the University of Toronto as Matthias Koenig was the Hannah Arendt Visiting Professor for German and European Studies at the time this chapter was written.

are rather different from the conventional norms practised by their parents, often adapting to the Canadian context. More ethnographical studies have highlighted the importance of religious contexts of reception; for instance, as Margarita Mooney shows in this volume, the incorporation of Haitian immigrants in Montréal is strongly influenced by religious institutional arrangements and how these institutions are viewed by the state. And migration scholars have also analysed how religion and race, respectively, affect life satisfaction, social trust, and civic participation among immigrants (Reitz, Banerjee, Phan, and Thompson 2009).

However, just as migration scholarship has long overlooked religion in evaluating immigrant integration (Ebaugh 2003), the role of religion in immigrants' *socio-economic* or structural integration has only rarely been examined in the Canadian context (for exceptions see Model and Lin 2002; Reitz et al. 2009). This is all the more astonishing as knowledge of whether and how religion tangibly affects immigrants' socio-economic or structural integration would be crucial to controversies over "reasonable accommodation" of religious difference (Bouchard and Taylor 2008) or the role of religion in the public sphere more generally.

In this chapter, we aim to shed some light on how religion affects immigrants' socio-economic or structural integration in Canada. In particular, we analyse the effects of religious affiliation and religious participation on the educational and occupational attainment of both first- and second-generation immigrants. We do so by drawing on Statistics Canada's 2002 Ethnic Diversity Survey (EDS). Although this survey is somewhat dated, it remains the best available data source to conduct comprehensive analyses of immigrant integration by religion in Canada. In fact, the survey continues to be used in current research dealing with religion and immigrant integration (see for example Connor and Koenig 2013 and Reitz et al. 2009). The sample size of this survey allows to examine differences in educational achievement (completion of a university degree) and occupational attainment (having a professional/managerial job) between natives and immigrants across different religious groups and across levels of religious participation (attending a religious service monthly or more frequently), net of other variables (sex, marital status, age, education, parental socio-economic status, visible minority status, and city of residence).[1] Moreover, the survey permits us to test whether religious context characteristics often assumed to distinguish Québec from the rest of Canada actually translate into differential effects of religion upon immigrant socio-economic success.

We begin with a brief overview of the role of religion in immigrant integration as theorized in the wider literature. Having laid out a series of hypotheses on how different religious groups and different habits of religious participation may result in variable socio-economic outcomes, we turn to how religious effects on immigrant integration may differ in Québec and the rest of Canada. The analyses begin with baseline estimates of educational and occupational attainment as conditioned by religious affiliation and participation among the native-born population in Québec and the rest of Canada. Using this contextual comparison, we then analyse religious effects on educational and occupational attainment among immigrants, with separate analyses for the first and second generation. We conclude with a summary of findings and theoretical implications.

Theoretical Background

Recent scholarship on the role of religion in immigrant integration has put strong emphasis on contextual differences between North America and Europe (for reviews, see Cadge and Ecklund 2007; Voas and Fleischmann 2012). In transatlantic comparison, Foner and Alba (2008) have prominently contrasted the rather dissimilar functions of religion as a "bridge" to the mainstream in the United States while constituting a "barrier" to immigrant integration in Western Europe. Building on this metaphor of "bridge" versus "barrier," we have elsewhere attempted to specify causal mechanisms through which religious participation and affiliation, respectively, may affect socio-economic outcomes of immigrant integration (Connor and Koenig 2013). While the "bridging" mechanism operates through the social resources embedded in religious organizations, the "barrier" mechanism presumes religion to constitute a diacritical marker of ethnic or cultural difference. Our core theoretical argument is thus that both mechanisms depend on contextual religious field characteristics and religious boundary configurations.

Religious participation may be related to socio-economic integration through a causal mechanism that is triggered by specific religious field characteristics. It has often been noted that the United States is not only far more religious than Europe (Norris and Inglehart 2004) but has a rather congregational, voluntaristic, or "Toquevillian" religious field. Many studies in the United States (Hirschman 2004) have thus demonstrated how immigrants actively involved in local religious organizations have greater access to social capital (knowledge of job openings, self-employment coaching, language courses, social networks for business opportunities, etc.). It is in this sense that religious participation constitutes a "bridge" to the societal mainstream for immigrants, although one may arguably assume the "bridging" function to be more pronounced among religious majorities than among minorities. Indeed, several studies point to this "religious" advantage in the United States (Connor 2011), particularly among the second generation (Bankston and Zhou 1995). The European context, by contrast, is not characterized by such actively religious civil society but by highly state-regulated religious economies; in fact, individual religious attendance rates have been plummeting throughout Europe during the past few decades (Norris and Inglehart 2004). As a consequence, religious attendance should provide only little assistance to immigrants; if anything, active involvement in religious organizations could even be regarded as a penalty for immigrants in secularizing Europe.

The mechanism captured in the "bridge" metaphor depends less on religious field characteristics than on religious boundary configurations. As Gordon (1964) noted years ago, symbolic boundaries constitute important contextual conditions for immigrant integration. Drawing from the American experience during the early twentieth century, he recounts how racial, and to some degree religious, differences from the majority population can serve as structural barriers for immigrant incorporation. Alba (2005) further elaborates that immigrant societies have an array of "bright" and "blurred" boundaries for different immigrant groups; "bright" boundaries can be religious in some contexts, while in others racial or linguistic differences may be of greater relevance. For example, Alba considers racial differences to be a "bright" boundary in the United States, whereas in Europe religion constituted a salient boundary separating immigrants from natives. That such boundaries do indeed translate into tangible socio-economic integration outcomes is suggested by empirical findings that religious minorities in Europe, particularly Muslims, are less likely to be called for a job interview (Adida, Laitin, and Valfort 2010), to be employed (Model and Lin 2002), and to succeed socio-economically in general.

While much debate on different integration contexts focuses on US-European comparisons, Canada provides an interesting case in that it combines moderate religious boundaries with a moderately active religious civil society (see also Connor and Koenig 2013). We therefore turn to a more detailed discussion of the Canadian case.

The Canadian Integration Context

As often noted by historians and sociologists alike, Canada lies somewhere between the United States and Western Europe in terms of both religious boundary configurations and religious field characteristics (Lyon and Van Die 2000). Assessing whether and how these contextual factors impinge on the ways religious affiliation and participation are related to socio-economic attainment of immigrants at the individual level therefore promises to shed some new light on above-mentioned scholarly debates.

Within Canadian public debates, it is often presupposed that long-standing historical differences between French and English settlement and centre-periphery relations have left a lasting impact upon the reception of immigrants. Thus, it has been argued that the transition from ethnic or more civic codes of national identity has proceeded differently in Québec than in the rest of Canada (Breton 1988). Indeed, in reversal of previous expectations of Anglo-conformity, the rest of Canada outside of Québec has since the 1970s adopted a policy of "multiculturalism" that in rather liberal fashion allows immigrants to retain or not retain their particular cultural identities (Kymlicka 1996; Li 2003a). Québec, defending her own peripheral national identity within a hegemonic English-speaking polity has , by contrast, pursued a more proactive strategy of integrating immigrants through active French-language programs and the like (Maclure 2003; Milot 2009).

Québec has also been argued to differ substantively from the rest of Canada in terms of religious boundary configurations. Until the Quiet Revolution, Catholicism was the main pillar of Québec's imagined identity as a peripheral nation. Although a rapid process of secularization has moved other linguistic and cultural markers to the core of Québécois national imaginations, new religious minorities are sometimes considered to face "bright" boundaries (Milot 2009; O'Toole 1996). Not accidentally, controversies over "reasonable accommodation" (Bouchard and Taylor 2008) emerged in the Québécois context. By contrast, religious diversity has more easily been embraced outside of Québec. Already by the time of Confederation (1867), the Anglican

Church was formally disestablished and put on equal terms with the other four major denominations in the country (Catholic, Presbyterian, Methodist, Baptist). While denominational diversity initially went hand in hand with imaginations of a "Christian nation," it provided fertile ground for religious diversification that came with new waves of immigration (Bramadat and Seljak 2009). We caution, however, that these internal differences may appear marginal once Canada is situated within broader transatlantic comparative perspective (Connor and Koenig 2013).

Diverging historical backgrounds are also sometimes argued to translate into different religious field characteristics, with religious organizations outside of Québec having adopted a congregational model since the nineteenth century, while in Québec a church model continued to be operative into the twentieth century. Worship attendance has also declined more sharply in Québec than in the rest of Canada (Clark 2003). Again, however, we note that in contrast to Western Europe the religious field in contemporary Québec can be regarded as considerably less regulated, more pluralistic, and to some degree still an important part of civil society. In the absence of a strong central state, religious organizations have historically been the most prominent institutions of civil society, including even the working classes, in both Québec and the rest of Canada (Bramadat and Seljak 2008; Christie and Gauvreau 2010). Moreover, a recent study actually found that worship attendance increases the likelihood of political engagement throughout Canada (Tossutti et al. 2008).

In sum, the existing literature would suggest to treat Québec and the rest of Canada as distinctive integration contexts. However, there are also arguments that caution not to overstate internal differences. After all, both contexts share similar labour-market characteristics, welfare regimes, and immigration policy; and both are generally known for rather successful integration of second-generation immigrants (Boyd and Greico 1998).

When we look at contemporary religious statistics, we do find some evidence for different contextual configurations in Québec and the rest of Canada. Thus, data from the 2002 Ethnic Diversity Survey (EDS; see table 13.1) suggest that provinces outside of Québec are more religiously diverse than Québec, with nearly half of the population claiming a Protestant affiliation, a quarter being Catholic, and slightly less than another quarter stating no affiliation.[2] In Québec, the population overwhelmingly states Catholicism as their religion. In terms of religious

Table 13.1 Descriptive statistics by context

Variable	Québec			Rest of Canada		
	Native born	First Gen Imm	Sec Gen Imm	Native born	First Gen Imm	Sec Gen Imm
Outcome Variable						
Completion of Post-secondary Education	0.58	0.68*	0.73*	0.61	0.63*	0.69*
Professional/Managerial Occupation[a]	0.53	0.57	0.65*	0.54	0.52*	0.57*
Religious Affiliation						
Unaffiliated	0.06	0.11*	0.17*	0.22	0.19*	0.22
Catholic	0.88	0.53*	0.68*	0.27	0.33*	0.29
Protestant	0.05	0.11*	0.09*	0.49	0.25*	0.43*
Muslim	0.00	0.08*	0.01*	0.00	0.06*	0.01*
Eastern Religions	0.00	0.04*	0.01*	0.00	0.12*	0.02*
Religious Attendance						
Monthly or more frequent	0.24	0.37*	0.23	0.34	0.46*	0.34
N	2,551	837	887	7,590	5,910	7,175

*t-test difference of $p < 0.05$ between from native born within each context
[a] Limited to those who are employed
Note: Descriptive statistics are unweighted; religious affiliation does not total 1 as other religions such as Judaism and Christian orthodox are not displayed

attendance, about a third of the native-born population in the rest of Canada attends religious services monthly or more often, whereas only a quarter of the native-born population in Québec does so.

Both Québec and the rest of Canada have likewise experienced religious diversification as a result of immigration from various non-European countries. In the EDS, this is reflected in the religious composition of both first- and second-generation immigrants. For first-generation immigrants outside of Québec, Catholics, Protestants, the religiously unaffiliated, and other non-Christian religions (Islam, Buddhism, Hinduism, etc.) each represent about a quarter of the immigrant population. In Québec, there are a slightly larger percentage of Muslim immigrants than in the rest of Canada, and also a larger percentage of Catholic immigrants. It also appears that although first-generation immigrants attend religious services more frequently than the native born in both Québec and the rest of Canada, second-generation immigrants have similar religious participation levels as their native-born counterparts.

Assuming that Québec and the rest of Canada would indeed be characterized by distinctive religious field characteristics and boundary configurations, how would these affect immigrants' socio-economic integration? Our arguments associated with the "bridge-versus-barrier" metaphor would suggest a number of expectations: Given the history and extent of religious diversity, one would expect fewer religious barriers outside of Québec than in Québec; religious minorities in Québec would indeed be expected to experience some socio-economic disadvantages compared to other religious groups. Furthermore, because of a more prominent role of religion within civil society in the rest of Canada as compared to Québec, one would expect religiously active immigrants to receive a slight boost in their educational and occupational attainment. Contextual differences within Canada, if there are any, should translate into religion operating more as a barrier for immigrants' socio-economic integration in Québec, while constituting a bridge in the rest of Canada.

For the remainder of this chapter we put these expectations to an empirical test by analyzing how religious affiliation and participation are related to educational and occupational attainments, net of other standard socio-demographic factors (sex, marital status, age, visible minority status, city of residence) known to affect these integration outcomes. In particular, moving beyond some existing studies (Beyer 2005), we control for immigrants' class background (more specifically parental education), which is known to be the most important factor impinging on both educational and occupational achievement (Heath and Cheung 2007). Given Canada's immigration policy which selectively privileges high-skill migrants, it is indeed crucial to control for socio-economic status when analyzing differences between native born and immigrants and their children. To get a visual sense of the multiple comparisons between religious groups, immigrant generations, levels of religious participation, and across the contexts of Québec and the rest of Canada, we display predicted probabilities. The lines on the following graphs indicate the predicted proportion of the population having the outcome (i.e., university degree, a professional/managerial job) at a 95 per cent confidence interval, all net of the factors already discussed.

Educational Attainment

Education is one of the major means through which immigrants and their children can gain equal access to socio-economic participation

(Li 2003b). It is therefore crucial to determine whether any ethnic or religious penalties exist for distinctive immigrant groups. Following the above hypotheses, we would expect that, due to religious boundaries in the receiving society, non-Christian immigrants are at a disadvantage educationally relative to Christians; and if conventional wisdom about internal Canadian differences was correct, we would expect this religious boundary effect to be stronger in Québec than in the rest of Canada. Moreover, we would also expect the religiously active population (for example, those attending religious services monthly or more frequently) to have higher educational attainment than the religiously inactive population. And this religious attendance premium should be more prominent outside than inside Québec.

Figure 13.1 displays the predicted probability (0 to 1) of completing a university degree by religious affiliation and participation, net of a number of socio-demographic controls.[3] Results for Québec are located on the left, results for the rest of Canada on the right. Horizontally, the figure subdivides native-born (top) from first-generation immigrants (middle) and the second-generation (bottom). Religious groups are subdivided by the religiously inactive (attending religious services less than monthly, including no religious attendance) and religiously active (attending religious services monthly or more).[4] Since respondents affiliated with no religion were not given the opportunity to respond to the religious attendance question, the "no religion" group is not disaggregated by religious attendance. Religious groups include Catholic, Protestant, Muslim, and Eastern Religions (Buddhism, Hinduism, and Sikhism combined).[5] Unfortunately, small sample sizes for non-Christian groups made for less-than-reliable estimates for native-born and second-generation analyses. In interpreting the graph, any overlapping value between religious groups (inactive or active) is not statistically significant. The varying ranges for confidence intervals are influenced by sample size, which explains why smaller groups have longer lines (first-generation Muslims for example).

The native-born population provides a baseline for comparing first- and second-generation immigrant educational attainment. A careful inspection of the graph finds that although the second generation's educational attainment is higher on average compared to the native born for most religious groups, first-generation educational attainment among Catholics, Protestants, and those with no religion is very similar to the same religious groups for the native-born population, both for Québec and the rest of Canada. However, in the first generation, Eastern religious groups are significantly less likely to have completed

Figure 13.1. Predicted probability of having a university degree by religiously active/inactive religious groups and by Québec and the rest of Canada

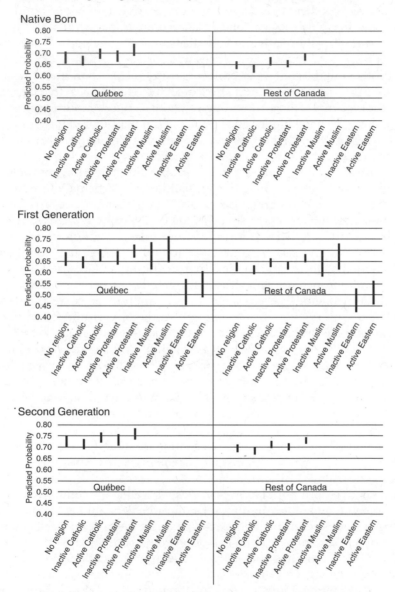

Source: 2002 Ethnic Diversity Survey, Statistics Canada. Predicted probabilities are based on the authors' calculations using logistic regression modeling.

a university degree compared to other religious groups. And, contrary to the above hypotheses, about equal penalties for Eastern religious groups occur for both Québec and the rest of Canada, net of other factors, including visible minority status that differentiates between major origin groups. To those assuming stark internal differences within Canada, it may come as a bit of a surprise that Muslim immigrants in Québec have similar levels of education as other religious groups and that this is not vastly different from the Muslim experience in the rest of Canada. In sum, only belonging to an Eastern religious group is associated with lower education compared to other religious groups, but the effects are similar throughout Canada.

Moving to religious participation, a quick snapshot of Figure 13.1 indicates that frequent religious attendance is generally associated with a higher probability of completing a university degree, even for non-Christian religious groups like Muslims and Eastern religions. Also, religiously active immigrants consistently have higher education than those with no religion (and hence religiously inactive).This is significantly the case for religiously active Protestants outside of Québec for all three groups – native born, first-generation immigrant, and second-generation immigrant. Religiously active Protestants are more educated than religiously inactive Protestants and those with no religion. Even in Québec, religious participation seems to provide a slight boost for all religious and immigrant/native-born groups, but their differences compared to those who do not regularly participate in religious organizations are not statistically significant. In sum, religious participation does seem to operate more as a bridge for immigrant educational attainment outside of Québec than in Québec, at least for Protestants.

Occupational Attainment

Immigrants arrive with varying levels and quality of education from their countries of origin which they may, or may not, turn into success on the labour market (on early placement trajectories, see Fuller and Martin 2012). For the second generation, in particular, who have been exposed to the same educational system as the native-born population, it is crucial to determine whether they face any particular penalties on the labour market. Therefore, occupational attainment is consistently used in migration literature as an indicator of structural integration (Chiswick and Miller 2010; Model and Lin 2002). Immigrants who can procure high-level occupations, either through their education, skills, or other means, have in many ways structurally adapted to the receiving society.

Figure 13.2 displays the predicted probability of having a professional/managerial job by religious group (both inactive and active) as well as across contexts (Québec and the rest of Canada). The same interpretation of the confidence interval lines for the education figure holds for occupational attainment.[6] The predicted probabilities for occupational attainment control for the same socio-demographic variables (gender, marital status, age, visible minority status, parental education, city of residence) but also add education.

Like educational achievement, second-generation occupational attainment is very similar to that of the native born, if not higher for some groups (see for similar findings, Boyd 2008). Many studies have found first-generation occupational attainment in Canada to be generally lower than that of the native-born population (Li 2003b), and this is also demonstrated in the results in Figure 13.2. But, in examining religious group differences, it is immediately clear that non-Christian groups like Muslims and Eastern religions are at a severe occupational disadvantage relative to Christian and religiously unaffiliated groups, net of other contributing factors. In fact, native born and immigrants alike who either have no religion or are Christian (Protestant or Catholic) have about the same probability of working in a professional/managerial job. In contrast, first-generation Muslims and those belonging to Eastern religions are significantly less likely to be in a high-level occupation, all net of educational attainment and visible minority status. Although the small number of respondents belonging to the same non-Christian religious groups in the second generation makes it impossible to see if this trend persists across generations, the religious differences in the first generation are quite striking. But, contrary to assumptions about distinctive integration contexts, there are no significant differences between the two regions for this non-Christian penalty in occupational attainment.

Religious participation presents a slightly higher probability of being in a professional/managerial job than those who are inactive in religious organizations, regardless of religious group. However, unlike educational attainment, none of the religious participation effects for occupation are significant, neither in comparison to the same religious group nor for those with no religion. Moreover, the generally higher probability of holding a professional/managerial job among the religiously active population is not significantly different in Québec than in the rest of Canada; the religious participation boost is equally realized

Figure 13.2. Predicted probability of being in a professional or managerial job by religiously active/inactive religious groups and by Québec and the rest of Canada

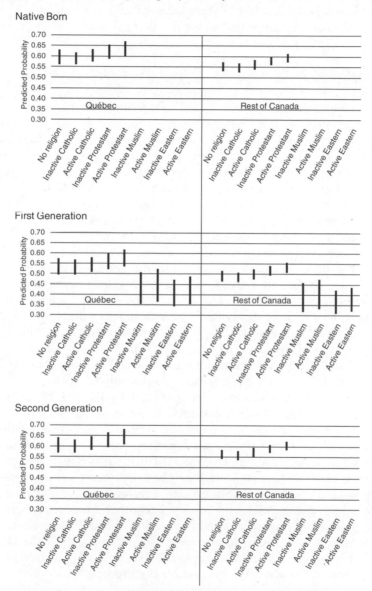

Source: 2002 Ethnic Diversity Survey, Statistics Canada. Predicted probabilities are based on the authors' calculations using logistic regression modelling.

in both contexts. In sum, it appears that regular religious participation is associated with a general uptick in the probability of having a professional/managerial job, but this advantage does not significantly differ across population groups (native born v. first generation v. second generation), religious groups, or across contexts.

Discussion

In this chapter, we have contributed to ongoing debates over contextual differences in how religion affects immigrants' socio-economic integration. These debates which typically focus on the United States and Europe, would in our view profit from greater attention to the unique case of Canada which, given its unique history of church-state relations, is characterized by remnants of bright religious boundaries while having also developed a congregational pattern of religious organization. Thus, Canada provides a crucial case to test the extent to which religious boundaries translate into barriers for religious minorities' socio-economic attainment and religious participation simultaneously constitutes bridges for immigrants' integration into the receiving society (see also Connor and Koenig 2013). We also engaged with the widely held perception that Québec and the rest of Canada differed markedly in both religious boundary configurations and religious field characteristics, although we cautioned against overstating these internal contextual differences. Indeed, our findings on immigrants' educational and occupational attainment as evinced in data from the 2002 Ethnic Diversity Survey yield rather mixed results.

At least for educational and occupational attainment, the religious contextual differences often assumed to exist between Québec and the rest of Canada were not associated with differential outcomes of immigrants' structural integration.[7] Rather, "barriers" and "bridges" seem to be present throughout Canada. Thus, Eastern religious groups were less likely to have completed a university degree in both contexts. Muslims and Eastern religious groups were also less likely to be in a professional/managerial job compared to other first-generation religious groups, net of socio-demographic variables. Furthermore, religious participation seems to provide a moderate boost to educational and occupational attainment, regardless of religious affiliation and immigrant generation. This integration premium associated with religious participation was most pronounced outside Québec, particularly for Protestants, but it still occurred to a moderate extent in Québec.

There are many limitations to this study, mostly related to the data itself. As data are not longitudinal, we cannot definitively state a causal direction to the observed correlations; reverse causation could be at work. Another limitation is time. As already mentioned, the study was conducted about 10 years ago, and much has changed in Canada and the world since then (e.g., Iraq and Afghan wars, religious accommodation debates). These changes as well as the recent economic downturn could potentially affect the role of religion on immigrant integration. Most importantly, the second-generation population belonging to religious minorities is only now reaching adult age; therefore, we were not able to reliably see whether religious affiliation differences present in the first generation persisted in the second. Although further analysis not shown in this chapter indicates that the integration experience for religious minorities among the second generation is on par with Christian children of immigrants, more time is needed to fully assess whether any perceived differences between religious groups in the first generation persist through the second generation. If the religious differences do persist in the years to come, then boundaries would seem to operate in Canada more generally; if not, this might suggest that religious penalties could be explained by omitted variables unique to first-generation immigrants such as time in country, citizenship, etc. In fact, in further tests of the first generation, we did find more muted differences for Muslims and Eastern religious groups when these types of immigrant variables were included in the models (see Connor and Koenig 2013).

However, despite these limitations, our study does shed some light on the debates over the religious dimensions of integration contexts. Standing between the extreme cases of the United States and Europe, the Canadian case suggests that the mechanisms of minority religious affiliation as a potential barrier and religious participation as a potential bridge may operate independently from each other. Even though results were not statistically significant, there was a slight improvement of integration outcomes for religiously active Muslims and Eastern religious groups in Canada compared to inactive people in the same religious groups. Although religious participation did not allow first-generation immigrants belonging to religious minorities to match educational and occupational levels of immigrants belonging to Christian groups or having no religion at all, it still improved their probability of having a university degree or a professional/managerial job relative to religiously inactive people belonging to the same religious group. In other words, religious participation may, in line with arguments from segmented assimilation theory (Portes and Rumbaut 2006; Warner 2007), be profitable even for those religious groups who might otherwise experience barriers because of their religious minority status.

In conclusion, religion seems to operate as a bridge for most immigrants seeking to make a better life in Canada, but at the same time as a barrier for religious minorities. Although we cannot present any definite conclusions, given the limitations of our data, we hope to have contributed to knowledge on the relationship between religion and immigrant integration by a few empirical steps. Until now, some may have assumed the putative religious contextual differences in Québec and the rest of Canada would be associated with differential immigrant outcomes when it comes to religion; however, this does not seem to be the case. And, although findings do point to some kind of religious-participation benefit for immigrant integration, it is small in size and does not provide the socio-economic gain needed for religious minorities to match native-born achievement.

As more recent data are made available, additional research should examine the second-generation experience, particularly among religious minorities. Also, more qualitative research examining the role of religion on immigrant outcomes across the Canadian context by religious group is needed. As Canada continues to receive new immigrant cohorts annually and the number of children among religious minorities grows, there will be plenty of additional research questions to answer, with the religious contextual differences between Québec and the rest of Canada only one part of the story.

NOTES

1 The Ethnic Diversity Survey (EDS) was conducted in 2002 by Statistics Canada and represents the national population with oversampling for ethnic minorities ($N > 40,000$). The EDS was conducted in English, French, and Canada's seven largest nonofficial languages: Mandarin, Cantonese, Italian, Punjabi, Portuguese, Vietnamese, and Spanish. Analyses presented in this paper are limited to participants of working age (ages 25–64). Occupational attainment is limited to those who are employed, while educational attainment is for the complete sample. Missing cases (< 5 per cent) for outcome variables, religion variables, or control variables were removed through list wise deletion and considered missing at random. Since publicly available

data do not include a code for province, Québec residents are considered to be those who either live in Montréal or responded to the survey in French (except for those respondents responding in French but living in Toronto or Vancouver). Although a small number of French-speaking respondents in other provinces outside Québec are considered residents of Québec, it would be a negligible number of respondents and would not affect the general findings in this study. Furthermore, very few immigrants living outside of Toronto, Montréal, and Vancouver would respond to a survey in French. The EDS was conducted April through August 2002; therefore, no period effects related to September 11, 2001, are known to exist.

2 Authors' calculations from the 2001 Census by native-born and first-generation immigrants mirror the religious breakdown found in the Ethnic Diversity Survey. For 2001 Census data on religion and immigrant status, see http://www12.statcan.ca/English/census01/products/standard/themes/Rp-eng.cfm?LANG=E&APATH=3&DETAIL=0&DIM=0&FL=A&FREE=0&GC=0&GID=0&GK=0&GRP=1&PID=55824&PRID=0&PTYPE=55430,53293,55440,55496,71090&S=0&SHOWALL=0&SUB=0&Temporal=2001&THEME=56&VID=0&VNAMEE=&VNAMEF=

3 Completion of a university degree rather than some college was selected because of the differing post-secondary educational systems in Québec and the rest of Canada. Educational attainment is drawn from the EDS question: "What is the highest level of education you have attained?"

4 The "monthly or more" division for religious participation was selected to allow for a greater range of religious participation for religious groups that may not expect the weekly attendance typical in Christianity. Religious activity is drawn from the EDS question: In the past twelve months, "How often did you participate in religious activities or attend religious services or meetings with other people, other than for events such as weddings and funerals?"

5 Religious affiliation was drawn from the following EDS question: "For some people, religion may be an important part of their ethnicity or culture, while for others it is not. What is your religion, if any?" Respondent religion was recoded into the categories presented in this paper.

6 Occupational attainment was derived from several EDS questions collapsed by Statistics Canada into the Standard Occupational Classification (SOC) 1991 categories. Management, business, finance, administrative, natural and applied sciences, health, social sciences, education, government service, and religious occupations were coded as professional/managerial jobs. Occupations in art, culture, recreation, sport, sales and service, trade, transport, primary industry, processing, manufacturing, and utilities were coded as not being professional/managerial jobs.

7 In their analysis of other integration variables, including life satisfaction, identification with Canada, and social engagement, Reitz et al. (2009) also found few differences between Québec and the rest of Canada.

REFERENCES

Adida, Claire, David Laitin, and Marie-Anne Valfort. 2010. *Proceedings of the National Academy of Sciences of the United States of America* 107: 22384–90.

Alba, Richard. 2005. "Bright vs. Blurred Boundaries: Second Generation Assimilation and Exclusion in France, Germany, and the United States." *Ethnic and Racial Studies* 28(1): 20–49.

Bankston, Carl L., and Min Zhou. 1995. "Religious Participation, Ethnic Identification, and Adaptation of Vietnamese Adolescents in an Immigrant Community." *Sociological Quarterly* 36: 523–34.

Beaman, Lori G., and Peter Beyer, eds. 2008. *Religion and Diversity in Canada.* Leiden: Brill Academic Press.

Beyer, Peter. 2005. "Religious Identity and Educational Attainment among Recent Immigrants to Canada: Gender, Age, and 2nd Generation." *Journal of International Migration and Integration* 6(2): 177–99.

Bouchard, Gérard, and Charles Taylor. 2008. "Building the Future: A Time for Reconciliation." Québec: Québec Government, 22 May.

Boyd, Monica. 2008. "A Socioeconomic Scale for Canada: Measuring Occupational Status from the Census." *Canadian Review of Sociology* 45(1): 51–91.

Boyd, Monica, and Elizabeth M. Greico. 1998. "Triumphant Transitions: Socioeconomic Achievements of the Second Generation in Canada." *International Migration Review* 32(4): 853–76.

Bramadat, Paul, and Matthias Koenig, eds. 2009. *International Migration and the Governance of Religious Diversity.* Montreal: McGill-Queens University Press.

Bramadat, Paul, and David Seljak. 2009. *Religion and Ethnicity in Canada.* Toronto: University of Toronto Press.

Bramadat, Paul, and David Seljak. 2008. *Christianity and Ethnicity in Canada.* Toronto: University of Toronto Press.

Breton, Raymond. 1988. "From Ethnic to Civic Nationalism: English Canada and Québec." *Ethnic and Racial Studies* 1: 85–102.

Breton, Raymond. 2012. *Different Gods: Integrating Non-Christian Minorities into a Primarily Christian Society.* Montréal and Kingston: McGill-Queen's University Press.

Cadge, Wendy, and Elaine Howard Ecklund. 2007. "Immigration and Religion." *Annual Review of Sociology* 33(17): 359–79.

Chiswick, Barry R., and Paul E. Miller. 2010. "Occupational Language Requirements and the Value of English in the US Labor Market." *Journal of Population Economics* 23(1): 353–72.

Christie, Nicole, and Michael Gauvreau. 2010. "Secularisation or Resacralisation? The Canadian Case, 1760–2000." In *Secularisation in the Christian World*, edited by Callum G. Brown and Michael Snape, 93–117. Aldershot: Ashgate.

Clark, Warren. 2003. "Pockets of Belief: Religious Attendance Patterns in Canada." *Canadian Social Trends* (Spring): 2–5.

Connor, Phillip. 2008. "Increase or Decrease? The Impact of the International Migratory Event on Immigrant Religious Participation." *Journal for the Scientific Study of Religion* 47(2): 243–57.

Connor, Phillip. 2009. "Immigrant Religiosity in Canada: Multiple Trajectories." *Journal of International Migration and Integration* 10: 159–75.

Connor, Phillip. 2010. *A Theory of Immigrant Religious Adaptation: Disruption, Assimilation, and Facilitation*. Princeton: Princeton University Press.

Connor, Phillip. 2011. "Religion as Resource: Religion and Immigrant Economic Incorporation." *Social Science Research* 40(5): 1350–61.

Connor, Phillip, and Matthias Koenig. 2013. "Bridge and Barrier – Religion and Immigrant Occupational Attainment Across Integration Contexts," *International Migration Review* 36(1): 3–38.

Ebaugh, Helen R. 2003. "Religion and the New Immigrants." In *Handbook of the Sociology of Religion*, edited by Michele Dillon. Cambridge: Cambridge University Press.

Foner, Nancy, and Richard Alba. 2008. "Immigrant Religion in the U.S. and Western Europe: Bridge or Barrier to Inclusion?" *International Migration Review* 42(2): 360–92.

Fuller, Sylvia, and Todd F. Martin. 2012. "Predicting Immigrant Employment Sequences in the First Years of Settlement." *International Migration Review* 46(1): 138–90.

Gordon, Milton. 1964. *Assimilation in American Life: The Role of Race, Religion, and National Origins*. New York: Oxford University Press.

Heath, Anthony, and Sin Yi Cheung, eds. 2007. *Unequal chances: Ethnic Minorities in Western Labour Markets* (vol. 137). London: The British Academy.

Hirschman, Charles. 2004. "The Role of Religion in the Origins and Adaptation of Immigrant Groups in the United States." *The International Migration Review* 28(3): 1206–34.

Kelley, Ninette, and M.J. Trebilcock. 1998. *The Making of the Mosaic: A History of Canadian Immigration Policy*. Toronto: University of Toronto Press.

Kymlicka, Will. 1996. *Multicultural Citizenship*. New York: Oxford University Press.

Li, Peter S. 2003a. "Deconstructing Canada's Discourse of Immigrant Integration." *Journal of International Migration and Integration* 4(3): 315–33.

Li, Peter S. 2003b. *Destination Canada*. Oxford: Oxford University Press.

Lyon, David, and Maguerite Van Die, eds. 2000. *Rethinking Church, State and Modernity*. Toronto: University of Toronto Press.

Maclure, Jocelyn. 2003. *Québec Identity: The Challenge of Pluralism*. Montréal and Kingston: McGill-Queen's University Press.

Milot, Micheline. 2009. "Modus Co-vivendi: Religious Diversity in Canada." In *International Migration and the Governance of Religious Diversity*, edited by Paul Bramadat and Matthias Koenig. Montréal and Kingston: McGill-Queen's University Press.

Model, Suzanne, and Lang Lin. 2002. "The Cost of Not Being Christian: Hindus, Sikhs and Muslims in Britain and Canada." *International Migration Review* 36: 1061–92.

Mooney, Margarita. 2009. *Faith Makes us Live: Surviving and Thriving in the Haitian Diaspora*. Berkeley: University of California Press.

Norris, Pippa, and Ronald Inglehart. 2004. *Sacred and Secular: Religion and Politics Worldwide*. Cambridge: Cambridge University Press.

O'Toole, Roger. 1996. "Religion in Canada: Its Development and Contemporary Situation." *Social Compass* 43(1): 119–34.

Portes, Alejandro, and Ruben Rumbaut. 2006. *Immigrant America: A Portrait* (3rd ed.). Berkeley: University of California Press.

Reitz, Jeffrey, G., Rupa Banerjee, Mai Phan, and Jordan Thompson. 2009. "Race, Religion, and the Social Integration of New Immigrant Minorities in Canada." *International Migration Review* 43: 695–726.

Statistics Canada. 2003. "Ethnic Diversity Survey 2002." Available at: http://www23.statcan.gc.ca/imdb/p2SV.pl?Function=getSurvey&SDDS=4508&Item_Id=1717&lang=en

Tossutti, Livianna S., Ding Ming Wang, and Sanne Kaas-Mason. 2008. "Family, Religion and Civic Engagement in Canada." *Canadian Ethnic Studies/études ethniques au Canada* 40(3): 60–95.

Voas, David, and Fenella Fleischmann. 2012. "Islam Moves West: Religion Change in the First and Second Generation." *Annual Review of Sociology* 38, 525–45.

Warner, R. Stephen. 2007. "The Role of Religion in the Process of Segmented Assimilation." *The ANNALS of the American Academy of Political and Social Science* 612: 102–14.

Conclusion

SOLANGE LEFEBVRE AND LORI G. BEAMAN

This volume has demonstrated the degree to which in-depth case studies shed light on the complex relationships between religion and the public and private spheres. As the discussions here have demonstrated, religion blurs the boundaries between the public and the private, and presses us to think in new ways about what these categories mean, the work they do, and the power relations embedded in them. Accordingly, the reflections contained in this book have revealed the interrelationship between a range of core concepts: identities, ethnicities, values, multiculturalism and interculturalism, new media, law, youth and society, family, domestic violence, immigration, the voluntary sector, academia, the workplace, theology and religion, politics and power, and healing. Each case study blurs the line between the private and the public spheres, challenging the neatness of this categorization and reminding us that individuals engage in a complex socioreligious universe between and within the public and private spheres. For this reason, allow us to reiterate the polythetic nature of the chapter groupings related to the relationships of the public and private spheres. Indeed, a broad set of concerns resides at the intersection of religion, public, and private.

Several chapters included in this book, for example, point to the gendered dimensions of the discussions on religion in the public sphere (Cohen and Scioldo-Zürcher, Beaman, Nason-Clark, Fournier and See). Their texts explore the ways in which women's bodies have been disproportionately targeted for regulation by a patriarchy that operates to shape the very definition of the public sphere and the activities that take place within it. Yet, in the discussion, we are asked to evaluate what is more acceptable to society, a married woman who has covered her face or one gyrating nude for tips among strangers. While many works in this collection that stem from feminist discourses related the gendered power dynamics to constructed boundaries of the public and the private that have been largely defined by a Christian legalistic ethos, in contrast, Banack's findings on the matter of religion, politics, and sexuality identify the conservative Christian heritage of Alberta as a force of skepticism about government policymaking. Thus, the same bill that included protection of gays and lesbians under human rights legislation included a prohibition against "gay friendly" education in schools. Understanding this contradiction requires a sophisticated read of Albertan history and politics that implicates both private and public spheres, religion and big government suspicion.

The driving forces that shape public–private relations and the place of religion are diverse. For example, the reciprocal relationship between law and society is also imbued with religion. Moreover, law is not only shaped, challenged, and limited by religion, it also shapes, challenges, and limits religion in turn (Banack, Bowlby, Lefebvre, Fournier and See). We must also remember that multiculturalism represents an imaginary filter through which issues of religion in the public sphere are broached, thus limiting those aspects of the religion which are emphasized for non-adherents. Many of these traces can be linked to the Christian patriarchal paradigms built into the legal system itself. Yet, we cannot forget the ongoing influence of "competing imaginaries" in these dynamics and that these imaginaries themselves are not static entities. In the increasingly complex global world, Ramji demonstrates that individual identities are intimately connected to family and local community, but also to a broader network of international communities that can be easily accessed via the internet. The role of social location and social relations are also central in shaping society and identity in both the public and private spheres.

While it remains trite to suggest that history shapes the present, the importance of findings from historical excavations cannot be ignored. Too often questions about religion are supported by a limited engagement with the historical aspects and development of contemporary issues. Some of our authors have attempted to remedy this (see Bowlby, Beyer, Cohen and Scioldo-Zürcher in particular). The chain of memory that impacts responses to religious involvement in immigrant settlement in Québec, for example, is a key explanatory factor in understanding the reluctance to open space for religion in the public sphere.

Immigration represents an important element of this discussion, but focusing on this aspect can somehow frame these issues as being solely

related to the religions of immigrants. Religious diversity and the negotiation of the public sphere have a long history in Canada. Jehovah's
Witnesses have long advocated around this issue; the *Hutterian Brethren* decision concerns a minority group installed in Canada for many
decades. The fear of religious difference also helps blur the distinction
between ethnic and religious minorities, and recent immigrants. In the
context of a global world, the "Other" has become a somewhat vague,
but still very powerful category.

In Canada today, multiculturalism and interculturalism remain shadows cast on any discussion of the public sphere. In most discussions
on religion and the public legitimacy of its presence, power relations
between different cultural, ethnic, and religious groups are at stake
(Beyer, Connor and Koenig). If the belief in multiculturalism has characterized Canada since the 1970s, the debates that have agitated Québec
on the issue of interculturalism have reverberated in other provinces,
especially through criticisms of multiculturalism. On this particular
point, Canada can be compared to Europe, where similar perspectives
crisscross. Further, the historic majority remains a watermark whose
contours are both ethnic and religious in nature and is sometimes threatened by the recent waves of immigration. However, webs of tensions
between those who wish to keep their religious lives private and those
who wish to carry aspects of their religion with them into public spaces
endure. Nayar's contribution highlights that politics of resistance also
ruminate in our schoolyards. On the issue of religious paraphernalia
and clothing, that the private world seeks to exist in public is clear. Our
policies on religious diversity will of course shape how the youth of
today fare in an increasingly complex society. In this regard, alienating
either established religious and ethnic groups or minorities will have
devastating consequences.

Of course, there are limitations to establishing a focus on religion.
The cases we have explored herein raise the problem of foreground-
ing religion. While we obviously think that religion is worth examining
as a category that operates in particular ways in relation to the public
sphere, Lefebvre, Mooney, Nayar, and Ramji highlight the intersection-
ality of religion and other identity markers. For example, ethnicity, gender, and language may come together to include or exclude individuals
and groups. In so doing, there occurs a certain de-problematization
of religion, understood less as the problem at the source of many current conflicts and more as one challenge among others. In this regard,
the problem is not so much religion itself, even if many public debates

present religion as such, but the manner in which diversity is managed and/or included.

Our volume is one contribution to a broader discussion that is underway in relation to religion and its presence in the public sphere. The case studies we have presented offer valuable insights, but they also point to the need to expand research to more fully engage with the notions of the public and the private and their intersections with religion. Despite all of the insight we have gained into matters of religion, what a "diverse Canada" actually means requires further examination.

Debates in Canada have been too focused on a duality, or a binary relation, between Québec and the "Rest of Canada" (ROC), French and English, Catholic and Protestant (Beyer, Connor and Koenig), and more recently the acknowledgment of a ternary relation, the third pole, the First Nations. One reason for the former could be that Québec invested considerable time and resources in defining itself, through involved processes like governmental commissions, but also a formidable body of scholarly work. Along the way, we seemed to have forgotten that each province and region was also shaped by a unique set of historical forces that helped to build diverse and specific characters (see Banack, Bowlby, Nayar, Allen).

Nonetheless, there are still too few scholarly works on how the interaction of immigration, law, education, public policy, and history shapes religion and vice versa. If the focus was initially on different areas of the Canadian landscape, we realized through the editing process that most of the case studies go beyond provincial borders. The Maritimes, Québec, and Alberta could be grasped as areas where specific forces shaped the provincial character in a number of central ways, but it was difficult to pinpoint similar trends in other provinces. With this work, even though we could not include the topic of indigeneity within its covers (a vast topic in and of itself), we believe that we have nonetheless helped unpack some key aspects of the Québec/ROC binary and provided a number of tandem points from which to broach future issues related to diversity in Canada over the next decades.

Index

9/11 (United States), 86, 114, 186, 223, 241; post-9/11, 10

Abbotsford (BC), 221
Aberhart, William "Bible Bill," 257, 264–6, 271n4
Aboriginal people/person, 31, 33, 37, 89, 178, 187, 193, 195. *See also* First Nations
abuse, 14, 46, 150–2, 155–6, 158, 161–3, 166, 238; abuser, 13–14, 152, 155–6, 158, 161–3, 6, 238. *See also* domestic violence
accommodation: administrative, 37; cases, 175, 190; direction of, 38; duty of, 176–7; guidance on, 278; institutional, 223, 230; intercultur-alism and, 7; issues of, 6; language of, 7, 55; management/ing of, 177, 187; political, 56; practices, 7, 182; in public institutions, 175; reasonable, 7, 173–5, 177–9, 182, 186, 188–90, 193, 198n11–12, 250, 278–80, 287, 294; religious, 9, 15, 173–4, 180, 182–3, 192, 307; of religious diversity, 180, 231; of a religious nature, 182, 195; request,

175, 182, 186, 188–9, 195, 275, 277, 287; rooms, 187; subject of, 193; tolerance and, 49, 149
activists, 150, 165, 258, 293
adolescence, 153, 225, 228–9
advocate, 149, 151–2, 154, 161, 163, 178, 202, 204, 251n6, 259, 270, 277, 284, 315
Afghanistan, 6
Africville (Halifax), 37
Alberta: Alberta Human Rights Commission, 258, 261; Alberta hu-man rights legislation, 18, 258–60, 314; Albertans, 261–3, 270; govern-ment, 257, 260, 269; province of, 6; Reform Party, 267–8; Social Credit, 257, 264–8, 271n3; United Farmers of, 264
Alberta Individual Rights Protection Act, 257
Alberta v. Hutterian Brethren of Wilson Colony, 2009 SCC 37 (Canada), 20n2, 59n11
Algeria, 121–3, 127–9, 131, 144n3
Ali, Ayan Hirsi, 237
alienation, 16, 18, 230
Allen, Paul, 9, 17, 237, 316

IslamOnline.net, 101–2; Islamophobia, 186, 287; language of, 97;
practice of, 104, 107, 115
Islamic: Council on American-
Islamic Relations, 279–80; faith,
99; identity, 14, 97, 99; sites, 100–1;
theology, 246n1; tradition, 98–99
Israel, 122, 127
Italy, 44, 54, 57, 277

Jamaica, 14, 163
Jarnail Singh Brar (Bhindramwale),
225
Jehovah's Witnesses, 50, 315
Jesuits, 204–5, 242
Jewish: community, 14, 121–4, 135–8,
140–1, 143, 144n4, 145n19; community centre, 124, 138; immigrants,
10; immigration, 122, 127, 136,
144n2; institutions, 124, 134, 142;
migration, 14, 121, 123, 138, 141–3;
neighbourhood, 45, 123–4, 146n20;
population, 122, 140; practices,
122–3
Jews: Algerian, 121, 131; Iraqi, 128;
Moroccan, 121–2, 124, 128, 135,
137–8, 141, 144n7, 145n17; North
African, 114, 121–3, 127, 132, 142,
164n20; Orthodox, 45, 50, 176;
Shephardic, 13, 121, 137, 142–3;
Tunisian, 121, 131
Jilbab, 108, 110
job, 83–4, 121, 182, 204, 207–8, 212,
241, 249, 294, 296, 300, 304–6,
308, 309n6. See also employment;
labour; workforce
Judaism, 29, 123, 125, 127–8, 131–4,
137, 142–3, 145n13, 146n20, 299
judge, 152, 154–5, 162
jurisdictions, 150–1, 167

jurisprudence, 9, 177, 245
justice, 53, 81, 149–55, 161–2, 165,
167, 222, 233n12, 281, 286

Kant, Immanuel, 249
Khaled, Amr, 111–12
Khalistan: politics, 16, 224, 227,
233n14; t-shirt, 16, 219, 224–7,
229–30
Khalsa: Oder, 218–19, 232n11; school,
223
Kirpan, 27, 45, 50–1, 82, 88, 173
Klein, Ralph, 257, 267–8
Knott, Kim, 49
Koenig, Matthias, 9, 10, 19, 203, 293,
315–16
Kronman, Anthony, 244–5

labour: force, 181–2; labour market,
298, 303; labour shortage, 180,
194, 196. See also employment; job;
workforce
laïcité, 47, 49, 56, 212, 276; laïcisation,
47; laïcité ouverte, 47, 55, 91; laicization, 138; Mouvement laïque
(Québec), 279. See also secular;
secularism; secularity; secularization
Laurier, Wilfrid, 32, 34
Lautsi v. Italy App. no. 30814/06, Eur.
Ct. H.R. 2009 (Italy), 54
Laval (QC), 204
leadership, 29, 155, 165–6, 168n8,
205, 205, 262
legality: legal status, 204; legal
system, 175, 314; of the practice of
polygamy, 6
legislation, 18, 33, 37, 58, 104, 121,
178–9, 182, 194, 220, 258–61, 270,
275–7, 279, 282–3, 285, 288, 314

rites, 100, 123
ritual, 112, 115, 124, 127–8, 131, 134,
    140–2, 145n14, 156, 228
rural: areas, 88, 181, 264; regions,
    183, 195
Russia, 128

Sabbath, 173
safety, 60n21, 85–6, 92, 152, 155, 158,
    164, 166, 232n10
Saguenay (QC), 6, 183
Salvation Army, 42, 46, 167n7
same-sex: couple, 48, 262; marriage,
    5, 258, 262, 269; *Reference re Same-
    Sex Marriage* (2004), 48; relation/
    ship, 27, 260, 270n1. *See also* gay;
    homosexuality
Saskatoon (SK), 240
Saudi Arabia, 105
school: administrators, 224, 229;
    board, 8, 37–8, 50–1; Catholic,
    36–7; denominational, 34, 36;
    divinity, 240; high school, 16,
    38–9, 105, 156, 204, 219, 223–4;
    Maimonides, 137; professional,
    163; public, 18, 35–9, 45, 173, 229,
    232n10, 258–62, 269, 270n1; *Public
    School Act*, 36; residential, 37, 46.
    See also education(al), institutions
Scioldo-Zürcher, Yann, 9–10, 13–14,
    121, 144n2, 131–4
second-generation, 10, 12, 14, 66–7,
    92, 97–100, 133–4, 116, 118n3, 196,
    210, 212, 293–6, 298–9, 301–8. *See
    also* first-generation; generations
secular: agency, 162, 164–6; between
    the secular and the sacred, 15;
    exclusion, 18, 275; imaginary, 38;
    institution, 205; program, 153, 155;
    and the religious, 15, 282; sacred/

secular, 14, 160; society, 33, 53–4,
    67, 215, 277; state, 283, 285. *See also
    laïcité*
secularism, 8, 12, 18, 90–1, 100,
    211–13, 215, 245, 249, 276, 283,
    286–7. *See also laïcité*
secularity, 16, 213, 284. *See also laïcité*
secularization, 7, 9–11, 25–9, 39, 165,
    202, 214, 239, 247, 282, 297. *See also
    laïcité*
security, 11, 51, 60n21, 92, 157–8,
    222–3, 278, 280
See, Erica, 9, 18, 52, 56–7, 215, 275,
    313–14
segregation, 25, 34
Seljak, David, 5, 29
Sephardic: identity, 130, 137, 143;
    Jews, 121, 137; Judaism, 128, 137;
    traditions, 137, 143
Serbia, 77; Serbian Orthodox group,
    79, 92
sexual orientation, 15, 18, 179,
    257–61, 286
sharia, 246, 270
Shi'a, 104, 108–9, 112–14
Sikh: community, 10, 16, 218–19,
    221–3, 232n9, 233n14; identity, 69,
    223, 231n3, 232n8; immigrants,
    219, 221, 223; religion, 223, 230;
    Sikhs, 9, 16, 29, 31, 39, 51, 68, 71,
    82, 88, 93n4, 182, 218–19, 221–5,
    227, 232n11, 233n14; student, 219,
    225, 227, 229, 232n9–10; tradition,
    220, 225–8, 232n11; youth, 16,
    218–19, 222, 224–8, 230
Snowdon (Montréal, QC), 124, 138–40
socialism, 266, 268
Social Sciences and Humanities
    Research Council (SSHRC), 19n1,
    118n2, 167n1, 197n1, 231n1, 288n1